Praise for **Down to This**

"The book stinks of cigarettes and ch[...]
ditchwater and soggy cardboard. It sti[...] [...] or us
have never known, and will probably ne[...] [...], but that Mr. Bishop-
Stall has learned about, and unflinchingly describes. . . . But Mr. Bishop-
Stall's rocky cruise along the edge of hell is not the usual post-graduate's
drug binge and writerly outpouring. He has given us, instead, a painfully
frank, clearly and excellently written report about Torontonians we live
among, occasionally hear about, but do not know, and—face it—do not
want to know. It's high time we knew everything this remarkable book
has to teach us."
—John Bentley Mays in *The Globe and Mail*

"One of the book's surprise strengths is its comic, wiseass tone—a device
that in lesser hands might have been disastrous. . . . A genuine accom-
plishment, brilliantly balancing humour and horror, steadfastly refusing
to stereotype or simplify. I have no idea who Shaughnessy Bishop-Stall
really is, but he had a lot of guts to set out on this project, and he has
even more talent to have pulled it off."
—*National Post*

"It's a wondrous book, a sad and funny, dark and joyous tale that starts
out as an observer's view of the homeless and evolves, without being
maudlin, into a man's journey to mend his broken spirit. . . . A roller-
coaster ride of pain and despair, acceptance and healing. *Down to This*
might have a lot to say about the homeless, but it has more to say about
our own personal humanity."
—*Edmonton Journal*

"It's impossible not to be transfixed because, like the best social docu-
mentarists, Bishop-Stall is deep inside his story and doesn't preach or get
mired in clichés."
—*The Gazette* (Montreal)

"Tent City's golf club beatings, tuberculosis and soiled bedding make cable television's *Trailer Park Boys* seem like a Hallmark presentation. . . . The Pit of Despair, notes Bishop-Stall along the way, is not a conical one, but a spherical hole with no eventual bottom. Writing a book, on the way down, especially one as uplifting as *Down to This*, must've been one hell of a task."
—*Calgary Herald*

"The book is compelling, often ugly and full of squalor, but it shows real compassion for those who have hit bottom."
—*Times Colonist* (Victoria)

"Finely written and bitterly honest, it's also a moving depiction of the contradictions embedded in our common humanity."
—*Maclean's*

"By turns harrowing, hilarious and touching. He has produced nothing less than a masterpiece of urban anthropology—a must-read for anyone who pretends to understand the roots of homelessness."
—Jonathan Kay in the *National Post*

"The array of carefully drawn and fully rounded portrayals of the spectrum of Tent City residents are the stinking, breathing, laughing, fighting heart of *Down to This*."
—*eye Weekly*

DOWN TO THIS

squalor and splendour
in a big-city
shantytown

SHAUGHNESSY BISHOP-STALL

vintage canada

VINTAGE CANADA EDITION, 2005

Published in Canada by Vintage Canada, a division of Random House of Canada
Limited, Toronto. Originally published in hardcover in Canada by Random House
Canada, a division of Random House of Canada Limited, Toronto, in 2004.
Distributed by Random House of Canada Limited, Toronto.

Vintage Canada and colophon are registered trademarks of
Random House of Canada Limited.

www.randomhouse.ca

Library and Archives Canada Cataloguing in Publication

Bishop-Stall, Shaughnessy, 1974–
Down to this : squalor and splendour in a big-city shantytown /
Shaughnessy Bishop-Stall.

ISBN 0-679-31228-5

1. Squatter settlements—Ontario—Toronto. 2. Poor—Ontario—Toronto.
3. Homeless persons—Ontario—Toronto. 4. Beggars—Ontario—Toronto.
5. Homelessness—Ontario—Toronto. 6. Bishop-Stall, Shaughnessy, 1974–
—Homes and haunts—Ontario—Toronto. I. Title.

HV4050.T6B58 2005   362.5'09713'541   C2004-905218-7

In this book, certain names and identifying details have been changed
to protect identities.

Text Design: Daniel Cullen

Cover photo: Goran Petkovski
Inside photos: Goran Petkovski (pages 1, 7, 61, 105, 149, 181, 229, 337, 417, 469)
Amy Sedgwick (pages 286, 377, 477)
Marc Lemyre (page 10)

Printed and bound in the United States of America

2 4 6 8 9 7 5 3 1

For Bob Stall and Jacqui Bishop,
the most understanding parents a boy could have.
And for the Dirty Thirty,
the best bunch of derelicts in town.

Tent City is not a city and we don't live in tents. We live in shacks and shanties on the edge of Canada's largest metropolis where the river meets the lake. There's a fence dividing these 27 acres from the rest of Toronto, and on this side we've built what dwellings we can with the rubble of a scrapyard, a no-man's landfill caught in confusion between the city and private business. Sometimes it seems like a community and sometimes like chaos. Junk Town would be a better name.

Picture a dump, littered with the cast-outs of the last millennium. Refrigerators, stuffed animals, shoes, original paintings on torn canvasses, photo albums, three hundred broken bicycles and toboggans and hockey sticks, TVs and microwaves, lamps and cash registers, headless Cabbage Patch Kids and enough books to start a library or a bookstore or your own education.

Now picture dozens of the country's thieves and drug addicts, vagabonds and ex-cons. They're drunk, hungry and tired of running. It's getting old and getting cold, and one night they find themselves in this place, with the rest of the discards, on the edge of the world but smack in the middle of it all.

They look around and realize that everything they've been hustling for is right here: stereos and VCRs, room to move, a perfect hideout and waterfront property. They aren't way out in the lonesome countryside or the goddamn suburbs or trapped in the same old city. In fact, the city looks perfect from here—the lake, the downtown high-rises, the sun setting beneath the tallest free-standing structure in the world—it's like a picture postcard. And best of all, there are no laws and no cops—as long as they stay this side of the fence. It's all private property. No one can tell them what to do, no one but Home Depot, the company that owns this land.

So they dig into a corner of the rubble for something they can use to build. There's so much, they could make anything. But for now they just throw together a few shelters using tarps and old office furniture. They buy some beer, light a fire, call it Tent City and decide to stay. The smoke rises for everyone to see, like a warning or an invitation. They drink and wait.

For almost four years people have been squatting here, and now some days the population reaches sixty or so. The singularity of this place has drawn media attention from all over the world, as well as a flood of well-meaning, but mostly redundant, donations—if only salvation could be bought with wool hats and toothbrushes. This remains, as much as such a thing is possible, a society of anarchy.

The rules are made up nightly. Repercussions are rarely considered in advance, or recorded for future reference. It is a useful, using and sometimes useless place. The castoffs of the megacity are snatched up, played with, eaten, worn, painted over and tossed into the mud. China plates are disposable, pillowcases never washed. If this place has a credo, it is: Grab what you can, stay drunk and mind your own damn business.

The protocol for moving into Tent City is one of invitation or recommendation. I unknowingly broke protocol. I came without a clue and nothing to lose, to learn about this place, write a book and live rent free. During the month I've spent so far, I've realized there is no one way to live here and a hundred possible stories to be written. Some people beg, some squeegee windows, some steal, some work jobs, some sell themselves, sell others, sell drugs. Most do drugs, some do nothing at all. I don't yet know what I'm going to do.

The rules I've set for myself are simple: no money or friends, except those I might find from here on in. I'll do what others do to get by, be whatever bum I choose: vagrant, beggar, wino, criminal, busker, con man or tramp, on any given day.

What follows is a record of my time in Tent City.

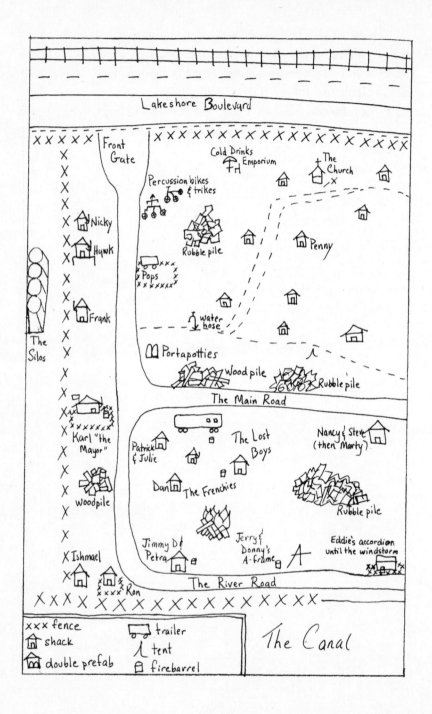

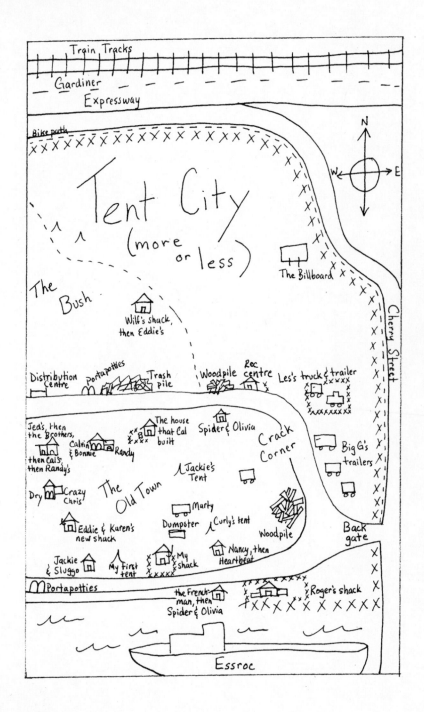

November:
The Invisible Streetcar

November 15

I'd hoped to start writing yesterday, but then the soldiers were coming at us across the field, I couldn't find a pen or paper, and I started to shake.

It was my first night in Toronto and I stayed at the Salvation Army shelter down on Sherbourne Street on the east side of Moss Park. On the west side of the park is the Department of National Defence Military Academy. Across from that is an army surplus store where I plan to get my supplies.

The DND trains teenage militia on the turf of Moss Park. Being the Canadian army, they practise strategic advance without even blanks in their rifles. Late at night they charge across the football field toward the homeless shelter, giggling as they shoot each other, yelling, "Bang! Bang! Bang!"

This span of Queen Street, running along the south edge of the park, is covered with junkies, dealers, hookers and cops. And last night I sat among them, smoking and shaking on the Salvation Army steps—trying to alert the others to the attacking soldiers. In no condition to fight, I gave out as many cigarettes as I could and wedged myself in between the toughest and craziest—to my right, 300 pounds of muscle just released from prison, to my left, some guy trying to think of every B word he could and yelling them out in bursts of triumph: "Beer! Beaver! Bread! Bobby Brown!" The soldiers were firing. As if shot, an old man with a nicotine Santa beard lay on his back on the sidewalk singing demonic opera in a dozen voices from falsetto to basso profundo. "*O solo frio.* Me loony! Me loony! Old man shiver!"

"Barbecue! Blister! Baby brother! Banana!"

"I'm going to kill you, you bitch!"

"Bang! Bang! I got you, dude."

I dropped my head and stared into the dark space between my knees, shivering and shaking.

Later it got worse. I was lying on a cot and it was as if there were small quakes inside me, my right arm jumping all over, my hand like an electrocuted squid. *Even if I could find a pen,* I thought, *I couldn't hold one long enough to write.* And I couldn't sleep either, with the sweats and the sound of the guy on the cot next to me alternating all night between violent snoring and savage masturbation, like a man trying to tear himself apart.

I left there as soon as the sun came up, and now I've got myself a room at Filmores—a cheap hotel and strip club on Dundas Street. I kind of like the place. It's an old brick building with a streetcar track out front, so that every seven minutes or so my room shakes, and then for a moment it's as if I'm at peace and I belong here, shaking in a shaking room.

November 22

I've been in this room for a week now, leaving only to stock up on food, Aspirin, cigarettes and antibiotics for what a walk-in doctor diagnosed as the flu. I never pictured myself like this at 27, trying to detox in a third-rate strip club in a strange city, waiting for an invisible streetcar to shake the walls.

I've talked to nobody in all this time except the strippers, who live on the main floor and change between songs in the laundry room. I made the mistake of telling them that I'm going to write a book and now they keep asking me to come up with stage names for the new girls.

"I don't know . . . Isis?" I say. They shake their heads. "Mississauga

Magdalena?" I try. "Rehab Rhonda? . . . Sweet Sally the Soul Destroyer? . . . Sorry, I'm no good at making up names—that's why the book's non-fiction." Then I close the door and go fetal on the bed. I can feel the rats in my head, the toxins tearing through my blood.

If you follow it long enough you'll see there's no bottom to a downward spiral. It's not a conical shape descending to some deep final point. It's actually a cylindrical helix—a shape that exists nowhere in nature but our own DNA—the unbuilding blocks of life. Since this descending helix won't ever stop itself, it's up to you to do it. So I attempted the jump, and somehow landed here—on a bed above a strip club, choking on the stench of talcum powder and gin.

November 27

This is what I'm bringing to Tent City, most of which I bought at the army surplus store by Moss Park: a Norwegian army rucksack ($29), a Canadian army satchel ($4), Canadian army long-johns ($19), a no-name army knife ($6), a fleece jacket, a hooded sweatshirt, a turtleneck and sleeping bag (all from Goodwill for $22), a toque ($2), a scarf ($2), a flashlight ($1), an alarm clock ($1), a pup tent ($130), two pairs of jeans, shorts, three T-shirts, a leather jacket, leather gloves, a pair of beat-up 7-year-old leather boots resoled three times and in need of another repair, basic toiletries and this pad of writing paper. I seem to have forgotten my hunting knife back in my old apartment. But knives are messy. Instead I've bought an adjustable steel baton ($45) that telescopes out 26 inches with the flick of a wrist.

I'll spend most of the money I have before I leave here tomorrow. The girls have dragged me down to the bar, and now I just feel like an idiot—tears running down my face as I stare at them dancing naked under the lights. I'm drunk for the first time in two weeks, and I've realized I don't even know where Tent City is.

December:
A Wonderful Life

December 1

Just three days in Tent City so far and I'm already a mess, my old boots leaking sewer water, the knees of my jeans two moons of mud, my leather jacket all beaten down like a moth in the rain. There's a small cut or bite above my left eye, my hair is curling into chaos, and I feel better than I have in months.

It's been raining steadily since the day I left the hotel. I walked into the downpour, my rucksack covered by a garbage bag flapping in the wind—weak and wobbly from the sickness and the bourbon—and still didn't know which way to go.

If you're looking for it, Tent City is on Lakeshore Boulevard, between Cherry Street and Parliament. It's right on the edge of downtown, just a few kilometres from Filmores. But following the directions I got from someone on the street, it took me about three hours and six miles of walking, and even then I didn't know I was there.

After trudging through warehouses, over train tracks, under the expressway, over the boulevard and along the bike path to the harbour, I couldn't see anything like a city of tents. I saw a narrow inlet with a drawbridge stretching across to ships and tankers and giant concrete silos. On this side there was just a fenced-in wasteland of garbage, wild grass, trees and bushes. I looked around, across to the lake, up to an airplane descending through the sky and again at the scrapyard before me. Then, as I stared through the chain-link fence, the rubble began to take shape, and slowly I could see roofs of plastic and sheet metal, walls of plywood, a garden of hubcaps, flags of all colours and puffs of white smoke. I could see Tent City rising in the rain.

Places, like people, are rarely how you imagine them. Tent City is both more beautiful and more revolting than I pictured. As I crossed through the fence there was garbage and sewage and rats all around. But it was somehow picturesque, like a Popeye shantytown or the romantic sepia of Hooverville transposed to the future. It was quiet. I could hear my breathing and my boot heels, and there wasn't a soul to be seen.

A dog barked. The door of a nearby shack opened and a big smiling woman stepped into the rain. I waved to her as I crossed the lake of mud and trash between us.

"Hi," she said. "I'm Jackie."

"That's my mum's name," I said.

"Okay . . . and what's yours?"

I'd planned on playing it tough at first—like the new convict in a prison movie—so people would be intrigued but think twice before messing with me. I hadn't planned on the first thing out of my mouth being a reference to my mother. I also hadn't planned on there being any women.

"Are you scared of dogs?"

"No, not at all," I said, trying to recover. "They're usually scared of me."

Jackie giggled and motioned for me to come inside. "Well, Cleo's a Rottweiler," she said. "She's only just turned 3, but she's 130 pounds already . . . *Aren't* you, puppy? *Good* girl! *Good* Cleo!"

Between the dog and Jackie's disarming manner, I decided to give up on the tough-convict thing for the time being, and asked if I could dry my socks by the wood stove.

We sat and talked until a motor sounded outside and Jackie looked out the window. "Get your shoes on," she said. "Wood's here."

Some contractors, not wanting to pay dumping fees, unloaded a truckful of construction scraps and we started going through it in the mud, searching for anything small and dry enough to burn. An older woman showed up and fell into the middle of the woodpile. I dropped the wood I'd gathered and reached to pick her up. "That's Nancy," said Jackie as Nancy fell back into the pile. "Watch where you're grabbin' her. She'll be covered in piss."

By the time we'd got some firewood and had gone back inside, more people were showing up—home from doing whatever they do in the city. Jackie said, "My Sluggo'll be here soon. He built this place for me when I was sick for nine weeks."

Although her blue eyes sparkle, you wouldn't want to mess with Jackie, a Viking demigod—her blond hair a shining helmet, her arms war hammers. She's almost my height but twice my weight, and it's not easy for her to get around. She's also like a child—amused, defensive and vulnerable. She's the first person I met in Tent City, and I liked her immediately. I hadn't expected that, and I hadn't expected a shack with a warm wood stove.

"Nice place," I said, and she told me how the owner of a construction company brought some lumber and tools to Tent City last month and helped some of the men build their own homes. Sluggo had never done anything like it before, but within two weeks he'd constructed a 12-by-7-foot, insulated, wood-heated, waterproof shack with two backwards windows, an upside-down door and a roof shingled the wrong way around.

"You did a great job on the place," I said when Sluggo got home.

"I was *really* stoned by the time I got to the roof," said Sluggo. "But I'm still hoping to make the cover of *Better Slums and Hovels* . . . Hey! Who the hell are you?"

"This is Shaun!" said Jackie. "He's okay." Sluggo was staring at my socks as they steamed on a chair by his stove.

"I've got $30," I said quickly. "Where can we buy some beer around here?"

"There's a store on Cherry Street," said Sluggo. "I'll show you." And the two of us walked out into the rain.

Sluggo is a tall, thin middle-aged man. He's got long hair down his back in a ponytail and a dark beard that covers half his chest. He walks fast on his long skinny legs, and you can tell he doesn't like to talk much—although on the way to the store he told me twice that he's never smoked crack. He said he was a junkie for twenty years, but he kicked all that.

We brought beer and sandwiches back to the shack. I asked him why he's called Sluggo and he said that some guy's jaw crushed his knuckles so badly the blood was poisoned all the way up to his shoulder and he couldn't drink for a month. "Worst good punch I ever threw," he said, and slugged on his beer.

Jackie said she did eighteen months for robbery and is now looking at another thirty days for screwing up her parole. She's due in court next Thursday. Sluggo said he got ten years for something to do with an axe, served four and a half, and isn't allowed to touch any sort of weapon for the rest of his life. He's nervous about all the news footage of Tent City, especially one shot where he can be seen working on his shack, a hammer in his hand.

Nancy showed up while we were eating the sandwiches, her red eyes swimming in the rain. "Where're my spices?" she slurred.

"We gave 'em back to Marty," said Jackie.

Nancy looked around, almost falling over with the turning of her head. "Where's my beer?" she said.

"You just got here—you don't have a beer," said Sluggo.

Nancy muttered something incoherent and stomped away.

"I'll close the door," I said.

After we finished eating, Nancy returned. "I want my spices back!"

"I just told you!" said Jackie. "Marty has them!"

"Where's my beer?" said Nancy.

"Fuck off!" said Jackie.

"She can be very redundant," said Sluggo.

All I could think was, *They have spices?*

I was waiting for the rain to stop before trying to set up my tent, but apparently the rain never stops in this city. Jackie suggested that instead of staying in the tent I should take one of the dollhouses.

"The what?"

"The dollhouses." She pointed out the window. Near the narrow road that runs through the centre of Tent City were two small plastic sheds with white walls and blue pitched roofs. "You can't stand up in them, but they're good for sleeping, and they're warm." Apparently an organization called the Toronto Disaster Relief Committee (TDRC) brought a few of them down a couple days ago, and there was still one unclaimed. By the time the beers were gone, however, so was the last dollhouse, and it was still pouring.

"Damnit!" said Jackie, looking out the window. "I'll find out who took it. That was yours!" Sluggo rolled his eyes. I was touched, if a bit surprised, by Jackie's concern, but I stopped her from charging off to repo the dollhouse.

"It's okay, Jackie," I said. "I'll be fine in my tent."

Even in the dark rain there was almost enough light from downtown, the highway overpass and the ships in port to see what I was doing. After half an hour of groping in the mud and slamming pegs with a rock, I had something that looked kind of like a tent. I found some squares of Styrofoam insulation and wedged them beneath the floor.

Just as I finished, a van came around with sandwiches and blankets, people tossing them to us like relief workers in news footage after an earthquake. I got a blanket, and Jackie got me a blanket, and then Nancy came over and got me one, too. She seemed to have balanced out a bit, and patted my cheek when she handed it to me. "Here, kid," she said. "Stay warm. It's raining."

In the dark, I'd set up camp at a low point, in the path of all the runoff flowing down into the lake. The rain kept up all night until I was in a river of mud, piss, rats, needles, candy wrappers, the heads of stuffed animals, dog shit and bottle caps. It rained forty hours and forty inches but somehow, like a self-absorbed miracle, I stayed warm and dry. I felt good, until I slept and dreamt of her.

December 2

Even with the nightmares and the rain, everything seems to be going pretty well. After my first night in Tent City I went to breakfast with Sluggo at a nearby community centre called Dixon Hall. Every Friday they serve bacon and eggs to anyone who shows up by 9 a.m. I sat across the table from a guy named Eddie, who also lives in Tent City.

"Welcome to the neighbourhood," he said, grinning. Eddie's grin echoes in your eyes. He looks like he's been through hell and brought a lot of it back with him. He and Beetlejuice have the same demonic barber, and if his eyes weren't so expressive and his grin so charming, his head would look like a skull still sprouting hair after death. He shook my hand, long arm muscles rippling beneath his shirt. "Yeah, you're all right," he said, and laughed, though I hadn't said a word.

When we got back, Eddie brought me some squares of insulation. He lives with his old lady, Karen, in a bizarre structure on the other side of Sluggo and Jackie's shack. He's built a front and back wall on what appears to be a tunnel of corrugated plastic. People call it the accordion. Next to it he's built a frame for a new shack, and says they plan on moving into it when it's done.

With the new squares of insulation, I was able to get my tent off the ground. Then I dug a storm trench around the perimeter with an old soup ladle, so now the runoff circles the tent and drains into the lake. So far, it's kept out the water, but I don't like the idea of spending many more nights in this zip-lock coffin, without room to even sit up and write.

Mine is the only tent in Tent City, and all the shanty dwellers shake their heads when they see it, like they feel sorry for me. They tell me I'm crazy if I think I can survive the winter in a tent. You know you're in trouble when people living in a garbage dump think you're nuts.

x
x
x

Last night I thought the war had come to Toronto. The rain had finally stopped, there was a full moon and everyone was beating each other up. I had no idea what the fights were about, and didn't want to drink too much (it being my last day on antibiotics), so I squeezed into my pocket-sized tent and tried to fall asleep. Then the explosions began.

By the time I pulled on my boots and got out of my tent, everyone around me was gazing up at fireworks in the sky. It was a strange moment—all these fighters and drunks on a full-moon binge, all these squatters emerging from their shanties, staring up in awe as showers of coloured light rained over the city like celestial spores.

After the grand finale, a voice behind me bellowed, "Merry fucking Christmas!" Then, "Who the hell is *this* guy?" I turned around, and there was a giant of a man glaring at me, his eyes narrowed in his massive round head. He was wearing a longshoreman's wool hat, black snow pants and a red sweater.

"Hey there!" I said. "I just moved in! Didja see the fireworks?" In retrospect, this may have been the right time for my convict persona.

"No, I'm fucking blind," he said, still staring right into my eyes. I stared back. There was something scary in there. He looked well taken care of, overfed and pumped up like he'd just come from the gym. He would have made a good enforcer for Bizarro Santa Claus. *He's the biggest man I've ever seen,* I thought.

"Uh, do you live here?"

He snorted a laugh and stepped toward me, grinding his hands together. "I'm Hawk," he said, as if that explained everything. "I break legs. Break necks if I have to—if there's somebody on the wrong side of the fence. You know what I mean? What about you? You on the right side?"

"Um . . ." Before I could say more, Eddie was between us, slapping Hawk on the back.

"Don't worry about young Shaun," said Eddie. "He's a good guy. Trust me."

I have no idea why Eddie did that, but suddenly Hawk switched gears.

"I don't gotta be down here, you know," he said, rocking back on his heels and looping his thumbs through his snow pant suspenders like mayors in the old movies do. "I make $80,000 a year, contracting. But I've lived on the streets since I was 14. Through gangs, prison, murder, you name it. But now I'm doing it right. I watch over this place—you got it?"

"Yeah, sure," I said. "Like the sheriff."

"That's right. Just like the fucking sheriff. You need a snowsuit for the winter?"

"No, I got clothes. Thanks."

"I'll get you a suit," he said, like I really had no choice in the matter. "You don't know what it's like when the wind comes off the lake in January, –50 fucking degrees, and you'll be crying like a girl all night. I'll get you a suit."

"Okay. Thanks."

I stayed outside until it got too cold and the fighting started up again. Then I scurried back into my tent to sleep among the rats.

December 3

Chris, whom Jackie lovingly refers to as Crazy Chris, has a pet raccoon. He found it lying by the train tracks a few days ago, whimpering and barely alive.

"I almost killed him," he said. "Was going to bash his head in with a rock—to, you know, save him from the misery. But then I thought, hell, I'd never want to be saved from the misery that way. I'd just want to be saved from dying. So now look at him, eh?"

The raccoon had eaten so much by this point he wasn't even interested in the remaining plates of tuna laid out for him, and had moved on to Claudette, nuzzling into her chest, groping at her hair.

"Careful," I said. "Those things can be vicious."

"Yeah? What do you know?" said Claudette. She lives next to Chris, in a prefab she shares with this big beer-bellied guy named Jed. "I've had three raccoons," she said. "And they all loved me just fine."

And it's true, I guess I don't know much. She kissed and snuggled with that raccoon for ages, and the thing was gentle as a kitten.

"What's his name?" Everyone just stared at me.

"We don't name the fucking raccoons," said Jed.

I drank a beer and talked to Crazy Chris, also known as Tattooed Chris. I'm not sure why, since everyone down here has tattoos. Maybe he just has more of them, or maybe some people are scared to call him Crazy. He's got that glint in his eye, that broken-toothed grin that suggests he'd go ten steps further than anyone else, into anything. He's the only guy I've met here who's as young as me. With a few less scars he'd have boyish good looks. He's got leather pants, motorcycle boots, the kind of muscles that look like they've been beaten into shape with a tire iron, and now a pet raccoon he just couldn't kill.

A group of U of T students showed up while we were still playing with the raccoon, to hand out food and snacks and give us their best wishes. Everyone was pretty drunk, and Jed kept yelling at them, "Look at that! Now you can go back to your university and tell 'em how we're all *nice* to animals. You see that! That's being *nice!*" I guess Jed's had some bad experiences with animals and college kids. To their credit, they kept smiling and looking around. They didn't stay long.

x x x

I'm sitting here in a second-hand, two-room, bright red tent. Someone brought it down here as a donation, and I spent all day setting it up. Another night in that stupid nylon coffin and I might have chewed right through it.

Although there's a lot of room in Tent City and it feels about 5 degrees colder by the water, I've decided to stay here in the crowd. I'd rather listen to the waves than the traffic, and I've already got to know my neighbours. They call this part the old town—where Jackie and Sluggo's shack, Eddie and Karen's accordion, Nancy and her man Marty's trailer, and two prefabs belonging to Crazy Chris and this guy Randy all form a messy horseshoe—so there's sort of an accidental town square in the middle. The area I chose completes the circle. It's barricaded by an abandoned A-frame on one side and a huge Dumpster on the other. I'm surrounded by sparse trees and bushes, and the front flap of my tent is about 20 feet from the edge of the water.

I started on my new home by trying to level out the land with a shovel and a broken pickaxe. I laid down a base for the floor with eight skids roughly the same size, then covered the skids with squares of insulation cut with a hatchet. It took the rest of the day to set up the tent itself. It's a confusing contraption, with about fifty different pole parts, and is so large that there's a dividing wall inside, splitting it into two big rooms.

In one room, I put down my bedding—a few blankets and a sleeping bag. In the other, I put a chair and a small octagonal table raised up on bricks, so I can write. I also fit in some stand-up shelving and a short filing cabinet to keep food and other stuff away from the rats and the rain. Unfortunately, the fly is missing and so I've tied an old ripped-up tarp over the roof.

This'll do for the time being. I've left my old tent set up for anyone to use—with all the domestic fighting down here, I'm sure people get tossed into the cold all the time.

December 4

I feel like I spent all night in the lake. With this huge monster of a tent my body heat left me alone to go and create condensation all over the walls, making everything wet as well as cold, especially me. If I did sleep, I dreamt of being wet and cold.

So today I had to ignore everyone around me and just work on surviving the night. First I scrounged some more Styrofoam insulation and propped it against the walls of the tent, then covered it all with whatever sheets of wood I could find for a windbreak. I put barricades of plywood on the front, then brought in my pup tent and set it up as a sleeping cave on the other side of the curtain divider. I figure this should restrict the loss of body heat. My neighbour Randy gave me a mattress that fits in my newly blanketed sleeping womb, and just to make sure, I covered the small interior tent with blankets.

Randy's a funny one. He looks like Popeye, and tends to act like him, too, clicking his heels together, singing silly songs, glugging down bottles of whatever he can find as though alcohol were spinach. He lives in a double-size prefab he shares with a woman named Brenda—whom I've never seen—and he spends a lot of time dancing with his dog, Chaos.

There are four prefabs—ugly pink plastic houses that the TDRC brought down here about a year ago. Two are doubles, with a door for each room, and two are singles. The two doubles and one of the single prefabs are all on the main Tent City road. Crazy Chris and some other guy share one of the doubles, surrounded with piles of car parts and broken bicycles. The whole front of the house is covered in hubcaps, and Chris has built an addition, which he calls the garage, on to the back. Jed and Claudette live together in the single-room prefab, and Randy lives in the other double. He's built a large windbreak, two walls and a half-roof, on the side, where people huddle around his fire barrel. One of his inside walls is covered in cartoon characters—stuffed animals, plastic figurines and cardboard cut-outs of everyone from Yosemite Sam to Spider-Man, Tweety Bird to Mickey Mouse. In the centre of them all hangs Popeye, crucified on the wall with roofing nails. "You can come over any time," said Randy, waving at the wall behind him. "You'll fit right in."

In addition to the mattress, he also gave me a big blue tarp that I've used to cover my whole tent, fastening it down with railway spikes and bricks. After finishing the renovations, I dug a firepit out front. Eventually I want to get a barrel, like everyone else has. With luck, I can prove to all these naysaying shack dwellers that a man can survive the winter in a tent.

December 5

I slept like a premature newborn in an incubator, emerging finally from my souped-up tent to bright streaks of sunlight and ducks and geese on the smiling mouth of the Don River. It was warm, and I was in a T-shirt the whole day. I spent most of it hunting through the piles for firewood and anything else I could use. I've now got four sizes of firewood sorted into buckets and drawers—enough for at least a week. There's no better feeling than standing atop the highest trash pile in the dump, your shirt off in December, watching the sun set over the city. And I ended the day with a big steak dinner.

Every Wednesday, the lawyers at Osgoode Hall serve a supper for the homeless. Sluggo and I walked over there together, and on the way he showed me how to get a free paper out of a *Toronto Sun* box: three jiggles and a quick punch. "The one right outside the *Sun* building works the same way," he said. "So you can add insult to injury."

Osgoode Hall is right next to City Hall, which is all done up in thousands of lights and Christmas trees. Cute little couples skate on the outdoor ice rink, gazing into each other's eyes as Christmas carols play in the background. We waited to be let into the dining hall with the other two hundred or so who'd shown up, all the hungry men analyzing, in painful lonely detail, each move of every girl who skated by.

Before sitting down to dinner I went into the bathroom to wash up. It was the first time I'd seen a mirror in days, and it was a bit of a shock. My face was red from windburn and streaked with mud. My hair was matted and my beard looked even thicker with all the soot and dirt. I scrubbed at my face, then tried to clean the cuts on my hands. And in the clean bathroom—a lawyer's bathroom—I could tell how really bad I smelled.

The law student who served our meal looked like a young Lauren Bacall. Although dizzy with hunger, I felt so self-conscious—her hands reaching over my plate and filling my cup with juice—that it was a while before I could eat. She served us steak and salad and french fries, with fruit and ice cream for dessert. But all the men went on about her ass the whole time and how none of us could ever have anything like that, ever—and I had this sad sick feeling in my stomach through the whole damn dinner.

I wanted to stand up and yell: "You're full of shit! Just because you stink and you're dirty and you live on the street doesn't mean you can't have a beautiful woman. And if it does, then I'm different! She could love me with all her heart!" But, really, it's only been a week and I could barely look this girl in the eyes. If I'm going to be here for a year, I've got to figure out how to keep myself together, keep my pride, keep that light shining like a new loonie in the gutter, or a bare-chested bum atop a trash heap at sunset.

I've got a fire going now. And the waves are soft against the shore.

December 6

Both Crazy Chris and his raccoon are behind bars now. It seems he was driving around on a stolen motorcycle, with the raccoon on the back, when he stopped at the corner of Queen and Sherbourne to throw some guy through the front window of Coffee Time. A couple of cops were in there buying doughnuts, and now the raccoon's in the pound, Chris is in jail, and the police are busy going through all his warrants and failures-to-appear.

When I suggested that if a fugitive from justice happens to be sharing a stolen motorcycle with a raccoon, he probably shouldn't stop in the busiest intersection this side of town long enough to throw someone through a window, Sluggo patiently informed me that the guy had called Chris a goof.

"Oh," I said. "That explains it."

I don't know if it's a Toronto thing, a prison thing or what, but "goof" is a pretty serious slur around here. So far I've met three Tent City residents, Sluggo included, who have ended up in jail due to goof-related incidents.

Mike says he's going to post bail for Chris tomorrow—and that he's already done so for half of Tent City. Mike might be as close to a saint as this place is ever going to get. He doesn't live here but comes down each day with a truckload of donations he picks up from all over the city. Today I helped him set up what he's calling the Distribution Centre. He is a uniquely optimistic and overeducated man, and could easily get on my nerves. Today his monologue went something like this:

"Are you good at hammering? You look like you're good at it. Here, you can use these . . . It'll be good when the Distribution Centre's up. A lot of the time I bring down a load of really good donations—clothes and dinnerware and what have you. But then, of course, the boys get into the crack and the booze and things end up all over the place, and then it all gets rained upon.

"This way, we'll have a system for it. We'll have shelving and boxes and it'll all be much simpler for everyone . . . So what's your background? I mean, do you have an education? . . . Writing? Well, you've certainly come to the right place. Do you realize where you are? I mean really, what you've entered into? You should write about it. Do you have a computer? . . . No, right, of course. Well, the way I see it, this is really the centre of the world now. And I don't mean Toronto. I mean Tent City. It's absolutely fantastic! Just look at it!

"First of all, from a writer's perspective, you have this great metaphor of the trash, the scrapyard—and all these people who have just sort of gravitated here. You see what I mean? But more than that, you have archaeology and sociology and all the wonders of the world. On one side we have a grain elevator, on the other a concrete plant. On one side the CN railroad, on the other a canal so deep that ocean liners from the other side of the globe come and dock so close you can almost touch them. On one side, the largest city in the country, on the other a bicycle path that stretches clear across that country. Do you have a bicycle, Shaun? . . . No, but you see what I mean?

"I am fortunate enough to have the background, the education, to put all this in perspective—but can you grasp what I'm getting at? . . . I really believe the people here—without even knowing it—are tapping into some sort of bridge to the future, like pioneers. They're all, in some way, part of a community that exists above law . . . First, on a basic level, they can do things—light fires, drink and take drugs right out in the open—all of which is illegal. And yet no one does a thing about it.

Because it's private property? Maybe. But perhaps there are other reasons. I mean, the news stations do stories on this place, interviews with the 'residents of Tent City,' their names underneath their faces on the news. And these are guys with *warrants* out for them—some of them for murder. And yet nobody puts it together, or at least nobody ever shows up. As if there's some sort of force field over Tent City. Do you see what I mean?

"I mean, this is one of the most photographed, written about places in the country. I alone have fifteen thousand digital photos on my computer. In fact, I've already taken four of you while you were hammering. I hope you don't mind . . . But instead of all this attention bringing the police, we have so many donations from so many organizations that we have to set up the Distribution Centre here to keep track of it all.

"And have you noticed that practically everybody here is white? And almost all Canadian? And they've all spent time in jail. This makes for a very specific, very interesting demographic—a strangely isolated part of the population. You see what I mean? This is the most fascinating place in the world, as far as I'm concerned. Although I don't live here—and the boys, they sometimes give me a hard time for that—I'm quite certain I'm going to spend the rest of my life down here.

"This truck I'm using, it's from an organization called Friends of Agape. Do you know what that means? It's a Greek word for the fourth level of love. There's *philios, sterge, eros* and *agape*. Fraternal love, maternal love, sexual love and selfless love. You know what I'd really like to do? I'd like to set up a computer centre down here—give the boys the opportunity to communicate with everything else going on out there. Do you smoke pot?"

At this point, Hawk and two of his men strolled by with clubs in their hands "to go and tear down Jimmy D's place"—something about a new wood stove and debts unpaid. Jimmy D lives in a shack by the water on the other side of town, past Eddie's place. He's got a crew of lost boys down there, a couple of vicious dogs and an old lady named Petra. As Mike kept talking, Petra came out of the shack with a two-by-four, swinging and yelling, the dogs going crazy.

"Uh . . . don't you think a computer wouldn't last very long?"

"Why do you say that?"

"Even if you managed to set one up and keep it out of the mud— powered, I guess, by a generator—don't you think someone would trash it, or sell it for drugs?"

"Well . . . I don't think so, Shaun. And not if they knew they'd be on camera. We could put surveillance equipment right on the computer, if you think that's necessary."

"Uh, I'm not sure that would make a difference."

"Well, like Chris, for instance. You know what his original warrant was for? He robbed a convenience store—or tried to—where he knew the guy behind the counter. And when the guy wouldn't give him the money, Chris started grabbing cans off the shelves and throwing them at him—all this while the cameras were videotaping him. But, you see, the cameras were unnecessary, since the employee knew exactly who Chris was, had even been to his place the day before. I guess that's what the crack'll do."

"Well, that's sort of my point—about the computer, I mean."

"Hmm. Well, that's interesting. But you've got to look at the big picture. Do you know much about architecture?"

Most of the people down here can't really stand Mike. Part of it, I guess, is that they don't know why he spends all his time trying to help them out—as if there's got to be an angle. Then there's all the photos. "I swear, Mikey, I'm going to shove that camera right up your ass" is a popular refrain around here. But more than that, I think they resent feeling like subjects in Mike's ongoing study of the fantastic unwashed.

By the time we finished my architectural tour of Tent City, featuring the many ways to build a shack and the various schools of organic design mirrored therein, a moratorium had been declared on Hawk's muscling of Jimmy D and everyone was milling around in the old town square.

"Mike says he'll help me build a place," I said to the guys and they started to laugh.

"You'd be better to live in there," said Sluggo, gesturing at the fire barrel we were warming our hands over.

"Nothing he's built so far has stayed up twenty-four hours," said Jackie. Mike didn't say anything. Hawk and his snowsuited storm troopers had left, but Petra was still out—all adrenalized and cracked-up, breaking dishes that had been brought down as donations. Everyone was yelling again. Mike looked over at me and smiled in a boys-will-be-boys kind of way.

"Stop fucking smiling," said Jed. "You're just a fucking garbageman, Mikey. You know that, don't you? Just a fucking garbageman!" Mike carried on smiling like it was all a joke. I haven't seen him once stand up for himself. "Drive us to the beer store, Mikey," they say, and he does. No matter how painful it is to watch, I'm not going to be standing up for him either—not until he tries to do so himself, or until I get my bearings a bit more down here.

December 7

This holiday season is hard enough without listening to the *Peanuts Christmas* album while Rambo the wino tries to read the bingo balls in Dixon Hall.

Rambo's other name is Willy, or Billy, and he lives under the bridge outside Tent City. He looks insane, with a leather jacket too small even for his tiny warped torso, and straggly rings of silver hair, a gin-blossom face and four teeth. His little body is like a broken wind-up toy that can only function, albeit in a Tin-Man-on-acid sort of way, if he keeps it fuelled with alcohol. His slur is impossible, his laugh a hopeless war cry.

As far as I can tell, however, he's not called Rambo ironically. According to his own lore, even the cops refer to him this way, due to his lifelong habit of squaring his shoulders, looping his arms behind his back and pulling two big guns at once from his 26-inch waistband. Never mind that it's hard to imagine him being able to pull a poppy seed from his own teeth.

"One goes blam-blam," he says. "And the other's like a vibrating bed in hell, man. That automatic, that's the one that got me in the most trouble—'cause I'd never just let it go. Drop that gun? Not me—not Rambo. No fuckin' way." At least I think that's what he's saying. With Rambo, you only recognize every fourth word or so, and have to make up your own version of a sentence.

For the time being, it seems Rambo's two-gun days are over. He grabs liquor-store bottles and runs, or kicks in barroom doors and dives at the shelves. He mostly gets caught.

Right now, though, we've drunk just enough to get Rambo off the street, up the stairs and into Dixon Hall for the big Christmas dinner. We're sitting in the dining room under dimmed fluorescent lights, wearing faded paper crowns, off-pink and pale grey, from Christmas crackers with no bang. The walls have been decorated for us by the kids who come in for daycare—messages scrawled in red and green crayon under stick drawings of reindeer: "Santa Claws loves you too!" "Have a Mary Christmas homeless people!"

After dessert, we play bingo. Jerry the cook spins the cage, pulls out the balls and hands them to Rambo to read. Rambo growls and slurs incoherently. This is about as close as we come to tradition: "M–forty-two. Under them over there, four and oh . . . shit. G–two. No! Wait! Just fucking wait, you hear! There's two of them. G–twenty-two! Gee, fuck, I'm seeing single!" At least this is what he might be saying.

I win a half-pack of cigarettes, and then a skinny Santa shows up with thermal socks for everyone. An old man in the corner is crying as we leave.

December 8

I guess I got too smug about my tent, and maybe about everything down here. A storm came in last night and blew my stuff all over the place. I couldn't sleep—which at least meant no dreams of her. I think I'm sick. I'm finding it hard to write, or move.

December 10

I've still got a fever. I drag myself out of Tent City and head downtown until I come to the Paramount—one of those new mega movie pleasure palaces with plush seats and cup holders, a dry warm world where time stands still. I stand at the concession and watch the ticket taker for a while, then manage to get past him just in time for the 3:15 showing of *Harry Potter*.

By midnight I've seen *Black Knight*, *The Heist* and *Ocean's Eleven*, too. I have no idea where one movie ends and another begins—wizards double-crossing gangsters, people slipping in and out of British accents, the past and present colliding and, strangely enough, a lot of jokes about shoes.

By the time I get back to Tent City I'm feeling a bit better. As I bend down to unzip my tent, something big and hairy busts out of the flap then scurries off between my legs. There are two animals I hate: chickens and rats. Chickens at least you can eat. Part of me feels like this is just another movie. But the tent is shaking. There's a hissing sound, like claws and teeth on nylon. I pull the zipper open a bit more, then smack my hand against the tent and stand back. Two more rats come running out, but still the walls are moving.

I drop my bag and look up at the sky. I just want to sleep. But the rats have taken over my home.

Finally I open the tent and step in. It takes me far too long to locate the flashlight and during that time I'm in a dark and feverish place. There are rats everywhere and, although I can't see, I can smell them and hear them—the noise they make is loud and frantic—and I feel the weight of them running across my feet.

By the time I switch on the light, it seems they've gone. I turn the flashlight off again, and lie down in the cold darkness. But they are still there in the night, circling me, running over my chest, through my hair, scratching and scurrying into my sleep. So now I also dream of rats.

December 11

When I woke up I decided to build a house. There's nothing like rats to get you moving.

I tore down what was left of the windbreaks, then tossed everything out of the tent, pulled it down and went looking for building materials. Within an hour I had a new floor built, and by noon Hawk had showed up. He likes to know what's going on.

"Rats," I said.

"I told you not to set up down here."

"I know."

He shrugged and left. A while later he came back with four guys, carrying a half-built frame for a small shack. "Here," he said. "I was building it for this other guy, but he's outta luck."

I borrowed a hammer, saw and nails from Sluggo, set the frame on the floor and hammered it down. I worked non-stop, and by sundown I had a floor, three insulated walls and even the makings of a storage space at the back. Considering the scraps at my disposal, and my never having built a house before, it looks pretty good. The only problem is I've torn down my tent, haven't finished my shack, and it's starting to rain.

December 12

One day is never like the one before, or the one after, and the worst thing you can do is let yourself think things are going well. Nothing is ever "going." There is no continuous tense, and if you think there is, you're screwed.

I came out of that three-day flu with some rat-fuelled moxie—nothing would stop me. But the rain stops you. Dreams and stupid heartbreak stop you. Hunger and booze and all this ugliness stop you. You can't function, can't really move, but have nowhere to sit and rest. It's wet and cold wherever you try.

I thought I'd be smart, the best bum on the block—thought I'd comb my hair every day, cook my greens, count my pennies. I pictured myself taking care of people, helping the downtrodden, the schizos, walking like a displaced prince through the alleys, writing like a poet beneath the eves of a church, feeding the pigeons, an apple and a jug of water in my knapsack, a knowing glint in my bright eyes.

I can't remember the last time I talked to a lucid human. I ramble on to myself all the time: "Okay, boy, come on, just try to find the part that's dry. Okay, is that wet or just cold? Wet and warm is worse than cold and dry. Don't sleep yet. Come on, boy, don't sleep . . . Okay, just get into the bathroom before they see you. Pick up your feet. Take off your shirt first . . . Wash as much as you can. More soap, come on, where's your deodorant? There, is that it? . . . Okay, come on, roll it on your pants, too. God, you stink. Flatten down your hair a bit . . . Okay. Find something to wrap that muffin in. No, don't eat it yet. You're going to be okay, I promise. Just don't think about that, no don't. Don't think about any of that."

Everything I have is wet. I am a cold, wet man. I try to grab sleep in ATM cubicles, in bus shelters, in law office corridors. But I can't sleep for too long. And I don't want to sleep. I don't want the dreams.

I run into her at a supermarket, or she meets me in a bar, or we're in our old apartment, but it's always the same. She tells me she's lonely, too—she loves me and I should come home now, out of the cold, and we can start our life again. It is a state-of-the-art nightmare—it knows all the loopholes.

"Is this a dream?" I say.

"No, of course not, baby."

"Please, really. I have to know. Because it's just too much for me if this is a dream."

"No, no. I love you. You're just tired. You're hungry. Don't worry. Everything'll be okay. We're together now. It's okay."

"But I keep having these dreams. And they feel so real . . ."

"Ssshhh. Be quiet, darling." And she kisses me again.

"Do you promise?"

"I promise. I will love you forever. I'm sorry about everything. Just be happy now. Just hold me."

And then some guy is kicking me. And I wake up.

December 13

I'm rich. Until yesterday, I'd been living off handouts and drinking off some cash I won in a pool game, as well as a stereo I acquired for $5 and sold for $25. But now I've got some real money.

Last week Jackie brought me up to the welfare office on Wellesley to apply for a homeless cheque of $195—which she and everyone else gets every month. I got mine yesterday, and so far I've spent about half of it on a slice of pizza, Band-Aids and alcohol.

It's customary to drink your cheque away as quickly as possible. With the endless rain now morphing into a sleet and hail storm, and me still without a roof or third wall, maximum intoxication appears to be a necessity. I'd rather be building a home, but apparently winter has other plans.

As a result of all this, I've finally decided on a favourite bar. Except for a truly unfortunate name—Who's on First?—it's otherwise perfect. Not only is it close to Tent City and has both Billy Idol and Frank Sinatra on the jukebox, but it's large enough that you aren't obliged to partake in every single bar fight. There's karaoke on Wednesday nights—and it's not your grandma's karaoke. As the clientele is mostly crackheads and winos, the performances are as tragic and haunting as a Mexican bullfight.

December 14

The violence here is constant. It encompasses everything and stays with you far outside the gates of Tent City, ready to sucker-punch you on every corner.

Usually I can't help but get involved in whatever's going on. What with the self-absorption of my recent heartbroken stumblings, however—as well as the knowledge that I have an entire year in which to learn the truths, redeem the downtrodden and save the kingdom—I figured I was being downright inconspicuous. Apparently, that isn't so.

"You're going to hit some real trouble if you're not careful," Hawk said today, giving me one of his ominous winks.

"Why's that?" I said.

"Well, for one, there was that thing with Nancy the other day."

"That thing," as Hawk put it, was just me running to a pay phone to call an ambulance when I noticed that Nancy was lying on the ground bleeding from her head.

"Fuck that," I said.

"People don't like it if you get involved."

"I'm not getting involved in anything. I just figured it would be pointless—and probably more trouble—if Nancy went ahead and died because everyone else was too drunk."

"But it's not your business."

"Well, if anyone's pissed off about that, they can come to me themselves."

"They just might," said Hawk. "You gotta watch yourself. You know Randy's woman thinks you're a narc?"

"Yeah, I met her the other day. Me and Randy had a laugh about it."

"And do you know why she thinks that?"

"He said it's because I'm the only person who just showed up here, without knowing someone first."

"You are."

"And because I watch people."

"You do."

"Yeah, well, we talked about it. Randy says she's paranoid."

"Of course she's paranoid. Everyone's paranoid. And there's no point you looking out for any of 'em. 'Cause they won't look out for you."

"I don't expect them to," I said. "If I look out for people, that's *my* business."

"They'll stab you in the back," said Hawk. "They'll come into your tent—or your shack if you ever finish it—and they'll stab you while you're sleeping. So don't bother caring. Nobody else does, remember that. And I won't be able to help you. The Hawkster can't be everywhere at once, lookin' out for every one of you fools."

This is the great contradiction of Hawk. It's not that he doesn't believe in helping people, it's that he wants to be the only one doing it. He wants you to fear him and need him and distrust everyone else. And he's very persuasive.

It's snowing now—huge, soft flakes falling from the grey sky, covering the trash, the mud and my half-built house. Even the overpass is suddenly quiet.

December 15

A first snow will make even Toronto as romantic as Venice for a few hours, women dragging their men into misty doorways, laughing, candlelight refracting through frost and steam, fringing restaurant windows like a frame of gentle fire, the inside world warming in relation to the outside cold.

You, however, will never be that warm—not without a place of your own, a woman laughing with you and a plate of candlelit food on the good side of an uncracked window. A first snowfall makes your whole body vibrate with longing and the most precise self-pity. Your fingers go numb against the cold bottle in your hand.

I walked north out of Tent City until the blizzard was so heavy I was snow-blind. You can't get a bed in a shelter if you take a homeless cheque—apparently they cross-reference you against the shelter's intake lists. And in Toronto all but the bars close early—earlier if it's snowing. By the time the snow comes it's a good idea to have a fourth wall, and maybe a roof.

Fortunately, most people look a bit like a bum when they come in out of a snowstorm. So I didn't feel too out of place walking into a middle-class bar where the beers are more than a buck, the finger food is free, every couple of hours the pretty bartender sets up a round on the house, the sound system's thumping, the dancing doesn't turn to fighting and your last $60 lasts all night—even when they disregard the liquor laws and stay open two extra hours like they know you've got no home and could do with an early Christmas present.

By 4 a.m. the snow was still blowing and I knew I was drunk enough to pass out in the street. I stumbled down Yonge Street looking for some shelter, and finally came to the entrance of a shopping mall parking garage. There was a sign that said "Enter Here" and so I did. There were red arrows on the wall and I followed them like markings on a treasure map, up the car ramps, all the way to the third level. I came to a door that said "Mall—Upper Level" and gave it a pull, just for the hell of it. It opened.

A mall at 4:30 in the morning echoes like a church and shines like a deserted casino. I kept close to the walls at first, trying to hide from the surveillance cameras and the janitors who were walking the concourse like zombies in *Return of the Living Dead*. But then the holiday season got the best of me. I went window shopping at the finest stores, sledded down the ramp between the escalators and sat for a while in Santa's chair. I decided it would be too much for the kiddies in the morning if I were to pass out in the big man's throne, and so I stumbled away and lay down by one of the exit doors instead.

I awoke from a particularly poignant dream of her on Christmas to someone kicking at my leg. When I opened my eyes, I saw three clean white faces—a girl and two guys—staring down at me, tin-can voices talking into my muddled brain. With the fluorescence and the uniforms I thought for a moment I was in a hospital, or a morgue.

"Oh, hello," I said. "Am I okay?"

"Get up, sir," said the woman.

"How'd you get in here?" said one of the men. He looked about 15, with small mean eyes.

"Uh . . . The sign said 'Enter Here,' so I did. There were even these arrows, and—"

He grabbed me and pulled me to my feet. "I'm writing him up. I'm taking him in," he said, still holding my arm. I yanked away and he pulled out his billy club. "Easy, Todd," said the girl. "We gotta find out how he got in, okay?"

So I walked around with them, trying to figure out how I got into the mall. By 7 a.m. we'd found four breaches in security, and then Todd pushed me once more as I walked out the doors. "And don't come back," he said. It sounded so corny I had to laugh.

It was still cold outside, and on the way back to Tent City I counted fifty-eight people on the street, waking up homeless to a new winter day.

December 18

A couple of days ago I found a ready-made front wall in one of the scrap piles, with a space for a window and a door and scorch marks up the outside where a barrel fire apparently got a bit out of hand. After I spent a few hours cutting the bottom off with Sluggo's $2 saw, it fit perfectly against my side walls. I hammered the base down on to the floor, and the sides into the four-by-fours I'd put up. And just like that I had four walls.

I found a narrow six-paned window over near Randy's and nailed that over the one opening. Then I found a big wooden door and cut a half foot off the bottom so it would fit. It's particularly difficult to put in a door by yourself. Luckily, some guy showed up to hand out pamphlets on yogic meditation—a change from all the flyers with Jesus crucified on the front—and I asked him to hold the door steady for me as I put in the hinges.

Before I made a roof, I finished insulating the place with the stuff Eddie gave me, then began building the inside walls. I amassed dozens of different pieces of wood—plywood, hardwood, oak cabinet fronts, tops of cable spools, varnished desktops, painted drawer fronts—and pieced them together over the insulation like a life-sized jigsaw puzzle. The hammer split on me, and I started using a rock. I worked with the door closed, inside my four walls, looking up once in a while at the bright open sky above. I was tired and hungry and it felt like I was in a box placed on this earth by some god, so that only he could see me, and he laughed as I bashed at the walls with a rock, trying to hammer in nails scrounged from the frozen ground.

Finally I cut some planks I'd found and fit them together to form a roof, then I nailed them down. Closed the box. Covered it with Randy's tarp. And now the guy in the sky can laugh at someone else.

It's a small shack, and the bed that Randy gave me barely fits against one wall. I dragged in all my other stuff that's been sitting out there in the mud and snow.

"Lookit that," I said to Sluggo, who hadn't lifted a finger to help, even the few times I bothered to ask him. "I done got myself a roof. And now I'm gonna sleep under it."

He nodded, and I closed the door.

x   x   x

The freezing rain starts falling at midnight. The largest leaks in my flat stupid roof are right over the bed, and soon the blankets are soaked right through. I lie there, swearing to that smug god in the sky that I'll sleep in this bed if it kills me. And so I pull the blankets tight around me and curl into a ball, each drop of rain a heartbeat in utero.

For once, there are no dreams of her, just half-conscious battles in my brain between the evil of falling water and the goodness of dry cloth. I try at least to keep my mind dry, sheltered from the flood . . . but finally there's nothing left but the shivering instinct of a fetal fox. By the time the sun comes up, the drops are splashing as they hit the bed.

December 19

Like a first-year sociology student I keep coming back to Maslow's hierarchy of needs. I know there are five levels, and that the first must be something like food, water and shelter, because that's what I work at all day. But the second? Human contact, a good book and pinball? The third, I guess, is the stuff you get jailed for: fast cars, cocaine and kisses that end in a sunlit morning by the sea. Above that would be enlightenment, an

Academy Award and true love. And then finally, I guess, redemption.

I've been working cold and mostly unfed, not stopping until I sleep.

Sun-up to -down yesterday I built an attic with a slanted roof to save myself from the rain and snow. I raised three two-by-fours up the front wall, nailed a plank for a cantilever awning to the tops, hauled two eight-foot plywood sheets up, nailed them to the awning, filled in the sides with some pressboard and covered it all with the same old tarp.

I couldn't have done it so fast if it weren't for Mike, really the only guy so far who's given me a hand, like he's trying to realize his utopia—the Amish village of his own mind. He's a terrible carpenter, but he stayed through the rain and smiled good-naturedly every time he hit his thumb or fell in the mud.

"See," he said as the sun went down. "People help each other here."

December 20

In my life so far, these are the things I've done for money: mowed lawns, dug ditches, worked in a video store, built adobe houses in Mexico, telemarketed, sunk eight balls, picked olives in Spain, painted villas in Italy, written stories, edited ESL proposals for the Department of National Defence and the RCMP, edited poetry, bashed down walls, constructed bleachers for the Grand Prix, taught English to CEOs and hairdressers, sold my body for clinical drug testing, led a convoy of models and deejays to college campuses across the country for frosh week, played poker and installed toilets in Arizona. But the hardest work I've ever done is begging for change in a Santa hat.

This morning I woke up freezing but dry and walked to the Metropolitan Church for lunch. The Out of the Cold Program serves lunch on Tuesdays and Thursdays and dinner on Mondays, all winter long. This was my first time there. Until now I've been living mostly off the baloney sandwiches and soup that the Street Help vans bring down to Tent City. I didn't know if my stomach could handle real food, but the young woman who served me gave me all the energy I needed to face the day. She put a plate of turkey casserole and apple salad on the table in front of me, then promptly sat down, smiling disarmingly. "Do you want some more?" she said, though I hadn't yet taken a bite.

"Uh, maybe after," I said. "Thanks."

"Sorry, yeah. I mean after." She was quite lovely and I couldn't help smiling back at her. "It's my first day here," she said.

"Me too," I said. "It seems like a very nice place. Is this your, uh, church?"

"Yes. I'm Lori." The tag on her sweater read "Lori."

"Are you going to be here every Thursday, Lori?"

"I hope so. If I can find the time. I have two businesses to run as well."

"What are your, um, businesses?"

"One's communications, and the other is therapy training."

She had a funny way of talking, like she was trying to find the words tucked into her smile, stored there on loan by someone with greater authority. A "business in communications," for instance, turned out to mean she writes articles she hopes to sell to women's magazines, but on topics "more meaningful, like spirituality and identity and the responsibilities of being a woman, not just the usual stuff."

"Like bikini waxes?" I offered, trying to show I understood.

"Um . . . yes, like that," said Lori.

"Therapy training" meant that she's a certified reiki master, qualified to teach the Japanese art of healing through touch.

"Like a laying on of hands," I tried again. "In a samurai sort of way?"

"Yes, exactly," she said. "And what do you do?"

I looked around at the other homeless people, unsure for a moment if I was in the right place, if maybe a bill would come at the end of the meal.

"I, uh . . ."

She nodded, still smiling. I didn't know what to say. I didn't want to scare away this smiley churchgoing reiki master by pointing out what should have been obvious—that I'm a bum among other bums, here to beg for food. "I'm trying to get back on my feet," I said. "You know . . ."

She nodded sweetly, and said, "Where are you living?"

"I just finished building a shack," I said. "Down by the water."

She didn't seem to find this strange, just nodded again, as if we're all pioneers here, exploring the new world.

"You'll be just fine," she said. "It's good to be you."

That one threw me. It felt like a scene from *Touched by an Angel,* and

I glanced around quickly to see if anyone was staring at me as if I was talking to an empty seat. I started to laugh, then saw she was serious. "Uh, yeah," I said. "I'm going to be fine."

"I'm dancing at the church here on Sunday night. To harp music. It should be sort of mythical, or mystical. You should come, if you don't have plans."

"No plans," I said.

Throughout the meal Lori kept coming back to see me. When I finally got up to leave she said, "I'll see you on Sunday," and put her arms around me. I hugged her awkwardly and walked quickly out of the church.

I headed up Yonge Street feeling kind of high, then walked through the malls among the crowds of holiday shoppers. I bought a Santa hat with my last $2 and decided it was time to stop messing around. I once vowed to myself never to beg. I also told myself I'd never take welfare, but it's funny how things work out.

I figured if I was going to do it, I'd start right at the nerve centre. City Hall is the hub not only of municipal politics, but also the homeless population. There's usually about a dozen in sleeping bags outside the main doors. Some people go back and forth between Tent City and City Hall; when things get too sticky in one place, they head to the other.

After ten minutes out front, however, I was ready to leave. The problem was simple: I couldn't ask for money. I just stood there opening the door, wishing people a merry Christmas with my toque bunched in my hand and all the other homeless people looking at me like I was nuts.

"Just opening doors," I said to them. "Merry Christmas."

I crossed Queen and decided to try again, in front of a TD Bank/Starbucks Coffee building. I held the door open, wishing people a merry Christmas until a security guard came out and told me to leave.

"Just opening doors," I said.

"Well, do it somewhere else."

I figured if I gave up now, I'd have to squeegee windows or steal if I wanted money. So I went back to the mall, found a subway entrance with a nice pair of doors, and started pulling them open for the holiday shoppers.

"Merry Christmas, ladies," I said. "Merry Christmas, sir . . . Have a happy Christmas, buddy." Then finally it just came out: "Spare some change if you can . . ."

When someone finally fished into a pocket for a loonie I was so surprised—trying to quickly unbunch the hat in my hand—that I let go of the door and it banged against him.

"Oh, sorry," I said. "Damnit! Don't worry about the loonie." But he gave it to me anyway.

Eventually I figured out how to hold the hat and the door at the same time, to wish people a merry Christmas and mention spare change in the same breath.

I know that if I let myself, I could be really good at this. If I treat it as an acting gig and just go with it, making people laugh, dancing, telling jokes and opening doors, I know I could make a bit of money. But I also realize that it's not an act for anyone else, that it's my hand holding out the hat, my voice begging for money. And I don't know if you can divide yourself from your actions. If you beg from someone, can you ever be anything but a beggar in their eyes? If you stand with your hat in your hand for weeks, or even months, will you eventually cancel the eyes of a whole city?

Whatever the case, within an hour I got $11 and a woman gave me a bag of sandwiches left over from a business conference.

"They've got mayonnaise," she said. "So you shouldn't save them." Little does she know I live in a deep-freeze.

To balance out my karma and justify the Santa hat, I spent the rest of the evening giving the sandwiches to other beggars. As I should have expected, however, most barely acknowledged them and asked for a buck or two instead. You can find food, but you can't find booze or drugs. Those you have to pay for. When the sandwiches were gone I bought a mickey of whisky, then came back here to write by candlelight in my freezing new shack by the river.

December 21

Like hunger, thirst and loneliness, the cold can make you temporarily insane. And so, in the deep chill of winter, fathers gas their families to death trying to heat a one-room apartment with a two-burner stove. Pensioners set fire to a chair and choke on the smoke. Winos, usually more careful, take a gulp of lighter fluid to thaw out their stomach. I sit here nights, trying to write, taking quick slugs of whisky and burning each page of rough copy, dropping them flaming into a bowl at my feet. The shack fills with flame and floating embers and smoke and for a few moments my eyes burn rather than freeze. My fingers warm up, I write another line and try not to choke on the words.

I light a fire outside my door, and stand in the middle of it until I can feel my toes again, stepping out before my soles melt too much. Then I go back to writing and drinking and dropping burning pages into a bowl. There's no point in trying to sleep until you are exhausted enough to pass out. You can't just drift off when your face is too cold to feel your nose. You wet your lips, and your mouth is like a slash of fire.

x   x   x

When I woke up this morning I decided to start using my head.

I think I've been under the impression that I have an advantage over others on the street—that I am smarter, stronger and more in control. And so, as if to take away this edge, I've been handicapping myself almost subconsciously, letting myself slip into a state of half-thinking unresourcefulness. I've let others go first and take all they can. When people come down with donations I end up with nothing. Almost every shack in Tent City now has a wood-burning stove except for mine. I go out on the street and pass out sandwiches and cigarettes, then come back and shiver in my shack, as if this will allow me the full disaster of homelessness, and teach me something. But I'm just being stupid. Everyone finds an edge.

First I went looking for food. After talking to the old boys and following different leads, I realized there's no reason to go hungry in a city like Toronto. As long as you can walk and don't mind eating poorly, you won't starve. Within walking distance of my shack, the Good Shepherd serves lunch and dinner every day. The food is terrible, and the crowd's pretty rough, but you can have as much as you like until they kick you out. For better food, Dixon Hall has breakfast on Fridays, and Osgoode serves dinner on Wednesday, breakfast on Thursday and brunch on Sunday. The Salvation Army on Sherbourne has a nightly dinner, except Fridays, but you have to pick up a ticket at 1 p.m. There are also a half-dozen churches downtown that serve dinner through the Out of the Cold Program during the winter.

I ate at the Good Shepherd, where I got to witness two fights, then went looking for a place to shower. My hasty wash-ups in gas station bathrooms have been doing little more than smearing the dirt around and leaving me cold. I found a community centre with a gym right near Tent City, and went in to talk to the girl behind the counter. She gave me a free membership to the gym, pool and shower rooms. At first I assumed it was my immeasurable charm that had done it, but it turns out it's their policy—anyone who can prove need of assistance can get a year-long pass.

So I took a shower—the most blessed long shower of my life—and then went around the corner to the library, where I found I can get half an hour a day of free Internet access to check my e-mail. By the time it started getting dark, I wasn't feeling like a bum at all, although I only had $2 in my pocket. I decided I could do with some more money and started walking.

On Queen East, in the window of a bar called East on Queen, I found two words so ominous and full of possibility that I stopped to study them, trying to put them together in as many contexts as I could: *Killer Pool. Killer . . . Pool . . .*

I opened the door and walked in.

"Hey there," I said to a slightly dishevelled Chinese man behind the bar. "What does Killer Pool mean?"

"We're playing it now," he said. "Easiest game in the world."

In killer pool, any number of people can play. Each puts in a couple of bucks and their name on the board. After the break, you get one shot to sink any ball, or you have to chalk an X next to your name. Three Xs and you're dead. The last one alive takes the pot.

I've never been patient enough to be a consistent money player, too often scratching the eight, shooting too hard, passing up a good hook in favour of a fancy, implausible shot. The only things I've got going for me are that I can sink the balls and I get better the more I drink—the right skills for a simple bar game like killer pool.

The Chinese guy is the owner. His name is Henry and so everyone calls it Henry's Place. By closing time—after ten games with an average of twelve players per game—I'd paid my bar tab and cleared $60. I'd also learned a lot about the neighbourhood from the Irish delivery drivers, Indians with junked-out teeth, dirty-bearded bikers and alcoholic ex-athletes who handle the cues like broken hockey sticks. The last game of the night I even got applause, killing fourteen players without a single X on the board.

December 22

Hawk's shack is like a Spartan military checkpoint. It sits high on a trailer bed right at the front gates, so he can see who's coming and going. The small sleeping room he's built off the main room is angled to a point, so that from outside it looks like a beak. His door is made of glass and shines like a big watchful eye.

I was on my way to get water today when he called me over. "Come on in," he said. "I want to talk to you."

His shack is immaculate. There's never anything in view but two chairs, and a stove. I don't know where he keeps his clothes, or the guns he's always talking about.

"What's up?" I said.

Hawk told me to sit down. He narrowed his eyes at me and leaned his massive body forward. "I'll give you this one chance, you got it?"

"Uh ..."

"Are you, in any way, involved with the police?"

"I ..."

"I don't mean this out of disrespect, Shauny, but I *will* bust you up if you don't use this chance properly. You can walk away now, and nothing will happen."

"Hawk," I said, trying to keep my voice even, "I've got nothing to do with the police."

"Because if you stay here and I find out different, I *will* kill you—you understand?"

Just being near Hawk, you feel the presence of a threat. Hearing one come from his lips shook me physically. I kept my eyes on him and said, "I understand. But why are you asking me this?"

"Ah," he said, waving one big arm in the air, "people are talking."

"Who's talking?"

"I told you the other day—Randy's old lady, what's-her-name, just people. But the thing is, I don't see it. I like you, you understand? It doesn't fit for me. And not for my brother Nicky, neither."

Nicky lives next door, in a shack that Hawk built. He doesn't say much, but looks dangerous.

"Like Nicky says, you've got that face, like you've been on the street a while, or maybe on the road, I don't know. I'm good at reading stuff like that, so I shouldn't even be listening to those bitches. But I said I'd find out. So I've asked you straight up, you hear what I'm saying?"

"Sure," I said. "Thanks for telling me there's a problem. I'll try to deal with it."

x   x   x

As I walked back through Tent City there was a lot going on around me. The TDRC had brought down some guys to install donated stoves, Street Help was distributing boxes of food, and there was a documentary film crew handing out $10 bills in exchange for a few minutes of inane interview. The drinking had started a bit earlier than usual and there were already a few fights breaking out. But all I could see were people looking at me, like they thought I was a narc.

Randy's girlfriend, Brenda, is one of a few Native women who live in Tent City. I met her a couple weeks ago, and she's been nice to me. But like everyone down here her sense of humour gets skewed when she's been drinking, and her voice gets loud.

"Hey, Shaun!" she yelled as I walked toward her. The documentary crew had moved over to Randy's barrel. Randy had a big foam cowboy hat on his head, and was lifting Chaos's front paws so he could dance for the camera.

"You've been saying I'm a narc, Brenda," I said, and the camera swung around to film me.

Brenda looked at me for a moment, then started dancing with Randy and Chaos, singing, "Narky, narky, narc . . ." Randy was laughing, but then I stepped forward and grabbed the big foam hat off his head. I felt a bit silly holding it and gave it to Chaos, who started to chew.

"Hey!" said Randy. Brenda was still singing, "Narky, narky," and I could almost hear the cameraman drooling.

"You explain to her when she sobers up," I said. "She can't say things like that."

Randy looked down at Chaos devouring his hat, then turned to Brenda. "Shut up," he said. She stopped singing and threw a bottle at the sky. "You're right," he said to me, serious for just a moment. "I'll make sure she understands."

x   x
x

Eddie gave me the best Christmas present I could have hoped for. Jed and Claudette have taken off somewhere, and Eddie gave me their propane heater until they get back. I put it by the table where I write, heated myself up for a while, then went up to Henry's Place for another night of killer pool.

December 23

At 7:30 this morning Sluggo came banging on my door. He was already drunk, and looking for someone to commiserate with. Jackie started on a crack binge yesterday and came back around midnight with two guys in a truck. They rolled Sluggo for the last $50 of his welfare cheque, then the three of them sat in the truck smoking and laughing at him before driving away.

"That's pretty rough, Sluggo," I said.

"Yeah. That's what you get for living with a crackhead."

It's hard for me to reconcile these two sides of Jackie. She's sweet to me, but her anger is quick and strong and bursts unsuspectedly. I've seen her go after three men at a time. She swings a two-by-four like it's no heavier than a pool cue, and her voice cuts them down even before she can cover the ground. She's 31 and has already borne six children, one of whom is dead, and none living within range of her anger or sweetness. But for all that, I feel safe around Jackie.

"That bitch!" said Sluggo, staggering over to his fire barrel. "That crackhead!"

"I'm sure she'll be back, Sluggo."

"I know," he said, and fell on his ass.

x   x
x

In a place like this it's hard to meet a nice girl, and there aren't many pretty ones either. There is Julie, however. She lives on the other side of Tent City with Jimmy D's crew. There's a bunch of lost boys over there, who live in and around a big grey trailer. They stick close to Jimmy D, and I've been warned by the old boys not to go over there when they're partying. My first week in Tent City I got into an argument about some wood with Julie's boyfriend, Patrick. When she came out of the shack to yell at me too, however, I lost the focus of our argument in her long legs and lovely moving mouth.

Today, as I was on my way to the liquor store, she called out to me. "I'll come with you," she said, pulling on a jacket. We walked along Lakeshore Boulevard.

Julie is from the Czech Republic, where her family still lives. Patrick works construction during the day while she smokes pot. She's off the other drugs now, and when she smiles her dark eyes flash. There's nothing that can lift your spirits faster than going for a walk with a pretty girl.

I spent most of the money I'd won on whisky and wine, and when we got back to Tent City I helped Julie set up a Christmas tree that some-one had stolen. I left before she started decorating it, though. I had to get to church before the reiki master started dancing.

By the time I arrived, the only seats left were in the back of the upper balcony, right in front of the choir. As I sat down, the harp music rose up through the church, and three barefoot dancers with long dark hair and velvet dresses appeared. They looked so eerily similar to each other that from that distance I couldn't be sure which one was Lori. And as they danced in the candlelight, I damned myself softly for thinking of Filmores.

Once the dancing was over, the singing began, and eventually it became too lovely to bear. When the choir began to file out, I thought they'd finished and chose that moment to excuse myself, working my way to the centre aisle. As I reached the end of the pew, however, another song began and I found myself standing in front of a soprano solo, the whole congregation staring up at me. I nodded to the singer and tried to walk away. But suddenly Lori appeared, and her hand was on my arm.

"Are you staying for the rest?" she said.

I shook my head and she hugged me tightly. When I got outside it was pouring rain.

December 24

There is blood on the floor and on the bed, and it's dripping on the page. I think my nose is broken, and maybe a few ribs. My face feels like pulp when I touch it.

There were three of them, and one of them had a two-by-four. Nothing really hurts right now, but I know it will. I feel numb, and sort of high, like I'm falling through the air. My whole body tightens when I breathe. There's blood in my eyes and I can taste it in my mouth.

It is almost midnight. Merry Christmas.

December 25

Although I don't feel like reliving it, I'll try to explain what happened yesterday.

People are supposed to be generous on Christmas Eve, so I went downtown with my Santa hat on. I opened doors, told jokes and wished people a merry Christmas, dancing around and stomping my feet to keep warm. I made $27.25 in three and a half hours, and when it was dark I headed back to Tent City.

As I passed Who's on First? I noticed a woman in the doorway, though she only barely looked like a woman. Her face was smeared in garish cabaret makeup, the skin snow white, a circle of red ringing her mouth, a halo of blue around each eye, a pink spot on each cheek. Her chest was bare and a thin white shirt lay crumpled at her feet. Her body was so emaciated it didn't seem like a body at all. Her ribs stuck out like daggers, her breasts were translucent packets of sagging skin. They looked like wings folded against a fallen bird.

"Are you all right?" I asked, moving toward the doorway, but she just stared at me with her blue-rimmed bloodshot eyes. "You're going to freeze," I said. "You have to put some clothes on." The men on the street were circling behind us like jackals.

"You're going to get hurt if you stay here," I said. "Come on. I'll find somewhere for you to go."

"You're scaring me," she said, but she let me guide the sleeves of her shirt back over her arms. It hung open and she wouldn't let me touch the buttons.

"Do you have a quarter?" she said. On top of the face paint, her skin was streaked with sparkles, like my darling used to wear when we'd go out dancing.

"Yeah," I said, "I've got a quarter. Come with me." I guided her down the street, but as we passed another bar she pulled away and slipped through the door. I tried to follow her, but two men stopped me just inside. It was crowded and I couldn't see her.

"There's a woman," I said. "I have to . . ."

"Get out, buddy."

"But she . . ."

"Out."

I stood outside the bar for a while, then finally left.

All the way back to Tent City I could see her junkie-angel skeleton—the streaks down her face, the lines up her arms, her sparkling skin, inward wings hanging useless in the cold, waiting for the dogs to chew her bones.

As I walked through the gates, into Tent City, a car pulled up and a man handed me a stack of pizzas. "Merry Christmas," he said, and drove away.

On my side of town everyone was passed out, except for Sluggo. I gave him one of the pizzas, but there were still four left. Julie had told me to come by for their Christmas Eve bonfire party. I hadn't intended to, but now I had pizzas and no one to eat them. So I took them to Jimmy D's.

I'd been warned about those guys, but I figured it was Christmas and I knocked on the door. "Who the hell is that?" growled Jimmy D. He is famous for this growl, which sounds like the demented raving of a Muppet lost in the desert with nothing to drink but kerosene. Some people just call him The Voice. He is famous for three other things as well: he used to be a professional boxer, he is never sober, and he is crazy.

Once a year Jimmy D gets to cry. Every Christmas Eve—no matter what—Jimmy D watches *It's a Wonderful Life* on TV. He watched it every Christmas he was in the pen, and now, as I opened the door, he was staring at a stolen TV. A small generator was humming against the wall and Jimmy Stewart was approaching the bridge.

I passed around the pizzas and Petra handed me a beer. Apart from her and Jimmy D, there was Julie and Patrick, and Dan and his girlfriend, Jen, who scowled when I came in. Around Tent City, Patrick and Dan are known as the Frenchies, since they're from Quebec. They're about my age, and as far as I can tell they act as capos for Jimmy D.

Then there was Karl, who had brought the generator over. He's about twice my age and lives at the first turn of the road through Tent City, in a long house with a big fence around it and a German flag tied to a pole. He has a thick German accent and army boots, and if his dog responds to anyone but him he gives it a kick. This was the first time I'd met Karl, and he sure seemed like a Nazi to me. Everyone was drunk. Julie was wearing a tight, festive red outfit. "For Christmas!" she said.

I sat down on a crate between Julie and Karl, and right away he started pissing me off. He told me I should be scared of him because he used to be an assassin, and somehow that led to an argument over the origin of the word.

"Iz word in Latin," said Karl, sneering like it was tiresome to explain things to dolts like me.

"No it's not," I said. "It comes from the Islamic . . ."

"You sink you know somesings?" said Karl. "You sink you are smart? You know somesings?"

"I know you were never an assassin."

Here are some words of advice: Beware of anyone with whom you get into an argument over a word like "assassin." And if you're dumb enough to go somewhere you've been warned against merely because of a pretty girl, beware even more.

"You sink you know somesings?" said Karl once more. "You know no sings!"

It went on like this for a while, until he spat on the floor near my feet. I told him to go spit somewhere else and Julie laughed in his face. He walked across the room muttering under his breath and crouched down next to Dan. I could see him eyeing me as I talked with Julie. Patrick tried to join our conversation, but apparently his English gets lost when he's drinking.

During the movie's intermission we got a bonfire going outside and Julie wanted to listen to some music, so I went over and got the radio I won in a pool game the other night. I brought over a bottle of whisky, too, and passed it around as I plugged in the radio. "Who Are You?" by The Who was playing, and Julie turned it up.

"Change ze fucking music," said Karl, still hunkered down next to Dan by the door.

"I like this song," I said.

"Iz my fucking generator," said Karl.

I pulled the plug, the battery power kicked in, and then I did something truly stupid. I turned to Karl and smiled.

We listened to the music, drank beer and whisky, and everyone got even more hammered. I told Julie about the junkie with a painted face and broken wings for breasts. Jimmy D was shadowboxing on the couch with a bottle in each hand as Petra shook her breasts in his face. Karl was still muttering in Dan's ear. Patrick was drinking from my bottle of rye and trying to focus on what Julie and I were talking about.

It's a Wonderful Life started up again, and I decided to go invite Sluggo for the bonfire. I grabbed my bottle and made my way across the crowded shack. When I reached the door, Karl stood up and said, "You never take ze ozer man's bottle!"

"It's my bottle," I said, and as I reached past him for the door he shouldered me into Jen. I caught myself before falling on her, but she let out a yell anyway.

"Get the fuck away from her!" shouted Dan, who was on his feet now too. "She's pregnant!"

I turned toward her to apologize. But before I could, Dan punched me in the mouth. The only thing that flashed through my head was, *Pregnant? But she looks so skinny.* And then I was outside, on the ground.

I tried to cover up, but there was only so much I could do. I finally managed to get to my feet, but Karl had a two-by-four and they took me down again. I could see the wood descending in the firelight, the smoke curling around it as it cut through the air.

Julie was out there now too, trying to get them off me. But that just made things worse. Patrick followed her out and started kicking me. My nose had burst and there was blood in my eyes, and I could hear Julie's voice yelling, "Look at him! Look what you've done to his face!" And then she was on the ground beside me. I tried to grab for her, but my arm went into the bonfire and I could hear blood sizzling on my sleeve.

"Go with him, bitch!" yelled Patrick. "Go with him if you like his face!" I rolled over on the burning sleeve, and suddenly everything was crimson—Julie's red party dress in a glow of blood and fire. My arms had gone numb from deflecting the blows, and felt like someone else's arms—someone else who was taking this beating.

A woman's voice called out.

It was Eddie's girlfriend, Karen. "Leave him alone!" she yelled. She is small and slight and pregnant, too, and apparently very brave.

"That's my friend!" she shouted. And for a moment everything stopped, as if it hadn't occurred to them I might have a friend. It was a surprise to me as well.

Then, in the momentary stillness, Karl's true self rose up. Like the opposite of the Grinch's heart growing three sizes, Karl's sick soul began to swell. He turned, took a swing, and hit Karen across the side with the two-by-four.

Even before she yelled out, I was up and at him. No one moved to stop me, and now Karl was under my fist as it worked up and down, the sleeve still smoking on my arm.

By the time the Frenchies finally snapped out of it and came for me again, Eddie was there too, and he reached me first.

"Hi, Eddie."

"Hey, young Shaun," he said, then pulled me to my feet and dragged me down the shore to my shack. I was dizzy, and he propped me against the door. "Don't go back there tonight," he said. "You got that, Shaun?"

"But I—"

"You can deal with them in the morning."

"The morning," I said, blood gurgling in my mouth. Eddie pulled the door open and helped me inside.

"Karl's mine, though," he said. "You understand?"

"All right, Eddie. Merry Christmas."

"Thanks. And it's my birthday, too."

"Happy birthday."

My hands were swollen and shaking, and by the time I got a candle lit there was blood on the floor and the bed. I pulled open my notebook and blood dripped on the page. My face felt like pulp when I touched it. I tried to breathe and my whole body tightened. It didn't feel like my body, or my eyes—like I'd been turned into a monster. I wrote a few lines and the blood froze where it landed. I lay down on my back and looked up at the wooden planks of my roof. My body didn't hurt yet, but I knew it would. And like children all over the world, I couldn't fall asleep, just thinking of the morning to come.

December 26

I woke Christmas morning in my clothes. My whole body hurt, but I got myself upright and walked out of my shack. There was a group of people over by Randy's fire barrel.

"Merry Christmas," I said. I could feel the cuts cracking open on my lips.

"Holy shit!" said Randy. "You look like you been hit by a truck."

"Yeah," said Marty. "But you seen Karl? Looks like he was hit by *all* the trucks, and the teamsters, too. The ambulance just left."

"The ambulance?"

"Yeah, half his fucking head is gone."

I put my hands over the fire. They were dark with dried blood. Then Eddie was standing beside me. "You gave me your word, Shaun."

"Huh?"

"You said you'd leave Karl for me—it's my birthday, remember?"

"Yeah, and Jesus' too. But I didn't do it."

x
 x
  x

I can't tell you who told me, but I got it on good account that this is what happened:

After Eddie helped me home, Karl was still out by the bonfire, frothing at the mouth and circling the flames. He was mad that I'd got in a few licks and went into Jimmy D's shouting at the Frenchies to go after me, to drag me out of my shack.

Until then, Jimmy D had stayed out of it. But now he stood up from the couch and put his arm around Karl. He cupped the back of Karl's head with one hand and hammered the other into his face. Karl hit the floor and Jimmy D pulled a five-iron from behind the couch.

When he'd finished, Jimmy D looked down at the mess on the floor. "You fuckin' ruined the movie," he growled. "I didn't even get to cry."

x x x

I just wanted to forget what had happened, and let it slide. But of course I couldn't. The crews here have formed over decades in the pen and on the street, and though Karen saved me last night and Eddie helped me out, I knew I was on my own. If I did nothing I'd be a mark—and wouldn't last the year with any dignity left, nor many teeth.

Because it was Christmas, one of the outreach programs had set up a stage and got some local musicians to play for us. There was hot turkey, apple pie, boxes of chocolate and a couple dozen smiling strangers here to help us celebrate.

I sat down on the ground as a woman onstage began singing "Little Drummer Boy" without a drum. I took off my Santa hat, and by the time I could stand up again, I'd had my Christmas revelation. Beat up as I was, now was the perfect time to deal with things. Even after all my self-destruction, after jumping off that downward double spiral, quitting drugs and running away from my life to detoxify myself, I'd still retained one last superpower: an invincibility to hangovers. And although Jimmy D is the most infamous drinker in town, the Frenchies were no doubt feeling fragile this morning.

According to Eddie, Julie had locked Patrick out of their shack, so I figured he and Dan were still at Jimmy D's. The door opened before I could try my most intimidating knock, and I could see Patrick and Dan lying on a bed near the back.

"Merry Christmas," I called to them. "How you boys feeling?"

"Leave it," said Petra. "You shouldn't be here." Jimmy D stepped forward.

"I just want my bottle," I said. "And the radio. And you guys got any pizza left?"

Petra pointed to the bottle and radio sitting by the door, and I picked them up.

"All right, guys," I said, still calling into the back of the shack. "We'll talk later, okay?" And the door closed in my face.

At least I went there, even if all I got to show for it is whisky, my radio and the coming of the Lord.

x x x

The old crew say there haven't always been rats in Tent City. They got them for Christmas just last year.

There were less than a dozen people here last winter, and it just so happened that they all had somewhere to go for the holidays. There'd already been a lot of media attention and someone brought down a dozen cooked turkeys and left one on each doorstep. By the time the residents returned to their shacks a couple days later, the turkeys were gone and the place was crawling with vermin.

December 27

Some things move fast once you start them—like cars and the progression of sin. On Christmas Eve I got beat up. By Boxing Day, I was boosting minivans.

Jake came down here a couple of weeks ago with his girlfriend, Joanne, whom everyone calls Jo-Jo. Jake and Jo-Jo. But they ain't no puppet show. Jake is a very big guy. Not as big as Hawk, but bigger than the rest of us. He's got a thick beard over a thick jaw and plenty of jailhouse tattoos. He's a thief, and he's a smart guy, but he really plays up the psycho bit. He's got teeth broken into points at all the right places and that Nicholson grin down just perfect. He's practised his laugh, so that now it's the kind that says he's got no fears—he's crazy and loving it, and you better watch out.

But of course he does have fears. Jake's scared because he's got no strong connections down here, and he saw we were in the same boat long before I did. He came by each day while I was finishing my shack, bringing me tools he'd stolen—so now, if I want, I could build a new home somewhere else. When he said we should go do a job together, he was offering that as a gift, too. He usually takes Jo-Jo with him, but he was willing to give me a shot. "We could watch each other's back," he said, but at the time I didn't think much of it.

On Christmas Day, after I got my radio and bottle back, Jake came by with a staple gun for me, and started right in: "We get ahold of a truck," he said. "I can have one in twenty minutes, and tonight we roll right over their fucking shacks, chase 'em into that trailer of theirs at the back. Then we just Molotov the fucking thing. A bottle in each window. No messing around, you hear what I'm saying? Even if they get out alive, they won't be fucking with us again." Us. It was pretty clear he saw his own future reflected in my bruises.

"Uh," I said. "I hear what you're saying . . . But I don't want a war. Thanks, though. I'll deal with it myself."

"Whatever you say," said Jake, handing me the staple gun. "But you're just one guy."

Which is true.

"You know, I was thinking . . . ," I said when he came over again this morning. "It'd probably be smart if we looked out for each other."

"That's just what I was thinking," said Jake. "You ready for a job?"

"What do I need?"

"Just some gloves and a hat. With that face you better put some shades on too."

I knew this would be the price of his trust, but as we walked through the gates I wanted to turn back. I was no more born a thief than a beggar. Jake, on the other hand, has a real passion for stealing.

"I been on the run two years now, eh? But how you gonna catch up with a guy who changes cars three times a day? You hear what I'm saying? I always got 'em beat."

We walked up Cherry Street and turned into an alley. "There she is," he said, nodding at a Honda van parked in the snow. "Picked her up yesterday. Look like anyone been near her?" There were no footprints, and an even layer of snow on the roof and hood.

"Not to me."

"Me neither. Get in and keep your gloves on—I already wiped her down."

He stabbed a flat screwdriver into the popped-out ignition and turned the engine.

"There's a baby seat back there," I said.

"Yeah." He handed me a cigarette and we waited for the engine to warm up. I kept glancing into the back seat, like the invisible baby might wake up. "You okay?" he said, flicking ashes on the floor as we finally pulled away.

"Yeah . . . It's just the broken nose. Can't breathe right." He gave me a sideways smirk as I pulled out the ashtray.

"Just don't leave any butts in here. We'll have a fresh one soon and then you don't have to worry. You'll see how I scrub 'em down. You should see how I do."

I realized pretty quickly that this, mostly, was why I was here—to see how he does. If it didn't jeopardize the operation so much, Jake would love an audience for every car he boosts. As we drove toward Yonge he pointed out all the best "victims" parked on the street. "That's what I call 'em," he said. "Every car's a victim, but some are easier, you know? Plymouths are the best. Ignition slides out like butter. I can do her in forty seconds."

He pulled us into a back lane off Bloor and cut the engine. "You want to go for coffee?"

"Sure," I said, with a bit too much enthusiasm.

"Stay here." He got out of the car and disappeared up a fire escape. I sat there for a minute, then got out and stood about 12 feet from the car. He was back soon with money in his fist. "Grab my bag, will you," he said, ignoring the fact that I wasn't in the car.

We walked around the corner to a Second Cup, got a couple of coffees and sat down.

"Ain't this civilized!" said Jake. "I almost feel like a real person."

"Yeah, it's nice," I said, hoping the coffee would last all day, that closing time would eventually roll around and he'd say, "Well, too late for robbing now."

"You're still drinking, eh?" he said when he'd finished his cup.

"Yeah," I said, looking down at my half-full mug, and shrugged like there wasn't much I could do about it.

"Okay. Wait here. I'll be back in ten."

I nursed my coffee, checking the status of my swelling head with my hands. I could feel people staring at me. Not a good way to start my career as a thief.

"How long was that?" said Jake as he strode toward the table. "Ten minutes?"

"Damn. I thought I was faster." Apparently time is very important to a car thief.

We walked back down the street. "It's two laneways over," he said. "A blue Voyager. I just got to get something from the last one. Go in through the driver's side." I walked down the two blocks and stood about 12 feet from the blue Voyager.

He stopped for just a moment when he saw me, then opened the door. "After you," he said.

He gave me another smoke and cranked up the radio. This time he drove fast, spinning on the icy corners as he grabbed pieces of loose paper and business cards off the dash, throwing them out the open window.

"Don't worry 'bout your gloves," he said. "I'm wiping her down."

"How many cars you think you've taken?" I said, trying to relax a bit.

"Shit, no idea," he said, though you could see he appreciated the question. "Four hundred, maybe five?"

We drove around for a while, with him talking through his psycho grin, pointing out unmarked police cars, honking at girls on the sidewalk. We stopped in front of a store with an ATM. "Lookit that," he said, grinning even larger under his mirrored sunglasses. "Never seen one so close to the door. Think we could slide it into the back of this thing?"

"Yeah," I said, trying to grin as big as him. "But after dark."

"Maybe we'll come back. Must be twenty, thirty grand in that thing."

"Yeah." A bank machine, in fact, appealed to me much more than baby seats and some poor guy's power drill.

We circled an apartment building until he found someone turning into the parking garage. He pulled in behind, passed a business card over the security monitor for the benefit of any surveillance cameras and slipped us under the gate as it was coming down. We drove up a few levels, then pulled into a corner.

"Wait here," he said. "If you see anyone coming just open your door. I'll hear it." He hit four cars quickly, popping the locks like he had a key for every one, and grabbing stuff from inside. A door opened on the other side of the garage, and a nice little family started walking toward us. I opened my door, but he'd already seen them, and was coming back low behind the bumpers. He opened the driver's door and got in.

While we waited for the parents to get their kids in, buckle down, start up and drive away, Jake went through the bags, swearing at all the candles, children's clothes and boxes of chocolate. I wasn't prepared for this. I didn't know we'd be stealing kids' Christmas presents—I didn't even think there'd *be* Christmas presents on Boxing Day. I expected Cindy Lou Who to start knocking on the door, looking up at me with her big round eyes, puzzled and inquisitive: "Mister? What are you doing?"

"It's all crap," said Jake, throwing the ripped-open presents into the back. "But Jo-Jo likes chocolate. You take the candles."

When the nice family left, he hit three more cars, then we drove to another level. We stopped again and he went for the nearest car, peering in the windows, circling it once before strutting back to the van.

"See that car there?"

"Yeah."

"That's the feds."

"Doesn't look like it."

"No, it doesn't. But it is. Got the red light and markers inside. Think we should take the light? Man, that'd be fine, eh? Driving 'round town with the colours flashing."

"Probably not . . . That's the Mounties, eh? Guess we shouldn't stick around too long."

"You kidding? I could spend all day here," said Jake, sucking on his teeth. "Takes more than that to scare me." And it was true. As the day went on, Jake did things that seemed fearless. And yet he was obviously scared of what had happened to me, sneaking glances at my face.

"Never got a beating like that," he finally said.

We're all scared of different stuff, I guess. For him, that was the fear—that the wolves would get a hold of him. I'm not that scared of people and places. Some of the things I do make others think I'm fearless. But I've got lots of fear.

I'm scared of losing the people I love—and some of them I already have. And I'm scared of losing my freedom—not just being locked up for a while (because this time in Tent City feels a bit like that)—but losing the freedom to go wherever I want.

When I was a teenager, learning how to drink, my friends and I had a game in which we'd run through the neighbourhood ripping off hood ornaments. The one with the most after an hour got a case of beer. We thought it was a noble crime against vanity and the bastardized peace symbol of Mercedes. But one night someone caught me and held on. Instead of roughing me up or calling the cops, he took me on a walk down to the beach. "I got caught stealing when I was 19," he said. "And now I'm 38 and I've never been anywhere. I've got a record and I can't leave the country. You hear what I'm trying to tell you?"

I've been scared of that one ever since.

I'm also scared of being a bad person and hurting people—of taking their kiddie's Christmas clothes and candy, of breaking my mother's heart. I hope she'll understand that I went along with Jake as a matter of survival—not to eat, or to get enough for a warm bed, but to form a tricky sort of alliance, to get backup so I wouldn't get beaten again, or something worse.

On the bottom level of the parking garage, we pulled in next to a big green van. Jake circled it once, tried both doors, then smashed the passenger-side window. The crash and shower of falling glass echoed through the garage.

He got the sliding door open and started pulling stuff out—a pair of skis, a meat cutter, chainsaw, a halogen lamp. I was grabbing it all in through the driver's-side door and struggling the stuff over the seats into the back. Suddenly headlights appeared and I started yelling, "Jake, Jake! A car!" He just ignored me, and the car turned onto the exit ramp.

When he got in and closed the door, he didn't mention that I'd freaked out. "That's enough for now," he said.

I gave his chest a good thump. "Good job, Jake," I said. And he grinned.

I thought maybe now—with the stolen van full of stolen goods—would be the time for caution, but Jake cranked the music even louder, rolled down the windows and stood on the gas. We sped through the city and onto the expressway, singing "Good Times, Bad Times" along with the radio until my bruised head hurt so bad I could barely look at the road.

"You okay?"

"Just the head. Double vision." I pulled some painkillers from my pocket and swallowed them dry.

When we got where we were going, Jake went in to talk with his fence. I got out of the van and stood about 12 feet away.

He grinned when he came back out, shook his head and said, "It ain't gonna bite you."

On the way back through town he pulled out some cash.

"You keep it," I said, thinking maybe I could still salvage my soul. "Just watch my back, eh?"

"And you watch mine," said Jake, burning the tires as we sped into Tent City.

December 31

I don't know how to write this. I've been staring at this page for hours, but I can barely put a sentence together.

The past four days have been hell.

I came here to write a book.

No, that's too fucking easy.

I came here to escape the mess I made of my life. I thought that if I could plunge into the destruction of other people's lives I could forget my own. And there was a chance, I thought, that if I could write a good enough book it would open up something else for me. And failing that, I could just drown here—in this new mess—and disappear.

But then, four days ago, the life I left came and found me. And now I can't do a fucking thing.

I came back to this shack to give it another chance. But I'm still just staring at this page.

What am I supposed to write? That I've spent the past four days wandering through the streets drunk and sobbing my eyes out, stumbling into doughnut shops to sing to myself in the bathroom mirror, stealing and gambling with nothing to back up a bet, running through the malls shouting at people to look at the moon, waking up in alleys to yell at the bugs in my hair? Why should I humiliate myself further by writing this down?

I don't know how I came to this. If I'm really going to write, I should just start this book over.

Call me Shaughnessy. I'm a fuck-up with no excuses. I was given a great life. I was born healthy and happy, to the best parents anyone could ask for. We lived in the nicest part of Vancouver, just blocks from the ocean, and the streets were lined with chestnut trees. My dad went for runs in the woods nearby, and I raced ahead of him on my BMX. My mother read to me at night. They gave my sisters and me names they would have liked for themselves, and trusted us to make of them whatever we wanted.

But that wasn't good enough for me. I wanted to prove that I could be great even without a lucky life—that I could live anywhere, do anything, under any circumstances. I wanted the whole damn world.

When I graduated from high school I left home with a few hundred bucks and hitchhiked to Costa Rica. It took a long time, and there were stretches of months when I didn't call home once. I broke my parents' hearts, and never even realized it.

By the time I finally came back I could speak another language. I was a drinker and a smoker. I thought I knew things that other people didn't, and that I'd learned how to move through any kind of life. But there's always another one out there.

After a month or so I left again. I bought a car and drove through sixteen states, a few provinces, then finally crashed into a highway pole on the outskirts of Montreal. And that's where I met her.

I fell in love with her instantly. I don't care how that sounds—I fell in love when I saw her wolf eyes. I saw the whole world in there, and decided to stop running.

But a couple of years later we broke up, and I was right back out there. I dragged my broken heart down to Mexico, then over to Europe, through a half-dozen more lives, until she finally called me home.

"Let's make sure that doesn't happen again," I said, and we drank to it as we held each other.

Over the next few years we made the nicest kind of life for ourselves. We lived in a Montreal apartment with high ceilings. We got university degrees, lots of good friends, and we visited our parents on holidays. I was learning to cook, she was learning to drive, our careers were slowly taking off, and when we went out we danced together all night—even after the music had stopped.

But then I screwed it up.

I still don't know why I did it. I guess that part of me that always wants more rose up, and it wanted more than a good life with this beautiful woman I loved, more than my family and friends and that expanse of possibility that stretched out before us. Like Aesop's dumb, greedy dog, I kept going for another bone—for that reflection in the lake. I dove in until I was cold, then lost feeling altogether.

And by the time I finally thawed out I had nothing at all. I'd lost her, and my life was broken into splinters. Everything just started gushing out of me and I became the worst kind of cowboy song. Nobody wants to hear that. So eventually I came here, to this place.

She kept living in our apartment in Montreal, but she has a new boyfriend now, and nice new clothes. She was wearing them four days ago when she came to see me.

"Just to make sure you're all right," she said. "To wish you a merry Christmas." But I couldn't stop shaking. She looked as beautiful as the first time I saw her, and I could see the whole world in her eyes, every bit of it that's not mine anymore.

And I hate to think of what she saw—this beaten-up bum in a shack by the river who couldn't even look at her without shaking. She tried to keep warm by the kerosene heater as she talked to me softly, telling me about what our friends are doing now, and how she finally got her driver's licence. And though she thought she was doing me good, it almost killed me.

But even then I somehow thought there was a chance that I could win her back—if only I could say the right thing.

"I love you . . . ," I said. "I've learned all sorts of things . . . I'm stronger than I ever was . . . I'm clean now. I've been clean since I left Montreal." And even filthy as I was, neither of us laughed.

When she finally got up to leave, I fell to the floor. I begged her to stay. I begged her all the way to Lakeshore Boulevard, and then she climbed into a taxi.

Why would I want to write this down, where someone could read it?

I'm going to get out of here now. It's New Year's Eve, and who knows? Maybe someone out there wants to kiss a lonely bum at midnight.

January 5

Most of the women seem to have left Tent City, like getting out of here was a collective New Year's resolution. Randy's lady, Brenda, has taken off. Jackie is still MIA. Nancy left her husband, Marty. Jo-Jo left Jake. They got in a long fight about whether or not she's a crack whore until finally she just left. And now Jake has disappeared too.

I somehow hadn't realized until now that most of the women here sell themselves at night for money and drugs. The cars that come down, if they're not bringing donations or looking for a quick news story, are driven by johns. It's hard to keep your girlfriend through the holiday season when she's a crack whore.

The ladies seem to have taken any warmth we had with them. The nights are bitter now, none kinder than -15 degrees. I've scored an old kerosene heater that shines a sort of hallucinogenic flower pattern on my wood-plank ceiling. The propane one wasn't doing much and Eddie gave it to a couple guys who've moved into Jed's old place. Unfortunately, I'm running out of kerosene fast and still haven't achieved anything that could be described as warmth.

Money has been pretty scarce, too. People aren't as appreciative of my door-opening abilities as they were before Christmas, and the killer pool has pretty well dried up. They're playing only once a week for a dollar a game each, so I'm making just enough to cover my drinks. The last game ended with some guy being thrown through the fish tank. Since Christmas, I haven't crossed into a new morning with money in my pocket.

I seem to have settled things with the Frenchies, though. I'm not exactly sure what did it. It may have been the visit Hawk paid them on my behalf. When I finally went to confront them—pumped up on that brand-new, same-old, love-lost rage—they did the one thing that would stop all this—they apologized. They said they knew Karl had set me up, and were sorry it had happened.

"Well, good," I said. "'Cause I don't have time for this shit."

"Yeah, of course not," Dan said, as if there are plenty of other people who have more time to get beat up.

"Fuck that," said Jake when it was done, pacing the canal and sucking on his teeth. "Let's take 'em down anyway."

"Forget it," I said.

"Well let's do *something.*"

The last day I saw Jake we went for lunch at the Metropolitan Church. One thing about car thieves, they never like to walk anywhere. Just keeping him on course was a trial. Now that Jo-Jo was gone, his grin had turned to a constant snarl.

"I'm kamikaze today," he said, in case I hadn't noticed.

On the way back he boosted a car, but I wouldn't go with him. I hate this mean, petty theft more than just about anything. I'd rather beg, even if it's harder on the pride. If he were stealing from big companies or store chains, that would be different. But Jake doesn't get my take on this.

"I'm not stealing with you, Jake. Not today."

"Why not?"

"Because you're kamikaze." The night before, he'd taken a Plymouth hatchback up to 160, outrunning the cops down the DVP. He's exploding, just as I'm trying to put myself back together.

"Fuck you," he said, then turned the screwdriver in the ignition and drove off.

Later that night he burst into my shack, dumped a bunch of useless stolen stuff on the floor and sat down on my bed.

"What's up, Jake?" I asked. But he didn't answer. He just stared at the wall as if he could see right through into some distant fire. He was breathing heavily and shaking, as if working himself up to one last criminal frenzy, until finally he burst out the door and stumbled back into the cold night. I haven't seen him since.

January 6

Yesterday was a bad one. There are these two guys, Derek and Lenny, who came down at Christmas and moved into Jed's prefab between Randy and Crazy Chris. They lived down here last summer and seem well-connected with the old crew. They're known as the Brothers. Derek, as far as I can tell, is the bigger brother. They're both mean, but he's meaner. They're both loud, but he's louder. Lenny follows Derek around but has trouble keeping up. They're both dumb, but Lenny's dumber. They're both ugly, but Lenny looks like a bloated ferret. They're equally drunk all the time.

They are good with their hands, though, and have already built a new room, larger than the prefab itself, on to the front—as well as a porch with a windbreak where they make their own booze from apples and sugar, which they boil on a fire barrel. They start drinking at 8 a.m. and go until they pass out.

Then there's Jerry and Donny. They are supposedly half-brothers—which I guess explains why they put up with each other. They're about my age and live in a ramshackle A-frame over by Jimmy D's, but they spend most of their time at the Brothers' place. The four of them together are a formidably stupid force.

Yesterday morning I was coming out of my shack to head downtown and do some panning, when Jerry and Donny called me over to sit in on their drinking circle. They'd already been going for a while and were getting some air on the Brothers' porch. Donny vomited as we went inside.

"I'll sit in for a while," I said, nodding to the Brothers as I sat down, "but I got no cash." The Brothers didn't introduce themselves, and neither did I.

Jerry handed me the bottle. As I took a sip, Derek said, "You gotta throw in."

I'd already had a drink. "Sorry," I said, holding the bottle out to Lenny. "I got no coin,"

"Then get the fuck out," said Derek. "I don't drink with suckers."

"Not a sucker," I said. "They asked me in."

Jerry, to his credit, stuttered something like, "N-n-n-not a sucker," but shut up fast when Derek and Lenny found their feet.

"This ain't a free fucking boat," said Derek, swaying like the whole room was being rocked by giant waves of moonshine as he tried to stare me down. He's not that tall but he's built. He's got a Fu Manchu that stretches around his snarling mouth, which is always open. One front tooth is silver, and the other isn't there.

"I don't need this shit," I said, and walked out of the shack.

I opened doors for a couple of hours, until this old guy, who pans down in the subway, came up and told me to get away from the doors.

"Security," he said. "They just got me."

So far I've been lucky, putting my hat on fast whenever I see the guards coming, stepping through my doors like I've got somewhere to go. It's a $150 fine for "loitering." Having made barely $10, I thanked him and left.

I went for dinner at a nearby church, which sounds much cozier than it ever is. Most soup kitchens are set up like prison cafeterias. We line up single file with our plastic trays, then walk slow and thick-shouldered back to our tables to hunker down over plates of meat and pasta. Most sit with the same crew they sat with in the pen, so it just goes on—the same unwritten rules, the same glances, the same quick violence— just like prison.

I moved the food around on my plate until the guy across from me got punched off his chair by a big Native with teardrop tattoos. Then I went to a bar near the church and made a few drinks playing pool. On the way back to Tent City I stopped in at Who's on First? (which I've since renamed Who's on Crack?). As I came in the door, Rick the bartender was bellowing. He's always bellowing at someone. He used to be the bouncer, and the current one spends most of his time trying to stop him from killing the customers.

Tonight Rick was in an especially bad mood. A country band was playing and as I walked in, he leapt across the bar at a black guy, his fists flying. The guy headed for the door and Rick bellowed out, "Don't fuckin' come back. I should just make this an all-white bar—keep all you niggers out."

Then things really got nasty with all the country boys getting up on their boot heels, and Rick following the guy outside with a club in his hand. By the time I'd finished my beer, he was tossing black guys out at random and, like schoolchildren who think they're suddenly allowed to say "shit" because the teacher stubbed her toe, the cowboys were throwing around the N word like it was a Ku Klux Klan Christmas.

I felt like I'd been angry all day, all week—for as long as it mattered. I was angry at being called a sucker. Angry that I couldn't have a beer without someone being clubbed, or eat dinner without some guy being punched in the head, couldn't play pool without flying fish and shards of glass.

I headed home with $5 in my pocket, drunk and all geared up to confront the Brothers—to throw my $5 down on their barrel and tell them to crack a bottle of apple swill. When I got there the fire was out, their cabin dark, and I was about to pound on the door.

"Hello, young Shaun." It was Eddie, walking toward me over the ice and snow.

"Do you know these guys?" I said.

"Forget them, buddy. What are you doing? Or what do you want to do?"

"Cocaine." It just came out. I looked down at the snow between my feet.

"You got five bucks?" I walked with him to Street City—a harm-reduction housing complex just a block from Tent City. It's essentially a government-run crack house and whorehouse, and it's also where those in Tent City get their drugs. I waited outside while Eddie went in to score. When we got back, he opened the door to the almost-completed shack into which he and Karen intend to move. He finished the roof yesterday, and Hawk helped him install a stove. We sat down on the floor and Eddie pulled out a dime bag.

"What is that?" I said.

"Don't worry, I only get the good stuff," said Eddie.

He smoked, then packed the pipe again and handed it to me. And that's how I ended up smoking crack for the first time. As Eddie got up to stoke the wood stove he was grinning, and the light from the fire glowed in the lines on his face, his white hair like electric currents shooting from his head.

When I handed back the pipe, he laughed and said, "There's still half a rock in here, you moron."

"Oh," I said. "Sorry. I haven't really smoked this stuff before."

He stared at me for a moment, like a man who'd just stabbed his best friend.

"I shouldn't have done that . . . ," he said. He turned toward the stove, put the pipe in his mouth and smoked the rest of the rock.

I really like Eddie. He's a good man. I would have banged on the Brothers' door and got myself into trouble, but Eddie took the fight out of me, sitting there on his new plywood floor next to his warm wood stove, talking about nothing. I trust Eddie. I know he means what he says, and his smile is really a smile.

Before he went back to Karen in their old accordion, he said, "You're great, young Shaun. Don't let anyone tell you different." From someone else it would have sounded cheesy, but from him it got me through the night. Even though the crack made me sick.

January 8

Nancy is back, with a new guy and an eye infection. The doctor says she got it from the soil here. There's an ongoing debate as to whether the ground is contaminated, dangerous, deadly or just dirty. Everyone's always sick, but there's a lot more than this earth to blame for that.

Marty doesn't seem bothered that Nancy's come back with another man, like it happens all the time. They're staying in the prefab next door to my shack, while Marty's still in the little trailer behind the Dumpster.

The new guy, Steve, is a tall, thin man with straggly hair and a flattened nose. When he's sober he's lucid, and when he's drunk he talks in song lyrics that aren't quite right. He hangs around with a little guy named Calvin, who's always smiling, looks like a leprechaun, and develops a Newfie accent whenever he gets drunk or excited.

The three of them keep hours similar to mine—huddled around a fire barrel through the night while the rest of Tent City is passed out drunk—so we're getting to know each other. They seem like the kind of thieves I can stomach. They've got a scam going whereby Steve shoplifts from Canadian Tire and Home Depot, and then Calvin returns the stuff for a cash refund.

"And no little guys get hurt," says Calvin, who's about 5 foot 3. "They even get their stuff back." It's not just this sort of logic that makes me like these two. They're nice guys. Last night I brought over a bottle of whisky at four in the morning, and the three of us, along with Nancy, drank the sun up, cooking eggs over a barrel in the early-morning light.

Nancy told me that she also has hepatitis B, cirrhosis of the liver and intestinal cancer. "I don't have long," she said, her smiling eyes shining through the red mess of infection.

When the sun was all the way up and the whisky finished, Steve handed me $10. "For the next bottle. We good guys gotta stick together."

January 10

If absolute power corrupts absolutely, then powerlessness does the same. Down here it's hard to find goodness that lasts. Everywhere you look, the eyes turn small, the teeth begin to show, and then poison drips from the gums.

Over the past two months I've watched Sluggo's bitterness slowly eating him. I've ignored it until now, like I try to ignore so much these days. Today as I walked through town, he was drinking with the Brothers. Lately, when Sluggo's drunk, his face gets all glassy and mean.

"The tool box is empty," he said. The Brothers were sitting on either side of him, glaring at me.

"What's that, Sluggo?"

"The tool box . . . is . . . *empty*."

"Oh," I said. "How come?"

"I took the tools out," he said, jutting his big beard in the air as if challenging me to something.

A couple weeks ago Jake gave me a large construction box full of saws, ratchets and chisels. I didn't have room for it and suggested we share it with Sluggo, who put it out front of his place beneath a tarp. I hadn't thought about the box since.

"Okay, Sluggo," I said, trying to play along. "Why'd you take the tools out?"

"'Cause you keep fuckin' giving 'em away. That's why." The Brothers were nodding in agreement.

"What are you talking about?"

"Hammers and fucking saws," he slurred, slamming down his bottle. "That's what I'm talking about." Since Jackie left, Sluggo never goes anywhere. He's always right here, yelling at his dog, Cleo. He was here when I lent Eddie my saw to finish his shack. He was here when I gave Randy back a hammer I'd borrowed—neither of which were ever in that tool box.

"Listen to me, Sluggo . . ."

"No, you listen to me!" he said, trying to stand.

Brother Derek got to his feet first, puffing his chest at me. "I seen you!" he said.

"You seen me what?"

"Get out of my face," he growled. And then once again, like his Spidey senses were tingling, Eddie appeared. He put his arm around my shoulder and walked me away.

"Man!" he said, handing me a cigarette. "People either like you or they really don't."

"I don't know. I met a guy once who was indifferent to me."

"What happened?"

"I kicked his ass."

Imagine how long that must have been burning inside poor Sluggo—the idea of his precious tool box being compromised, and by the new kid! He could just picture the no-good punk lifting the lid and smiling—all those men grabbing his ratchets and hammers, laughing at him like those crackheads had laughed as they squealed their tires and sped off with Jackie and his fifty bucks. And then finally one night, it had all become too much. Under the cold cover of darkness, he scurried out to the big plastic box and gathered the precious tools in his long shaking arms . . .

"Sluggo's going on about you and his tools to anyone who'll listen," said Randy after I got back from a shower at the community centre.

"Yep," I said, and we stood there warming our hands over his fire barrel, waiting for the Street Patrol van to come down with some baloney sandwiches.

"You see the Mayor's back?" he said, smirking disdainfully.

Ever since I came down here, I've been hearing offhand, facetious mentions of the Mayor of Tent City, but couldn't figure out who people were talking about. It wasn't until yesterday, when Karl was released from hospital, that I finally put it all together. Somehow, over the years, Karl the Fascist has become known through the media as the Mayor of Tent City. He probably just declared himself so to a reporter one day and no one bothered to dispute it.

Since his return, however, Karl's been lying pretty low. He's moving slow and his face looks grey. Another blow to the head would probably kill him. The mayorship, I presume, is open.

Today an old Chinese man tried to beat up a prostitute in the lunch-room of the Metropolitan Church. Lori wasn't there. I haven't seen her since before Christmas, when she hugged me in front of a one-woman choir.

January 11

It's been four months since the terrorist attacks on the United States, but the people here don't talk about that stuff. Down here, the breach of this once-secure Western world and the forewarnings of apocalypse happened long ago. People on the streets haven't become overnight experts on Osama and Bush, and airplanes turned to missiles. Instead, when they rant, they expound on God, and the end of it all.

Tonight the man across from me at the Salvation Army dinner had a white Hemingway beard and clean, pressed clothes. He was talking when I sat down, and the others at the table seemed accustomed to listening.

" . . . the body duality of Jesus," he was saying, "like I was telling you before. Very much like what happened to me."

"What's that?" I blurted over my plate of spaghetti, then apologized. "Can I ask what happened to you?"

"I would tell you anyways," he said, turning to look at me. "It's what I'm supposed to do."

"Okay. Thanks."

"I just happened to pick up this book yesterday, in which appears a passage describing how—when Christ was brought down off the cross—he split in two. He left his body and stood next to his dying, dead form, looking down on himself. He could see what they'd done to him and for a moment there were two of him. Two Christs." He spoke carefully and clearly, nodding a rhythmic affirmation of his own intelligence as he looked around the table.

"And that is precisely what happened to me," he continued. "Before God brought me here—to show me 2005."

"Sorry, I'm not sure I follow you," I said.

"I was shot, on a street in Montreal. And as I lay there, as I died, I found myself rising from my body, looking down on myself bleeding. And for a moment, as with Christ, there were two of me. But then the body disappeared, and God brought me to Toronto."

"You just sort of appeared here?"

"No. I took the bus."

"Oh."

"I knew the man who shot me was going to prison, and to his own hell. And *I* . . . was going to Toronto." He had a way of saying "Toronto" that made it sound like the land of milk and honey. "But when I came out of the bus station, there was almost no one in the streets. And God let me understand that it was the year 2005. The only people left were bad—the Fourth Reich, and all the evil men. But there were angels too."

"Angels?" I said. Someone asked if I was going to eat my brownie, and I waved him away. "The Fourth Reich?"

"The Fourth Reich, you see, will form very soon. It will be a coming together of the warlords and the biker gangs and the Mafia. And they will make a pact to slaughter all the good people of Earth. But God will fool them. Like separating the wheat from the chaff, he will bring the good people home before the slaughter begins. He will harvest the good—and so condemn the bad to their final satanic feast."

"Um, how?"

"How what?"

"How, uh, about the satanic feast thing?"

"On the day the Fourth Reich is to begin the killing they will wake to find the good people already gone. There will be no bodies, and they will be angry, confused. And then their hell will begin. They will have nothing to do but look at each other, and wait for the devil. But of course the devil will already be there, feasting on their souls."

"And God told you all this?"

"He showed me. I am the fourth—and I am riding a blue horse."

"You'll be riding a blue horse when the apocalypse comes?"

"No, I *am* riding a blue horse. And I am the fourth."

"And this will happen in 2005—in three years?"

"It will *begin* in 2005," he said, looking around at the whole table to make sure everyone understood. "But it will not end until 2012. When you wake into 2005, you will look around to see that all the good is gone. And it will be a long seven years to follow."

"You don't think God will take any of us?" I asked. "We'll all be left behind?"

He glanced around the room and shrugged. "If you last that long," he said. "The devil is hungry."

x   x
x

I didn't grow up in a religious environment, and was taught to distrust the idea of good and evil—the real truth a murky grey. Even after years of roaming through such Catholic countries as Mexico and Italy, religion has remained an abstraction for me.

But here it feels so real. Not only do many of us spend part of most days in a church—fed by the parishioners, or trying to nap on gym mats beneath the fluorescent light of the Lord—and not only are we preached to on the streets, God's name given out like the address of a year-round safe house, but the spiritual struggle is actually happening, and is far more concrete than the war on TV. Good and evil, salvation and redemption, heaven and hell aren't just concepts here. They feel as real as anything.

On the wall of the Metropolitan Church dining hall is a year-by-year tally of the homeless dead, dating back to 1985. Under 1989 there are five names with dates next to them, and the same for 1990. Ten headings later, there are fifty entries for 1999, and another fifty for the year 2000—a couple dozen of them named John Doe.

The 2001 list is not yet finished and verified. The people who eat here are still adding to the typed script with crayons and markers, scrawling the names of friends and enemies who've recently died. Those who can't read or write, but for their own name, scribble that down in place of the dead. They write their names on the wall of the church dining hall, adding themselves to the devil's breakfast menu.

January 12

I'd been waiting for Sluggo to come out of his beady-eyed animal drunk before confronting him about the tool box stupidity. I'd also come down with a full-day hangover—the last of my superpowers gone—and so finally this morning, wanting nothing more than a day of peace, I walked over to Sluggo's and asked him why he was tossing this shit at my back. He apologized right off, pleading the obvious, that he'd just been drunk and was sorry he hadn't listened to me. Happy the confrontation was behind me, I headed for the gates of Tent City.

A journalist who did a story on this place for a men's magazine came down a couple days ago to drop off an issue each for Hawk and this old guy Pops, who lives across from Hawk and Nicky. Since neither of them was home, I took the magazines, and told him I'd be sure they got them.

Eddie wanted to read the article, so I gave him one to give to Pops. And then, still unable to locate Hawk, I ran into Crazy Chris. I showed him the photo of his place in the magazine and he asked if he could borrow it to photocopy.

"As long as you get it to Hawk tomorrow," I said.

So on my way out of Tent City today I went to check if Hawk had got the magazine. Before I could reach his door, however, he and Nicky were out of the shack, coming right at me.

"Hey, Hawk," I said. "Did you get the—" And then I saw the look in his eyes, his hands in fists as he charged toward me. I jumped back.

He was snarling, saying something like, "And *you're* the other one," his huge body still lunging after me. "You gonna take me, eh? You gonna straighten *me* out? I'm gonna break you in two!"

I kept jumping around, trying to hold off his advance and talk him down at the same time. But Nick was coming at me too. "Hawk! Hawk!"

I blubbered. "What're you doing? What are you talking about? Stop! Goddammit!"

"You gonna straighten *me* out, boy?"

"No . . . No . . . Just stop, Hawk!"

Amazingly he did, but his fists were still clenched, chest still out, eyes still staring through my skull. His jowls were vibrating and beginning to flare. This is what happens when Hawk gets mad. He's got some weird muscles back there, behind each side of his jaw, that begin to pulse when he's angry. And then they swell beneath each ear and start to move in and out like gills.

"What's going on?" I said, trying to keep my voice steady and my arms still, just inches away from his 300-pound body. I could see the muscles vibrating underneath his snowsuit.

"I hear you and Chris are going to straighten *me* out," he said, pronouncing the word "me" like an angry evangelist bellowing the name of God.

"What?"

"That's right. Everyone is talkin' about how, 'cause of this article, you two boys are going to straighten me out. Straighten *me* out."

"Whoa!" I said, Hawk's jaws twitching like he was about to bite. "I really have no idea where this has come from. I mean, I'd have to be a total idiot to go up against you. Do I seem like a moron?" I figured I only had this one moment to convince him not to kill me, and I was talking fast. "You helped me out, right? You talked to me straight about that narc stuff, and I know you went to bat for me when I got beat up—and you're Hawk! I'd have to be stupid and insane to start after you. Why would I?"

"Well, there's one thing, Shauny," he said. His voice was still harsh, his eyes still glaring, but the twitching gills had started to settle. "I train every day. Me and Nicky train every day—don't we, Nicky?"

"Yep," said Nicky.

"And there's one thing that gets me madder than anything—and that's someone threatening me. A cop threatens me—you've seen this, eh Nicky?—Boom! He goes down."

"Yep."

"I'm not that stupid, Hawk," I said. "I wouldn't threaten you."

"Well maybe," he said, rocking back on his heels for a moment, finally dropping his gaze. "But I'm going to find out. Chris is dragging your name in. And he, at least, is going down. I'm going to give him every combination—take him every which way, the whole nine yards. He's going to feel this—you can be sure. And if you're—"

But before he could threaten me again, two vans full of church kids from New York State drove through the gates to hand out peanut butter sandwiches, cookies and juice boxes. We put on our nice Canadian-hobo smiles, and as they swarmed around us I shook Hawk's hand and walked quickly through the gates.

I wandered around the city for a while, trying to figure out what to do. According to Hawk, long before Tent City was founded, he used to come and camp on this land. He says that he, his brother Nicky and old man Pops have been here longer than anyone. He's got a lot of pride in this place, and a very particular view of it. The line he gives every reporter, journalist or photographer is always the same. And usually, as the keeper of the gates, he talks to them first. "Nobody writes the truth about this place," he says. "So if you're going to do a story, you should write the truth about it, even though you don't want to write what I have to say."

"Why?" they ask.

"Because it's the truth."

"Okay. What is it?"

"I'll tell you, everyone comes down here to write about the poor and the homeless. But we're not poor. Most of us work. There's people down here who make $80,000 a year. And this other fellow pulls in $150 a day panhandling. But money is money, right? The thing is, we live down here because we want to. We want to live like folks in olden times—like the Mennonites. See these houses? I helped build most of 'em. This is a community, and when we build a new place it's like a barn-raising, whole nine yards. But you don't want to hear that. You want to hear the sob stories. Well, the people who give you those—you know what that is? It's called a scam."

I've heard this speech, pretty much word for word, a half-dozen times, bestowed like a golden scoop onto journalists who came from as far away as Australia for the story of Tent City. Hawk's view, of course, is not shared by most people down here. Although it's his town, and he knows a lot about the old boys, he doesn't seem to realize how many people are squatting here now, and how the desperation for drugs tends to distract them from tilling the community soil. And I still can't identify the mythical panhandler pulling in $150 a day. Mine, however, is not to question Hawk—especially out loud.

It's interesting, though, how close his view of Tent City is to Mike's. And yet Hawk dislikes Mike even more than the others do. He calls him an old junk man and insists this place was pristine before Mike started hauling all this garbage down here. Of course, when Hawk negotiates a truckload of lumber or clothes, it's never "garbage."

And now Crazy Chris, who's under Mike's obscure wing, and is rarely down here since his latest arrest, has supposedly been using my name in a threat to Hawk, because of what was written in the magazine I'd put in his trust. I have no idea why he shot his mouth off like this— if in fact he did—or why he's brought me into it. Even if I manage to get to him before Hawk, I can see no way to save us both.

In the early evening I came back in through the Cherry Street gates to avoid Hawk and went to Chris's prefab. He wasn't there, but a half-dozen guys were sitting around the fire barrel on the Brothers' porch.

"You guys seen Chris?" I said.

"Chris who?" said Derek.

"Chris," I said again. "You know—lives right here."

Jerry tried to stutter something, but Derek cut him off. "No, I don't know," he said, narrowing his Doberman eyes. I muttered a farewell, and started to walk away. "Get the fuck away from my fire," he slurred, just loud enough for me to hear. I stopped for a moment, then kept on walking. As I neared my shack, I could hear him saying, "I don't like that fucking guy."

"Well, do you know him?" someone said.

"I know enough. And you watch—that fucking prick's going down." Lenny, Jerry and Donny grunted in agreement like henchmen in a Mad Max movie.

I sat on the bed in my shack and lit a candle. I stared at the floor for an hour, then left Tent City through the back gates and came to this bar. I've been here for a while.

I've always assumed that other people's fears don't apply to me—

that as long as I decide not to be afraid, I'll be okay. But now I'm scared.

I don't know what made me think I could do this—go in on my own and hope to last, in a place like Tent City.

I feel like if I write enough, I'll stop being afraid, or at least figure out what to do, though it doesn't seem to be working. I'm not scared of another beating, or having my shack torn down or being thrown out of town. I'm scared of being the first John Doe on the church wall, 2002. I want to run. There are just too many of them who might be against me now—the Brothers, Hawk and Nicky, Sluggo, the Frenchies, Karl and God knows who else. Jake's gone and Eddie's on a crack binge. I can't fight them all or even talk my way out, especially since I don't know what I've done wrong.

Practically the only sane voices I hear these days come from my radio, which I listen to at night. On the CBC program *Ideas*, Paul Kennedy has been doing a series on the philosopher René Girard, entitled "Scapegoat." It's primarily about the theory of mimesis, and the idea that the history of religion is the history of violence—that the world was built on a system of sacrificing one to create a temporary peace for the rest. An innocent would be demonized, killed, then redeemed in memory during the time of peace to follow—the angers, hostilities and frustrations of the masses momentarily relieved by the act of murder.

Girard believes the world was trapped in this cycle of sacrificial violence until Jesus showed up to offer himself as the ultimate scapegoat. And then everything changed. In the New Testament, for the first time in literary history, violence was represented as something tragic and cruel rather than a heroic necessity.

Part of the idea of mimesis is that all violence is facilitated through a pattern of imitation. On a basic level, one man raises his voice, another copies him, and soon they're beating the shit out of each other. When Jesus says to turn the other cheek, he is showing us a way to break this cycle. Instead of copying your aggressor, you offer the other side of your head for a clobbering too, and thus unplug the power of mimetic violence.

I don't know if any of this can help me, but it's all I've got—the advice of Christ as read by a smart French guy beamed over the airwaves, through my radio and into my shack.

January 13

After the bar closes I go back to Tent City, in through the gates on Cherry Street. I don't want to be here, but figure I might be able to catch Chris on one of his late-night visits. I wait for him in the cold for about an hour, then go back to my shack to lie down.

I haven't been asleep for long when I'm awoken by the Brothers howling along with Jim Morrison on their radio. I've slept in my clothes again.

Like some people do sit-ups in the morning, take a shower and make a pot of coffee, the Brothers howl and yell and break a few things, gearing themselves up for a new day of drinking. I lie there for a while, sunlight coming in through my window. Over at the Brothers' the song has changed, but it's still The Doors.

I'm still scared. I'll have to get that under control. If I'm to go over there, I've got to do it before they get drunk. I pull on my boots and a baseball cap, open the door, and I walk toward the music. It's loud, and they're still howling.

Not only do the Brothers have a wood stove in their new addition to the prefab, but out on the porch they've got two fire barrels. I step up to one of them and stand as I did the night before, holding my hands up to the fire. It's just the two of them now. As Derek turns toward me, Lenny is still howling.

"I know you don't want me at your fire," I say, loud enough to be heard over the music. "But I'm here."

"Who said I don't want—"

"You did. Last night."

"Don't listen to me when I'm drunk," Derek says, and starts to turn away.

"I don't give a fuck if you like me. But if you're going to go on about how you don't, you should meet me first." I nod my head toward his brother. "What're your names?" I say, though of course I know their names.

"I'm Derek," he says, and gets up to turn down the music. "This is my brother, Lenny."

"I'm Shaun," I say, holding my hand out over the fire.

"We know who you are," says Derek, and shakes it.

"And do you know who Chris is?"

"Tattooed Chris?"

"I guess. He lives right next to you. Have you seen him?"

"Not for a long time. Why?"

"Somebody's put Hawk on to us. Said we were threatening him."

"You don't want Hawk mad at you," says Derek. "Anyone but him."

"I know."

"Here," he says, turning around. "Try this . . . Hey, Lenny, pass me a bottle." Derek hands me a 1.5-litre bottle, half-full.

"What is it?" I say.

"Just try it."

"If I end up drinking your piss I'm not gonna be happy." It isn't that funny, but Lenny giggles as I take a gulp of the thick, cream-coloured swill. "It's not bad," I say, though it's not good either.

"Apples," says Derek, and points to the huge pot that's bubbling on the fire barrel behind him. "You should sit in sometime."

"Sure," I say. "I'll bring an apple." I nod to them both and walk back to my shack.

A few minutes later a woman comes to my door. I won't tell you her name, since she's taking a risk by coming to me like this.

"You shouldn't trust those guys," she says.

"I don't."

"Hawk should know better than to listen to them," she says. "If somebody comes to you, talking about someone else—you got to ask yourself why . . ." I wait. "I was there the other night . . . It was the Brothers who told him about you and Chris."

"Why?"

She shrugs her shoulders. "I guess they don't like you?"

"And why are you telling me this?"

"I guess I like you."

"Oh," I say. "Thanks."

I put some things I might need in a small bag and leave through the back gates. I might not be back for a while.

January 15

I've been looking for Crazy Chris, but it's hard to find someone who doesn't want to be found. I've been mostly roaming the Queen-

Sherbourne area—the bars and shelters and alleys—and sleeping when I can. Apparently the cops are looking for Chris too, and I don't think he even knows about this thing with Hawk. If I don't find him soon, I'll have to go back and confront Hawk and the Brothers on my own—or not go back at all.

January 16

Last night, still unable to find Chris, I tried to get some sleep in a church. A TB epidemic is flourishing in the Toronto shelters. I lay on a tiny blue mat among ill unwashed men, the sound of their flooded lungs hacking. We had just inches between us and the whole place reeked of fear. What else would drive men into such wretched sanctuary?

After a time I got up and stepped over the moaning, coughing bodies to the door. Once out on the street, however, I remembered the other reason we were in there—the cold. I huddled in a doorway until the mall opened, then sat inside, watching the store clerks pulling up the security gates to open the shops for the day. I was sitting across from a magazine store, and by the time the gate folded to the ceiling, I knew what I should do.

x   x   x

When I got to Tent City, there was smoke rising from Hawk's chimney. I walked up and knocked on the door. "It's Shaun," I said. "If you've got time, I'd like to talk to you."

He opened the door and squinted at me, then said, "Come on in. Sit down."

"You've done a lot for me since I came here," I said after I settled myself in one of his two chairs. "And although I'm angry about whatever bullshit someone's saying about me, there is one thing I do feel responsible for. I told that guy I'd get the magazine to you—and I haven't done that. So I picked this up for you." I handed him the magazine, letting the receipt fall out so he could see that I had paid for it. It had taken me over an hour of door opening to get the $4.16. "The photo of you and Pops is real nice."

"Thanks." He leaned back to study the magazine at arm's length, then flipped it open to the article. "Will you look at that!" He seemed impressed, as if I'd published it myself. "That's good of you, Shauny. I appreciate it."

"No problem . . . This all just pisses me off, you know, that feeling I've been set up—and that they used you to do it . . . you know what I mean?" This part was a bit dicey. I glanced over to make sure the door was unlocked.

"What do you mean?" said Hawk, lifting his gaze from the magazine. His jaw was tightening.

"Well, I just don't know where this bullshit came from."

"It came from Chris," said Hawk, nodding his massive head. "And he's going to get it, whole nine yards, Shauny."

"Yeah . . ." I got up and stepped over to the door. "Have you seen him?"

"Not yet."

"Me neither. I went down after talking to you the other day, and asked around—asked those brothers . . . what're their names, Derek and Lenny?" I opened the door. "They say they haven't seen him since Christmas . . . Anyway, thanks for your time, Hawk." I started down the stairs.

"Um . . . yeah." I could almost hear the question forming in the shack behind me. "Since Christmas?" he called out.

"Yeah—you know who I'm talking about? Those two brothers— that's what they said."

"Tell you what . . . ," said Hawk. "If I do get that other copy from Chris, I'll give it to you, okay?"

"Don't worry about that."

"No. You should have one. You're part of this place now. Who knows, maybe someone'll do a story on you one day."

"Yeah. Maybe. See ya, Hawk."

I didn't feel like hanging around, not if the Brothers were there, not if Chris was going to come waltzing in, and not if Hawk came down to have a talk with any of them. I headed back out the gates and uptown, to pick up my $195 from the welfare office. The cheques aren't issued until 2 p.m., and while I was waiting around, some beggar I know from downtown told me about a dinner party for the homeless at St. Lawrence Market tonight. I'd been planning on going to Osgoode for supper, then out on the town with my $195, but a beggar's banquet is hard to resist.

x
  x
    x

In the St. Lawrence Market there is a large hall where they have a flea and farmer's market on the weekends. Tonight it's a banquet hall, and by the time I arrive, there are a couple hundred people seated at the tables like peasants at the palace. Several street charities have gotten together on this one, and the abundance is awesome. Everywhere you look there are trays of chicken and fresh fruit and sushi. "Sushi," I whisper in awe. A band is playing.

I walk down the centre aisle, and at every table there are people I've met on the streets, in shelters and soup kitchens. I wave to them as I pass, and someone calls out, "Young Shaun! Over here!"

They're all seated at one long table—Eddie and Karen, Sluggo and Jackie, Nancy and Steve, Calvin, Rambo, Randy, Mike, Pops, Jimmy D, Jerry and Donny. The Frenchies, however, are nowhere to be seen, nor Hawk, nor the Brothers, nor Crazy Chris.

"You're back among the living," I say to Eddie as I pull out a chair.

"No, here," says Steve, and they slide a seat to the head of the table for me. I move over and sit down. Everyone is smiling.

"It's good to see you, kid," says Eddie. Everything seems different, everyone is happy. I realize the troubles of the past few days have only been mine.

"Jackie!" I say. "How've you been?"

Her massive face goes crimson as she smiles. "Aw, Shauny," she says. Only she and Hawk call me Shauny, though in different ways. "I guess I was a bad girl there for a while." Sluggo laughs and she punches his arm. "But I'm back now! And I got baptized, eh?"

"You what?"

"Baptized! It was great! I'd never been baptized before!"

"Well . . . way to go! It's good to see you, Jacks. And you too, Nancy— your eyes look good!"

"All the better to see you with," she cackles and pinches my cheek.

Everyone is piling food onto my plate. Even some of Jimmy D's crew are nodding to me in welcome. I can't figure out what's going on.

"So," I say. "Where are the Brothers?"

"You didn't hear?" says Steve.

"Hear what?"

"They're gone," says little Calvin.

"Gone? What happened—they run out of apples?" This gets more laughs than warranted and I can see Jerry and Donny staring in disbelief—their leaders gone.

"And I got the place!" says Calvin, smiling. "You gotta come over and drink!"

A circle of Native drummers and singers begins to play. As their song rises up like a storm inside the hall, the toughest boys at our table get up to dance. This good mood, though, isn't just because the Brothers have left. A lot of them couldn't give a damn about that. It's this sudden unity. It might not feel like it down in Tent City, but on this side of the fence, we're a band, a brotherhood—surviving the winter on our own terms. We're sitting at the same table and, miraculously, we are sober. People keep bringing up this fact like frat boys go on about how drunk they are: "Man, this is great! We're all so sober! Listen to that music!" It's not like they planned it this way—there just wasn't much booze today, and now everyone's eating.

After the drummers, a huge black woman starts belting out some Motown tunes. Jerry gets up. As he walks by me, he says, "Sh-Sh-Shaun," as if in greeting, and slaps my forehead. It is the kind of slap that could be taken as friendly by a very close friend, or a brother—but not so by anyone else. I grab his wrist and, still seated, bend his arm into a hammerlock.

"What's your name?" I say. As with the Brothers, the half-brothers have never actually introduced themselves to me, and I think maybe this can be my new thing, like a catchphrase: *Go ahead, punk, what's your name?*

"Y-you know my n-n-name," he says. Jerry's got the kind of stutter that fails to elicit any empathy. Instead, it makes his mix of cocky aggression and simple charmlessness that much more annoying.

"Tell it to me," I say.

"Why?"

"So I can say it while I slap your head."

"S-s-starts with J."

"Okay, Jackass," I say, and let go of his arm. "Don't touch me like that again."

"W-w-whatever," he says.

Half our table is on the dance floor by now. The rest are still eating and telling stories in loud laughing voices. People are shuffling in out of the cold by the dozens and waving at each other across the hall. They come over to our table to say hi as though we, of Tent City, are the vagrant celebrities, the nobility of the bums. While others slip into the shelters, we're building our own houses with our hands. While they crowd around the TV in a community centre, we're stoking the fire barrel, watching sparks rise like new stars in the cold night. They're under a blanket of rules, and we're making up our own then tossing them off with a laugh. Some of them keep it tough—they live alone beneath viaducts and bridges. But we live together on the banks of the river and the lake. We've fought each other, and we'll fight each other again. But not just now.

Jo-Jo comes out of the crowd and kisses my cheek.

"Jo-Jo!" I say "Where you been? Where's Jake?"

"He's in jail, honey," she says, eyes darting around the hall. "They popped him up near Street City. He got set up, honey."

"He had a car?"

"Bicycle."

"What?"

"Don't ask. But he's gone for a long time. Five years at least." Behind her fast talking, she is trying not to cry. Someone slaps me on the back and I turn to see Crazy Chris standing beside me. He's wearing a studded leather headband.

"Hawk . . . ," I begin, but he just laughs.

"Don't worry, don't worry, I got it under control." He dances around for a minute, and disappears.

Apparently neither my enemies nor my worries have been invited tonight. It's too bad about Jake, but almost everyone else I've met over the past two months is here. Looking around, I have such a sudden strong love for all these people it shocks me.

An a cappella group is singing "Stand by Me" and everyone is clapping along. If God were to drop in on the St. Lawrence Market tonight and take a look around, I can't imagine him condemning us. Surely he would take us home.

Randy is up on a chair now. Sluggo is dancing with Jackie. Jerry is stuttering to one of the volunteer girls. Eddie and Karen are shovelling cookies into their pockets, and Nancy is singing off-key with Steve and Calvin. It's like the last scene of a ridiculous Hollywood movie—the bad bums off in some limbo, the good hobos happy and victorious.

But of course this isn't a movie, and tomorrow's another day.

January 18

Bonnie is the antithesis of everyone down here. She is conscientious, political, eloquent, law-abiding, educated, non-drinking and non-drugging. She is a tall, bone-thin Metis woman with long dark hair and bangs that brush the top of her glasses. She refers to herself as a Nish, short for Anishnawbe, which means "the people" in Ojibway. According to her, she worked for fifteen years in some social-work capacity on the front lines of what she calls "the poverty industry." Then, this Christmas, dumped by her man, out of a job and broke, she came over to this side of the fence, and has ended up in the other half of Randy's double prefab.

She started talking when she got here, and hasn't stopped since. She talks about class struggle and political systems and harm reduction and aikido and her music career and the formation of a Tent City council and a donation wish list and human rights and community development and addiction psychology and homeless trauma and viable cottage industries and gender divisions and quilting and PR for squatters and self-empowerment programs.

Much of what she says I don't understand, because she insists on speaking in acronyms, euphemisms and catchphrases. She's always referring to her ADHD. She uses the names of her ex-co-workers like everyone knows them. She calls hookers sex trade workers and refers to drug addiction and alcoholism as self-medication. She also refers to her own near-genius IQ a lot.

Rather than being annoyed, which was *my* first reaction, most of the guys down here seem bewildered by Bonnie. A few have sought my opinion.

"What's she talking about?"

"Is she with an agency or something?"

"Why's she here?"

"Do you think she's a dyke?"

"You know, Shaun," Bonnie said to me after a few days, "I get the feeling I'm talking over people's heads."

"Perhaps."

"I just want to help. But it's difficult sometimes when you've got an IQ two points off genius."

"I'm sure. But maybe you can just relax a bit, get a feel for the—"

"I've *got* a feel. I've got too much of a feel. I was a caseworker for fifteen years on the front lines. You wouldn't believe the shit I've—"

"I know. I'm just saying—"

"But I feel I can talk to you. At least you respond."

She's been talking to me a lot. And while she talks she dresses the men's long-festering wounds, makes tea out of cedar bark, dish soap out of lye, ash and water, washes the dishes that have been thrown in the mud. And already some of the men have grown to love her, like lost boys reaching out for a kind, though manic and self-absorbed, den mother.

Little Calvin and his brother Spider always have some disgusting wound or another. Calvin is a good, if always self-medicated, listener, and it seems over the course of trying to divert the blood poison, lessen the gangrene, slow the infection and reduce the swelling, he and Bonnie are becoming friends.

Since the Brothers left, we've created a sort of sanctuary in the house they built, getting together in the evenings to roll cigarettes, drink and play cards by the heat of the wood stove. If I can, I bring whisky. Jerry and Donny, the fairweatherest sons of bitches I've ever met, bring beer. Steve brings food. Bonnie cooks it and Calvin sits there cackling at his own jokes while he tries to keep the fire going.

January 19

It looks like Calvin's already lost the place the Brothers left. Randy and some of the old boys got together and kicked him out of there, ostensibly because Angel, one of the prostitutes, was staying there too, but really it was just because Randy wanted the place for himself. It shows how little they respect Calvin that they didn't even bother coming up with an excuse that makes any sense—there's hardly a Tent City rule against shacking up with ladies of ill repute.

By the time I learned what had happened, Bonnie was ranting and crying, and Calvin had taken off. I found him trudging along the railway tracks, and convinced him to come back. So now he's in Randy's old place, drinking double time to quell his anger. Randy—on the second day of a Cough-X high—has moved into the Brothers' renovated, stove-heated shack, Jimmy D is doing the rounds, claw hammer in hand, to discuss recently remembered debts, Eddie's off on another crack binge, Bonnie is still trying to impress upon everybody the folly of misogynistic in-fighting among the oppressed as she boils soup on Randy's old barrel, and those of us still standing at the end of the day join her by the fire.

January 21

I woke this morning to women yelling at each other, but figured it was just Petra arguing with Jackie, or Nancy going at Spider's old lady, Olivia, and pulled the covers over my head. But the yelling got worse, and then I could hear the deeper voices of men, angry and aggressive. And dogs barking. Then silence, like a breath pulled in, and heavy scuffing, grunting, thuds, a few sharp yells—the overly familiar soundtrack to a fight.

I dragged myself up, pulled on my jeans and boots and went out the door. As I rounded the side of my shack, over the rubble and between the trees, I could see Dan the Frenchy coming at Jackie with a stick. He got her on the side of the leg, but then Sluggo was on him, pulling his jacket over his head like a hockey jersey and pummelling him with his fist. He let him go, and Dan fell back into the crowd.

The younger faction of Jimmy D's crew—which has been growing over on the other side of Tent City for the past few weeks—were all here now, the guys holding sticks, the girls yelling about crack whores and sluts, crowding in on Sluggo, Jackie and Bonnie. Off to the side, Jimmy D and Hawk stood looking on. Jimmy D held a machete and Hawk's hands were curling at his sides.

As I crossed over to them, Dan came up off the ground, grabbing a piece of wood, Hawk stepped forward, and Jimmy D's famous voice barked out: "Enough, you little shits! Get yer asses out of here." And slowly—the girls still yelling "crack whore" at Jackie, the guys shouting threats at Sluggo, Dan foaming at the mouth and bleeding from the nose—they shuffled back to their side of town. I walked over to Hawk and stood there until everyone had dispersed.

"Twenty-seven acres!" he said, waving his arm at all the brush and trees behind us. "And you guys have built so close you're farting on each other. I don't get it, Shauny. I'd end up killing all of you if I lived in this circle-jerk."

"I know. Have a good day, Hawk."

I walked over to Randy's old windbreak, where Bonnie was sitting by the fire barrel, tears running down her cheeks.

"Hey, Bonnie."

"I don't see crying as a sign of weakness," she said, wiping her eyes. I nodded. "I'm human. Trying to treat people like humans. I mean, the issue isn't if so-and-so is a crack whore, or so-and-so called the cops. I mean, do you see any phones around? It's just basic respect . . ."

"Bonnie . . ."

"It's a question of respect, and of us not wanting to have our houses burnt down, and voicing that concern in a legitimate—"

"Bonnie. Please tell me what's going on."

"I mean, seriously, they're not just endangering themselves. They're going to take the whole place with them—"

"Bonnie! Explain to me what happened, like I'm a child—a really stupid child."

"Okay, Shaun. Just calm down."

x   x
x

I know first-hand how Jimmy D's boys like their bonfires. I've still got the burn marks. And I can easily picture what happened last night:

They're bent on crack and smashed on beer, and the flames just keep getting higher. They're throwing everything they can find onto the pyre—barrels and doors, an easy chair, a mattress, until the whole sky is filled with fire. The wind is blowing east, walls of smoke rolling like black lava over the huts, embers the size of hands slapping the roofs. Jackie stumbles out of her shack, wheezing. Bonnie is hacking. Nancy's eyes are puffing up again. And fire is falling on the dry timber of our shacks.

The smoke is thick enough to see from downtown. The flames are reflecting off cars on the overpass. A helicopter flies in and hovers over-head, searchlight beaming down on Tent City. And still they're yelling, howling, breaking bottles, throwing chairs on the fire. The chopper rises, flies off, and the sky is red with flame.

The old boys aren't around, and the three women walk together through the smoke to the blazing bonfire. Bonnie tries to reason with the boys. Jackie and Nancy yell. The gang growls at them all to fuck off, grabbing flaming sticks from the edges of the fire. The women decide to go get Hawk. But Hawk isn't home. (He happens, at this moment, to be sharing a bowl of popcorn with me, watching *Hannibal* in the basement of a church on St. Patrick Street.)

As the women walk back to their shacks, engulfed in smoke, sirens sound and a convoy of police cars and fire trucks rolls through the gates of Tent City.

x   x
x

"And so they come over this morning to fight," said Bonnie. "Because they've got the IQs of turnips, and they think we called the cops on them. As if we've all got cellphones! We don't want the cops down here either—they're not the only ones with warrants. Jackie's got her failure-to-appear. I tried to explain . . ."

"Bonnie," I said, "you can't talk to most people down here in the manner you're used to—not when they're drunk. You just gotta try and stay away from them." And suddenly I realized how much I've already changed—how much I sound like Hawk. I could see a part of me disap-pearing even as I spoke.

"I just wish I could explain to them," said Bonnie, her face dis-traught in the light of the fire barrel, "the real enemy is this goddamn system that makes it impossible for us to find affordable housing, and illegal for us to squat. I mean, no matter what people say, it's not our choice to live like this. For choice you need the options of equally beneficial possibilities. Are our options beneficial? In aikido there's a saying: If you're thrown, the only choice you have is how you hit the mat. If they could just see the real issue . . ."

"No, Bonnie. There *are* no issues. And they don't see you as being in a position of authority. Once they start picking up weapons, they're not interested in listening. And when they're yelling 'crack whore' and all that crap, they're not trying to communicate with you, okay? That's just more violence. They *will* beat you if you get in the way."

"I know, I know! But I hate it! I mean, poor Jackie. She's trying to stay clean, you know. Even got baptized—although I think that's all a crock of shit; Jesus was a capitalist, you know . . ." But now Jackie had joined us at the fire barrel.

"Hey, killer," I said, trying to make her smile. But she still looked so scared. She took a step forward and stopped.

"I'm trying to be good," she said, and her face just broke, tears welling in her eyes like she was remembering every beating she'd ever given or got. "I'm trying. It's just so . . ."

And now Bonnie was on her feet, hugging Jackie, and both of them were crying, their faces streaked with mud and dirt. A rat ran past their feet. There were piles of scrap and garbage behind them. I muttered something about more wood for the fire and walked away.

"They hugging?" said Sluggo as I passed his shack.

"Yeah."

"And crying?" He was squinting over at them as if trying to make out the tears.

"Yep."

"Wow. Don't see that every day."

"Maybe times are changing. Want me to stick around in case the boys come back?"

"Nah. Fuck off. I think it's done for the day."

"Yeah."

But neither of us sounded too sure.

x
x
x

I walk around downtown, try to write a bit, have dinner at the Salvation Army and come back to Tent City in the late evening. There is a big bonfire burning down near Jimmy D's.

"That's nothing," says Bonnie. "Twenty feet lower than last night."

"Anything new?"

"Nothing much. Dan got drunk and threw some bottles at Sluggo's shack for a while. But eventually he gave up. I'm making tea."

"Where's Calvin and Steve? Haven't seen them all day."

"Off drinking somewhere."

"You okay?"

"Yeah. I've been trained in anger manage—"

"Hey, Sluggo."

Every evening, Sluggo walks Cleo along the fenceline and back.

"Hey there," he says as Bonnie's wiry little dog, whose name I can never pronounce to her satisfaction, leaps up to greet Cleo.

"You know," starts Bonnie, "I was proud of how Jackie conducted herself earlier. After she got all her yelling under control, she was really trying to communi—"

"What the fuck?" growls Sluggo all of a sudden, and starts toward his shack. Bonnie and I stand up. There are almost a dozen of them, and they have the place surrounded, beating on the walls with sticks and pipes. By the time we get there, they've got the door open and I can see Jackie's face full of fear in the candlelight. And again the women are yelling. "You five-dollar slut!" "You cunt!" "Crack whore!" "Bitch!" And Dan is shouting for Sluggo to come out. But Sluggo is behind him.

He grabs Dan by the jacket and throws him away from the door. The crowd surges after them. I step forward as Sluggo is surrounded. But I move slow, I can feel the fear holding me back, my voice too quiet, saying, "Hey, hey . . ." *What's happened to me?* I think as my hands hang uselessly. *When did I become a coward?*

A bright light glares through the dark, and I can see Sluggo's scared and angry snarl, Dan's broken nose—all the mindless thugs glaring at each other as Hawk comes charging through the crowd, a Maglite in his hand.

"I should get one of my Uzis and blow you all away!" he bellows. "Maybe that would teach you somethin'." He grabs Dan and ushers

Sluggo with him into the open. "Enough of this crap. If you're gonna do this, you do it one-on-one, whole nine yards. We get a circle around you and get it done."

I see Jimmy D standing off to the side. "Hey, Jimmy," I say, and stretch out my hand. I want to see if he'll give up the hammer he's holding to shake with me. "Haven't seen you in a while."

"Hey, guy," he growls. I'm pretty sure he doesn't remember my name. "Good to see you." He passes the hammer from his right to his left and shakes my hand.

"What the hell's going on?" I say, waving at his crew.

"Ah, kids," he says in his cartoon-Tom-Waits-drunk-in-the-desert voice. "Hawk's got it right. Nothin' more fun than one-on-one." He's shuffling on his feet. "Or two-on-two! Or three-on-three! When it's just you and him and you're moving and moving, and boom! And boom, boom, boom!" His fists are shooting out fast combinations, head bobbing and weaving. "I used to be a boxer."

"Then why do you need the hammer?" I say, and regret it immediately. Whether or not he used to be a boxer, Jimmy D, like Hawk and so many others down here, is still a killer.

"I don't need the hammer." He's stopped moving now, and stopped smiling.

"I'm sure you don't," I say. "So why you got it?" I'm not sure what I'm doing, maybe trying to make up for my earlier cowardice.

He stares at me hard. "Because," he says, and suddenly his face breaks back into a grin. "Because things are more fun when you've got a hammer!" He howls, and then starts laughing, shuffling double time toward the pugilists-to-be, calling for them to fight.

But now Hawk has given Dan pause to think, and Sluggo has used it to grab Jackie and slip back into their shack. And there's no way the mob is going to start all their stick-banging again with Hawk here.

Bonnie and I head back over to the fire barrel. Hawk and Jimmy D walk into the darkness. And suddenly the gang of thugs is standing out there on their own, looking at each other confused, like they've just woken up in 2005. Cursing and muttering, they slink back through the rubble to the other side of town. Tonight there'll be no one to fight but each other.

x
x
x

It's late, but I'm still writing when Randy comes over, his Popeye mouth pulled into a giant gleeful grin.

"Where you been all day?"

"Where YOU been?" he says, and sits down on the foot of my bed. Other than my ex-girlfriend that horrible night, and Jake who's now in jail, Randy is the only person who's ever been in here. He's looking around at the candles flickering on my little bookcase, the psychedelic light on my ceiling from the kerosene heater. He puts a cigarette in his mouth, but makes no move to light it. "Nice place. Where's the kitchen?"

"Cough-X?" I say.

"Yeppers. Three days now. It's nice, like my brain is glowing, or at least half of it." Randy's Cough-X hallucinations have led to more than a few misunderstandings in Tent City.

"How much do you take?"

"Eight ounces. Four, and then when it kicks in, another four. You should . . . ," he drifts off into a blissful gaze, staring up at the light on my ceiling, " . . . try it sometime."

"Sure. We'll do it together."

"Make sure you get DM. Those are the magic letters . . . You're the only one up, you know? A lot of yelling going on today, a lot of yelling." He shakes his head, still grinning. "Why do we live here?"

"I don't—"

"G'night, kid." He stands up and walks out of the shack, his cigarette still unlit. I get up and close the door.

January 23

Jackie says her church group is going to pay for her to go through a six-month drug rehab in Niagara Falls: $12,000 for the program, plus spending money and a new wardrobe for a drug-free Christian lifestyle.

Down here her church group is known as the Purple People Eaters. They arrive every Sunday morning, wearing these purple faux-medieval vests that read "Jesus did THIS just for you!!" with a depiction of Christ crucified underneath the catchy slogan. They hand out coffee, chocolate bars and cans of Zoodles, and invite you back to the church for the good food. "Chili!" they say, or "Glazed ham!" Some go with them, then come back full of lunch and scripture, itching to get drunk.

Spider has become the town celebrity this week. He pans out front of a radio station on Yonge Street, and a few days ago some gonzo programmer pulled him off the sidewalk to do the midday traffic report. Spider says they gave him $20 and a free lunch, then introduced him on the air as Homeless Dave. He's the type of guy who uses his real name as pseudonym.

Although he and Calvin are brothers, Spider seems much more feral, as if he's never heard a kind word in his life. When I ask Calvin about it, he—who lives with the death of his wife, the loss of his children, and a cancerous growth that's killing him—says, "I'm the lucky one."

"How so?"

"When I turned 11, my old man gave me $1000 and kicked me out on my own. There were eighteen of us, and not much room. But he held on to Spider."

With vocal cords almost as warped as Jimmy D's and a style as abstract as Rambo's, Spider might just redeem pop radio. He signed off his first live report with, "This, I guess, is Homeless Dave. Thank you very little, and fuck you very much."

Calvin has borrowed my tools. But rather than building his own place, he's started on one for Bonnie instead. He's laying down skids for a floor back by the main Tent City road, about 100 feet from the double prefab they're staying in now. I'd give him a hand, but right now I'm just so tired for some reason.

I spoke today with a man from the TDRC named Beric. He says they'll be bringing more wood stoves down the second week of February, but that I'll only be able to get one if I can make my place bigger. In my six-by-six shack, a stove would probably light the bed on fire—a painful, albeit dramatic, way to go.

Luckily it hasn't been too cold lately. In fact we've had one of the warmest Januarys on record and no real snow since December, although it is always about 5 degrees colder here than downtown. Eddie gave me a roll of aluminum foil bubble wrap insulation, which I've used to cover my ceiling in hopes of reflecting the heat back in.

Despite all this, I seem to be getting sick again.

January 24

I sleep for fifteen hours straight and still I'm exhausted. I stumble around downtown, then come back home and cough while I sleep. I wake up and try to write, but I can't concentrate. There's always someone yelling out there, someone fighting.

I stumble out of my shack and see the Brothers.

"What's going on?" I say.

"The Brothers want their place back," says Bonnie. "Lenny punched Randy, and then Randy punched Derek." They're stumbling around in the glare of the fire barrel on the porch as they yell at each other. I try to find my way back to my shack to rest. I'm sweating.

More yelling.

"What's up now?"

"Brenda pushed Lenny, and Derek punched Randy," says Calvin. "Are you all right?"

Back, and back again.

"And now?"

"I think Randy punched them both out, and they came back at Randy, and now Eddie's trying to get it all finished . . . You don't look good, you know? You should put on a jacket. And maybe some pants."

"I have pants."

"Well, you're not wearing them."

"Okay." I sit down on the ground by Bonnie and Calvin's fire barrel. The fighting has stopped, and the Brothers have left. Eventually Jerry and Donny come home from robbing people in the city.

"Y-y-y-you know what we just seen?" says Jerry. "The B-B-Brothers out on the highway, t-t-trying to double on a bike. B-b-but they're way too drunk, and they're b-bleeding!"

And now I'm laughing, and the laughing turns to coughing. I lie down next to the fire barrel until Bonnie and Calvin drag me back to my shack. I don't know if I'm laughing or coughing, and I can't stop.

January 25

I go to get water from the hose, but only make it as far as Randy's.

"Hey, asshole."

"Hey, shithead."

I stand around the barrel with them, laughing, coughing, talking about nothing. I feel like I'm swaying. A carload of churchies appear, and now they're trying to shake our hands, pushing into the circle around the fire like they're on a mission.

"Do you believe in God?" one of them asks.

Steve lifts his head and says, "I know that there's a devil, and I pray that there's a god." And then these people, who've come to save us with pamphlets and rainbow stickers, form a circle encircling our circle encircling the fire barrel, and begin to pray. Suddenly I'm trapped between them and the fire. There's no way out, and I fall to the ground.

January 26

In hell, you sweat and shiver. You burn with fever and your skin stings from the cold. You get 6 by 6 feet—just enough to lie down, so the fever dreams can consume you. Hell smells of human waste, contaminated soil and kerosene. The rats chew at the floor beneath you, scratch at the walls, screw in the attic. And beyond the sound of rats, you hear yelling, cursing, madness, sadness, the howling of intoxicated, wasted pain. In hell, the supply van comes once a day, someone hands you a baloney sandwich, a cup of orange liquid, then drives away, day after day, forever and ever. In hell, people drink because they think it will make them feel better. But instead, they feel worse, want to die, are already dead, forget in the morning, try to get drunk again, trade everything they can for booze and crack. They eat each other, drink each other's dreams and soul-remnants, gnaw at each other's lips until their mouths are bleeding. In hell, you get glimpses of Earth, but can never touch it.

January 27

I either sleep all the time, or live my life in darkness and dreams. My lips are blistered and it hurts to talk. I try to talk with my darling, who's here all the time now—as if she never got in that taxicab—but mostly I cough. She talks and talks, sweet soft words that sound so good coming out of her mouth but cut me up a moment later. And now Randy's here, too, sitting on my feet.

"Randy, have you met my darling?" I try to say, but I'm retching so hard my back muscles burn. "I think she's trying to kill me."

"Cough-X," he says. "You need Cough-X."

"Gimme some," I try to say.

"Cough-X," he says.

"I know, gimme."

"Cough-X," and his grin stretches into a Popeye twist. And now he's wearing a sailor suit, pulling out cans of Cough-X, squeezing them so that they pop like cartoon spinach into his gulping gullet. "Cough-X! Cough-X!" The rats have chewed through the floor, are swarming over me as Randy gulps down can after can of green glowing Cough-X.

"Help me, Randy," I try to say.

"I yam what I yam, kid. I yam what I yam."

January 28

She comes to me now in her sparkly blue dress.

"Stop it, baby," she says. "If you stop it, you can come home—I promise."

"Stop what?" I cough.

"Quit the kerosene, and you can come home with me right now. That's all, just quit the kerosene." The light from the heater is reflecting off the silver ceiling, shining a giant glowing flower across her face. "Just stop the kerosene."

"But . . . I'll freeze."

"No, no. I'll keep you warm." And now the fabric of her dress is bursting to flame, embers falling from her body like shooting stars. "Just quit the kerosene, babe." And she's standing before me naked, her smile so sweet, the floor catching fire.

As I open my mouth to tell her I love her, I begin to choke. I retch, and a clear, burning liquid comes gushing out of me. It burns like acid and I try to yell out, to warn her. But it's too late. The kerosene gushes from inside me onto the burning floor, and everything explodes into a ball of blue flame.

And now I'm floating on a clear burning river.

I float. And float.

My love has exploded. My shack is gone.

But someone is knocking. Knocking on the river? And now the world suddenly fills with light.

"Come on. Get the hell out of there." Hands are grabbing me, pulling me toward the light. "You've been in there too long."

"Jackie?"

"Yeah, numb-nuts, who'd you think? God, you look like shit. What's the matter with you?"

"My darling's dress. The sexy blue one."

"Come on. You're going to the doctor."

January 29

"Bronchitis. And flu," I explain, carefully repeating what the doctor told me. "Oh, and a bit of carbon monoxide poisoning."

"Carbon monoxide poisoning?" says Calvin. He and Bonnie are boiling something on the fire barrel.

"Just a bit."

"Well, you ain't using that kerosene heater no more. What'd they give you?"

"Pills. An inhaler. Oh, and Cough-X."

I am still feeling weak and tired, but at least I can stand on my own feet. It is dark now and I can hear yelling and laughing down near Jimmy D's.

"What's going on?"

"Tweedle Dumb and Tweedle Dumber." This is how Bonnie refers to Jerry and Donny. "They stole some golf clubs and a bucket of balls from the driving range. They're hitting them at the boats."

"Sounds fun!" I say, and walk toward the river.

"You sure you should?" Bonnie calls out. "In your condition?"

"It's only golf!"

They are down by the chain-link fence, with two six-irons, a five-iron and a three-wood. The first tanker is only about a hundred yards away, but most of the balls are hitting the dark water like invisible fish jumping.

"Can I hit a few?"

"I-I-I don't know. C-c-can you?"

"*May* I hit a few, Jerry?"

"S-s-see if you can hit the boat. If you can."

"Yeah, I get it." I usually just ignore Jerry, whose unique mix of ego and idiocy makes my palms sweat and my brain itch, but apparently my illness has altered my judgment. "Watch this," I say.

I take a half-swing with the five-iron and pop one off the deck of the closest ship, then a full swing and hit the one behind it. "Just one more," I say, and drive one with the three-wood all the way to the third tanker at the end of the docks. It pings like a muffled bell across the water.

"Fuckin' A, man," says Donny, and steps up with a six-iron. I stand back.

He hops with his swing, like he's trying to kill a gopher. The ball hits a fence post 4 feet to our right and rebounds straight into my kneecap—a clang then a crunch. I hit the ground. And now Bonnie and Calvin are standing beside the idiot halflings, the four of them looking down at me laughing.

"W-w-way to g-g-go, Shaun," says Jerry.

"Jesus," says Bonnie. "You really are the unluckiest son of a bitch I ever met."

"What?"

"Yep," says Calvin, still laughing. "Weren't we just saying that the other night?"

"What do you mean?"

"Come on," says Bonnie. "If something's going to happen, it's going to happen to you."

I lie there staring up at a Metis with ADHD, a tiny alcoholic widowed ex-biker with cancer, a toothless stuttering moron and his Newfie bail-jumping half-brother. "You guys think *I'm* unlucky," I say.

"Fuck yeah," they chorus as Calvin helps me to my feet.

"I mean who else," says Bonnie, "gets carbon monoxide poisoning and a golf injury in the same day?"

"But, but . . . I hit the third tanker," I say. My legs buckle and I fall back on my ass, on the cold wet ground.

January 30

I shake, sweat, guzzle Cough-X and cough up blood, red-stained scraps of toilet paper piling up in the dark corners of this tiny fucking shack. It's the end of the month, and so most everyone's got their $195s and are raging drunk out there, as I drift in and out of sleep.

"Come on, dickweed. It's daytime—get your ass out of bed."

"Jake?" I can see him sitting on my chair, staring at the wall, not looking at me. "I thought you were in jail."

"This *is* a fucking jail. My cell's bigger than this place! And fuck it's cold in here!"

"I quit the kerosene, Jake," I say.

"Yer sick. You gotta get one of those stoves. They'll be here soon, you know."

"I can't. The place is too small. You know, according to the Geneva Convention, even prisoners get rooms bigger than—"

"Then get off your ass, you moron. Get up and make it bigger." He's still not looking at me, and I notice that when he talks his mouth doesn't move.

And now Randy's here too, sitting on the foot of my bed. "Cough-X?" he says and looks around. "Nice place!"

I take a swig of Cough-X. "How do I make it bigger?" I say to Jake.

"Build, fucker, build! Cut through that back wall and build."

"There's no room back there. That old A-frame's there, and the tree."

"So turn it."

"Yeah," says Randy the Sailorman. "Turn it—that'd make it even nicer. Cough-X?"

"Turn it?"

"Turn your fucking house," says Jake, still glaring at the wall. "Turn the house, cut a hole in the back, build a bedroom, then you have room for the stove and can stop fuckin' killing yourself with kerosene."

I look up to see my darling in the blue dress. I wonder for the first time why she's not cold in that thing. "Baby," she says, "you said you'd quit it."

"I have! I did! I'm freezing!"

"Turn it," says Jake, not lifting his eyes. "I'd turn my fucking cell if I could, so I could see the river. I'd knock out that back wall if I could, and go boost a four-by-four, come back and Molotov every one of those fuckers . . ."

"He's right," says Randy.

"What do you mean he's right?"

"Cough-X?"

"They're right," says my darling. "Turn it . . . Turn it, baby. Please!"

I burst out of my empty shack. The day is bright. There are swans on the water, geese flying overhead. Rats scurry out of the rubble as I cross over to Calvin and Bonnie's fire barrel. Calvin is working on the floor for Bonnie's shack.

"Hey, Lucky!" calls Eddie. "Put on a jacket!"

"Who?"

"You," says Bonnie. "It seems to have stuck."

"I'm going to turn it," I say.

"What?"

"My shack. I'm turning it." I stagger back over to my place, pull the door open and start dragging everything out: books, clothes, table, mattress and box spring. I climb up on the ladder, unhook the side of the tarp and throw everything out of the attic: my tents, extra clothes, my rucksack, running shoes. When everything's strewn across the ground between my shack and the water, I stumble over to Sluggo's.

"Come on, Sluggo! You gotta help me turn my shack."

"Fuck off. I'm drunk."

"Everyone's drunk. Come on, let's go."

I limp over to Steve's, my knee throbbing. "Come on, Steve. I don't care if you're drunk. We're turning my shack."

I make my way back over to the barrel. "Let's go, goddammit! We're going to turn it! We're turning my shack!"

Within ten minutes there are a half-dozen drunken men at my shack: Eddie, Calvin, Jerry and Donny, Sluggo and Steve, all kicking at the skids beneath my floor, looking at the walls like they're searching for the button labelled "Shack Turning."

"How the fuck . . ."

"I don't know, just grab a corner. Put your weight into it. Come on!" I start pushing against the wall, bare arms sweating in the cold. The rest step up and begin tugging, pushing and swearing at my shack. "Turn! Turn!" And suddenly there's a loud crack like a rifle shot and Sluggo's lying on the ground behind me, the side wall of the woodshed/extension broken beneath him.

"Shit!" he yells. Everyone else is standing over him, laughing.

"Okay, okay. We need a plan." I start scrambling around, grabbing skids from nearby rubble heaps, placing them on the river side of the shack. "We'll try to turn it onto these," I say. "Off those skids onto these ones. Okay?" Everyone's looking at me like I'm crazy, but then Eddie steps up.

"Yeah, that might work," he says. "Those skids under there are embedded in the ground, they're not going to move. But we need some leverage."

"Leverage!" I say, and Eddie and I start digging for two-by-fours. We shove them under the house in the spaces between the skids, and prop each one up with bricks to create a sort of fulcrum.

"Lift and turn!" I yell, and start pushing down on the end of a two-by-four. Everyone's grunting and cursing, the walls rocking back and forth, skids cracking beneath. Eddie is bellowing orders, trying to co-ordinate the effort, as I keep yelling, "Lift and turn! Lift and turn!" Then slowly, magically, the shack shifts a foot to the left, tilts . . . and turns.

And now more people are stumbling over drunk, laying their hands on my shack, pushing this way and that. One of the walls is about to buckle, the door rips off its hinges, another man hits the ground, but we soldier on.

"Lift and turn! Lift and turn!" I shout. More men slip to the ground as the floor shifts out from beneath the walls, skids breaking. The shack turns another foot as the two-by-four snaps under my weight and I fall forward, my wrist bent beneath my chest. I get up quickly and start pulling at the doorway. The whole house is groaning, the floor is crack-ing, a sudden strong wind is blowing the waves onto the shore behind us, Jackie, Nancy and Bonnie are cackling from the sidelines, Sluggo is damning me loudly, everyone is yelling out with one last effort of sense-less brute force, "Turn!"

The house tips one last time, straightens out, and then stands facing the river. I step back. Everyone is still, quiet, gazing at my shack in awe.

"Fuck!" exclaims Randy, who's just shown up now. "We did it!"

"It turned, b'y," laughs Calvin.

"Y-y-you owe us big time," says Jerry.

"Big time," says Sluggo.

Eddie is smiling at me. "Well, there you go, you little prick," he says. "Hope you're happy."

My back to the rolling river, I take a step forward and stare at the front of my shack. It's like looking at a friend who's done something so out of character you can't even recognize him. "Thank you," I say.

When the guys have gone back to their drinking, I step up to where the door used to be, and look in.

The floor is completely destroyed, as if by a six-by-six-foot earthquake, the skids broken and twisted and jammed up against each other, insulation sticking out all over the place, the three pieces of floor pulled apart like continental plates, buckled, caught under the walls—half outside, half in.

"Shit," says Bonnie, looking in over my shoulder. "Way to go, Lucky."

I can't believe what I've done. I feel like I'm going to throw up.

"You can sleep in the dollhouse next to Randy's tonight," says Bonnie. "There's nobody in it . . . You coming to Osgoode with us?"

I suddenly realize how hungry I am, how exhausted. I can't think about what I've done to my shack. "Yeah. Let's go."

January 31

I am not unlucky. It's just that my instinct for self-preservation is outweighed by a subconscious urge to destroy myself. Although a good gambler when it comes to games (I know the odds and respect them), I delude myself when it comes to life.

I had a good life. I had a woman I was crazy about, a family that supported and loved me, money, friends and a sunlit bedroom that felt good to wake up in. Most any other fool would have been satisfied, but my reserves of idiocy run deep. I just kept throwing this simple bet to the sky: "All or nothing!"

I guess the Fates finally got sick of hearing this same stupidity, and one day I woke up with nothing—not even the sunlight.

The fact is, given enough time I will always sabotage myself. This is something I've never admitted before, and maybe I'm not owning up to it now—maybe I'm just delirious. Whatever the case, I have to accept that I've given myself carbon monoxide poisoning and bronchitis, wrecked my wrist, destroyed my shack, and once again lost everything I own under a foot of snow and ice.

Last night, the first snowstorm of this late-arriving winter came in full force. By the time I dragged myself out of the dollhouse the world was white, the snow bending sideways like a giant slap from the gods. I made my way down to the river, but other than my broken shack I could see nothing there—my clothes, books, bed and blankets, radio, table and chairs, tools, candles, dishes, filing cabinets, bookshelf and kerosene heater, all buried in the storm.

I stood at the doorless doorway. The wind whistled under the walls. I stepped inside with the waves crashing behind me and felt like I was on a shipwreck, my back sliding down the broken wall. I could see our apartment in Montreal, the living-room couch, the curtains I put up, the kitchen aglow in candlelight, our bedroom—two warm bodies beneath the blankets of our bed.

Fucking home wrecker. I began to head off through the snow, but then I remembered. I found a splintered two-by-four sticking up above the surface, returned to my front yard and started to dig. I got down on my knees by the birch tree, pulling out T-shirts, spoons and empty bottles. And finally I found what I was looking for, three spiral-bound notebooks: November, December, January—three cold chapters of a buried book. I tucked them inside my jacket and trudged through the snow once more, over the ice and away from the river.

A voice called out, "Where are you going, Lucky?" I didn't answer.

x   x   x

I don't know where I'm going. It seems I never do. People have told me that I run away from things—try to escape through travelling and alcohol and writing and whatever else. But that's always seemed too simple and pessimistic. Instead I've preferred to see myself as attempting the plunge to the heart of things—with movement, alcohol and writing as tools to dig. But now I've destroyed my home again, even if it was just a shack by the river, and there's got to be a reason for that.

Sure, I thought I was doing it to make room for a stove. But maybe it's more than that. Ever since she came to see me, that shack became just another thing that reminded me of her. I couldn't even look at that chair without seeing her sitting there, clean and beautiful, looking on me with those eyes. And so maybe I had to turn it, to get different light in through that window, and escape the vision of her.

x   x   x

I limp through the snowy streets, the only one out in this storm. I peer into windows and yell at buses. I have no money, and so can't stay any-where for long—a doorway, a foyer, a mall until the mall closes. And so once again I'm this stupid caricature of self-sorry vagrancy. But that's what it is to be homeless. It's hard to have insight into your all-consuming stumble through the streets. I want my old life back, but I'm scared I'm moving farther and farther from it, becoming invisible—like the man who I used to be is disappearing on the horizon. I want to go back to Montreal, back to my darling in our bed. I want to go see my family, find my life again before it's too late. I want to get drunk, but I've got no money.

Forget all this. I'm going to make it all the way through this damn city. I'm going to the highway. Going to Mexico. Going to hell. I'm going to walk until this storm beats me down.

Finally I find the entrance to an underground parking lot, and decide that's where I'm going—that good old carbon monoxide hover-ing in the air. I pass out and dream of snow, rolling in white powder, inhaling it, my mouth thickening, blood racing, from the heaven-dropped devil drug. I want more and more and more and more. But there's nothing left—just parked cars, and thick cold concrete.

February:
White Powder and Swimming Pool Blue

February 1

It took me a while to get back to Tent City, since I made a few detours—
to the highway on-ramps trying to hitchhike out of Toronto, to the train
tracks looking for open boxcars. But finally I went home through the
ongoing storm.

"Hey, Lucky, where you been?" Bonnie followed me as I trudged to
my shack. "Where's all your stuff?"

I pointed to the frozen snowdrifts and she muffled a laugh. "Oh
fuck, Lucky, you really are incredible," she said, and stared through the
doorway into the disaster of my home. "Tell you what, Calvin's not going
to work on my place today. The weather's too harsh, and he's gone on a
drunk. I'll give you a hand if you want."

"Really?" I said. "Thank you, Bonnie."

For half an hour, snow and wind beating against the shack and
whipping through the door, we tugged at the floorboards, trying to dis-
lodge and straighten the broken skids, until finally we were frustrated
and freezing.

"This is impossible, Lucky. It's just not working, you know? I don't think you can build a floor if the house is already sitting on the stuff you're supposed to build it with. It's like the Nish say, 'When the sky . . . '"

"Bonnie."

"Yeah?"

"You're right." I sat down in the snowy middle of my floor-that-once-was.

"I'm going to go back to the fire and warm up. If you think of something, come get me."

I stared at the floor for almost an hour. Finally I got up and walked back to Bonnie's.

"I don't know where to go," I said.

"What do you mean? Do you mean in spirit? If I had my tarot cards, I'd—"

"Will you help me, Bonnie? It'll be hard. We'll have to really persevere. We'll—"

"You're talking weird, Lucky."

"Yeah, well. I don't feel too good. You with me?"

We started by digging some two-by-fours out of the snow. I made some fulcrums and, corner by corner, wedged them under the insulation beneath the mess of floorboard. As she sat on the end of each lever, I tugged out what insulation I could, propped up the floor bit by bit and struggled the skids straight. It took a long time but finally we had something that almost resembled a floor.

"Thank you, Bonnie," I said.

But there are still problems. Trying to walk on this floor is like going to sea. It rises in the centre, sinks at the sides, waves popping up underfoot with every step. And I've shoved so much stuff under the boards, trying to level it out, that none of it'll budge an inch anymore, all stuck into this warped hilly mess. The stoves arrive tomorrow, but there's nothing more I can do.

February 2

I was woken by Beric from the TDRC and Dan the stove man, banging on the door of the dollhouse. We walked through the snow to my shack.

"Something's different," said Beric.

"Turned it," I mumbled, avoiding their eyes. Dan looked through the doorway.

"What the hell happened in here? We can't install a stove on that."

"I'll try to fix it," I said

"We got some others to do. We'll come back in a couple hours, okay?"

They left, and I stood in the doorway once more, waiting for a bit of strength. I made a decision—I would build another floor on top of this one. The only problem, of course, was that any building supplies lay under a foot and a half of snow.

After a quick survey I found a massive piece of heavy, coated, pressurized wood leaning against Randy's shack.

"Mind if I take it, old man? I'm in need of a floor."

"Go ahead, fucknuts—what's mine is yours." Randy was staggering pretty bad from the Cough-X, so I got Calvin to give me a hand with the wood. It was heavy as hell, and I dropped it edgewise onto my right foot as we struggled it through the door.

"Ow! Fuck!"

"Nice goin', Lucky."

At least now I'll be more symmetrical, limping with both legs, which I guess goes against the nature of a limp. I cut the wood to length, wedged it in against the walls, then scrounged for some scraps to prop up the parts that still wobbled. When it was done, the new floor covered only half of the old one, and I double-limped—staggering like the rest of the drunks down here—over to Eddie, who came up with some tongue-and-groove pressboard.

"Thanks, you big freak."

"You goddamn bum."

Calvin gave me a square piece of slate to go under the stove. I did a lot of wedging and propping and messy nailing, and somehow had a flat floor by the time Dan came back. In the process, however, I'd lost about six inches off the height of the ceiling.

"Watch your head," I said as he bumped it against the roof planks, then struggled the stove over to the corner. It was the most beautiful inanimate object I'd ever seen.

We cut a hole for the chimney in the left side wall with a small handsaw, hammered in a cylindrical metal casing, fit the piping in, stuffed the hole with insulation and bolted the chimney into the top of my beautiful, front-loading, sleek and sexy stove.

"Thank you," I said. "At this moment, you are my favourite person in the entire world, including people who are dead, like Van Gogh or Francis of Assisi."

"Are you okay?"

"I'm great now. Everything's going to be just fine. I have a stove."

"Hey," he said, finally taking the time to look around. "You didn't make this place any bigger. You just took all the stuff out. Where are you going to sleep?"

"Don't worry," I said. "I'm building another room."

"You sure you're okay?" he said.

"Can I light it now?"

x

x

x

The white smoke—a message of spirit and hope—like cardinals choosing a new pope, rose into the late-afternoon sky. For a moment, everyone stopped what they were doing. Nancy put down the bottle she was drinking and lifted her eyes. Sluggo stopped yelling at his dog. Calvin dropped a two-by-four as his measuring tape zapped back on his thumb. Randy stopped mid-stagger and pulled up his slipping pants. Bonnie put down the jar she was washing. Eddie, a joint in his mouth, fell to the ground and made a snow angel as he gazed at the sky. Smoke!

By early evening, drawn not by the promise of booze or drugs or even food, summoned by nothing but smoke, they came from all over, and gathered in my humble house by the river, to see the new wood stove.

"Way to go, Lucky," they said.

February 3

When I woke up this morning, my wrist, knee and foot were swollen, and I was coughing. I'd slept well, however, and felt hopeful for the first time in days.

I stepped out of the dollhouse and staggered straight as I could over to Hawk's.

"Morning, Hawk," I said. "How would you like to chainsaw my wall today?"

When he was done, I stood at the back of my shack, staring right through to the river on the other side.

"What you gonna do now?" he said.

"Build, I guess." Hawk glared around at the frozen ground, shook his head and walked away. It started blowing snow.

When I built the original shack, I had the luxury of an unfrozen ground strewn with all manner of wood, two wrists that worked, no fever and the absence of Nancy's spite.

Nancy is mad. She's mad at the world, for sure. But right now she's mostly mad at me, and Bonnie, and anyone else who got a stove this weekend. She's been down here a long time, but has never built her own place. Without a shack, there's nowhere to install a stove, and now she's in a rage—yelling and spitting and swinging a two-by-four. To his credit, I heard Steve say, "Can't you just be happy for them?"

"Fuck them and their fucking stoves," yelled Nancy and tried to heave a rock at the fire barrel, then fell down to have a seizure. Nancy's seizures are as infamous down here as Randy's Cough-X hallucinations, but far more dubious. They occur when she needs attention, then quickly dissipate.

After an hour of digging through the snow I had two large pieces of plywood, a couple lengths of two-by-four, some one-by-twos and some pieces of pressboard. Then it took a while to scrape and chip the ice off. I sawed a couple of ragged planks to size then laid them over the skids and began to hammer down the floor.

"Fuck you," yelled Nancy. "Some of us are trying to sleep!" It was one o'clock in the afternoon, but I stopped hammering nonetheless, since I'd run out of nails. It's hard enough scrounging for nails in a garbage pile, but doing so in the snow, during a snowstorm, is like searching for a nail in a snowstorm.

After staring at my feet for a while, I remembered seeing a broken speaker in one of Randy's milk crates. I pulled the magnet out, tied it to a string and put a large pot of water on Bonnie's fire barrel. When the water was hot enough I carried the pot over to a spot I remembered seeing lots of nails, and began sloshing the steaming water onto the ground.

As the snow and ice melted I dragged the magnet through the slush. Calvin came over, laughed at me for a while, then got down on his knees to help.

By the time we'd found enough straight ones, the snow had let up and you could see the glow of a winter sky over the water. Calvin gave me a hand building the walls, both of us trying to ignore Nancy's increasingly demonic threats.

"You bastard son of a bitch! I'm gonna fucking tear that fucking piece of shit down! You asshole! Some of us are trying to sleep!"

"Calvin, can you go tell her it's not sleeping time right now?"

"Fuck that, I ain't going near her."

"That roof is coming down, motherfucker!"

The two large pieces of plywood I'd found were almost the perfect size, and Calvin held them up for me as I hammered them crosswise onto the back of my shack. Then, working from inside, I nailed in one-by-twos as crossbars, measuring them to bracket some leftover squares of Eddie's Styrofoam insulation.

"You're still hammering! They're still hammering! You stole my fucking stove and now you're hammering!"

"We'll be finished soon, Nancy. And then you can come over for tea, okay?"

"You son of a bitch!"

As the glow of the sun began to fade in the sky I collapsed on my mattress in my new bedroom, hammer in hand, surrounded finally by walls.

x   x   x

Drip, drip . . . drip.

Drip, drip . . . drip.

Melting snow is falling from the ceiling and my skin is going cold. I sit up and watch the descent, ceiling to bed. Drip, drip . . . drip.

I decide that the problems with the roof are many, but solvable. Although I've stretched the existing tarp all the way across, the roof addition is flat. The snow has gathered and is melting where the new roof meets the slant of the attic.

For the time being at least, Crazy Chris has abandoned Tent City. A few of the guys pillaged his "garage" the same day they tore down Mike's Distribution Centre, and scavenged the wood and contents. I managed to salvage a roll of tarpaper Chris said I could have, and now I figure I need it.

I shovel the snow off the flat roof, then cut the tarpaper into strips the length of my bedroom ceiling. I shimmy it under the tarp as it whips in the wind, nail it over the gaps in the wood as best I can, then lay some plywood against the attic, trying to create a slant beneath the tarp all the way to the back wall. But still it doesn't seem enough to prevent the snow from accumulating.

I find a one-by-one long enough to span my entire roof, cut one end into a point, and slide it under the tarp until the point hooks into the front of the awning, so there's now a second pitch to the roof. Instead of pulling the tarp tight, I decide to leave some slack. Down here, rain or snow never falls without wind. And now my roof ripples like a sail, beating off the snow as it falls.

"Yeah, that's cool," says Calvin. "Maybe I'll do that for my roof. If I ever finish Bonnie's."

Bonnie is a neurotic perfectionist—a fine thing to be when somebody else is building your shack. She wants perfectly framed walls with a precisely pitched and shingled roof. Calvin is drinking less and working all day. He will get her house built as perfectly as he can, if it kills him. It may be the first act of platonic love I've witnessed down here.

Everyone rides Calvin because of it, but he doesn't seem to care. At the end of the day, tired as he is from building, and even though her constant chatter drives him almost as crazy as it does me, he sits at the fire barrel and brushes the knots from her long dark hair. The old boys make easy jokes and laugh in his face. But Calvin just smiles.

Having finished my revolutionary new roof, I finally put the front door back on. Jerry and Donny have stolen a couple of pizzas, so I dig out some chairs and we eat dinner by the wood stove in my renovated, two-room, waterfront shack.

February 4

The fire went out during the night, and the walls of my bedroom are not yet insulated. But still, it felt good to step out through my front door and see the swans, white as snow, spreading their wings on the sunlit canal. I gathered an armful of wood I'd stored, and lit a fire in the stove, smoke lifting into the early-morning sky, as white as the swans, as white as—

"Fuck yer fucking stove!"

"Good morning, Nancy."

I worked on insulating the walls until Eddie came by and invited me over for a cup of coffee. I pulled some ice from his doorstep and pressed it against my wrist as he poured me a cup. "What the fuck did you do now?"

"Don't know, but I don't think it's broken. I've busted them both a couple times, so I know what that feels like." This, of course, led to us trying to outdo each other with badly healed bones and messy scars.

"Check this out. I got that from cliff diving . . ."

"Knee popped right off—baseball bat . . ."

"How about this one?" I said, and showed Eddie the scar at the base of my right index finger, on the back of my hand.

"That thing's not so big."

"Yeah, but it's a duelling scar," I said. "Sword went halfway through my hand." I took a swig of coffee, satisfied that I had him.

"You want to see something?" said Eddie, his voice soft now. He unbuttoned the cuffs of his shirt and pulled them up as far as they'd go. "Remember a while ago? When you were drunk, and said you didn't care if you kept living or not?"

I didn't say anything. I was looking at his arms.

"I gotta tell you: one day you might get older, and then you'll be happy you're still alive." The scars looked like thick white worms, crossing each other in careful Xs all the way from his wrists to his biceps. "Set myself on fire, too . . . And hung myself."

"What? When?"

"All at once. Well, first I cut. Then—before I could bleed out—I poured the kerosene, and lit it just as I put the belt around my neck. Woke up six days later and asked for chicken fingers."

"Why?" I didn't know what else to say.

"Guess I was hungry."

"No, why did . . . ?"

"To beat a murder rap."

"Who? I mean, how?"

"I used to be real angry and fucked up, you know?"

I nodded.

"Anyone looked at my friends the wrong way and I just went for 'em. I've stabbed twenty-two guys—I counted. When I was 19, I got put in the pen. But then, you know, this guy raped a kid I was hanging with. So I stabbed him forty-four times. That's what I was like then."

"Uh-huh."

"So then I'm looking at life. But my lawyer thought I should plead insanity. So I did, and I tried to off myself to back up the plea. Didn't know just how to do it, but I managed to get myself a shiv, a can of juice and a belt. But you know what the thing is? Even though I was just going to do it for show, as soon as the blade cut into my skin, everything sort of changed." Eddie smiled, his eyes flickering as he looked at me.

"Shit."

"Yeah, so after I got out of the infirmary, they put me in the nut-house for three years—or it was supposed to be. But then I killed a guy with a shovel. And this was '78, right? So they just blanked me out for a year—they shocked me and drugged me, till I just turned right off. When I asked this guard if the son of a bitch I shovelled the day before had died, he said, 'Yeah, he died—but that was a year ago.' Then they put me back in the pen with my brain all mush. I did ten years in there."

"When did you . . . get your heart?" I knew this sounded like he was the Tin Man or something, but I was having trouble finding the right question.

"Always had a heart, Lucky." He smiled. "I guess I just realized that I'd spend my whole life in jail if I kept going at everybody who pissed me off. So I learned to talk . . ."

"You're a good talker. In fact you're the most diplomatic guy I ever met." I realized I was saying this to a man who'd stabbed twenty-two people, and had to laugh.

"You know what it is? I got out of the pen at 30. And instead of being pissed off at my wasted life . . ." He snorted and rolled down his sleeves, suddenly self-conscious. "I just try to do good to people, that's all. It's pretty simple."

"How come all these other guys go on about how you have to look out for yourself—tell you never to help anyone—like Hawk."

"Hawk." Eddie shook his head. "I'll tell you, I spent ten years in the pen, but I got out. Hawk's still in there—you hear what I'm saying? I'm the only one that ain't scared of him. Even Jimmy D is scared of Hawk. And Jimmy D's tough. But you know, really, why Hawk tells you to mind your own business?"

"Why?"

"He wants people to be assholes, not heroes. So that he's the only one who can help. Don't listen to that, Lucky. Just do what you're doing."

"I'm not doing anything."

"Then neither am I."

February 5

People down here can't drink. A bottle of wine, a few beer or a half mickey turns them into babbling maniacs.

Bonnie, who doesn't drink, has the explanation for this—the clinical diagnoses of cirrhosis of the liver and alcoholic dementia. I don't know about that, but I agree with her that booze, like drugs, is not the cause of this mess. It's just a symptom of our grief. It's grief that brings people here: the loss of love, childhood, livelihood; minds, dreams or faith. Some lost it all before they could even walk. They never had a chance.

If you're old enough, you know your grief fully by now, and have mostly drowned in it, spinning down angry and sad. If you're young, you might not know you're grieving yet, and still fly off angry and fighting until you get popped or offed, or survive long enough to become old and grieving.

There is no worse fate than to grieve for your life lonely in a room. And so even those who could have a roof and four walls end up on the street, where the struggle of living outside takes up some of the energy, fighting for a piece of ground—some of the fury. But you still beat at the walls, even when they're not there. You still drink when you can't anymore.

x
x
x

I decide I have to get drunk. The cough is a lot better, and I'm thinking too much. I go to a pawnshop carrying a drill set and snowboard that Jake had hidden away, and get more than I expected—enough for a twenty-sixer and two bottles of wine.

I finish the wine walking back to Tent City. The night is cold and late, and there's no one around, not even Calvin by the fire barrel. But by the time I get my stove lit, and step back out to watch the first soft clouds lifting into the sky, Steve and Nancy are out there, too.

"We're coming over!" says Steve. "And we're bringing beer!"

"Okay," I say. So they come on over, and they're not too drunk yet.

"*Mama told us not to come,*" sings Steve, and hands me a 2-litre bottle of Labatt Ice. "This is for all the drink you've given us," he says. "Or some of it."

We pass the bottle around, and Nancy grins at me with her probably-once-pretty, devil-red eyes. "She wants to say she's sorry," says Steve, then sings, "*You never give me your honey, you only give me your dirty faces. And in the middle of the masturbation . . .*"

"It's okay, Nancy." I pass the bottle back to her. "But like I said before, I'm not gonna listen when you yell. If you've got a problem, come over and tell me, and maybe I can do something. But not if you just stand over there and yell. Okay?"

"Okay . . . But I shoulda got a stove. I shoulda fuckin'—"

"You would have if you'd built a place. Even if you'd just started." I look at Steve.

"It's been fuckin' snowing."

"It's Canada, Nancy. And it's winter."

"I cut my fuckin' hand." She turns it over to show me as she passes the bottle, and beer sloshes on the floor.

"I'll fix that, Nancy," I say, then take a swig and pass the beer along to Steve.

"Yeah, baby," says Steve. "*Come on people now, spy on your mother . . .*"

I take her hand in mine and look down at the cuts on her palm. They're not too deep, but they're filthy, and one looks like it's getting infected. I pour hydrogen peroxide on some Kleenex and start to clean it up as Nancy squeals in pain.

"Come on lady make it hurt so good, sometimes the booze don't feel like it should . . ."

I get some Band-Aids and patch the cuts, then turn on the radio. When we're finished the beer, I pull out the bottle of whisky.

"Yes yes yes yes yes yes," says Steve, "Jimmy Beam, baby," and he howls, wide eyes staring at the bottle. Will I never learn? By now I've got the drinking rites down cold. I crack the bottle and pour the first drops on the floor—because the dead are thirsty, too. Then I take a slug and pass the bottle on to Steve, keeping the cap in my fist—it's up to me to close it. Steve cranks the radio louder. After a few rounds, Nancy is mumbling and grabbing at my hands, scratching at her bandages.

"You ever wonder what you're doin' down here?" says Steve. "You ever *wa-wa-wa-wa-wa-wonder* . . ."

"Yeah, sometimes."

Nancy is crying now, her hands over her face. I put my arm around her for a moment, then get up to shove more wood in the stove. As I sit down again, she burrows her head into my shoulder. "I, I . . . I . . . have nothing," she says and I hold her as she sobs.

"I'm going to get myself a cellphone," says Steve. "You want one?"

"Nothing!" Nancy yells. "I have nothing!"

"Nancy," I say, whispering into the top of her head as she digs into my chest. "It's okay . . . you have us, right? Look over there." I pull her chin up and try to make her look at Steve who is sitting on my bed playing air guitar to The Clash. "You've got a guy who loves you. That's more than most of us have, right, Steve?"

"Fuck yeah! And you got a brand-new Cadillac!"

Nancy starts punching herself in the head and I grab her hands. "You know what I got?" she says. "I got fucking cancer. I got cancer. I got—"

"I know. I know, sweetie. But . . . but I don't know what to do about it. I—"

"And I got fuckin' kids I never even seen. I got kids I killed. Abortion! You know what that is? I got cancer. I . . ." She is sobbing hysterically as I hold her, and Steve falls forward onto his knees and wraps his arms around us both, his busted, flattened nose pressed into my cheek, we hold her sobbing between us.

"Look at this," says Steve, finally. "Just look at all this love. I love you, you bitch," and he kisses her cheek. I get up to damper the stove and light a candle, keeping an eye on Nancy. She takes another swig of whisky, and so does Steve. Then the opening riff of "Gimme Shelter" burns out of the radio, and Steve is up and dancing.

"Watch the stove, Steve."

"You watch the stove . . . *It's just a piss away, piss away . . .*"

For a moment, neither of us are looking at Nancy—and that's all it takes. By the time I turn back to her, she is hyperventilating, gasping and choking as her body quivers like water about to boil. I grab the inhaler the doctor gave me for my bronchitis and press it into her mouth. As she breathes in, her eyes roll back in her head and she tumbles down. When she hits the floor she begins to writhe, her head striking the table, her legs kicking the chair down on top of her. And then she is still.

"Fuck!"

"Nancy," says Steve. He rolls his eyes.

"Fuck!"

"Just leave her," he says, and lights a cigarette. "She does this all the—"

"Not on *my* floor she doesn't! I'm not just leaving her there. Not on *my* fucking floor." She moans as I turn her over, and her tongue lolls out of her mouth. I bend my knees and try to pull her up by the arms, but she's immensely heavy.

"Come on, Nancy! Please get up . . ." But each time I get her almost standing, she shifts her weight and we crash back down, knocking over candles, the bookshelf, the radio hitting the floor. A new pain shoots through my wrist as I try to keep her from falling against the stove, and down we go again, my hand crunching between her head and the floor.

"No way, Nancy! I'm fucking sick of this! I'm the only asshole who ever helps you out, and you go and do this on *my* floor, with *my* booze!" I am yelling now, so that all of Tent City can probably hear. "We love you, Nancy. Just stop this! Get the hell up! We fucking love you, okay? We love you!" I turn to Steve, who is drinking, still seated on the bed: "Get over here and help me, you son of a bitch!"

"Captain, my captain," he says. "*Slide, Captain, slide.*" Then he puts the bottle on the floor and makes like he's stretching for the Olympic long jump—neck curls and arm pulls. "I've always liked you, Lucky. Yer a good kid, but I gotta tell you—"

"Just gimme a fucking hand, you moron!"

We manage to get her up long enough so we can angle her toward the bed. This time she falls straight back like a tree being felled, and when she hits the mattress her eyes spring open so wide and her body bounces so high that I can't help spitting out a laugh along with Steve. And then the shack fills with the hot smell of urine.

"She's pissing on your bed."

"Yeah."

"Hey, Pissy Pants!" yells Steve. "You're wetting the wrong bed!"

The smell gets worse. I take a swig from the bottle and hand it to Steve. Nancy is lying on my bed in her own piss, sobbing into my pillow. "Let the Good Times Roll" is playing on the radio, but Steve doesn't bother singing.

"Let's get her home," I say. "Can you try to help us, Nancy?"

We pull her to her feet, and slowly over to the door. I kick it open and she goes sprawling into the bright night snow, Steve tumbling out over her. I pull her arm over my shoulder, heave her up, and begin dragging her to the pink prefab. We veer toward the water, into the trees, over the rubble beneath the snow.

When we finally get her to the prefab, Steve fumbles the door open. We heave her through and she falls onto the stinking mattress inside. She is still crying. I fall on top of her and hold her for a moment, trying to say all the most gentle, comforting things I can think of, then stand up and close the door behind me. I can smell the piss on me.

"You coming for a drink?" I yell to Steve. I will never learn.

We sit in my shack with the door open, drinking the whisky.

"*We gotta get out into space, if it's the last thing we ne-ever do!*" slurs Steve, then he breaks from the song and shouts, "I can't take this shit right now! I'm going to go to jail tomorrow . . . Yeah, first thing tomorrow—I'm going to jail."

I nod like it's as good an idea as any. I keep stoking the stove, we keep drinking, and now Steve is making no sense at all, ranting against everything, kicking at my floor, trying to sing songs that never even existed, until finally he wants to fight—or he thinks he does—and I have to slam him back into his chair. I stare at him, sitting where Nancy was only an hour before, and think senselessly that maybe it's the chair—maybe the chair turns people into suffering angry animals.

I pull him out of the chair and out of the shack, on the pretense that I'm fighting with him. At least I think I'm pretending. I realize it's the only way he's going to move, and I get him across the snow to the prefab like that. I'm wearing only a T-shirt and jeans but can't feel a thing. We're hitting each other, wrestling each other down and down and down. Finally I get the door of the prefab open and let him lunge at me. His elbow smacks against my jaw as he tumbles in on top of Nancy, and I slam the door behind him.

I can hear them howling and crying inside as I turn and walk through the snow.

February 6

Bonnie said something to me a month or so ago that still scares the shit out of me:

"One year equals seven, you know?"

"What?"

"Everyone knows in the services, but they don't talk about it, of course. If someone's been on the streets a year—it's on average seven to undo it."

"Undo it?"

"If they can get their claws in you, get you off the street, just from the experience of one year—from living the shit you live, from seeing all that stuff—it takes on average seven years before you're a contributing, independent member of society."

"Oh."

"Yeah."

"Well, let's hope we're not average."

"Yeah," she said. "Or below."

x x x

I finally went to the doctor about my wrist, and Calvin walked with me up to Lakeshore Boulevard. It was a bright sunshiny day and he'd been planning on going thieving with Steve. But of course Steve is now in jail, just like he said he would be.

"You going for dinner at Osgoode?" said Calvin.

"Yeah, I'll hold a place in line . . . Calvin?"

"Yeah?"

"What'd you do time for?"

"You got a Caddy?"

"Yeah."

"Up it, Puppet." This is how Calvin talks, like he's an old grifter left over from a bygone era of speakeasies and flophouses. He calls booze "hooch" and trademark cigarettes "Cadillacs" or "Caddies." If he's not calling you "b'y," he refers to you as "Sport" and calls women "Dear." When something doesn't go your way he says "tough titty" as in, "Tough titty said the kitty, but the milk tastes good." I handed him a smoke. "Shotgun," he said. I wasn't sure what he was referring to, then realized he was answering my question.

"You shot someone?"

"No, b'y, shot a rapist."

"How long were you in?"

"Ten," he said, lighting the cigarette. "We all do at least a decade, one way or another—you'll do one too."

"How so?"

"You're like me, aren't you? Half Irish and half even more screwed."

"Yeah. Half Mick, half Jew."

"Half Mick, half Nish," Calvin grinned, then punched me in the chest. "The Jew and the Injun. Together we make one fucked-up Irishman." I punched him back in agreement, unsure of what this had to do with a shotgun blast.

But then Calvin said, "We're not killers," in his laughing, smiling, Newfie, Irish, Native lilt. "We just go all the way, that's all. We'll give a decade, probably give it all." And I realized Calvin was talking about kindness, not bravery. "By the way," he said, "you stink like piss."

"I know. You should smell my bed."

"Good luck at the doctor, Jewboy."

"See you in court, Kemo Sabe."

I took a long-overdue shower at the community centre, searching for my face beneath the beard and the grime. There was candle wax in my hair, and tree sap too. My knee was black, my foot was purple, and my wrist was blue. I scrubbed at my body until I was sure the stench of Nancy's urine was gone, then changed my clothes and dried my snow-boot liners under the hair dryer for the hundredth time this winter. I put the piss clothes in a plastic bag and did my two-legged limp back into the sunlight, heading toward the walk-in clinic on Yonge Street.

"It's never simple with you, is it?" said the doctor when I finally arrived.

"Huh?"

"You're the guy with the bronchitis and carbon monoxide, right?"

"Yeah . . ."

"And now you're also the guy with the sprained wrist and the tendonitis. It can't just be one thing, can it?"

"Tendonitis, too? But I gotta be able to use my wrist," I said. "For work."

"What do you do?" He looked down at my boots, up to my beard. "You work in the woods?"

"Sort of," I said. "But I also gotta be able to write . . . and play pool."

He gave me a look and left, then came back with some pills. "One of these a day, and try not to use your hand. And ice it. And you should buy a brace."

"I, uh, I've got no money for—"

"I thought you worked . . . in the woods."

"Yeah, but that's kind of on a voluntary basis, you see. And if I can't use it to play pool then I can't make any money—that's more like on commission, you know? I guess I could open doors, but it's kind of complica—"

"Okay, okay. This'll do," he said, and handed me a tensor bandage. I began to wind it around my wrist as he gathered together some papers. "Are you all right?" he said all of a sudden. "Do you want to talk to someone?"

"No thanks. I'm good now. I got a wood stove. It's a real nice one, you should—" He turned to leave. "Oh! I forgot. There is something else."

"Yes?"

"Can I get a flu shot?"

"Haven't I already treated you for flu this winter—twice?"

"Yeah. I don't want it a third time—guess I'm learning."

When the shot was ready he said, "It'll probably ache for a while . . . You left- or right-handed?"

"Right," I said, and he rolled up my left sleeve and swabbed the upper arm. But then, just as he was pressing the needle to my skin, I remembered. "Wait!" I called out, holding up my bandaged right hand.

"Oh yeah," said the doctor, and exhaled heavily, rolling his eyes and my other sleeve.

x   x   x

"How you gonna flog the dog now?" said Calvin as we sat down for burgers at Osgoode Hall.

"Why? You want the job?"

"Fuck you, sport," said Calvin and punched my right arm as Bonnie laughed.

"Aaah! Flu shot!" I showed him the small Snoopy Band-Aid on my arm.

"Poor baby," he said and smacked it again, but softer.

We ate seven burgers among the three of us, giddy and happy to be seated and served, all the beautiful people coming around to fill our cups. With my clumsy, bandaged hand I knocked over a cup of milk that spilled across the table, and then Calvin tried to spoon-feed me. I swiped his hat, attempted to polish his bald spot with a napkin, then tossed the cap to the security guard by the door. By the end of dinner, Bonnie had told every one of her bad lawyer jokes a few times over and Calvin was laughing so hard he blew Pepsi out his nose.

After almost three months out here, I've come to realize that the purest, happiest intoxication for a lot of people who live on the street is sometimes sobriety, a couple hours of warmth and a heavy dose of protein. And nobody gets drunk on ground beef like Calvin.

When we got back to Tent City, he told me to go to my shack and wait for him. I rolled a couple of smokes and took a glug from the left-over Jim Beam. It was a chilly night, but clear and beautiful. I could see the outline of boats halfway across Lake Ontario. There was a rumbling sound from back in the bushes, and then Calvin appeared, rolling an oil drum over the cold ground toward me.

"I found it today," he said. "Over by the train tracks. I popped the lid off before going to Osgoode." He rolled it a good 8 feet from my door, and stood it up. It was a perfect fire barrel—no holes, no dents, and the mouth bent just slightly oval, to better accommodate a cooking grill.

"It's a beauty," I said. Calvin was already bunching up newspaper to start the first fire. We gathered some wood and then I threw in a match. The oil residue burned in blue swirls deep in the barrel, and yellow and orange sparks rose into the sky like a hundred new stars. "Thanks, Cal."

"Yeah, you needed a barrel," he said. I held my hands out to the fire, the bright flame spiralling into smoke. Maybe there is hope. Maybe a year doesn't have to equal seven, or a decade a life.

February 7

This is where I live.

If you're on the deck of that huge tanker out there, my shack faces you across the water. The front wall is about 6 feet high and 6 feet wide, with a grey wooden door and a narrow window of six panes. The blue roof juts out like a square Elvis haircut. Smoke is rising from the stovepipe. There is a yellow glow through the window and the house looks content, like a one-eyed old man smoking a bowl of cheap tobacco.

If you decide on a whim to jump overboard, it's a short 100-yard swim to this shore. And when you pull yourself onto land, it's only seventeen steps to my plywood porch.

You stand there for a moment, and see that it's an old bathroom door; there are still the vestiges of a towel rack on the outside. You are freezing from the swim across the canal, and you knock once, then open the door. You feel the heat of the stove push against you, and as you step inside, the scent of burning wood brings you back to a hundred campfires. You sit down in the red chair by the door, and take a breath.

As you look around, steam rises from your clothes in the candlelight. Although the place is very small, with low ceilings, it is overwhelming at first glance, there is so much to look at—the haphazardness strikes you like a riddle.

The walls, though symmetrical and uniform on the outside, are made up on the inside of over forty different pieces of wood. There is green-painted plank, blood-red board, brown plywood, glossy stained oak. There are headboards, drawer fronts and the giant round top of a cable spool, all fitted together like you're sitting inside a homemade jigsaw puzzle.

To your right, tucked into the corner on the other side of the door, an old red tool box sits on the floor. On the wall above, the knobs of a blue-painted drawer serve as a coat rack. Beside the tool box are two card catalogues, one on top of the other, full of who knows what. And next to them, a wood stove crouches on a slab of stone. A metal shrimp-cocktail cup sits steaming atop the stove like an unholy grail, humidifying the air. On the floor between the stove and the dividing wall a large desk drawer is full of kindling and firewood. You get up, stoke the stove with hardwood, then sit back down.

You notice there are two pennies embedded in the door, like copper eyes watching you. Directly to your left is a table of sorts—an octagonal piece of enamelled wood nailed down crooked onto a small pine cabinet. You pull it open and find an almost empty bottle of rye and some pads of writing paper. You fill the cup on the table with whisky and take a sip. Also on the table is a lit candle dripping wax down an empty bourbon bottle, a pouch of tobacco and an ashtray. You roll yourself a smoke and turn to light it off another candle on the window ledge. The curtain—formerly a tablecloth—is rolled up and tied to a nail.

On the other side of the table, against the west wall, sits a metal chair with a green seat—beside that, a short black bookshelf. The shelves are overflowing with books, scraps of paper, candles, knives and more pads of writing paper. A small ghetto blaster sits on the top shelf. You move over to the other chair to switch on the radio, next to which sits a daily *Sports Illustrated* swimsuit desk calendar. "You Can't Always Get What You Want" is playing, and you feel a lump in your throat, like you always get when you hear this song. You take a long drink, and look at the calendar. February 7 reminds you of someone, and you refill the cup, take a longer swig and roll another smoke.

The shack is warming up now, the heat reflecting down off the aluminum-foil insulation that lines the ceiling. The ceiling is way too low. Maybe a midget lives here. You look around for clues, see mostly empty bottles—a midget who drinks a lot.

You take off your wet jacket and toss it on the bed. A large plywood shelf spans the foot of the bed, stretching from the back wall to the 2-foot-wide dividing wall. It is piled with clothes and newspapers. You pick up a pair of jeans: not a midget—just an inept architect.

You sit back down in the green chair and put your feet up on a small wooden spool beside the stove. "Little Wing" is playing. The wind whips against the walls.

You take a long drag off the cigarette and look out the window. You can see the candle's reflection, the crests of waves in the moonlight and the shadow of a loon—past that, the giant boat from which you swam. You lift your hand and wave to a man on deck.

February 8

It was sunny again today, and I helped Calvin with Bonnie's new shack. The halflings were there too, and at one point I was bracing a corner for Jerry to nail down when he missed the wood and hit my wrist. "You fucking goof!" I said.

We stopped, and stared at each other, both realizing what I'd just said. His eyes got small. "Y-y-y-you called me a g-g-goof."

"You hit my wrist."

He looked around and saw that nobody else was listening. Bonnie was going on about how she absolutely had to have her shack built in a Victorian style, and the window would have to be changed. Randy had just come by with a bottle of Bingo. Donny either hadn't heard what I'd said, or was choosing to ignore it.

"H-h-h-hold the wood straight," demanded Jerry and started banging again with the hammer.

x   x
    x
      x

A few hours ago, while I was sitting here trying to write, Bonnie came and knocked on my door. She was crying. I sat her down in the chair across from me.

"What's going on, Bonnie?"

"I don't know what to do. I just hate it, hate all of it."

"Bonnie, please. What happened?"

She took another breath and stared at me. "Jerry hit Calvin."

As I stood up, the blood rushed to my head. Calvin's almost 50, about 5 feet tall and 120 pounds. Jerry's half his age, a foot taller and twice his weight. And since the Brothers took off, Calvin's been like a father to Jerry and Donny.

"Fuck!" I said, starting for the door. "Where is he?""

"Who?" said Bonnie, looking at me like she'd just found some new worry.

"Jerry! . . . Calvin! . . . Calvin. Where is he?"

"I don't know. He left. He's drunk . . . Please just sit down, Lucky."

I sat down, then stood up again. "What happened?"

"You know he's dying? He's dying, Lucky, you know that, don't you?" Tears poured down her face. "He spends every minute on that house, even in the snow. And I think he's scared that he's going to get too sick to finish it. And . . ." She choked on another sob. "And it's for me . . . that house is for me. His whole heart is in there, Lucky . . ."

I sat down and took her hands, the long clean fingers so different from Nancy's scarred paws. "I know, Bonnie. Why did Jerry hit him?"

"He was . . . Calvin was collecting bottles to do a run, and the fucking idiot twins gave him some empties. I don't know, I guess he just thought it was a gift—or he didn't care and just wanted to get drunk, you know."

"I know."

"So of course he drank it all before he got back. It was a stupid thing to do, but he's been like a dad to them. And Jerry just smashed him in the face."

"Did he fall?" I said, a taste like iron nails in my mouth.

"Yeah. He fell . . . But you can't do anything, Shaun. Promise me you won't . . . He was really drunk, too. Came back over to the barrel bleeding. And then Jerry has the nerve to follow him, yelling that he called Calvin a goof and Calvin didn't do anything. Said he was going to get his machete. Said he didn't think Calvin had ever been in the pen, because he called him a goof, and Calvin didn't . . ."

Jerry and Donny have been staying in Eddie's new place until Eddie and Karen get it together to move in. I held the steel weapon in my bad hand as I walked through the snow, testing its weight against the stiffness of my wrist, unsure if I'd be able to manage the whip-action release. I put it in my front pocket, then hammered on the door with my fist. I knocked again. "Jerry!" I yelled. I pushed the door open. The cabin was empty. I circled it twice, trying to calm my breathing, a bit ashamed at the relief I felt, then walked through the snow to Bonnie's fire barrel. "Damnit, Lucky," said Bonnie. "You said you weren't going to do anything."

"I didn't."

We sat by the fire with Bonnie rambling on, the way she does—a stress-relieving oral fixation, maybe, like smoking or drinking, although she chain-smokes, too.

"Maybe you should take up drinking," I said.

"Fuck off, Lucky."

Finally Calvin walked out of the darkness.

"Hey, sport!" he said. When he's not happy, Calvin resembles a stocky elfin Druid more than a leprechaun. He circled the fire barrel. "So," he said. "What's going on?"

I stood up. "You okay, Calvin?"

"Yeah, I'm fine."

"What are we going to do?"

"Fuck!" he said, and turned to Bonnie. "You told him, didn't you? Fuck!" The right cheekbone under his eye was cut and swollen. "*We're* not doing anything," he said, turning back to me. "And *you're* not either. You're not! You got it?" He stared at me, then looked down at the snow. I got it.

"Well, I'm here," I said, "if you need me. Okay?"

"Yeah, b'y."

Finally the drink wore off and he passed out in his chair. Bonnie and I waited for the fire to burn down.

"You don't have to bother," she said. "I already got Jerry."

"What do you mean?"

"I didn't tell Calvin this, but I went over there before I came to your place. And I gave him the money—$3.80. I gave it to him."

"You what? Why?"

"So he could think about it."

"The only thing that's going to make him think about it is that he was right to do it. He's too stupid for that sort of psychology, Bonnie. Jesus!"

"It doesn't matter. I gave him some words along with the money— some very powerful words. He doesn't speak Ojibway of course—but I could see the fear in his eyes. Believe me, he's not going to be able to sleep tonight. It's coming to him, you hear what I'm saying? That was his blood money, that $3.80, that's it for him."

"I don't—"

"Just watch, you don't mess with those sort of spirits."

"But Calvin's going to freak about the money."

"He'll understand. He's a Nish, too."

"Whatever you say, Bonnie. Fire's out."

"'Night then, Lucky."

February 9

By the time I got up today, Calvin and Bonnie had left to do laundry at the Sally Ann, and Tent City was quiet. I worked on my shack for a while, then dug through the melting snow for firewood. Eddie came over while I was stocking the stove, with a guy named Frizz.

"Frizz used to live here. He just got out."

"Welcome home," I said, and Frizz winked.

"I wanted him to meet you," said Eddie. "He's one of the good ones."

"Good. You seen Jerry around today?"

"Yeah. I heard about that. Leave it alone, okay, Shaun?"

"Cal's my friend . . ."

"Leave it alone. Jerry's not worth it. And Calvin wasn't being too smart either. It's not your problem. Have I steered you wrong so far?"

"Nope," I said. And he hasn't. But I also know that Eddie doesn't like Calvin much, or at least he doesn't respect him, which is the same thing down here. In fact, nobody really respects Calvin. They think he's a sucker—just about the worst thing you can be.

x
x
x

I went to the Good Shepherd for lunch, and Pops waved me over to his table. I've been having a lot of dinners and lunches with Pops lately. He's always getting me in trouble, but I don't mind, because he makes me laugh. He looks sweet, innocent and harmless: everything he's not. Though tiny, bespectacled and always grinning, he is a lecherous, hell-raising, immoral thief. His skinny old frame—as I've discovered during his inappropriately timed stripteases—is covered in lewd jailhouse tattoos. But somehow even the most intelligent women can't see an inch through Pops. They think he's just a sweet, quirky old man, and they let him sit in their laps, stroke their hair, one arm surreptitiously brushing against their breasts. They laugh when he suggests they come home with him, and pinch his grizzled cheeks. Then, barely out of earshot, he turns to me and says, "Just you watch, I'll fuck her so hard her unborn daughters'll squeal!"

"God, you're sick!"

"I know! And it's sexually transmittable." He gives me his impish smile, giggling and slapping the table. "Security! Security!" he yells. "This man is trying to steal my muffin! Security!" And then I have to spend the rest of the mealtime trying to convince the guards that I have no designs on Pops's muffin.

"You're a bastard, you know."

"Security!"

As we walked away from the Good Shepherd, Pops lit up the joint he'd rolled on his food tray. "How things going for you?" I said.

"Good. Getting lots of fresh pussy, heh-heh."

"'Course you are."

"But my legs are pretty bad, eh? Got rheumatism in both, you know—sort of slows me down when I'm humpin'."

"You should try swimming."

"Where the fuck am I gonna go swimming? You having a pool installed down there?"

So I took Pops over to the community centre, and made him promise to behave. "I've got a good thing going here," I said. "So don't fuck it up." A good thing going is something Pops can understand.

On the way back to Tent City, he clutched his new membership in his hands and went on about how he was going to swim every day. "Don't you worry, Shaun," he said. "I know we got a good thing going." But he still couldn't help mentioning some nasty things he was going to do with the girl behind the counter. I thought of all those unsuspecting women in their bathing suits, wading into the pool. "And I guess I should get a lock," said Pops. "So I can lock my stuff up."

"Yeah, Pops," I said, and then I realized what I'd done. Not only had I acquired a free membership at the gym for Pops, but I'd given a veteran box thief open access to the locker room. "Don't you dare . . ."

"No worries, kid," he said, looking up at the sky. "I'll be good, heh-heh."

February 11

I guess I'm on a bit of a bender. I've been spending the days drinking and collecting wood and running shopping-cart races with Calvin. I've been trying to stay close to him ever since that crap with Jerry.

The Purple People Eaters came down yesterday with boxes of food and kindling, hot dogs and chili, playing their Jesus Loves You songs on a synthesizer and electric guitar. Jerry decided that Randy had taken more than his fair share of food. So while Randy weebled and wobbled in the sunshine, he lumbered over and punched him in the head.

"You see, it's working," said Bonnie.

"What, you put a spell on Jerry that made him punch Randy in the head?"

"No, but he's running out of drunk father figures. You'll see, he's going down."

Meanwhile, Spider has been hired by the radio station to do traffic and weather for a $100. As for Pops, he keeps going on about how somebody stole his bag from the community centre locker room.

"Kind of ironic, eh, Pops?"

"What's that supposed to mean?"

"I thought you were going to get a lock."

"Well, I didn't yet! I'm going to kill the motherfucker who . . . I told them that at the counter there, I swear—somebody's going to pay! I told them they better fucking find it."

I went over to the gym to see what was up and to apologize for Pops.

"Oh, he's such a sweet old guy," said the girl behind the counter. "We'll try our best to locate his bag. Tell him we're doing all we can. Poor guy."

"Yeah."

There's a lot more people moving into Tent City now. All of Eddie's buddies seem to be getting out of prison at the same time and a lot of people are drifting around, howling and yelling, drinking the day away and smoking crack at night. I bought some more booze, and a latch and lock for my front door.

February 13

Last night I walked to the beer store with Spider's old lady, Olivia. She was doing a run for Steve and Nancy. It was cold and snowing and I was tired after a long day, but Spider was off doing his radio bit and she didn't want to go alone. And now I know why.

When we got there we unloaded the empties on the side shelf, got our cash and went to the front counter. Olivia, who hadn't had a drink all day, asked for ten tall cans of Crest (also known as liquid crack) and a 2-litre bottle of Labatt Ice. The pimply kid behind the counter just looked at her. "Have you been drinking tonight, ma'am?" he said.

And Olivia, who's got a mouth on her five times too big for her roly-poly little body, who stirs up shit every chance she gets and cackles like the wickedest witch when the fur starts to fly—Olivia who knocks you down if you even look at her beer, then pinches your ass as you try to get up—couldn't say a word, struck dumb by this 20-year-old asshole in charge of the beer.

"What did you ask her?" I said.

"Sorry sir, it'll just be a moment." He turned back to Olivia. "We can't serve you if you've been—"

"She hasn't been drinking. That's why we're here—so she can start." The kid stared at me with a look of surprise on his face. Apparently he hadn't realized we were together—me and this small Metis woman with the booze-blasted face, so obviously a typical drunk.

"And what does it matter anyway? It's not like we drove here. In fact, we'll be lucky if we don't get run over on the way home by some drunk dickhead you *did* serve . . ." The more I talked, the angrier I got. I took the money from Olivia and stepped forward. "Ask me!" I said. "Ask me if I've been drinking!"

"Excuse me, sir?"

"Ask me!"

"Have you been . . . sir?"

"Yes I have. I have been drinking. But it doesn't matter, because *she* hasn't—and she's the one buying the beer." I gave the money back to Olivia as the kid called the order into the back.

"Not very bright, was he?" said Olivia as we made our way between the warehouses back to Tent City.

"An idiot, for sure." We cracked the bottle of Ice and I took her arm over the slippery parts. "How long you been on the streets?" I said.

"Only eight months," said Olivia. "I'm not used to this stuff. I had a business before, an apartment, went to school in France to be a chef. I'm educated, eh? More than everyone else down here."

"What happened?" I like Olivia, but I'm not sure I believe all this.

"Crack," she said. "My kids are nice and rich. You'd like my daughter."

"Yeah, maybe," I said. Spider is almost half Olivia's age. Together they are like a drunken mother and son. She's teaching him to read. And he practises live on the radio.

x x
    x

I went to get my $195 today, but my caseworker had already gone home. So I just wandered around downtown. It was bright and sunny and cold.

I've realized something lately—that the invisibility of street people blinds both ways. Those with houses and cars, DVD players and ThinkPads, don't really see us. To them, we are all one person with a yellow beard, a torn blue coat and gin blossoms. Our name is Homeless Dave.

But when you're on the street, when you've got no car or ThinkPad, those who do are faceless too. When you walk down Queen Street you see Igor and Heartattack, Friday, Sugar, Sunny and Dan. You see a guy you don't know and give him the nod, maybe even a solid—knocking fists like he's your brother, just for the hell of it. But you don't see the money people, the pretty ones. They're all the same person. And their name is Tom Cruise.

You start to think the other life only exists in one dimension, on a screen. After all, the shantytown in which you live is surrounded—yes, on the other side of the tracks—by film studios and production lots. Whenever you cross over, there they are, filming each other pretending to be junkies and cops and gang members, taking time off from their sitcom living rooms. A cop comes over to tell you this street is off limits right now (he's a real one, you've decided) and you turn and walk away.

x   x
x

I met Calvin, Bonnie and Pops at Osgoode this evening. We had steak sandwiches and were feeling pretty good in there, except of course for Bonnie, whose attention is never in deficit when she's got something to complain about. This time, it was the lack of napkins—the petty plot to keep her fingers sticky and her soul defeated, even as they served us steak.

"What the hell am I supposed to wipe my hands on?"

Pops giggled and wiped his greasy paws on my jacket. I turned and wiped my fingers on Calvin. Calvin, obviously not wanting to upset Bonnie any further, took a handful of my fries.

"It's not funny, guys. What do they expect me to do?"

It was cold when we got outside, the dark wind cutting right through us. As soon as we started home, painfully slow so Pops could keep up, Bonnie started in about the discomfort of her snow-pant linings, and Calvin came up with two transit tickets for Bonnie and Pops to take the streetcar home.

When they'd gone I said, "Sometimes I think she doesn't realize how lucky she is."

"What do you mean?" said Calvin.

"Well, just to come on down here without knowing anyone, and everyone takes care of her—well, mostly you. You even build her a house. And that's great and all, but it makes me wonder what would happen to her if it really got difficult. You know what I mean?"

"Hell, yeah. Like shitting your pants."

"Uh . . . what?"

"Like those days when you get so drunk you shit your pants—and you can't clean it up because you don't . . . live anywhere. You try to clean your ass in a frozen fountain, and you're just crying your eyes out."

"Yeah. Like that, I guess."

"You know, last time I shit my pants I wasn't even drunk," he said. "Ain't that a kicker!" He laughed.

"You sure you want to be telling me this, Calvin?"

"Sure. It's funny. I was sick from the cancer treatments, and I was on my way to the liquor store, right?" Only Calvin can start a funny story this way. "I guess I ate something I shouldn't have, 'cause suddenly it was like, *Boom!*" He stopped, a shocked look on his face like it had just happened. "And I'm like, *Fuck!* I mean, it's one thing if you're pissed, but when you're sober it really sucks, you know? But I just gotta get to the hooch barn—so I start walking fast, right?" And now Calvin's little legs were charging stiff down the sidewalk, his butt cheeks clenched, and I laughed while I tried to keep up.

"So I get there, and the girl at the counter goes, 'Hi, Calvin!' I try to give her a wink, but then everyone just stops, and they're looking at me. 'Gee!' I say, 'What stinks in here?' 'Uh, I don't think I can serve you this evening, Calvin,' she says. 'But darling,' I say, and I can really smell it strong now. 'I'm not even drunk. I shit my pants sober—I promise!'"

We were standing in the middle of the street laughing, cars honking all around us.

"Bonnie ain't got it so bad," Calvin said when we finally reached the curb. "But you know what?"

"What?"

"I'm glad about that."

February 16

Marty lives in a small trailer on the other side of the big Dumpster, just behind my place. He pans at Bay and Dundas to make money for the tall cans of Crest that keep him going. He also volunteers as a children's Bible-class teacher at a nearby church. Although he's supposedly married to Nancy, this only seems to apply when no one else can deal with her. He has a soft, kind voice, handsome eyes, a fisherman's beard and, today, a cracked and bleeding jaw.

"I was just sitting there, you know," he says. "Hat in my lap. I never ask, right—never ask. But I've got a lot of regulars. They know me, and they all give something. So this cop comes up—this goof—I'd seen him before. He came up to me about a month ago and said, 'There's a deal at the Greyhound station: you can get a ticket anywhere in Canada for $99. So when you bum enough, why don't you go over there and get yer ass out of town.' I just shrugged it off, you know." Marty spat out some blood and took a swig of Crest. "So yesterday I seen him coming toward me. And as he passes me he pulls his club and cracks me right in the side of the head. Didn't even stop. Just hit me and kept walking."

I tell him we've got to do something about it: hunt down this bastard cop, infiltrate the force, call up one of my old friends at the *Post*, sue the city, write a book.

"But I have to work that corner," he says. "That's my corner."

x x x

Calvin gave up on his cancer treatment months ago. You can't fight, scrounge firewood, sleep on a bench or hustle for food and booze when you're sick with radiation.

But his situation has changed. He has me and Bonnie now—mostly Bonnie—to look out for him. We've convinced him to go to the doctor, and made an appointment for next week. He's down to about a dozen drinks a week and spends all his time with Bonnie. I'm at about a dozen a day and spend my time writing and stoking the stove.

February 18

When I woke up this morning, the river was frozen over, the ducks sitting confused on top of the ice. I'd been drunk since I got my $195, and decided to try and get myself together a bit, so I went to the laundromat just around the corner from the community centre, up on the Esplanade. My clothes were in the dryer and I was copying out pages of writing when a voice spoke behind me.

"Wow!" it said. "Looks like you're writing your whole life story!"

I turned my head to see a tall, pretty woman. Her long coat looked like it was made from the feathers of alien birds. On someone else it might have been kitschy or tacky, but on her it had an exotic beauty incongruous in the laundromat.

"Always," I said, unsure of what I meant.

She laughed and filled the machine with clothes. She turned toward the soap dispenser, put in her coins and pulled out a small box of Tide. I sat and watched her, then turned back to my writing.

"It goes in here, right?" she said. "I usually use the liquid stuff."

"Yeah. But in the far slot." I watched her pour the detergent—white powder and swimming-pool blue—into the machine and then said, "They've got a deal here on Tuesdays, you know. You get free soap with every load. And . . . uh, today is Tuesday. You just gotta ask at the counter."

I realized I should have said this earlier, but she shrugged and said, "Oh well. Now I know for next time. Thanks."

She kept glancing over at me as I pretended to write. "What are you writing?" she said.

"Oh, you know. Stuff." I got up and walked across the laundromat to the dryers. Although the machine was still spinning, I opened the big round door and sifted my hands through the damp clothes. I didn't know what I was doing and just stood there, staring into the dryer until she called out to me.

"Thanks!" she said. "I'll see you later." I turned and waved to her as she left, her clothes sloshing around in a circle of soapy water.

I went into the bathroom and stared into the mirror. *Why did she have to see me like this? I wish she hadn't seen me this way.* I went back and grabbed my bag, stuck a few more quarters in the dryer and walked quickly over to the community centre.

I showered, scrubbing hard and fast, then stood in front of the large change-room mirror. Just a trim, I thought, and began snipping at my beard with the small scissors on my army knife. When I was done it looked uneven and patchy and sort of mangy. I dug out an old rusty razor and shaved my beard right off.

I washed my face and dried my long hair, then stared into the mirror again. But now I looked like a long-haired, creepy guy with fish-white cheeks.

I ran the twelve blocks to a place I'd seen advertising five-dollar haircuts, a haircutting school actually, in need of poor hairy guinea pigs. I laid down my money, trying to calculate how long it would take a pretty girl to dry her clothes. "Can you make it fast?" I said.

I ran back the dozen blocks, bits of hair itching inside my shirt, the wind cold on my newly shorn head, then stopped a street before the laundromat and just stood there.

"She's going to think I'm crazy," I said. "She's going to think I ran out and got a shave and a haircut just for her . . . That's okay, I'll just tell her I did. And then I'll help her fold her laundry."

But there was only a fat guy with a baseball cap in the laundromat—him and me and the guy behind the counter. I went to every washing machine and every dryer, looking for her colourful clothes, but couldn't find them. The guy behind the counter was watching me. I went back into the bathroom and stared at my clean-cut head for a long, long time.

February 20

Sluggo runs past my door with his pants on fire, yelling, "Stove! Sat on my stove! Stove!" After a few minutes he walks back past my shack in just his underwear, and when I go outside I can see his pants smouldering under a tree in the snow.

I walk through Tent City, past the piles of garbage and junk, the pigeons milling around on the ground, a broken TV with a burnt-out fire inside, sticks smoking where the screen used to be. But what stops me is an iron in a tree. Off a ways, I can see a small fleet of giant multicoloured steel trikes and bikes, with huge wooden wheels, their frames hung with all kinds of percussion instruments. A man is standing atop the largest one, and drumming like Dr. Seuss getting ready for some crazy hobo carnival. In the other direction I can see the remnants of a broken carousel, painted horses struggling out of the wild grass and frozen mud. Randy is lying on his new porch with a giant stuffed unicorn on top of him, giggling and giggling. But, for some reason, I can't stop staring at the iron in the tree. It's just hanging there, the long black cord wrapped around a bare limb.

Randy pushes the unicorn off his chest and stands up. He is wearing a pair of sweatpants, one large workman's glove on his right hand, a pair of ladies' underwear around his neck, and nothing else. It's −11 degrees. "Nice underwear," I say.

He grins. "I'm not wearing any," he says, and pulls down his pants. "See?"

I climb into my attic, the wind whipping the tarp, and find a dead rat in my baseball cap. I've lost my starter hat, and so I pluck the rat out by the tail, toss it into the canal and put the cap on. I could wash it first but I don't. There is something changing in my head.

February 22

Jerry is in jail, probably for quite a while. He and Donny got stopped for doubling on a bicycle. They both had warrants and, as they'd agreed, Donny gave the name and birth date of one of their brothers, who has no outstandings in Ontario. Jerry, however, couldn't remember which brother he was supposed to be, so he gave the same name, couldn't spell it, fucked up the birth date and started stuttering uncontrollably. So now he's in jail. According to Donny his outstanding warrant was for robbing $600 from a guy in a wheelchair.

"You see?" said Bonnie, nodding her head like the curse had finally done its work.

"Way to go, Bonnie."

Patrick and Julie both got popped in the city this week, for marijuana possession. They have a lot of outstandings, and will probably be gone for a while as well.

Bonnie is no longer speaking to Olivia (apparently she means this as punishment rather than mercy). She is, however, talking *about* Olivia.

"So she comes over last night, right, while Spidey's still uptown doing his radio shtick. Me and Cal are at the barrel, and she wants us to give her a heads-up if we see Spider coming. 'What the fuck?' I say, but she's already climbing into a van with some guy right there, in front of her shack, right? And she wants us to fucking watch her back! I mean, he's Calvin's brother!"

"He's my brother," says Calvin, shaking his head and sighing.

"She's screwing some guy for crack and expects us to help her!"

"But I don't want him to have to see that—you know, b'y."

"So Spider shows up," says Bonnie, really getting into it now, her long arms flapping, "and Calvin's trying to keep him over here. But he starts walking toward his place, so Calvin's trying to get in a fight with him, right? Yelling at him: 'Hey, shitface! Yer ugly and yer mother dresses you funny! Yer skinny and you can't dance!' So Spider turns around, and I guess they heard the yelling, 'cause the van takes off away from their shack, then it stops and Olivia's little body tumbles out of the passenger side. And meanwhile these two are rolling around on the ground now, but Calvin's trying not to hit him, 'cause Spider's too drunk. You should have seen it."

"Shoulda seen it, b'y."

Not only has Calvin begun repeating the last three words of whatever Bonnie says, but he is letting Jo-Jo and her colleague, Angel, use his half of the prefab—which I assume means he is sleeping in the other half, with Bonnie.

Jo-Jo, Jake's girlfriend, showed up again a few days ago. She and Angel walk the same stroll in the evening, and hang around the fire barrel during the day. I've been trying to work on my place, and they're always calling me over for one thing or another.

"You gotta check this out, Shaun! You got to see what we got!"

"What is it now?" I say, and walk slowly toward them.

"We were so high last night we couldn't stop laughing, you gotta see this thing!" They pull me into the prefab and shut the door. We're in a pink and white plastic room. There's light from a couple of candles and a small dirty window. "Look at it!" says Jo-Jo, pointing at the wall. "We found it under the bed!"

As my eyes adjust to the dark, I see a picture hanging on the wall. It's a painting of what appears to be a female archangel, her wings spread. She is holding a bow strung with a flaming arrow, and below her—in the distance—I can make out the ruins of a town or a city engulfed in flame.

"Isn't it horrible?" says Angel, and cackles out a laugh.

"It's great!"

"You think so?" says Jo-Jo.

"Yeah." There's something about it that gets me right away—the eyes of the avenging angel, her wings, the tiny roofs burning, the fire just a faint glow in the night. "But in a horrible kind of way," I add, to placate them.

And now Angel and Jo-Jo are both laughing for no apparent reason, pressing their bodies against me on either side.

"You got your hair cut," says Angel, and runs her hand through it.

"How you been doin'?" says Jo-Jo.

"All right," I say, still watching the archangel's eyes. "Any word from—"

"Who, Jake?" says Jo-Jo, cutting me off. "You keep asking me that! I don't know, all right? Jake left me with shit!"

"Your place is looking good," says Angel, still pressing against me on the other side. They have pleasant bodies, and I can't help but think how beautiful they must have been.

"Thanks," I say. I step away from them and open the door. The bright sunlight washes in across Angel's scarred and puffy eyes, Jo-Jo's rotted teeth, the archangel's spreading wings as she rises. "I really like the picture," I say. "Can I buy it off you?"

"Whatever, Shaun," says Jo-Jo. "You can have it when we leave."

February 25

My voice is gone, my head is throbbing and I'm broke and happy and proud to be a Canadian. Last night we beat the U.S. hockey team for the Olympic gold medal.

I won't go on about the game, since everyone—at least in this country—knows what happened. I'm only sorry I didn't get to see it with my father, and had to settle for hugging strangers in a bar instead, singing "O Canada" over and over.

Out on Yonge Street the party went all night. Everyone was drunk, and suddenly the streets weren't such a lonely place to be—the rich and poor and the homeless among them—people waving flags, high-fiving cops, riding on the roofs of buses and streetcars, and not one fight as far as I could see. I walked through the crowds for hours. Even after midnight there were little kids riding through the streets on their daddies' shoulders, everybody dancing and kissing. Not a thing wrong in the whole damn country.

By the time I got back to Tent City, everyone was already passed out.

I stood in the centre of the old town, my arms spread wide like wings, shouting "Ca-na-da! Ca-na-da!" until Sluggo came and joined me, yelling at the moon.

February 26

The TDRC has brought us a new house, and now it sits in the middle of Tent City: a large, fully furnished, propane-heated, plastiwood-panelled, one-room prefab. It was built—like the others that have ended up here—as a prototype for disaster-relief emergency shelters. I guess if we survive in it they'll be sending these things to flood and earthquake sites all over the world.

The TDRC, which over the past couple of years has arranged for the donation of our prefabs and dollhouses, our porta-potties and stoves, decided this fancy new model should go to Nancy and Steve, who is already out of jail. The criterion, apparently, was one of seniority combined with the frequency and decibel of whining. We can only hope Nancy will be happy now, or at least quiet for a while.

Bonnie went with Calvin to the doctor, and now he has a series of tests and X-rays next week, to decide on a method of treatment: chemotherapy or surgery.

"I think it should be chemo," said Bonnie.

"Why?"

She looked at me scornfully. The suggestion that there might be anything upon which Bonnie is not an expert is ridiculous to her.

"I dreamt it," she said. "I dreamt the chemo very clearly. And last night, after I worked on Calvin . . ."

"You *worked* on him?"

"Yes. It would be hard for you to understand. But after that, he dreamt of his grandfather—whom he's never met."

"Oh," I waited. "So . . . it should be chemo?"

"Yes."

We're having a birthday party this evening for both Bonnie and Jackie. It's being thrown by Jane, a woman who comes in from Hamilton on the weekends and a few evenings after work, bringing candles and batteries and things. Mostly she just comes to visit and she doesn't appear to have any ulterior motives—no media, politics or church behind her. When she heard about the double birthday, she decided to throw a party.

I hope things stay under control. Despite her open mind and genuine kindness, Jane's still a middle-class woman with little experience of the streets. I'm not sure of her squeamishness level, and it would be a shame to drive this refreshing bit of sanity back to the suburbs so soon.

February 27

To get ready for the birthday party, Calvin and I set up a picnic table we borrowed from a nearby park, testing its sturdiness with a game of full-contact table chicken until Bonnie got so mad we had to stop.

"You're going to kill each other and fuck up my party!" she said, and Calvin quickly got down off the table.

"Sorry, Bonnie," he said.

"Short leash, eh, Calvin?"

"Fuck off, b'y."

Jane drove in with a trunkload of burger patties, buns, potato chips, pop, birthday cake and ice cream. I gave Jackie a beanbag chair I'd found in an alley, and Bonnie a half-pack of tobacco. The burgers started sizzling. People were happy and everything was fine, until Spider showed up.

He came over drunk and yelling at Calvin, who yelled back. Bonnie's name kept coming up, and you could see Calvin about to lose it, his little fists curling at his sides. Then suddenly he stopped and looked at me. "You deal with this, Lucky," he said, and turned away.

It's no small thing to ask someone to deal with your brother, and I wasn't sure what to do. I grabbed Spider as diplomatically as possible and shuffled him away from the picnic table. "What's the matter, Spider?" I said.

"It's a birthday party!" he yelled over my head. "And Olivia should be here, too."

"Well, why isn't she?" The wincing behind me was actually audible.

"'Cause that *bitch* says she's not allowed!" yelled Spider, pointing his arm like a spear at Bonnie. Bonnie started jumping around behind me, shouting, "Ask her about the guy in the van, Spider! Ask her about the van guy!" Calvin was yelling, "Don't you call her a bitch!" And Spider was yelling, "You bitch! You bitch!"

Then, out of nowhere, Nancy appeared, and began circling us all in a large arc, shouting obscenities, charging around in circles until we were all getting dizzy and Steve hollered at her to give it a rest and come have a burger.

"Fuck your burger!" she yelled.

"Sorry, Jane," I said, still holding on to Spider.

"Is she okay?" said Jane.

"She thinks everybody hates her because of her new house," said Steve.

"Oh," said Jane.

"Come on over, darlin'," said Steve. "It's a birthday party!"

"Fuck yer fuckin' party!"

"She doesn't mean that."

The burgers were ready, and now Spider and Nancy were circling the party in separate directions, both of them yelling, "You fucking bitch!" as they passed.

"Looks like you're the birthday bitch," said Eddie to Bonnie.

"Me too!" said Jackie. "It's my birthday, too!"

"*You say it's your birthday,*" sang Steve. "*Well, it's her birthday too, yeah. Gonna have a good time . . .*"

"Fuck your birthday!"

"You bitch!"

"You okay, Jane? It's a nice party . . . really."

When everything had calmed down, Calvin got up on the table and lifted a bottle of Bingo. "To Bonnie," he said, and did a little jig. "Happy birthday! And to Jackie. And to my little brother, Lucky. I'm adopting you. Is that okay?"

On the street, if some guy says to you, "This is my brother," chances are they met in prison, or did something together that put them there. It took me a while to realize that Pops is not really Hawk's dad, and Nicky's just a guy he knows from the pen. I met Calvin's "son" and "daughter" on the street a few weeks ago, and later he told me he's known them almost six years. But if you ask, "Is he really your son?"

you'll get an answer like, "Fuck, don't he look real?" It's a sign of respect that Calvin, who's twice my age, has taken me as a brother, and not a son.

Jane was in the shadows, talking to Hawk, and when she came back into the light of the barrel fire she looked bemused, and slightly shaken.

"You met Hawk," I said.

"Yeah, he told me he could kill me if he wanted."

"He says that to everyone."

"He's really quite scary."

Not only did Jane stay through the birthday party, but she came into my shack with the others when it got cold and hung around right to the end, as comfortable as if she were sitting on her couch at home, sipping tea by the fireplace.

Before she finally left, she said, "We'll do it again next week. It's Calvin's birthday on Tuesday."

"Really? How do you know these things?"

"I ask."

As Calvin stumbled back to his prefab, he put his arm around me and got all serious. "You know I mean it, b'y?" he said. "You're my brother now."

"I know, Calvin."

"All right. Well good night, little brother."

February 28

Today, as I was walking back into Tent City, I noticed a tall, thin man trying to set up a tent between Karl's and Jimmy D's. The wind was blowing hard, and it was the kind of scene that should have been accompanied by player-piano music, the sepia film speeded up for frenetic comic effect: With each gust of wind the pup tent was blown into some extravagant new shape, pulling the man's long arms into contortions, sailing him back and forth, the tent slackening, wrapping around his neck, then expanding over his head like a giant helmet, fibre-glass poles dancing in the wind.

"Uh . . ." I called out to him. "You need a hand?"

He extracted himself, then tripped as he attempted to stomp the tent down. He fell on his knees, pinning it beneath him. "I don't think this is going to work," he said.

"No."

"It's windy down here."

"Yep. And cold at night. What are you doing here?"

He started to mash the tent into a big messy bundle.

"Oh, just thought I'd stay a few days."

"A few days? Look, I don't care either way, but people won't like it if you treat this place like a campground. You know what I mean?"

"Oh, it's not that. You see, I'm interested in alternative modes of living."

"Uh-huh."

"I spent a couple of weeks on the street last summer . . ."

"Yeah . . . Do you know anyone down here?"

"I just met Karl," he said, smiling and pulling at the tent poles. "He seems real nice."

"Hmm . . ."

"And I met Nancy and her husband last summer on the street. Is she still living here?"

"Yep. In fact, she just got a new house. Come on, I'll show you where it is."

"My name's John."

"Okay."

I walked him over to the big plastiwood demo house and pounded at the door. "Mine's the one down by the water, with the blue roof," I said. John had a brand-new seaman's duffle bag designed to look old and rustic. I left him at Nancy's door, dropped some stuff off at my shack and went over to Calvin and Bonnie's fire barrel for a coffee.

"What are you grinning about, little brother?"

"New guy," I said. "Interested in alternative modes of living."

"Oh shit," said Bonnie.

"I found him over by Jimmy D's, with a tent."

"Jesus. You get him out of there?"

"Yeah. Guess where he is now?"

"Where?" said Calvin, grinning expectantly.

"Nancy's. He says they're old friends, so I brought him over."

"You're so bad!" said Bonnie. Calvin was laughing.

"Are you kidding? I'm helping him out. You'll see. He'll be here in a minute."

When he showed up, the look on John's face was that of someone who'd just had a hallucination and was determined to keep it to himself.

"How's Nancy?"

"She . . . uh . . . I think she's sick or something."

I motioned for John to sit down at the picnic table, and Bonnie poured him a cup of coffee. He squeezed his tall, gangly legs between the bench and table, a brand-new toque on his head, a pinstriped button-down shirt poking out from beneath a light blue lumberjack flannel, a carefully trimmed goatee. It looked like he'd been studying *Beachcombers* reruns in preparation for Tent City.

"I'm John," he said to Bonnie and Calvin.

"Calvin," said Calvin. "This is my girlfriend, Bonnie." It looks like Bonnie finally decided it's all right for him to divulge the new nature of their relationship, and now Calvin is taking every opportunity he can to use the word "girlfriend," bouncing on his heels, grin stretching up to his eyes. Once in a while he gets so excited he just wraps his little arms around her waist and squeezes.

"This is your place?" said John.

"Yeah, sure," said Calvin. "But I just built a house, for my girlfriend." He pointed over to Bonnie's nearly completed new shack.

"Wow! That's nice!"

"Where you from, b'y?" said Calvin, now squinting at John like he couldn't quite see him.

"I, uh . . . I'm from London." Then he added, "Ontario," in case we'd mistaken him for British royalty.

"Yer to be careful down here," said Calvin.

"I'm sorry?"

"Look, kid," said Calvin, although the two men could have been born on the same day. "Yer not from the street."

"I, uh. I spent some time on the street . . . last summer."

"Why'd you do that, b'y?"

"I wanted . . . to get the experience . . . I wrote a piece about it for the *Toronto Star*." He swallowed, though he hadn't yet taken a sip of his coffee, and started to ramble: "It's funny, eh? When people—you know, friends—ask me what street people are really like, I say, they're just like everybody else—like you and me. You know?" Calvin looked like he was about to lose his Lucky Charms. Bonnie was staring at me like I should say something.

"So . . . you're a journalist?" I said.

"Well . . . freelance, I guess."

"If you camped over there, you'd sure have something to write about," said Bonnie. "You gotta be careful down here."

"Well, I thought people might ask what my story is, you know, and I'd—"

"People don't give a damn about your story," said Calvin. "And they might not ask anything. Might just go for you."

"Go for . . . ?"

"Yeah, not a lot of preliminary interviewing going on down here," said Bonnie. "Kind of a shoot-first-then-still-not-ask kind of place."

"What do you mean?"

I went back over to my shack to stoke the stove and just sit down for a while. Eventually, John came over and knocked on my door.

"Sorry to bother you," he said. "You made this place?"

"Yep."

"Wow!"

I didn't say anything, but motioned for him to come inside. "Can I ask you a question?" he said. "What'd they mean over there? They were talking about fighting and stuff, I think. So what's the story with that?"

"What do you mean?"

"Is that just like arguing and stuff? Or, you know, serious violence?"

"Any violence feels serious when it's pointed at you," I said. "How long you been writing?"

"Not long," he said. "I'm just learning, I guess. My wife died last year and I'm just trying to . . . live differently, learn some different things."

I nodded. I wonder what's happened to me that when a stranger opens up to me like this, I just nod. "You're welcome to try it out down here," I said. "But . . ."

"I have friends I can stay with in the city tonight," said John. "I guess

I'll go back home tomorrow. To London." We were both nodding.

I can't quite believe that just three months ago I came down here alone, a stranger with a tent on my back, smiling and waving. I can't believe anybody would do such a thing.

March:
A Vagrant's Teeth

March 1

I've been feeling morose these last few days. Yesterday Calvin came over with a joint. Since he's cut down the drinking, he and Bonnie have been spending any money he can find on food for their romantic dinners together, and a bit on pot for him.

"You know I can't smoke that stuff, Calvin. Not unless I'm loaded."

"It'll make you feel better, little brother."

"No, it won't, Calvin. It'll make me feel like a paranoid, itchy eggplant that wants to kill itself."

We smoked the joint.

"You just gotta get laid, little brother," said Calvin, blowing smoke trains through the air. Since he and Bonnie started sleeping together, this is the advice he gives to everyone.

"Yeah," I said, and tried to change the subject. "All your kids out in B.C., Calvin?"

"I got a girl in Sudbury, little brother."

"That's where they've got the nickel, right?" I meant the giant coin all the tourists stop for, but he shook his head.

"Used to. The mine's closed down now. I used to work that mine."

"Really?" It's hard to find something Calvin didn't used to do. He even told me he used to be a lifeguard, although I know he can't swim.

"Fourteen kilometres below the earth, b'y."

"That's deep."

"You're not kiddin'! Got trapped down there once. This cyclone come through and knocked out everything on the surface, and we're down there twenty-nine hours, with no fucking juice to move the lift."

"God!"

"More like the devil, b'y. Put on the oxygen masks and just sat there counting the minutes. Had thirty-six hours of air in the tanks, and so we start getting pretty nervous around twenty-six. Sweating pretty bad, eh?" He laughed. "You could really smell it. Nobody slept, and after a while nobody talked neither. But just knowing the others were there was good. Real hell would be sitting down there alone, you know."

I wanted to tell him about the time I went down into some abandoned mines in the Arizona desert with a couple of drifters I met on the road—that darkest dark when we hit the deepest cavern and switched off the flashlight, that silence more than silence, how when we finally climbed back to the surface the night sky was so blue I felt a fool to ever think it was black. But it felt like that had been someone else, in some other life, lying on the Arizona sand beneath the sky's gentle sheet.

"You and Bonnie . . . ," I said. "You love her, don't you?" He grinned.

"First time in eleven years I feel alive," he said. "First time in eleven years I want to live."

"First time in eleven years you been sober."

"That too."

"Just make sure you enjoy it, eh, Calvin?" I said, and then after he'd gone I lay on my bed, waiting for the darkness to leave me.

March 2

While I was collecting firewood today, Mike the martyr junkman—who, though he has an apartment downtown, spends most of his time in Tent City—came over and asked if I'd seen the church. The helmet he wears, even when his bicycle is nowhere to be seen, sat crooked on his head.

"A church?"

"It's truly amazing, Shaun!" he said, and so I walked with him up to the cluster of shacks by the boulevard fence. This little neighbourhood, like all of Tent City, has been growing a lot lately. Mike stopped and held out his hands. "The church!" he said.

The frame was up. The roof was tall and peaked, and looked a bit daunting hovering over walls that weren't yet there. We walked through one of them and stood in the centre of the floor.

"Everybody's getting together to build it!" he said. "A real community church, truly non-denominational! A Buddhist built the roof!" There was a stack of chairs in front of us to seat the parishioners, a podium behind them and a large free-standing cross.

"Who exactly is building this, Mike?" I said, walking toward the pulpit.

"Everyone!"

"But who?"

"Well, it was Dougan who started it." I've never met Dougan, but I've heard of him. He got drunk last summer and went around trying to break whatever windows there were in Tent City. "And me!" said Mike, as if he'd just remembered. "Come look at this!" I followed him through the non-existent back wall, where we came upon a second cross, standing midway between the church and the boulevard fence. A crown of thorns hung crooked over the crosspiece like Mike's persistent bike helmet. In front of the cross, on a makeshift altar, a bible lay open under a pane of glass—the glass held down by a punctured bicycle tire.

"Dougan was walking on the bike path and found this bible, open to this page," said Mike. "And that's when he knew he had to build a church."

"Yeah, it's great, Mike," I said, trying to make out the page of the bible, but Mike kept waving his arm over it as he spoke, and the print was small under the blurry glass.

"Do you really see what's going on here, Shaun?" said Mike, pointing back to the church. "The roof was built by a Buddhist! A Buddhist! And there's this cross. And this bible! Dougan *found* it!"

Mike has a habit of reiterating, but it was a powerful image—this half-built shanty church with a dirty bible under glass at the back of Tent City, the traffic going by on the other side of the chain-link fence. I planned to come back here, when Mike wasn't around, to read the open page.

On the way to my shack, I ran into Hawk, who was staring at the front gates with his arms folded. "Hey, Hawk," I said. "You see the church they're building?"

"What church?" he said, glaring at me like I'd just pissed in his private stock of holy water. "That's no fucking church! A bunch of crackheads and drunks get together and put up a shitty little shack, and they call it a fucking church! That ain't no fucking church!"

March 5

It was Calvin's birthday today, and I'd agreed to take him for some follow-up X-rays while Bonnie organized the party. You'd think she would have learned from her own birthday, but no such luck. She was determined to make an Irish stew and some traditional flatbread, to honour both the Nish and the Irish.

"Can't we just call him Inish, and get drunk?" I said, but she looked at me like I was the worst sort of imperialist—one who thinks he's funny.

"Just make sure you get him back by six o'clock," she said. "Everyone will be here by six."

"Who's everyone?"

"Jane and . . . I don't want the stew overcooked because you're late, okay?"

"You're *supposed* to overcook it, Bonnie. That's why they call it stew—so you let it just sit there—sort of *stewing*, you know."

Calvin pulled me away before I could say any more, and we headed for the gates. "Why do you have to kid her like that?"

"'Cause it's fun," I said. I was still a bit drunk from the night before. It was high noon and a beautiful day. As we crossed Dundas Street, I experimented with removing my sunglasses. "You nervous, Cal?"

"Nah . . . well, yeah. Just a couple months ago I didn't give a damn. But now, you know, I think I want to live some more. That's kind of fucked up, eh?"

"That's not fucked up, Cal."

All the way up Parliament, Calvin pointed out bars he'd been thrown out of, the abandoned buildings he'd slept in, the burn unit where he'd stayed after Spider torched their squat in the Don Valley.

It was mid-afternoon by the time we got out of the doctor's office. We went to the liquor store with the last of our $195s and bought some cans of Crest and a small mickey of Dr. McGillycuddy's Fireball. Then we headed over to the park at Bay and Dundas where Randy and Marty usually pan.

"Happy Birthday, Calvin," I said, cracking the tall cans. We sat down on the grass.

"Thanks, little brother. You know, today's also my son's birthday . . . and my daughter's, too."

"Uh . . . really?"

Calvin's life, as he tells it, often seems too ridiculously fateful to believe. But it's obviously been such a disaster that to doubt the suggestion of fatal design seems somehow cynical.

"Yeah. I wouldn't forget that, b'y," he said, shaking his head. "When my little girl was born I was drunk, and my old lady broke my jaw—even though she was paralyzed, eh?"

"Uh . . . how?"

Calvin then went on to tell me about when he was a drunken lumberjack in B.C. and how, after a logging run on his birthday, he got dragged out of the bar to witness the birth of his daughter, only to get beaten up by his paraplegic wife.

"But you know what, b'y?" he said. "I didn't fall. I just stood there with a broken jaw and held my little girl in my arms with my broken hand. And I didn't fall."

"Way to go, Calvin."

"Yeah. Guess I fucked up, eh?" We looked around at this shitty little downtown park and started laughing at whatever decades of fucking up had gotten Calvin to this particular birthday.

"I want to get a rose," he said. "For Bonnie."

"Good idea."

When we'd finished all but the Fireball, Calvin wanted to show me something, and I followed him—both of us a bit giggly—into the mall on Yonge Street. He took me to a small puppet shop on the lower concourse.

"Good afternoon, beautiful," he said to the girl behind the counter, then proceeded to peruse the puppets. "This is the one!" he said, holding up a fluorescent purple Muppet-style beast with floppy legs and a frizzy body.

Both Calvin and Spider consider themselves puppeteers, and do little shows on the street for spare change. According to them, they also go out and perform each week for the kids in the cancer ward at one of the hospitals. At least Calvin says he used to—before he got diagnosed with cancer himself and the reality of their fate took away his ability to entertain.

On the way down Yonge Street we kept running into Calvin's drinking buddies, but I was able to keep him on track because of the rose.

"Yep, I gotta get a rose, guys. It's my girlfriend's birthday!"

"It's *your* birthday, Calvin."

"Oh yeah. But I gotta get a rose!"

The flower lady on the corner of King came down from five to three bucks and Calvin held the flower with both hands as we headed back to Tent City, only letting go to take swigs of the Fireball. As we climbed over a fence into the rail yards, he zipped the rose under his jacket and we walked along the tracks.

"So it's your son's birthday, too?" I said.

"Yeah. But I ain't giving him nothing," said Calvin, as if it were really an option. "Kid's trying to blackmail me. He's got the whole ranch I left him when the old lady died. Whole 999 acres—except for 25 that I kept, right? And then he tells me he's sold all my horses, too." Sometimes it's as if this little sprite of a man has just fabricated his life from every tough-guy movie he's ever seen. If you're to trust every word, he's a biker, miner, logger, lifeguard—not to mention puppeteer and horse rancher.

"But he won't give me the money," said Calvin. "Until I come home. Home!" As the tracks crossed over Jarvis Street, he pointed to a dark patch of shade under the off-ramp and said, "I used to live under there."

By the time we got back to Tent City, everyone *was* there. Jane had shown up with a cake and ice cream. Goran, the Macedonian photographer who's been coming down here to take photos for the past couple of months, had brought his wife and some beer. Bonnie was going nuts as Randy, Jackie and Donny all dipped their fingers in the Irish stew.

"Fucking finally!" she said. It was ten past six. Calvin just stood there with a sheepish grin on his face, and reached into his jacket. He pulled out a few petals, then reached back in and came up with the crushed head of a red rose. He handed the mess of petals to Bonnie, and smiled. "I love you, babe," he whispered.

"Oh God!" said Bonnie, putting the flower in her pocket. "You guys are loaded!"

"It really was a nice rose," I said.

Everyone wished Calvin a happy birthday and we stood around eating Irish stew and bannock, except for Calvin.

"Boy!" he said. "It sure is hot!" It wasn't hot, but the bottle of Fireball was empty. He took off his jacket, then his T-shirt and just stood there grinning, his small, muscular torso covered in tattoos: a Hell's Angels skull with wings spreading large across his chest, the Grim Reaper on his side, a giant unicorn on his back, his tag—Sidewinder—in a crest on one upper arm, and the same crest, unfinished, on the other. I've wondered about that unfinished tag, the same as I've wondered at the fact that he has the L-O-V-E across the knuckles of one hand, but not the H-A-T-E on the other.

"Put your clothes on, little man!" said Bonnie.

"Happy birthday, baby," said Calvin. And then he passed out.

March 8

I don't know if it's just that winter is ending, but on all sides of me now there are new guys moving in, or rather, old guys who are new to me. A man called Heartbeat just took over Nancy's old prefab. He has long, reddish, biblical hair and a serious face. He just got out of the pen, and although he's quiet, very thin and unusually respectful, everyone assures me he's lethal.

"I've mellowed out a lot since I stopped drinking," he told me. "But if you ever need a hand, just give me a call. I got a shovel over there—no messing around."

"Thanks." I'm reluctant to ask why people call him Heartbeat.

Then there's Terry, who just got out of jail, too, and is building a place on the other side of me, behind the abandoned A-frame, which, it turns out, was built by Heartbeat a couple of years ago. He's one of Eddie's old-est friends, and has laid down a floor big enough for a mansion.

"Just don't be pissing on my house," I said when I saw where he was building.

"Don't worry," he said. "I'll aim for Randy's."

March 10

Three a.m., and it's impossible to fall asleep. My radio keeps saying "heavy wind warnings" and "over 100 kilometres per hour." In this law-less campground on the open lake any warning, and any speed, is increased by half again.

The place that Terry was building is already gone, the floors torn up, the walls blown down. Planks of plywood and pieces of garbage are fly-ing through the air. In the canal the waves are crashing right over the docks and slamming against the silos a hundred yards back. Two of the porta-potties have been blown over. Shingles off Sluggo's roof are shoot-ing past my window like clay pigeons sucked into a turbine. I guess that's what happens when you shingle your roof backwards.

My shack is shaking and the wind is screaming against the attic. To open the door I have to push my weight against it and then jump out into the storm as the door slams back. I've tightened the wires holding the tarp over my roof, but there's not much more I can do.

Maybe it ends like this—quick and simple—Tent City blown away like God getting rid of a piece of lint.

Bonnie (apprised on these matters by various spirits) has been con-vinced for a while that the whole place is going down. She says they'll come in here at 4 a.m. with armoured cars and Kevlar vests and dogs and guns. Break every door at the same moment and start clubbing people in their sleeping bags, dragging them out into paddy wagons. No chance for defence, for machetes, knives, clubs or two-by-fours. No time for Hawk to grab his guns. Quick and fast with no reporters asking ques-tions, no protestors chaining themselves to the fence.

Bonnie does admit they might try something else first, however: relocation. There's a building on Commissioners Street that Homes First, together with a few city councillors, has been trying to open up as permanent housing for Tent City residents: an address and electricity and running water, and everything else they think we want. But it doesn't make much sense to begin housing us, who have already housed ourselves, when there are thousands in the parks and streets and in the basements of churches. Sure the Tent City contingent might be nuts and drunk and poor and violent, but we're not really homeless anymore. We are blasted out of our minds, but also proud and strong and standing against this wind.

In a way there's something comforting about this hunkering down, the fire still crackling as the storm keeps on building. There's nothing I can do but sit here and ride it out, praying that I've built walls that can withstand this wolf of a wind, as he huffs and puffs and rages to get in.

x x x

The storm keeps up all night and all through the morning, but somehow my shack is still standing when Calvin and Bonnie come over, struggling the door open and stumbling inside with the seagulls screaming at their backs. The gulls have been shrieking all morning, their voices not like birds at all. They can't get off the ground. They try to lift off and are blown back so violently they barely manage to land again.

The door slams shut as Calvin takes off his hat, sparse grey hairs sticking up from his mostly bald head. "Told you!" he says.

Yesterday—before the storm started—the gulls were already earthbound. They walked up slowly to the fire barrels and stood among our feet, dozens of them. They stayed like that all afternoon. It was creepy—like that scene in *The Birds* when the people finally venture out of the schoolhouse. Calvin said it meant a storm was coming. I guess, sometimes, the little gnome is worth listening to.

"Holy shit!" says Bonnie when they've caught their breath. "Talk about divine justice!"

"What, the church?" I say. Supposedly the roof blew right off, and although it was built by a Buddhist, I don't feel like arguing the point with Bonnie, for whom any church is contentious.

"Not just that!" she says. "The accordion. That's *real* divine justice!"

"What do you mean?"

"Don't you know? She glances over at Calvin and smiles: "The Brothers were in it—Derek and Lenny! They came down last night and Eddie let them stay in the accordion. What fucking timing, eh!" Bonnie is slapping her knee as the wind beats against the walls. "The thing folded right up on them!"

By mid-afternoon the wind has died down enough so that you can walk around without being blasted off your feet. Calvin goes out to do a run with Spider, and I take a walk around town to assess the damage. As I come around the side of my shack, the Brothers are lifting up the tattered tarp of the old A-frame, peering in and kicking at all the junk inside.

"What are you doing?"

Derek lifts his head and glares at me. "Lookin' . . . ," he says.

"For somewhere to sleep," says Lenny, finishing the sentence.

"Not there," I say. Derek stands up and stares at me, then back at the A-frame.

"Yeah," he says. "Thing stinks. Fuckin' rats! Look at this shit!" He reaches out and rips a piece of plastic. I stand there until they've walked away, then climb over the strewn rubble of Terry's floor and walls. Sluggo's shingles are everywhere. The tarp on Randy's roof is blowing straight up one wall like a bad comb-over in a side wind. Eddie's old accordion will never play again. As I pass by the overturned porta-potties, the gulls are still screaming all around me.

Then, above the screech of the birds and the groan of the wind, I hear someone calling my name. Over near the water hose, a tarp is tearing itself free of what appears to be a half-built storage shelter, whipping around in the air. As I walk toward it, a hand darts out, trying to grab at the plastic.

"Shaun! Come here!"

I walk over to the shapeless construction and look inside. Mike is there, bicycle helmet strapped tightly to his head with some sort of telescopic sight protruding from the front like the single feeler of a wind-beaten bug. Over his spandex cycling apparel he is wearing a large blue plastic bag. There are holes cut out for his neck and arms, and the bag is cinched at the waist with a bungee cord. He is trying to do something with the flailing tarp and a piece of wood.

"Come in here, Shaun," he says. "Just step over that wall there."

"Mike," I say, not moving, "why don't you wait till the wind dies down?"

"Aha!" he announces, as if I've unknowingly proven some point of his. "That's the fascinating part! Look: the wind may be blowing out there, but you don't feel it—not in here! That's what I'm trying to show! You see, Shaun!"

I take a look, but there's barely even a "here" to be in, just four propped-up walls of pressboard and a couple of tarps whipping around like crazy.

"This doesn't make any sense, Mike. Just wait till the storm is over and—"

"Aha!" he says again. "That's exactly it!" Doing battle with a tarp, he looks like the caricature of a superhero, but it's funny only to a point. It is occurring to me that Mike—who doesn't live down here—is actually less sane than the people who do.

"It's just what I'm trying to prove!" he says. "I want to show I can do this, in this particular wind—this is a very strong wind you know, Shaun . . ."

"Do what, Mike?"

"What?" he yells over the wind.

"Forget it. I'm leaving. Have a good time." I turn to go.

"Oh, I will, Shaun! I want to have the experience of—" But a violent gust of wind whips the tarp around his head, and I don't get to learn the precise experience he is hoping for.

When Calvin and Bonnie come back over to my shack, I give them my assessment of Mike's mental stability, and tell them about my run-in with the Brothers. Calvin pulls out a bottle of Bingo he got on the run. "Gotta weather the storm, b'y," he says, splashing the first sip on the floor.

I don't like sherry at all, but try to drink as much as I can for Calvin's sake. I know what even half a bottle of the stuff will do to him since he "stopped" drinking. Despite my efforts, his ears are glowing by the time we've hit the last sips, and he's laughing too loud. Bonnie is glaring at him.

"I be back in a sec, b'y," he says, jumping up all of a sudden. "Save the spider for me." The spider is the heel of the bottle, which might be how Calvin's brother got his name. I haven't asked.

He is gone much longer than a second. When he comes back, he flops down in a chair and exhales like he's finally dealt with something. "Well, *that's* done," he says.

I hand him the almost empty bottle. "What's done?"

"Got the Brothers fixed up." He bolts back the spider. "I set 'em up in Chris's place."

There is a moment of stunned silence, in which even the seagulls and the storm go quiet. Then Bonnie jumps to her feet. "You did what?"

"I cut the lock for them. They're in Chris's now."

"Did what? You did *what*?" She is staring at him as if she and all her spirits are about to combust in a ball of hellfire.

"We're talking about Derek and Lenny here!" she yells.

"I . . . uh . . . I didn't want them staying here in the A-frame—for my little brother's sake." He looks at me for support.

"Didn't you hear what Shaun was saying? They'd given up on the A-frame!"

"It's cold out there . . . I . . . I guess I've just got a heart, is all," he says. I wince and look down at the floor.

"A heart! What are you talking about? They had a place for one night, and the roof came down!" shouts Bonnie. "They would have been gone, Cal!" She folds her arms over her chest and looks at me. I look at Cal, but still don't say anything. We listen to the wind. Finally the storm dies down a bit and we can hear shouting outside. It's the Brothers.

"You fucked up, Cal," I say.

"I'll fix it, b'y."

"No, Cal. Not now." But he's already through the door.

Bonnie takes a deep breath, about to start a speech with no end, and I follow Calvin into the storm.

x   x
x

Dry is an old guy with a long grey beard who's been down here for years, and whose last place burned to the ground. Although he lives in the other half of Chris's prefab duplex, you don't see him that much, since he's got a girlfriend who lives uptown. But he's here now, the Brothers on either side of him yelling in his face. Sparks from a fire barrel they've dragged over are blowing against the prefab.

"This place is made of cardboard!" Dry shouts. "You can't have a fire here—you just can't!"

"Get back in yer fuckin' house!" snaps Derek. "Before I fuck you up!"

I look up at the clouds speeding across the sky. Calvin stands there, waiting until Bonnie comes into view, and then he plunges right in, a windup toy spinning through the legs of angry dogs. "Hey guys!" he says. "C'mon!"

"Fuck off, Calvin!" growls Derek.

"Asswipe," says Lenny.

"Hey!" I say, stepping toward Lenny.

Derek turns. "Don't you talk to my brother that way!"

"Tell him not to talk to *my* brother that way," I say. Lenny looks at Calvin and laughs. I almost laugh, too. It all sounds so stupid, especially with us having to shout above the wind and the birds.

But then Derek says to me, "You should get yourself another brother," and Calvin goes for him, or at least he makes it seem that way. When I hold him back, his struggle is so slight I barely have to make an effort.

Ever since that thing with Jerry, I've realized that Calvin—no matter what he once was, or once did—is not a fighter. And now, thanks to him, I'm facing down the Brothers, trying to protect a place Calvin has broken into, pretending to hold him back while he pretends to fight so he can impress his new girlfriend.

The Brothers are baring their teeth, staring straight at me, and it seems it just isn't going to end without violence. So I sacrifice Dry's pride to save us all.

"The old guy's just scared," I say, nodding over to Dry. "He's been burnt out before, and it's got him spooked. Let's give him a break, okay."

Derek thinks about this, and the opportunity to belittle an old man finally wins him over. "Shit, yeah," he says, now turning to Dry and laughing. "Didn't want to *freak you out.*" He waves his hands like a drunken bogeyman. "Don't shit your pants, dude. We'll move the fucking barrel."

I lead Calvin away from the prefab, and he starts strutting around again. "Just one excuse," he says. "Just one excuse and I'll take 'em down!"

"Get a new lock for Chris's door," I say. "We'll deal with it tomorrow." And then I walk away.

x
x
x

As I'm nearing the front gates I take a glance at the church—or where the church used to be. The destruction is so precise and complete that it can't help but seem divine. All four walls have fallen straight back, like the sides of a magician's box. The large wooden cross is broken in half, a pencil snapped between the fingers of God. Dougan's bible, the glass and the podium have all vanished. As has the roof.

A hundred yards east of the ruins, I find the Buddhist roof, over-turned on the ground like the wreck of a poorly constructed ark. Not a good sign. Behind the screeching birds and shouting Brothers, I can hear the echo of Hawk's scorn carried on the wind.

March 11

When it's late and people want someone to drink with, they come by my shack. I'm usually up writing all night, and they see the light through my window. It was surprising, though, to find Spider at my door. He hasn't been too friendly since Calvin declared me his little brother.

"Saw yer candle, man. Just gotta talk to someone, that okay?"

"Yeah, Spidey. Come on in."

"That fuckin' bitch!" he said, growling in that now-famous radio voice, pulling a bottle of Bingo from his jacket. "Look what she fuckin' did to my new pants! Pushed me right into the stove! She's fuckin' nuts. She went at me with my own fuckin' knife."

"Olivia?"

"Yeah, Olivia," said Spider, and sat down. "And we got company over, too! Kelly and her boyfriend are trying to sleep on the floor while she's fuckin' beating on me—'cause they got no heat at the rec centre, eh?"

The rec centre is what we call the shack where Kelly and some of the other girls bring their tricks. Sometimes we'll stop a john in his car and ask to see his membership. We call shopping carts Tent City taxis and crack Tent City Tic-Tacs. I guess we think we're funny.

Spider handed me the bottle and leaned forward on his knees. I could see he was crying. "That's what really fuckin' gets me upset, you know," he said. "That she goes and acts like that when we got company over!"

Olivia and Spider live in a mouldy plywood box full of mangy cats and empty bottles. They've got no window, and use the stove to cook their food right in the can. I glugged the sherry, trying to save the second brother of the day from his sad old self.

"I'm cracking up, Shaun!" Spider said, still crying. "I think I'm having a real mental breakdown. What do you think I should do, Shaun?"

"If she's really trying to kill you, that's bad. Maybe you should kick her out."

"Nah. I can't do that. Then she'd burn the place down."

We drank for a while more, going over all Spider's options until he seemed to be feeling better, and started telling me all the crazy things that have happened to him since he became Homeless Dave, radio bum.

"This one day—you'll appreciate this one, Shaun—I'm heading down Yonge, and this woman starts calling out to me from behind. So I stop, and she's just running down the street after me. 'Homeless Dave!' she says, and she's just such a babe, and I go, 'Uh, yes, ma'am.' And she shoves this $20 bill right in my mouth and giggles, you know? And then she says, 'You wanna go for a beer?' So we go to the Peel Pub and she orders a large pitcher and a whole platter o' wings. And we're just having the best fuckin' time, right. And then I notice she's looking at me, eh? And suddenly she goes, 'Do you play hockey? Is that what happened to your teeth?' It takes me a minute. Then I say, 'Yeah, that's right. I play for the Devils, babe. I play for the fuckin' Devils.' Ha ha ha!"

When he laughed I could see his broken, missing teeth. Everyone here has broken, missing teeth, even the young guys, and yet everyone's are different. Sluggo's are grey and hollow. Jo-Jo's are brown and cracked. Derek's are silver and pointed. Olivia's seem shrivelled right up. Even Bonnie's are chipped and stained tobacco yellow. Only Eddie's and Calvin's teeth look somewhat healthy, but that's because they're not real—and sometimes they pop right out. Jane says when she first came down, she didn't think I lived here because I don't have a vagrant's teeth.

When he finally left, Spidey gave me a hug and said, "You come and get me in the morning if you guys need help with the Brothers."

"Yeah," I said. "We gotta deal with that—thanks to your stupid brother."

"All the stupid brothers," said Spidey, then staggered on home.

x
  x
    x

This morning, when Calvin and I went to deal with the Brothers, they'd already started building a new place on the site of the old accordion. Calvin put the chain back on Chris's door, and I locked it.

March 16

I've been spending a lot of my nights playing pool. Strangely enough, my game has gotten better since I wrecked my wrist, and I've been doing pretty well. I've even joined a Monday-night bar league. Although there's no money to be made until the playoffs, there's usually a free buffet and I'm building a list of places to play for cash the rest of the week.

Yesterday, after I went to pick up my $195, I was feeling pretty rich, and I wanted to do something nice for Calvin. So I bought the puppet he'd shown me on his birthday.

"Happy birthday, Cal," I said as he opened up the bag.

"Thank you . . . little brother," he said, just sort of mouthing the words. He seemed in a state of shock more intense than a purple puppet should ever warrant. He stared down at the fuzzy beast in his hands, danced the feet a bit, then swivelled the neck.

"What is it, Cal?"

"They can't find it," said Bonnie. I waited. The puppet's head was bobbing now, his left front foot popping out in time to some silent disco beat.

"Can't find what?"

"The cancer!" said Bonnie. "They can't find his cancer!"

The puppet now reared up on its back legs, front paws spinning as it did the shuffle. I looked at Calvin and he was grinning, bobbing his little head along with the non-existent dance music. "It's not there!" said Bonnie.

I turned back to Calvin. "You don't have cancer anymore?"

The puppet was grooving heavy now, like it was finally letting go.

"Can you get your radio?" said Calvin, looking up at me. "I need some music, b'y."

x
  x
    x

Today, as soon as I was up, Bonnie was at my door. She wanted to talk. The sun was out, so we sat by the water.

"God," she said, leaning her head into her hands. "This is just so hard to deal with."

"What?"

"All of this, Shaun. What with Cal's cancer being gone and every-thing. I don't know if I can deal with it. And now of course he's upset, and I'm trying to explain to him . . ."

"Bonnie . . . Bonnie, what are you talking about?"

"His *cancer* is *gone*, Shaun. *Gone!*"

"I know—that's great. Fuck, it's a miracle! So what's—"

"No it's not, Shaun! I've been through this before, you know? People think it's a miracle, or the power of God or some other shit. They think it discriminates! I mean, why Calvin? He's not *good*. He's not a *good* per-son. It's like hydro, okay? Hydro doesn't care if you're good or bad. It's not some moral force—it is power. You understand? Fuck!"

"Uh, Bonnie . . . do you think that you cured Calvin's cancer?"

She stopped for a moment, and looked at me. "It's a lot to deal with, Shaun. And that's what he doesn't understand. I mean, basically my work here is done. I can't control that. I can't go against the spirits, but he just doesn't—"

"Whoa, Bonnie! What are you saying?"

"You gotta respect the power, Shaun. I mean, obviously I was with him for a very specific reason . . ."

Yeah, I thought to myself, *to get your house built.*

" . . . and now he doesn't want to let go. But you can't have it both ways. You—"

"Bonnie, stop! Please! . . . Are you saying that you think you cured Calvin's cancer? And that now . . . that now, because of that, you're going to leave him—but it's not up to you, it's up to the spirits?"

"You don't understand, Shaun."

"No. I don't."

When she'd gone I went out and bought a flat of beer, and Calvin and I brought it around to Eddie and Karen, Sluggo and Jackie, Randy and the rest of the boys so we could toast the little man who somehow beat the cancer all on his own.

March 17

A while ago Goran the photographer asked if he could stay over at my place one night to get some shots of Tent City at sunrise. So last night he slept on my floor.

Goran is hard to describe. He is a kind, sensitive, cynical, dry-humoured, eccentric near-genius. Everything about him is contradictory. He is a down-to-earth conspiracy theorist—a rabidly political philosopher with a sense of humour.

Goran's camera manages to find things in people that are invisible to the naked eye: Randy, who is always grinning like the world is a joke and he's the sick punchline, is suddenly so desperately sad it hurts to look at his face, his brave but sunken shoulders.

Bonnie, her hard head held in her hands in desperate self-support, looks scared of the photo's silence.

Jackie's playful smile becomes devilish, like that of a 5-year-old girl realizing for the first time the possibilities of her own power.

Sluggo looks resigned, the game is over.

Calvin glows.

Eddie seems exactly what he is, only more so. I would never tell him this, but since James Dean bit the asphalt and Brando got fat and weird, I'd venture that Eddie is the coolest guy still kicking. In Goran's shots he is not just some charming, diplomatic drug fiend. He looks like a powerful rogue general, staring down the anarchy of war.

Long after everyone else had passed out for the night, Goran lay wrapped in blankets on my floor talking about photography and numerology, Freemasons and Incas, September 11 and the mysterious Dogstar people, the Chinese alphabet and pi, King Solomon's mines and the geometric angles of Washington D.C.'s streets, and what it all could mean. But then, at about 3:30 a.m., his cosmic-conspiracy thesis was interrupted by a knock at the door. I stepped over him to open it.

There was a woman standing there, small, blond and middle-aged, a black Cadillac idling its engine behind her. "How you doing, honey?" she said. One of her earrings, if pawned, could have fed me for a year.

"I'm okay."

"Where's Ed, honey?"

"Who, Eddie?" I saw there was a driver in the Caddy waiting for her, and stepped outside. "What do you want him for?"

"Just to talk, honey."

"Sorry. If you don't know which place is his, I'm not going to tell you, okay?"

"Aww, honey . . . ," she said, and batted her eyelids. "You got anything for me?"

"No, sorry."

"Do you mind if I pee?"

"No, I guess not," I said as she hiked up her skirt and began to squat against the front of my shack.

"Can you stand in front of me, honey? Don't want him to see me pee." She nodded to the Cadillac. I shrugged, and stood in front of her to block the driver's view. Her piss formed a narrow steaming river running into the lake. I moved my feet apart to let it flow on through.

"Gee, this is sort of embarrassing," she said, but not in a way that sounded embarrassed at all. I tried to picture her in a house up in Rosedale, going out to piss on the front lawn. When she was finished she pulled up her underwear, smoothed down her skirt, but stayed kneeling on the ground before me. I could see Goran peeking out through the window.

"Please get me some crack, honey," she said, reaching for the fly of my jeans.

"No, sorry." I stepped back to help her up. "I have company."

"Aww . . . that's all right, honey."

"And don't go knocking on anyone else's door, okay? Not everyone here is nice as me."

"Sure thing, sweetie."

"Good night."

The Cadillac drove away when I went back inside. Goran had nothing left to say.

March 19

I'm just now starting to get over St. Patrick's Day. I saved up and spent my drinking money in the Stone Cutter's Arms, a nice pub just a few blocks from Tent City. The band had neglected to wear green, so I gave my shirt to the singer, got drunk and fell a little bit in love with the bartender.

Her name is Sherry. She's cute and smart and didn't seem that put off by my vagrant chic or questionable behaviour. I told her (inaccurately) that I knew how to change kegs and ended up soaking both of us with beer. I offered to act as the bar's bouncer free of charge, then tried to kick out anyone who hit on her. But she put up with me all night, and even let me drink the overflow jugs when I ran out of money. I'd like to go back there sometime. I guess it's every lout's dream—a girlfriend and bartender rolled into one.

March 23

I think Jane's generosity might be getting her in trouble. She just turned 40 and seems to have hit a midlife crisis. She works for a company in Hamilton that makes documentaries, and has been with the same man for the last twelve years. She seems to believe that she can learn something from Tent City, and help out as well. But she's rarely taken a risk before, and this place is all about risk.

Most of the people who live here, however, haven't bothered to wonder about the complexity of Jane's presence. Many of them think she's just another churchy or charity worker and it's got to the point where they're writing her shopping lists and hitting her up for $20 "loans." Although she's made me promise to let her deal with this on her own, I did suggest she start coming here empty-handed, to break the pattern, so that people might see her more as a friend than a donation lady or—as Hawk would put it—a sucker. We came to the compromise that she would bring only candles.

Having followed my advice, however, Jane found herself surrounded today, the candles already distributed and a half-dozen drunk men still staring, waiting for her to open the trunk of her car.

"Don't think they've ever seen a white woman before," I said. "Just let them touch your hair."

"What the fuck's that supposed to mean?" said Hoyt. Hoyt is one of the old crew who's moved back down recently, and I've disliked him from the moment I met him.

"What are you doing here, Hoyt?" I said.

"I'm here for . . . stuff."

Jane grabbed my arm and said, in her firm yet polite voice, "I'm sorry, guys, I don't have anything more today . . ."

"Oh, *that's* how it is!" belched Hoyt. "Playing favourites, eh?" He backed off when I stepped toward him, and disappeared behind the Dumpster. But even as I shouted for him to get his ass back here, I could hear him slurring out the word "favourites." The others were good enough to apologize, and left Jane alone the rest of the day.

March 26

Yesterday evening I went with Jane to a showing of a documentary on Tent City in the ballroom of the Hyatt-Regency Hotel. The screening was sponsored by the Ontario Nurses' Union, and the heroes of the film are the members of the TDRC, the head of which—Cathy Crowe—is herself a nurse. It was surreal, sitting there among all these well-off, well-meaning professionals, listening to speeches and badly written poems about how we should all be nicer to bums and beggars.

Apart from detailing the efforts of the TDRC, the film—made before I moved into Tent City—tried to give a face to the "hard-core homeless" of Toronto. It focused on Karl (the ex-mayor of Tent City) and Patrick (who's still in jail), showing not only their valiant struggle to survive, but their efforts to help homeless people everywhere. Through clips of interviews, protests and meetings with the TDRC, these two guys who had given me a shit-kicking for Christmas came across as politically aware, humanitarian hobos with hearts of dented gold.

Strangely enough the only representative of Tent City invited to the screening by the filmmaker was Dry—who is there these days about as often as the cops.

It was interesting, however, to see what the place looked like a couple of years ago: a few shacks, a few tents, a dozen people and a remarkable lack of garbage. When the film was over, Jane drove me to a bar in the West End for my Monday night pool tournament. I shot okay, had a few drinks and got back to Tent City just after 1 a.m.

As I walked into town, I could see the red spinning lights of fire trucks, and started to walk faster. By the time I reached the main road the trucks were pulling away, and there was a pile of smoking wreckage where Randy's home should have been. I ran toward it, but my leg sank into a water-filled hole. I felt my ankle twist as I splashed down on the wet scorched ground.

x   x   x

As best I can reconstruct it, the fire starts just before 11 p.m. . . .

Randy is in an uncommonly sober state. He's only had a half-bottle of sherry and all he wants to do is curl up with his dog, Chaos, for a nice long sleep.

He stokes the stove with pieces of hardwood, then goes into the original prefab, which serves as his bedroom, and closes the door behind him. He lays down and Chaos curls at his feet.

For the past few days, Randy has been working on the front porch, trying to make it more welcoming. He's put up some shelves out there, hung some pots and pans, and even a velvet painting. He's just started on a roof for the deck, and that's why he's put off fixing the tarp that was torn in the windstorm—he wants to find a new one that will cover not only the addition the Brothers made, but the porch, too. And so he's left the old tarp out there, hanging off the roof. But now it isn't just hanging there, it is whipping around in the wind, and starts to wrap around the stovepipe.

Randy is finishing his last cigarette, about to blow out the candles, when he realizes something is wrong. The walls are suddenly too hot, and the room is filling with smoke. He jumps out of bed and opens the door. The roof is on fire.

He pulls Chaos out of the shack and starts yelling for Hoyt, who is sleeping in the dollhouse right next door, but he doesn't respond.

Calvin and Bonnie hear the yelling, but just figure Randy and Hoyt are drunk and fighting about something. Randy runs back in and grabs the two propane tanks so the whole place doesn't blow up. He goes in again and grabs the bag of dog food, bits of burning plastic falling on his shoulders. The smoke is thick. His lady, Brenda, left him two days ago, and still hasn't come back, but he pushes in once more to get her bag of "personal things." The ceiling is raining drops of fire now, zip bombs falling like flaming arrows on the floor. And as he comes out clutching Brenda's bag, Randy finally yells, "Fire!"

Within seconds, Eddie, Karen, Calvin and Bonnie are outside in their underwear, all of them looking for water, but the water is frozen—washing basins, and drinking bottles, all solid with ice. More people straggle out, some of them just standing around bewildered, others rushing over to the water hose to fill up buckets. But the prevailing mood is one of hesitation. There should be bucket lines down to the river by now. There should be people banging on doors.

Half an hour after the fire has sparked, someone finally calls the fire department on a cellphone. The trucks arrive within five minutes. They blast the shack with water cannons and chop at the walls with axes. They run out of water and, instead of driving to the hydrant on the corner, call for a water boat to come in onshore.

When it's over, there is nothing left but two smouldering spires of a burnt-out door frame, an overturned stove and a whole lot of water. An hour later, the water has created huge lakes of mud and hidden sink-holes—one of which I step in as I run through the wreckage of Randy's home.

x
   x
     x

Lifting my face from the sludge, I struggle to my feet then stumble over and knock on Bonnie's door. Calvin opens it. "Holy shit, b'y!" he says. "What happened to you?"

"Where's Randy?" I gasp. "Is he okay?"

"Yeah, he's on the other side now."

"What?"

"The other side of the prefab."

"Oh."

I grab a half-bottle of whisky and some cigarettes from my shack, head back over to the prefab and knock on the door. "Hey Randy," I say. "Thought you might like a drink."

"Thanks, Shaun."

Although Randy used to live in here, he had long since moved his stuff into the place that just burnt down. He had covered one wall with photos of everyone down here, and the opposite one with his stuffed-cartoon collection—Yosemite Sams, Supermen, Daffy Ducks and Popeyes—a mirror image of all of us, reflected off one wall onto another.

"That's what I'm really upset about," he says as we drink down the whisky. "All that—what do you call it?—memorabilia. All those photos and everything." The fact is, the only material objects he saved belong to others—Chaos's dog food and Brenda's bag. Anything Randy had is gone.

"But it doesn't matter, really. If I'd lost *him*," he says, kicking at Chaos, "that would have been the end. That would have killed me."

I look up and notice that the archangel is still on the wall, her wings spreading above the city in flames. I wonder when Angel and Jo-Jo took flight. Randy and I stay up talking and drinking, and then I go over to my shack to get him the last of the sleeping pills from my detox days at Filmores, as well as some of my clothes. "Thanks, Shaun. It's a hell of a thing," he says, stroking Chaos as he lights the last cigarette. But he doesn't mean the stuff I gave him, or even the fire. He means this life, and what you're able to save.

March 27

A pink, tagless pickup truck and trailer pulled in a couple weeks ago. The driver, Les, set himself up on the other side of Spider and Olivia's, next to the rec centre, and immediately got down to business. He cleaned up a half acre of land around the trailer, laid down a truckload of wood chips and built a nice log fence. He's even got a generator powering his TV and VCR, as well as running water from a tap into the water main. It was snowing late last night when he came and knocked on my door.

"I hear you're the man to talk to," he said.

"About what?"

"Nothing in particular, just to talk. Hmm-yeah. It's nice when you're talking—hmm-yeee—to have someone respond."

"I guess so."

"Yeah! Hmm-heee. See what I mean?"

Les talks non-stop, whether there's someone responding or not, and he adds in these little half-words, so that if you can't keep pace it starts to sound like babble. But the man's no moron. His eyes flash. His eyebrows shoot up like arrows to the sky. He grins and laughs when he's talking, and he's always talking. I lit a fire in the barrel outside and we drank a bottle of whisky as the snow covered the ruins of Randy's house.

"I would have, hmm-yeah, saved that place," said Les, "if someone had just knocked on my trailer or, uh-hmm, yelled 'Fire'—something like that. I would have found a hose that could reach all the way there. I could hear 'em at the tap I put in beside my trailer, filling up the buckets, yeah-hmm. They're telling each other to hurry, you know. I just, um-hmm, thought they were real thirsty or they suddenly realized, hmm-yeah, that they forgot to water the plants for a year, you know, hey-yeah. So I'm lying in there talking to myself, saying, 'The petunias are dead, boys. Give it up, let it go.' Would have been able to save his place, hmm-yeee. There should be a system, man."

Bonnie told me that when Les finally realized Randy's place was burning he not only found a hose, organized a bucket line and stayed out there fighting the blaze after the firemen had arrived, but somehow coerced others out of their shacks to do the same.

"A system would be good," I said, "but this is Tent—"

"Ah! I don't buy all that 'this is Tent City' talk."

"How about a bell?"

"There you go! Hmm-yeah. A bell would be good. People gotta get off their asses."

"Yeah. I know what you mean. How are things going for you so far?"

"Great. Always great, hmm-yeah. Long as I'm talking, I'm always good. I ever go quiet—yeah-hmm—*then* you gotta worry. I go quiet and I get depressed, or the other way around, it's cyclical, I think. I'm going to build a sports bar down here—you in? We could make a killing in the summertime. I'm gonna tap into that billboard out there, hmm-yee, for some real power, and we'll have cold beer and football on the tube. Whatya think?"

If one were to focus on each individual part of Les—his long, silver hair, the bushy white moustache, his jester's hat with bells on it, the ragged multicoloured jean jacket and pants, the way he walks, with this stocky, bowlegged, lackadaisical yet overconfident strut, the way he talks without a breath—he might seem a bit unappealing. But when it's all put together he's a quirky, dashing gypsy.

"What I really want to do is build some windmills. I been looking how to do it in the library, um-hmm, all I found so far is children's books—but it's all there, in pictures, yee-heee, so we'll just build junior windmills, like cute little Dutch kids. I know we can do it, hmm-yeah . . . And you know, that bell was a good idea," he said, passing me over the spider. "Wouldn't want our windmills to burn down, hmm-ha."

March 28

Sluggo and Jackie have been at each other since noon. When they go, they go all out, like they're trying to kill each other with their voices, and then they start swinging. You can't think when it's like this. They're not hitting each other now, but it's got to the point where Sluggo's just sitting in the shack with the door open, yelling in that hateful drunk voice, "Crackhead! You fucking crackhead!" over and over again. And Jackie keeps running back and forth, smoking crack in Eddie's place, then coming back to yell at Sluggo: "Drunk! You fucking drunk!"

Jackie's supposed to have a job gardening up at Street City, but she seems to be screwing that up pretty good. I guess that makes sense, since Street City is really just a crack house.

x
x
x

It's midnight when Eddie comes over and knocks his Fonzie knock at my door. He's the only one who can punch it just so the inside latch pops off the hook. This is how he wakes me up most days, smacking the door open, letting himself in and harassing me until I have to get out of bed to throw him out. And sometimes he comes over at night, when I'm trying to figure out how to sleep.

"Hey, young Jedi!" he says, pulling the pillow off my head. A few weeks ago he gave me a matching set of Star Wars bedsheets and pillowcases he'd scored—the same kind I had when I was 6. "Up off the bed, kid! I got something for you."

I follow him over to his shack. "Whatsamatter with your leg, Lucky?" he says as I limp through the door.

"I was late for Randy's fire—I had to really run."

Eddie pulls out a bottle of whisky and a white dime bag. "It's good stuff," he says. I tell him I've got no money. "Doesn't matter," he says. "Pay me when you can."

I pick up a book, empty the bag onto the cover and begin to chop it into powder.

x
x
x

I haven't been doing well lately. In writing this book, I've been untruthful by omission. I've wanted to record a clear vision of this place and the people here, and still come across as somewhat stoic in the process. But the fact is I'm a mess. I still spend my days mourning the loss of the life I had, and dreaming of my ex-girlfriend every night. I want to go back there, but I know if I did I'd still be fucked up and barely visible, a storm disintegrating on the horizon.

When things ended between us several months ago, I moved straight from our apartment into a bar. They let me keep some of my stuff in a back room, and the rest I kept with me in a duffle bag. I've always been a good drinker but have mostly avoided drugs—for fear of being swallowed by them. But this time I felt like I'd screwed up my life so thoroughly there was nothing left to lose. And so I dove right in.

After a couple months of this I was sure I needed no home, no food, no sleep, would never get a hangover and had the strength of a hundred normal happy men. And as long as I didn't look in the mirror, hear the wrong song or pass out for too long, I thought I could be this tough and ravenous and powerful forever.

Even without a home or much sanity, I managed to keep my job as a part-time English teacher. I dragged my duffle bag into class, high as a twisted kite, and my students never loved me more.

On the day I finally stopped teaching, I found myself in a library hours before I had to work. I hadn't written or read anything for months, and I felt there was something I needed to know. I started going through the stacks, starting with A, grabbing books and flipping through pages to find the right one. It wasn't until just before my class was to begin that I realized I'd misplaced $50 worth of cocaine somewhere in the Ds.

I spent the rest of the day going backwards through the whole stack—Dunne, Drake, Dillard, Dickens, DeLillo… I didn't come across the drugs and I never returned to work, but I did find some applicable wisdom—the one thing I already knew: "Hell is existence without love"—Dante. I walked back into the library bathroom with the book, and nothing to do but look in the mirror.

I spent those two weeks drying out at Filmores because I wanted to give myself a second chance, and I knew I couldn't do it if I was sick and jonesing. But I don't want to keep going like this. It's getting harder rather than easier. I think about her all the time, and I am getting weaker and more self-involved. I don't want to live like that and I don't want to write about it. I need to block out this stuff inside me and be fast and powerful again, whatever it takes. So yesterday I asked Eddie to find me some coke.

x
x
x

We are drinking Canadian Club and tall cans of Crest. While Eddie and Karen smoke a rock, I cut the powder into long white lines.

"Jesus," I say.

"Jedi."

"Bastard."

"Asshole."

"Old man."

Eddie leans toward me and tries to get serious. "You know I'm only giving you this so you don't smoke crack," he says.

"Okay."

"If I'd known you hadn't done it before, I never would have smoked you up that night—you know that, right?" he says as I take another line. "You're not buying any rock down here—you got it? I put the word out. I've seen how you've been kind of messed up lately, so I'm giving you this. But even this—if you come to my door wanting to buy every day, I'm cutting you off. Just once in a while, okay?"

"Okay," I say.

"I worry about you, kid," says Eddie. " 'Cause I'm your friend."

"Oh, Jesus!" says Karen, drawing on an empty stem, trying to find the crumbs in the ash. "You guys want me to leave so you can make out?"

Eddie pretends to smack her and refills the pipe.

I will always love Karen. She hardly knew me and got hit by a piece of lumber because she tried to help me. There are people I've known all my life who've never done anything like that. She's six months pregnant now, but it doesn't show at all. I don't know what they're going to do about this baby. Karen lives on cigarettes, beer, crack and Zoodles. I know all of this, and yet I do nothing. I don't say a word, I barely even think about it, really. I should want to shake them both, slap them and scream in their faces. Eddie looks out for *me* more than he does his own baby curled up clueless in Karen's tiny body.

"What are you thinking about, kid?" says Eddie, getting up to stoke the stove.

"Nothing, Pissy Ass. You worry about yourself," I say, and Karen starts to laugh. Eddie's been sitting in a puddle of urine left by Jackie, who apparently skipped a bathroom break earlier in the night for fear of missing a toke.

"That bitch," he says, trying to look at his own wet butt like a dog chasing his tail.

We drink until the sun comes up and, when I'm about to leave, Eddie and Karen put together a care package for me—a can of grape-juice concentrate, three ham sandwiches, a jar of instant coffee, an airplane bottle of rye and a half gram of cocaine. Eddie grabs my shoulder as we're standing in the doorway and says, "I hate the man who smoked me my first rock."

We've drunk a bit more than necessary, and now Eddie is grinning at his feet. "I hate that man like I hate the prick who raped me. Who would rape a fucking kid?" he says softly, like I'm not even there. Then he lifts his head and says, "Oops . . . Fuck, eh?"

"Ed . . . ?" I say.

"Go home, young Shaun. The sun's getting bright."

March 30

Cocaine is not the devil, but I'm sure he likes it. Cocaine gives you strength and ferocity and focus. You move with purpose, spin the cigarette in your fingers like a pool cue before the perfect eight-ball shot. It makes your game just wicked, the slate and felt rising up to meet your bridge, balls dropping like meteorites with white-streak tails. It puts a slide guitar in your brain, a glint in your eye, a rose in your teeth. It makes you the coolest, sharpest son of a bitch in your whole damn head. And even though this is all periphery, clothing, the snuggest-fitting sunglasses, the devil's quick snack, you can't help but smile, bare your teeth, crack open your jaw and take a bloody bite out of everything.

March 31

I do love this squalor—every day a little more. I love busting out of this shack in the cold sun, wearing just jeans and unmatching boots. I love pissing by the river with a great Canadian goose on either side of me, my body covered in goosebumps. I love listening to the giant concrete tanker unloading its bowels into the canal, like a clear mountain water-fall tumbling through my nightmares.

I love the dock lights, the highway lights, the railway lights, the starlight, the light of the skyscrapers downtown, of the giant bill-boards—Nikon and Canadian Club and Guess?—the firelight in barrels and the moonlight on water through my window.

I love the rats. They live beneath my floor, still scurry back under when they see me coming—as if I don't know they're there, like we don't lie awake at night (me and the rats) listening to each other breathe, scratching and scraping, and sharpening our teeth.

I love the ducks, pigeons, seagulls, geese and doves, all flying and fighting for bits of bread, singing and squawking—how it seems they're copying our every move.

I love Eddie coming over to "check on me" all the time, bringing drinks or bumming them, dragging me out of bed, trying to talk like even more of an asshole 'cause he's embarrassed by how well we get along. We raise some hell then take it down again—like those good days in junior high—shuffling back into class a bit cut up, and laughing, like you don't care if you're in trouble. Anyone comes near my shack and he's on them like the clubhouse lookout with a peashooter and a puffed-out chest.

I love my little big brother, Calvin. I love his smiling shiny eyes and that he asks me if I'm doing okay whenever he's not. I love that he laughs if I hit him a bit too hard when we're jousting with two-by-fours or fighting in the woodpile. I love that we can't hurt each other, no matter how much we bruise and bleed.

I love Randy spinning into my shack, then staggering out. I love his hungry, sad Popeye grin, his wrapped-up heartbreak like a present he'll never give you. I love how he announces, when we're in my shack, "We're in Shaun's place! We're okay, no worries—we're in Shaun's shack!" I love how he weebles and wobbles but never falls down—how he can walk on his heels with his body leaning so far back there must be an angel with her hands on his shoulders. I love the way you point him to his door and he starts off on a roundabout route like those *Family Circus* comics with little Billy's footprints winding all over the place: through the trees, over the woodpile, down to the water, over the garbage, through the trash, between the Johnny-on-the-Spots, onto a bike, into another pile of garbage, off the bike, around a fire barrel, through the ruins of his old home, into a puddle, and finally to the door of his prefab for the night. And then he comes back an hour later to offer a cigarette he found beneath his pillow.

I love the hookers who come over and hang out at my barrel, laughing and making jokes all the time, offering themselves gently without saying a thing, not the least bit disappointed to leave with chocolate and candles instead of money and crack. They laugh and dance and throw their candy wrappers on the ground, tell me I'm the nicest guy around—probably because I don't have sex with them—then they bring me clothes the johns have left behind.

I love Les's constant babble, his cowboy walk and his silly-hat collection.

I love going to lunch with the boys up at the Good Shepherd, all of us pulling each other out of fights, laughing our asses off, sitting at the same table then racing the streetcars home—jumping across the tracks at the last second like Superboy on his way to school.

I love Violet, who is 6 years old and Brenda's daughter. Her father brings her to Tent City to see her mother at least once a month, driving up in a nice new car. Violet has coffee-coloured skin and crazy pigtails and an angel face so sweet that the ducks waddle up in pairs to see her. She tries to walk through the rubble like we do, and we guide her small feet past the nails and cut metal. Or we sweep her into our arms and carry her. Calvin collects stuffed animals in a large bag and gives her one every time she visits. He turns her upside down and spins her with her pigtails flying.

Usually Brenda gets very drunk when Violet comes to see her. When she's gone, Randy and Brenda come over to my shack. Brenda's so blasted she's not sure where we are. "We're at Shaun's place!" says Randy.

"It was good to see Violet," I say.

"Don't you talk about my baby!" she growls. "Don't talk about Violet! I can't . . ." And then she sobs until I suggest to Randy that he take her home to bed.

I can hear her crying for her daughter as she stumbles back to their prefab. I can hear a half-dozen barrel fires crackling. I can hear the tanker in the canal getting ready to pull out, chains clanking, the boat rising. I can hear Sluggo and Jackie yelling, seagulls flapping through the sky. I can hear the rats beneath the floor, the wood popping in my stove, the rye pouring into my glass, the cigarette smoke rushing past my lips, and the wind against my roof. I am surprised, and a bit scared, that I love it here so much.

April 3

The woman ahead of me in the soup line today was laughing in a Hollywood approximation of madness. She turned to me, still cackling, and we stared at each other for a long time, both a bit out of our heads—monsters meeting in a desert world.

She put a cigarette in each of our mouths, and I lit them. She stopped laughing and said, "You have nice eyes." She said it like you might say, "You've shot me."

"Thank you."

She took a drag off her cigarette, then punched me hard in the stomach.

Everything's kind of like that these days.

x
x
x

Crazy Chris is back. It was snowing this morning and I gave him my kerosene heater to try and warm up his half of the prefab. "You should have the window open a bit so you don't go crazy from the fumes."

"Sure thing."

I showed him how to light it and he gave me a cigarette.

"How things going?"

"Fuckin' A. I'm bringing a bike in here tomorrow."

Things are always going fuckin' A for Chris.

"Not the Harley," I said. Word is, he stole a bike from the Hell's Angels. But if they're after him, he doesn't seem worried.

"Nah, different one."

"How you going to fit it in here?" I looked around at his tiny room filled with TVs, stereos and road signs. "Where you going to sleep?"

He shrugged. "Kerosene smells fuckin' A."

"Just don't sell the heater. I'll kick your ass if you do, okay?"

"Fuckin' A," he said, and laughed.

April 4

Strangely enough, most of the people here have cellphones now. Apparently a store up on Dundas and Sherbourne is giving them away with the first four months of calling free. I find this hard to believe, and yet everyone's got one—and I know they're not paying the bills. Mostly they use them to call dealers or emergency welfare. Steve, for some reason, has two, and talks into them both at the same time. Even on the phone he talks in misremembered song lyrics.

Jackie and Bonnie have been going at it for the past couple of days, fighting over some cans of milk that Jane brought down.

"It's only milk," I try to tell them. But of course it's never only milk.

April 6

There was a bad brawl at the brothel today.

A drinking buddy of a friend of Les's had a half-dozen too many and started smacking Kelly around, and pretty soon everyone was bleeding from ring cuts, broken bottles and knife wounds. Then the ambulances showed up, with the cops in tow, which really pissed people off. So now everyone's mad at somebody and the tributary fights are flowing into the night.

April 8

I always seem to miss the fires—the Lord of the Flies trash fires, the Act of God stovepipe-stupidity fires, and now the kerosene, matches and a flick-of-the-wrist fire.

Last night I was dancing and drinking in the Horseshoe Tavern. Goran and his wife, Julie—under the impression that I'm a writer rather than a bum, and that writers like other writers—took me to their friend's book launch on Queen Street West.

I felt kind of like Greystoke, out of the jungle and into the drawing room—surrounded by beautiful artists, hot little rocker chicks, people with degrees and perfect hair—like for a night I'd been dropped back into my life before Tent City. Luckily I made a $100 playing pool before the launch, and was able to divert attention from my smudged and feral appearance by buying people drinks. The drugs I'd scored let me dance without stopping, so that no one could get a careful look, and actually I did like the writer—she was pretty, and a pretty good dancer, and she even called me Cowboy, which I could never grow tired of. And so once again I missed the fire.

x
   x
     x

It was just after midnight and Crazy Chris was driving drunk. He had Mike's old junk truck and was doing doughnuts around the trash piles, until finally he crashed right into a couple of porta-potties. The shitters went flying, the truck got stuck, and Crazy Chris dived out the door and rolled like James Dean in *Rebel Without a Cause.* Instead of getting up and running a comb through his hair, however, he passed out in a puddle. When he came to, it was a couple of hours later. He stumbled over to Jimmy D's shack and asked to borrow a pack of matches.

That is all anybody knows for sure. That's all they saw. The problem is this: By the time the sun had risen, three of the plastic dollhouses had crude windows cut out of them with a knife and Frenchy Dan's shack had been burnt to the ground. Fortunately Dan was in the hospital with an abscessed tooth and nobody was hurt.

x
   x
     x

When I get home this morning, everyone is still on edge. They've added Chris's drunk driving to a packet of matches, come up with a guilty verdict, and again Crazy Chris has left Tent City.

"But no one saw him do it?" I say.

"No, but . . ."

"Then why's he run out of town? For crashing into the crappers?"

"He's not run out," says Eddie. "It's just better he's not here till we know for sure."

"I already know for sure," says Steve.

"Me, too," says Marty

"Not 100 percent, you don't," says Eddie.

"I know 99 percent," says Steve.

"Me too, b'y," says Calvin.

And now everyone's staying close to their shacks. "It's all I got," says Sluggo. It's all any of us have. There's a reason that most fights end up with someone yelling that they'll burn your place down—and a reason they usually don't.

"Nobody goes after Chris till we know for sure," says Eddie. Everybody grumbles. Burnt ash drifts by on the wind. I get my heater out of Chris's prefab before it's looted, and I can't help but think of his casual observation: Kerosene smells fuckin' A.

April 9

Randy and Jimmy D are always going at each other these days because of their dogs. Jimmy D has two mean sons of bitches who go for Chaos every time they're loose. I was over at Randy's prefab today, admiring the bruises from his most recent scrap with Jimmy D. The avenging angel was still hanging on the wall.

"You can have it if you want," he said, shaking his head. "I don't even know what the hell it's supposed to be." He took it down and replaced it with a poster of Budweiser babes in bikinis he got from Chris's place.

So now I've got this angel of vengeance on my wall, only she's not as I remember—or at least not as I described. I didn't do her justice:

She takes up the whole width of the frame, wings brushing against each side. Her long green hair is writhing like a nest of a hundred snakes.

Her open wings and short-cut dress are made entirely of peacock feathers, a mock-peacock eye in each one, as if she can see with every inch of her body. She is holding a long, straight, trumpet to her lips. In her other hand she has—not a bow and arrow as I'd thought—but a fletched spear, taller than herself. Her eyes are like wolf eyes. Her feet are on fire.

At the bottom of the picture, a small city is burning in the distance. There are rivers of fire flowing from the shacks and houses. The flames are rushing toward us.

April 10

I signed a book contract today. Some guy from the publishing house sat across from me and went over the whole thing, section by section, although I was a bit too dazed to focus. "How does it feel to have a contract with the largest publisher in the world?" he said.

"Um . . . I don't know," I said, but I couldn't stop smiling. I signed my name in a few different places, then thanked him.

"Don't thank me. Just keep writing. And get out of there alive, okay?"

But it's too much to think about—getting out of Tent City. I don't know if I'll be able to last the full year, or leave when it's over. A contract is a strange thing that way. It makes you do disturbing things, like expect a future. It makes you hope.

Along the same lines, I'd suggested we meet at the Stone Cutter's Arms in the hope that the cute bartender would be there, but it was her night off.

After the bar we went to Staples and bought a hand-held tape recorder. I'd decided to see if I could do some interviews down here, like a journalist would. When I got back to Tent City I told Bonnie and Calvin, Sluggo and Jackie, and Eddie and Karen about the book, but they didn't seem to really get it. I'm not sure I do either, but I asked Calvin if he'd mind doing an interview. "Sure, b'y," he said. "Long as you get the hooch."

x   x   x

An Interview with Calvin:

(The following dialogue is culled from seventy pages of transcribed audio-tape. The interview with Calvin took place in my shack over approximately six hours, a bottle of Jim Beam and a dime bag of cocaine. Whether or not this affected the progressively mythic proportions of Calvin's memory, it probably explains why our conversation became less and less coherent. As in our usual conversations, the more Calvin tried to explain his life the less clear it became. I have tried to edit and summarize this interview not only for length and clarity, but also for the reader's sanity. I have not been able to verify his facts.)

S: Tell me about your family.

C: There's Spider . . . there was fourteen girls and three boys. My older brother's dead . . . drove his bike into a wall . . .

S: What did your folks do?

C: My old man was an explosives technician . . . blew himself up when I was about 10 . . . took out half the fucking windows in Parry Sound.

S: Kill anybody?

C: I think sixteen died and I don't know how many others were injured.

(Calvin goes on to explain that after his dad died they all moved in with their dad's best friend, whom his dad had caught in bed with their mum just before he blew up himself and half the town).

C: Yeah, it sounds fucking weird but basically that's what happened. But it was an accident.

S: Uh-huh.

C: I wasn't around there very long. Took too many beatings . . . My stepdad put a really good beating on me and then I shot him with a crossbow and everything. It was good . . .

(Calvin tells a long, gory story about how, while his stepdad was beating him almost to death with a baseball bat, Calvin somehow got hold of a

*crossbow and stuck him to the barn wall, then dragged himself 16 miles to
his grandmother's house and moved in with her.)*

S: So you shot him with a crossbow and then went to live with your
grandma?

C: More or less . . . He was a goof . . . He wasn't even with my mother
fucking three months and he was beating on her, beating on me . . . Spider
was born, man, that fucking kid, no wonder he's so fucked up today . . .
Sometimes he reminds me so much of my stepdad I just want to fucking
choke him. That's why I think you're more my brother than he is. We get
along better . . . I'm pretty proud of that motherfucker too though, eh?
He's got a job up at Sick Kids . . . and he wants me to go back. I don't know,
can't do Sick Kids no more. Fuck, buddy, I got them a portable lung
machine, you know, I got them a portable kidney machine . . .

*(He explains how he organized all of the beggars and drug dealers in the
Ottawa area to donate part of their earnings to the Sick Kids Hospital.
According to him, this vagrant fundraising also involved a honey stand, and
eventually puppet shows for the kids themselves.)*

S: Okay, now bring me back to when you met your old lady . . .

C: I was only 14. All I did was kiss her and hold her hand, you know
fucking 14-year-olds, you know, b'y, good shit. I figured, okay, this is
going to last, right. But I got drunk, pissed her off, so she didn't want
to be with a fucking drunk . . . Wouldn't quit for my own fucking
mother, why would I quit for you? . . . Got a picture of my mom pouring a fucking beer into a baby bottle and passing me that fucking baby
bottle, and that's the only thing I would take.

S: Okay, so you're 14. You ditch your old lady because she wants you to
quit drinking . . .

*(Calvin explains that they got back together, and that Elaine became preg-
nant the first time they had sex. But because he was not yet 16, he had to
get his parents' permission to make an honest woman of her. His stepdad,
of course, refused—which gave 15-year-old Calvin the perfect excuse to
exercise his vengeance. He describes how he beat his stepdad until he finally
signed the permission form.)*

C: So I go and get married and three months later I'm a happy proud father of a baby girl: My little devil heart, my little devil child. (*He shows me his tattoo.*) . . . She's my favourite girl . . .

S: Okay, so what happened?

C: I told you before that my niece was raped and the guy that raped her got six days in jail.

(*He tells me a story about leaving Kamloops and going to Nova Scotia to avenge his niece, him being her favourite uncle. He had this confusing and elaborate plan whereby he would hang around the town—where apparently everybody knew him, except for the rapist in question—until he gained the man's trust, at which point they would go do some partying at Calvin's secluded campsite, where Calvin would then torture him to death and bury him in a lion pit. The plan didn't work out though, and instead—according to Calvin—he cut the guy in half with a shotgun blast in the middle of a crowded bar.*)

C: When I shot the cocksucker, man, it was funny, because the upper part of his body was going backwards, right, and his legs were still coming at me . . . I mean, yeah, you had to be there. Some people were. My brother says some of the friends we have in Nova Scotia still talk about it. It's funny as fuck. It was like a puppet show, b'y (*laughter*) . . . but it fucked me up for a long time . . .

S: So did they pop you that night?

C: Oh fuck, buddy man, there was wall-to-wall cops in fucking twenty minutes. Everywhere, fuck . . . I sat in the bar, I sat in the bar, buddy, I'll tell you, I sat in the fucking bar . . .

(*Calvin tells me about sitting in the bar. Supposedly the police chief and the bartender had been friends with Cal's father, respected what Calvin had done to the rapist and were unsure as to whether there was still a shot in the double barrel that Calvin held in his hands. And so they let him drink on the house for the next four hours before finally taking him to jail.*)

C: Judge says twenty-five, no parole . . . The sentence comes down and all of a sudden my knees went, they just went. I'll never see my daughter, I'll never see my wife, I lost everything I fucking own, yadda yadda, all this going through my head . . .

S: What was it like in there for you?

C: Ah it was scary at first . . . I had no crew, bud. I was in there alone, on my own. But when I walked, when I walked in there, they'd all read about me in the paper, they all knew who I was, right, so a lot of the guys were respecting me for what I did . . .

(Calvin talks about all the respect he got in jail. And then about the appeal that brought his sentence down to ten years. He then embarks on a long, convoluted description of how he brewed and hid hundreds of gallons of hooch all over the jail, which—about an hour later—somehow gets us to a guy four floors up who not only helped with brewing, distribution and trade of Cal's moonshine, but did so via a pet mouse on a string. I'm trying my best to understand, but it's all pretty complicated.)

S: So he'd send the mouse down with the hash or the pot and he'd be dragging brew bags?

C: No no not the mouse, the mouse is dragging the string.

S: No no, yeah yeah . . . So the string's attached to the mouse, the string when you get it in your cell, you'd tie it to the brew bag.

C: Yeah—

S: And he drags the brew all the way back to his house.

C: No no—I'd take my dope off. So I tie a little string onto him for him to go back to the guy's cell . . .

S: So you've traded each other's strings at this point?

C: No, he sent dope down to me, so I emptied the dope off the mouse—

S: Yeah, talk to me like I'm an idiot here 'cause I'm trying to figure—

C: I'm not talking to you like an idiot.

S: No, I'm asking you to.

(Calvin tries to talk to me like I'm an idiot until I almost get it, but then he starts talking about how his ceramic factory was the perfect cover for his moonshine operation because of all the equipment—and not only that, but he made over $20,000 selling Tiffany lamps and ceramic Dobermans to the prison guards. Finally I decide to move on.)

S: . . . Anyway, okay . . . So you get out of prison. How old are you?

C: Fuck, I was 17, 27, 28, 27 when I got out.

S: Twenty-seven? So you were my age? . . . That's weird, eh? . . . Okay so you're still married . . .

C: Fuck, I had two kids when I was in there.

S: Conjugal visits?

C: Yeah.

(Calvin then switches to talking about the Hell's Angels. He explains that most of his family is "connected," and that he was the first-ever lifetime member—insofar as he was the first person to be born in a clubhouse and thus instantly made an honorary Hell's Angel. He talks about "the riders" for a while, then his second prison stretch, which he says was a favour to the club.)

C: Ah . . . But ah see my old lady, right, my old lady and I, we had an accident . . . I was drunk, so she was driving. We were in a T-bird. And, uh, she rolled three times. So she was like paralyzed from the neck down . . . So I was in a bit of a financial bind, right. Surgeries and all that shit.

S: So your old lady hit the shoulder, rolled, paralyzed herself from the neck down?

C: Yeah . . . My first daughter . . .

S: Was in the car, too? What happened to her?

C: She broke a hip. They took a piece out of her shoulder and put it in her hip. You know the funny part about that is? I was the drunkest one. I didn't have no seat belt on. My daughter had a seat belt on, Elaine had a seat belt on, and she was ripped right out of her seat belt . . .

S: And you were fine.

(Calvin explains that he took the rap for another Hell's Angel's attempted murder charge in exchange for money for all the surgeries that were needed following the accident. He talks about the next five years he did inside, then his eventual release, whereupon the entire B.C. chapter of the Hell's Angels showed up to greet him with four limousines full of scantily clad women, Jack Daniel's and cocaine, as well as a briefcase full of cash. He then proceeds to describe in lengthy and graphic detail all the sex he had with all the women on the way home. I try to speed up this part of the story, to little avail.)

S: So you got home . . .

C: Oh yeah, b'y . . . I had all four fucking women on me when we pulled into the old lady's yard . . . And the old lady, she wheels out in her chair . . . and says to me, "Did you enjoy yourself?"

S: And how many kids you got at this point?

C: I only got four.

S: And, uh, you got a woman in a wheelchair.

C: Yeah.

S: So how'd you hit the streets?

C: My woman in the wheelchair died—

S: Do you want to tell me about that?

C: Ah bud, I loved her right through . . . I didn't even tell you half the beatings she gave me, b'y . . . and it came Christmas and my birthday and special days, she'd go buy me a hooker . . . Street people were always our people . . . so she'd pick a girl for me, bud. I'd go home with this fucking hooker, with her in the living room smoking a joint. I'm in the fucking bedroom with the hooker, doing coke, whatever the fuck, drinking. I'd have a 40 pounder, have some coke . . . Half the time we didn't fuck, we just sat in there and talked, come out fucking glowing. Did you have a good time, sweetie? No, baby, it was better with you . . .

S: So then what happened?

C: So then she died, b'y.

(We keep talking for a couple more hours. Neither Calvin's enunciation nor his life, however, become any clearer.)

April 11

About a month ago, a guy with a Gore-Tex jacket and a dippy little goatee came by while we were sitting around Bonnie and Calvin's picnic table having some beers. We offered him a drink, he took a coffee and smoked a few of my cigarettes. He said he lived in the neighbourhood and wanted to check this place out. When I asked him what he did for a living, he said something about ecology work and farming-aid programs, and that he was going to South America next month, for work.

And then, today, I picked up a copy of the *Toronto Sun*—belting the box three times, a quick yank at the handle—and started flipping through. I'm not in the habit of reading the *Sun*. Usually I just glance once at the Sunshine Girl then bunch it up to start a fire. But this week they're doing a seven-part series on the "homeless problem" in Toronto, and I figured it might be good for a few laughs.

Today was installment number five: "The Hardcore Homeless." And there, under the simple headline "Tent City," was our friendly ecologist neighbour, who'd somehow failed to mention that he was a writer for the *Sun.*

There's no shortage of reporters coming down to Tent City, but usually they identify themselves as such. Marty says the first story he can remember was by a woman from the *Sun* who came looking for interviews. There were only about a dozen people and a few makeshift tents back then, and the boys told her they'd answer her questions if she bought a case of beer. Instead, she promptly left and wrote a piece on the depravity of Tent City residents. And it seems that's been their angle ever since.

In contrast, a reporter and photographer from the *Toronto Star* came down on New Year's 2001 with a bottle of rum. Marty told them he'd do an interview, with only one condition: the first stupid question they asked he could dismiss them immediately.

"Some people consider this the real beginning of the new millennium," said the reporter. "What does this historical change mean to you guys down here?"

"Sorry, but you'll have to leave now," said Marty, smiling. They thanked him, laughing, and left the bottle behind.

It doesn't surprise me that most journalists don't get this place. It's taken me five months living here to see the good stuff running like a hidden stream under toxic earth.

At Easter, Jackie and Sluggo gave me a broiled salmon they'd got from the Purple People Eaters—"'Cause it's from B.C., like you, Shauny." I told Randy I liked his army pants and he gave them to me. I told him I liked the angel on his wall and he gave me that, too. Calvin has given me the shirt right off his back three times so far. Eddie gave me the bedsheets from my childhood, and whenever he has a bit extra he brings me food and booze.

I don't know if everyone has changed over the past few months, or if it's just me. Or it's just taken this long for people to trust me.

But no—some of these guys have been good to me ever since I came down here, though for some reason I couldn't see it then.

This place is both chaos and community—chaos by design and community by accident. And by accident Tent City might answer some of the dilemmas and questions put forward by social workers, poverty professionals, harm-reduction specialists, housing activists and even the editorial board of certain conservative publications. It is a place where people have housed themselves with no direct cost to taxpayers, and in doing so have grabbed themselves a bit of pride and self-esteem. It is a place where support systems that *do* exist can do their thing without bureaucracy and at minimal cost; health-care workers can come down here and help out dozens of people at once; same with those who have donations of food or clothing. And some who first come down to help end up spending a lot more time than they planned because they like it here.

From the outside looking in, it is hard to tell what we're up to. You might see Randy coming into town with more bread than anyone could eat, but not see that it's all stale, and miss him tossing the crumbs to the ducks and geese, talking to them with the gentleness he usually saves for Chaos. You could see Terry walking around with his head down, eyes to the ground, and you might think he's crazy, or defeated, or looking for cigarette butts. But really he's searching for pennies to take to Sick Kids Hospital; he only needs eighteen more to give them a full five hundred.

Sure, there's lots of drugs and violence and basic badness down here. But isn't it better that these eighty or so hard-living shit disturbers are keeping to themselves? The life that moves back and forth between prison and the streets is a violent one, and Tent City is a town built by alpha dogs—they've got well-practised growls and won't back down too easily. With this kind of atmosphere, and a constantly high level of inebriation, it's surprising that kindness and generosity hang around at all. But they do.

I guess I'm realizing that for the first time in a while I've actually got a political opinion: I believe that squatting should be legalized. And that tasteless tabloids are best used as kindling.

One good result of this latest newspaper piece is that Bonnie and Jackie are finally friends again—brought together by their common enemy. Angry that we were all quoted without being told the score, Jackie gave Bonnie her cellphone to call the *Sun*. But our neighbourhood reporter is presently on vacation.

April 12

I wanted to tell Hawk about my book contract as soon as I signed it, but he's been in the hospital for the past few days. Apparently he was in a bathhouse downtown and got burns on his legs and arms from too many chemicals in the water.

In the meantime, I've discovered that Hawk claims to be the nephew of Johnny "Pops" Papalia. Johnny Pops—until someone shot him dead in a Hamilton parking lot—was the head of Canada's largest crime syndicate. He is a Mafia legend, on and off the street, and Hawk is scary enough without being a lost son of the Mob. He's back now, and on painkillers—and so he's smiling.

"I don't do drugs—you know that, eh, Shauny?" says Hawk. "Never even smoked a marijuana cigarette. So when the doctor gives me pills, man, they work!"

I figure now's a good time to tell him about the book.

"Well, good for you, Shauny," he says. "But you make sure you do a good job on it, eh? You tell the truth about this place, Shaun."

"I will, Hawk."

Frenchy Dan just got out of hospital, too.

"Think he'll go after Chris?" I say. I've learned in the past few days that unless you're the Hell's Angels or Hawk, you tend not to go after Chris. Even the old crew say he's too tough and too crazy.

"I don't think so, Shauny," says Hawk, grinning from that Percocet glow. "Chris didn't burn him out. I'll tell you what happened: Last summer—this was before you come down here—there's this guy in a tent by the water. And he and Dan get into it, and this guy kicks Dan's ass pretty good, okay? So what happens, Shauny? Well, you know the score, ha, ha! Dan and Patrick go over there with baseball bats while he's sleeping and just give it to him, whole nine yards, you know?"

"Uh-huh."

"So I ain't seen this guy for some time, you understand, and he comes up to me the other day and he says, 'Hey, Hawk, how'd you like that little show I put on in Tent City? Just tell me they were in there. Tell me the suckers fried.'" Hawk's body is shaking with laughter. "Man, you should have seen his face when I told him that place was empty! But you know, I respect what he was trying to do, Shaun. What those boys did was wrong." It was exactly what he said when they kicked me around: What those boys did was wrong. I wonder if Hawk is disappointed in me for not setting any vengeful fires.

"So what about Chris?" I say.

"What about him?" laughs Hawk. "Guy just chose a bad night to drive through some crappers."

"Shitty luck," I say, and we sit there laughing on Hawk's porch in the cold sun.

April 13

Eddie pounded my door open at noon today.

"Up, you crazy little asshole!"

"Fuck off. Please."

"Just looking out for you, you prick. The Purple People Eaters are here with hot dogs and chili. You gotta put something in that gut of yours."

There were about twenty of them, all in their purple "Jesus did THIS just for you!" vests. Usually they camp out in front of Hawk's place, but today they pulled the vans and trailers all the way down here to the old part of town. It was cold and drizzly and they set up their amps and synthesizer inside the plywood box shelter next to Sluggo and Jackie's, with the vats of chili on a big round table that's recently materialized in the town square.

When there were enough of us standing out in the rain they formed a circle and prayed for us. Jackie held hands with them, as did a Native woman who had been drinking all night at Steve and Nancy's. She kept falling down in the middle of the circle, then apologizing. "I'm sorry. I'm sorry for my soul!" she said as they pulled her out of the mud once more, like they were playing some game of religious Red Rover.

When the praying was done, a few of the purple men strapped guitars over their vests and one of them started plinking away at the keyboard, singing about the bright light of Jesus as the cold rain fell. In between songs the lead singer bantered about how God's love is like a bank where your credit is always good and your account can never be overdrawn.

"Wouldn't that be nice, brothers and sisters?" he called out. "To have a bank account like that? Well, with Jesus you can. Jesus gives and gives. All you have to do is open an account. Any time of day or night, the Bank of Jesus is always open. Do you hear what I'm saying, brothers and sisters? Do you hear what I'm saying?"

"Hot dogs!" said Randy.

"They're good if you put the chili on 'em," I said.

"Chili dogs!" said Randy.

I somehow broke the spout of the juice keg and it started gushing all over the place. I was even more hungover than I'd realized, and just stood there with the bright pink juice spraying from between my fingers as everyone laughed and danced to the crummy music in the strawberry rain.

As I was working on my third chili dog, a young girl in a Purple People vest appeared from behind one of the vans. She was much younger than the others, in fact she reminded me of my youngest sister, and she looked as if she was about to cry. She took two steps toward a blond middle-aged woman in a purple vest and burst into tears. As I walked over to them, they were talking to each other quickly, the girl gasping for air.

"Are you okay?" I said. She looked up and her eyes locked on me. She couldn't have been more than 16 years old.

"Yes, she's okay," said the woman, and at the same time the girl said, "He didn't really do anything. He just grabbed me." She was shaking, and the woman put her arm around her.

"Don't be scared," I said to the girl. "Just tell me what happened. It's going to be—"

She stepped away from the woman and took hold of my arm. I was so surprised by this that it took me a moment to hear what she was saying: "Pray for him. Pray for him. We should all just pray . . ."

"Who was it?" I said. Did he hurt you?" She shook her head, then laid it against my shoulder and began to sob. She had pale freckled skin and long dark hair, just like my sister. I wanted to hold her, but I didn't move.

"Someone grabbed her. He scared her, that's all," said the blond purple woman, putting her arm on the girl's shoulder to gently pull her away. "She said it was somebody who was drunk." The other Purple People began crowding around us. I told the girl that I'd come right back, and went over to Eddie who was standing in his doorway.

"What's up, young Shaun?" he said, putting a half can of Crest in my hand.

I told him, and his eyes began to narrow. "That's not right," he said. "No fucking way. That's not going to happen down here. No fucking way . . ."

"Who would do that?" I said, looking out at Marty, Heartbeat, Randy, Terry and Frizz. They were all sober, and I knew it couldn't be any of them.

"Steve," said Eddie. "He's drunk as shit."

Steve is a bad drunk. It takes him into a blackout world where even the best songs become warped. The girl had been walking away from Nancy and Steve's plastiwood house when she came around the van.

"That's it for him," said Eddie. "But we won't do it now. Unless he comes out, we'll leave it till he's sober. He's gotta know, otherwise we'll just have to do it again."

"We gotta make sure it's him though," I said, thinking of Crazy Chris.

I walked back over to the small crowd—some of them Purple People, some of them Tent City boys. The girl's face was streaked with tears and her nose was running. "What's your name?" I said.

"Angie."

"It's okay, Angie. Just tell me—was it the tall guy in the house over there?"

She hiccuped as she looked at me. "I don't want you to do anything," she said, her eyes tearing up again. "Just pray for him." The Purple People Eaters nodded.

"*Better* pray for him!" said Heartbeat, and the other boys started throwing out threats, bouncing around and getting ready.

"I'm sorry this happened," I said. "We have to make sure it doesn't happen again, okay, Angie? Just tell me if I'm wrong. Was it the tall guy?"

As Steve stumbled out from behind the van, Hawk strode toward us.

"What's going on?" said Hawk. "I hear something about a girl—"

"You let me deal with it, Hawk," said Eddie, "I got it under control." Hawk squared his feet and smiled. Only Eddie can talk to Hawk like this. Steve stumbled past us as Angie dug her fingers into my arm. Eddie went after Steve, and Hawk began bellowing for explanations like some displaced Sicilian king.

As I tried to explain, one of the braver purple men stepped forward and suggested that Hawk was scaring the poor girl, which—despite his intentions—appeared to be true. I could feel her arm shaking.

"Who the FUCK do you think you are?" Hawk yelled. "I'll break you with one hand, you little fucking goof." The Purple Man folded like a K-way jacket into a hip sack, and the girl moved closer to me.

"There! You see!" said Hawk. "She knows we can protect her. I told you idiots not to set up down here—in this fucking circle jerk! Didn't I tell you?"

Hawk turned back to us. "Look, angel," he said. "That wasn't right what that man did." Angie let out a fearful sob.

"She shouldn't be here," I said. "These idiots should have got her out of here by now."

Hawk liked that. "Who has the keys to that van?" he shouted, glaring at the Purple People Eaters until someone held up a set of keys.

"You okay?" I said when we got her into the van.

"I'm sorry," said Angie. They drove off and Eddie came over rubbing his knuckles the way he does when he's just punched someone.

"Had to punch him," he said. "Wouldn't stay in there. Nice hit, too. Tried for a second as he was going down, but just kicked him instead."

Hawk laughed, then said, "Real shame . . . she was such a good kid," and walked away.

When the rest of the Purple People Eaters had left, Eddie, Heartbeat, Jackie and I stood around a tub of leftover chili, drinking cans of Crest.

"When he wakes up he's out of here," said Eddie. "But we should do it together. No fucking around. We all get together and walk him out."

"But—" I said.

"Nobody touches him," said Eddie, "as long as he does it easy. We'll go over there in an hour. He'll be awake by then."

"Come and get me," I said, and went into my shack to write.

x   x   x

I've only been writing for half an hour when Jane, who hasn't been down here for a few days, comes running to my door.

"You gotta get out there!" she says. "There's something bad happening! I mean really bad! Hurry!"

Why my hurrying would prevent badness from happening, I'm not quite sure. Putting on my best hero voice I say, "You stay here!" and leap out through the mud, reaching Steve's house in a few brave but awkward bounds.

About a dozen of them are there. Steve is in the doorway, with Nancy in front of him, screaming obscenities. Her eyes are like pools of pig's blood sizzling on a fire.

"I thought you were going to come get me," I say, stepping up next to Eddie.

"Nancy came out yelling and it just sort of happened . . . Steve already said he'll go."

"Really?"

"Yeah. He said, 'Tell me what I did, and if it's bad enough I'll go.'" And now, behind Nancy's screaming face, I can see that Steve is mouthing the words, "I gotta go. I gotta go now, Nancy."

"Nancy's going to be a problem."

"Yep," says Eddie, and then—as if to prove it—he moves toward the door saying, "Shut the fuck up, Nancy! Steve is going now."

"Noooooo!" she yells and she has a hammer in her hands, swinging it over her head.

"Hey, Shaun!" shouts Steve, looking straight at me. "That's the hammer I borrowed from you!" He sounds so good-natured it catches me off guard.

"Yeah! That's my hammer!" I say, and smile at him despite myself.

"Now might be a good time to get it back," he says, and Nancy starts toward us still swinging. If she'd aimed at one of us, she might have connected, but she swings for all of us at once, and Heartbeat grabs her arm. I get her wrist, and pry the hammer out of her hand. She tries to kick me in the balls, but I jump back so that she hits my thigh. I can see the hammer in my hand above her head.

"Are you insane?" I yell. "I've got the hammer!" But of course Nancy *is* insane—her brain has been boiled by drugs and booze and hopelessness. She turns and kicks Eddie square in the nuts, and he punches her in the side of the head.

I can see he regrets it immediately. "Fight like a man and I'll hit you like a man!" he yells. Nancy turns and goes for Jackie. But Jackie takes her down, her fist working like a piston, Nancy's head bouncing off the concrete.

Finally Eddie pulls Jackie off. We hold her back as Nancy gets to her feet, her eyes and cheeks already puffing up, the skin cracking like blisters on an overcooked hot dog.

We let Steve get whatever he needs from the house, and he takes a cellphone and his jacket. He isn't quite drunk anymore, and he's not quite sober. Nancy is trying to fight us and drag him back home. Steve looks at me in confusion as we move down the road, and I feel myself about to say something kind, or apologetic.

"Yeah," he says. "I gotta go. I know I gotta go."

At the corner in front of Karl's place we split up and Hawk walks him the rest of the way. I can hear Steve half-singing on the way to the gates. *"If I go I'll find some trouble. But if I stay I'll make it double. So come on and let me go . . . ,"* with Nancy still yelling behind him.

April 15

I went to get tested at the Regent Park Health Centre today, to see if I have TB, hep A, B, C, or all of the above. Although the TB outbreak in the shelters is getting worse, people down here don't seem to be getting it. The hepatitis I'm more concerned about. I've recently found out that pretty well everyone in Tent City is hep C positive. And I'm always sharing bottles.

"Oh, yeah, we've all got it," says Randy. "Assumed you had it too, Shaun."

"No."

"Oh. Well, you might have it now."

I won't know until next week.

x   x   x

It's hotter than hell right now, even the swans look like they're sweating, and the population rises with the temperature. There are four new places being built over where the church almost was, a shack next to Karl's, and a large three-room mess of metal, tarp and plywood in the field behind the porta-potties, put together by some young guys with tattoos and tiny girlfriends.

There are new dogs down here as well. Heartbeat's got a sweet little malamute puppy who howls like the world is ending whenever he's left alone. And the Brothers have a new dog, too, since Derek's old lady has moved in with her rat-size terrier. They all share an apartment uptown, but have decided to spend the summer down here where it's easier to boil up their barrels of appleshine.

Terry, on the other hand, has given up on the place he was building since Eddie sold his wood stove for drugs.

"That was my fucking stove, Eddie!" says Terry.

"Sorry, buddy," says Eddie, holding up his empty hands and smiling like a little kid with a 60-year-old skull. "What can I say? I'm a crack addict."

According to Eddie, the difference between a crack addict and a crackhead is this: An addict is an addict, but can still be an okay guy. A crackhead will do anything to get it—steal from people, or sell his friend's stuff.

"Like Terry's stove?" I say to him.

"But that's different," he says. "That doesn't mean I'm a crackhead."

"How so?"

"'Cause I'm more complex, you know. I've got heart." He says it with that smile that makes you want to believe. "It's not that I'm a crackhead. It's that I'm an asshole."

"Right."

"Like you."

"I see."

And it's true—though Eddie's an asshole, he's one crack addict I'd trust with my life. Though maybe not my stove.

x
  x
    x

Calvin's been doing some roofing with Les the past few days. They plan to work until they've got enough money for Les to put his truck on the road, then I'm going to drive it, as I'm the only one with a valid licence. According to Les we're going to make lots of cash—doing what exactly I'm not yet sure. So far, however, most of the money is going toward drugs and alcohol rather than plates and insurance.

Pops hasn't been down here for a while. Supposedly he and his dog are living with a woman and her daughter in an apartment uptown. I run into him at a church kitchen once in a while and he tells me about all the nasty sex he's having. Hawk just shakes his head like he can't believe I'm such a chump. According to him, Pops is nowhere but on a crack binge.

"Thought he was over all that, you know . . . Beautiful day, though, eh, Shaun?"

I ask Hawk if he'd mind doing an interview with me tomorrow and he agrees to it. I want to get him in this good mood of his, all sunshine and painkillers.

April 16

An Interview with Hawk

(Hawk and I begin the interview sitting on the front steps of his shack. I've brought a six-pack of Coca-Cola Classic for him, and some beer for me. I have drastically edited our conversation for length and clarity, and I haven't verified his facts.)

S: Where were you born?

H: Uh . . . Sicily . . . I came to Canada when I was 5 years old. Then raised in Hamilton, Ontario . . . But I used to go back every year when I was growing up . . . That's a cool place, Shaun—you ever been there?

S: I spent a year in Italy, but not Sicily.

H: Oh, you have to go there.

S: What was growing up in Hamilton like for you?

H: It was hard, I guess I could say, yeah it was hard. Hamilton's a very big, uh, how do you say it . . . it's a gangster city. You know what I'm saying? . . . And by the time I was, uh, I guess say 9 years old, I got into that gang. It was called the North Enders. Ran with them for several years.

S: What'd that entail, being in a gang?

H: (*Pause.*) Violence, I guess you could say. Shaun, I was raised in violence, you know what I mean? It was nothing for me to get kicked in the face. Dad was very old-fashioned—step out of line that's the way it was, you know what I mean? I'll tell you a story: My head's right through a wall and I'm screaming to get out of the wall, and I couldn't get out of the wall. So my dad turned and went into the room on the other side and booted me in the face with steel-toed boots back through that wall, so I could get out.

S: How old were you then?

H: (*Clears throat*) I was 8.

S: Is your dad still alive?

H: Nope. No . . . no. Dad's moved on now.

S: How'd you get along with him eventually?

H: (*Pause.*) I don't think I ever did, Shaun, to be honest . . . I loved my dad, don't get me wrong. I loved my mum, too. They brought me into this world, but I didn't *like* them, you know what I mean?

S: What's the worst thing you ever did in a gang?

H: Worst thing I ever did? (*Pause.*) Honestly I gotta . . . ah . . . (*deliberating*) . . . no, no I'm just thinking, there's so many different ones . . . I'd say the worst one I ever did was when I took a .44 Winchester . . . and took this guy's legs out . . . just demolished his legs, eh? Just kept fucking firing and firing and firing and firing and firing . . . I didn't stop. Just took the guy's legs right out . . . That was because one of the hos—gangs always have hos, brother, you know what I mean? He went nuts on her and this is why I went so bad because it reminded me of me when I was young. I'll never forget it, because he had a pair of Kodiak workboots on. And those were my favourite. I'd just love 'em, because for a big guy like me they're really good support, you know what I mean? They really stand up. And this guy had a pair of Kodiak workboots on and . . . he booted her in the chest and the face and everything, so I just flipped my lid and that was that . . . pulled out a .44 Winchester and fucking went to heaven and back, you know what I mean? It was, like, a *flashback.* How do you say it, brother? It was like a . . . a *flashback.*

S: You think that's when you get angriest—when you get brought back to beatings your father put on you, when something reminds you of that?

H: It's just, I dunno, I . . . uh . . . It's like I always say: You might think you're big and bad. But I'm fucking sick and sad—and that's just the way my saying is . . . It's not about the violence, 'cause the violence is real fucking easy, you know what I mean?

S: How many—and again, just shake your head if you don't want to answer this—but, how many guys, uh . . . Have you killed anybody?

H: Yeah . . . yeah, I have, Shaun. I got two murder beefs on my record, to be honest with you. And that's what I did ten years for in prison. Collins Bay Penitentiary. A-27, left-hand side, One Block—otherwise known as Gladiator School. I spent ten years there. For two first-degree murder beefs. But I'll be honest with you, Shaun—I'd do it again. 'Cause I think I told you the story about what happened to my mum . . .

S: No, you didn't tell me that.

H: I did not tell you that?

S: I would have remembered.

(Hawk tells me a long and extremely graphic story about how, shortly after winning the world championship in kung fu, he went to visit his parents and came upon the scene of his mother being attacked by two men with two-by-fours, and then beat them to death with his bare hands.)

H: Don't forget, I was wicked eh, Shaun . . . I was in top shape—*zero* body fat . . . I'm not talking as, uh, as bragging, but the one guy was really really really fast. I hit him twice and then I boot him, and I broke the guy's neck, eh? . . . He died right there on the sidewalk. And the other guy, well he was the tricky one, 'cause he was running around with this two-by-four . . . But when I finally got him, that was a bad scene, I'll tell you. I, uh, I fractured his spine. I broke both his legs. I cracked his jaw . . . I'll tell you honestly, I was picking him off the ground and throwing him up in the air so's I could still kind of hit him, eh? Yeah. That's the kind of thing I was doing. *(Sighs.)* They give me fifteen years . . . I did ten and I walked out of there as a free man. That'd be, uh, let's see, this is my third year out so this is a really good time for me. You know, you asked about, about doing good. Well, the last eighteen months I'm doing great.

S: What changed?

H: I left society, Shaun. *(Laughs.)* That's straight up—I left society. Left that world up there where the bank owns everything, and all you do is live by a goddamn mayor's rules . . . I left all that. And then I come to Tent City.

S: Tell me about your idea of what this place is.

H: Tent City's a bunch of people who want to live free. But freedom and being *mooches* is two different things, brother. Okay, 'cause don't get me wrong, Shaun, there's a lot of people who live here that just want to be left alone and go out and make their bucks and everything, but then we got people here who don't care and all they want to do is be crackheads and dirty hos and pieces of shit. So that's the facts, brother. It's not me to judge anybody, but hey, I think there's more to life than just being like this too, right? You know I went away last summer to a Mennonite village that lived just like this—old-fashioned ways. But hey, they *lived*, Shaun. You know what? They *lived*. Here, some of us live. But some of us just . . . just scum . . . That's the way it is.

S: You want to explain to the folks at home what a crew is?

H: Crew. Well, a crew is, Shaun—I guess you could say some solid people, huh? Like guys like Eddie and Heartbeat. Like Eddie's done time with my uncle, right? Which you probably know. And uh, you gotta remember, Shaun—I come from a family that's got lots and lots of power, too, eh? Lots of power. And it's funny, eh, 'cause I learned about a crew—it's about guys, girls, doesn't matter—that'll stick together, like real solid . . . Funny you ask me that, Shaun—because down here we have a little bit of it. *You* know that . . . But then we have some people who just don't care . . .

S: Hawk, you said Eddie was in jail with your uncle . . . You want to tell me about him?

H: Um . . . my uncle got shot in 1997. Shot in the head and everything. By a fellow named Kenny Murdoch. And they wrote an article about my uncle, about the gangster world and the Mob world, guns and drugs and everything—the whole nine yards. But they didn't write in the articles about how he fed Hamilton and how he fed all the homeless . . . and they don't talk about none of that, you know what I mean?

I told you how I spent the $10,000 on the streets of Toronto and Hamilton and handed out winter coats and boots and long johns . . . They don't talk about stuff like that my uncles have done, my dad's done, and my brothers . . . that's what bothers me.

S: Do you want to tell us his name?

H: Johnny Papalia.

S: You were in jail when he died?

H: Yes. Yes, I was, Shaun . . . And then, it all broke loose—1998. Guess who gets shipped to Collins Bay Pen? Kenny Murdoch . . . and that was a real bad scene, Shaun . . .

(Hawk tells me how Kenny Murdoch tried to get the jump on him by shanking him in the gym, but that the blade got stuck in his arm and Hawk was able to pull it out and stab Murdoch twenty-two times before retreating to his cell and stitching up his wound with a needle and thread. Somehow Murdoch survived, however, and was transferred to Kingston Pen, far away from Hawk.)

S: Do you know why he went at your uncle?

H: Yeah, Shaun. 'Cause he was the top. He was the godfather for Canada. That's the bottom line—that's it: He was *the man* . . . I don't know. Still today, my brother Gino doesn't, uh . . . he doesn't talk to me about it. So I don't know the whole, uh, throw down of it . . . I know there's things my brother hides from me—'cause I'm the baby of the family. It's like my brother says, I've always been the fucking nut of the family too, and that's 'cause there's things I believe in, eh? I believe in a lot of respect: You don't want to give it, I'll come and fucking take it, you know what I mean? . . . Shaun, there's history about me: I was the only guy in the city of Toronto to punch out fifteen cops in one week . . .

(Hawk describes how once, from a Monday to a Friday, he tracked down fifteen policemen who had beaten up some of his crew, and punched them all out, then got arrested on Saturday morning. He then tells me several other stories involving him beating up various bikers and drug lords.)

S: Uh . . . I heard you say the other day that . . . well, your addiction has always been scrapping . . .

H: Yeah . . . That's my rut, Shaun.

S: You never got into the drugs and booze too hard.

H: No, I never ever smoked a drug in my life, not even a marijuana joint. I take children's Aspirin for a headache and I'm stoned for two days. That's how clean my body is.

S: Do you think you've gotten over your addiction to scrapping?

H: Yeah, I could say that. I can honestly say, yeah I do deal with it different and I do step back and think between right and wrong. Yeah, I can say that.

S: Like that day you were mad at me, you could have chopped my head off right away. But you stopped long enough to let me try to talk to you.

H: That's right—that's what I mean. If I come right at you, you just talk to me straight up. I don't want nothing BS bullshit going on. Speak to me like I'm speaking to you: I'm asking you, now answer me—no "maybe" or "might be," just say yes or no. And that's why I got so much high respect for you, Shaun. And I do, I really respect you a lot. And I hope we're friends for a long time, I'll tell you the honest truth. It's because I've noticed that a lot about you—you're very straightforward. It's the way I think Canada—the country of Canada—needs to turn back to, Shaun.

S: Okay, can I ask you . . . Ah, as far as I can see—having known you only five months—there's a big fear factor surrounding you. You're good at intimidating, you know that . . . Are you ever scared of anybody?

H: I . . . I don't know, Shaun . . . I've never . . . To be honest with you, I don't really know about . . . how do you say this . . . atmospheres of, of . . . uh, nervyness—ah, uh . . . fear or frightness, uh . . . you know, I don't really know, Shaun—to be honest with you . . . It's like, Shaun . . . you know what Christmas Day is like? You know what it's like to have a birthday?

S: Uh . . . I mean, I know what it was like for me when I was a kid— that feeling . . .

H: Okay, see—I don't know. So you talk about feelings, you talk about, uh, birthdays—or *I* talk about birthdays—Christmases, and uh, *giving* and . . . uh, opening our Christmas presents and, uh, opening beneath the tree and all that . . . hmm—I've watched some good movies about that . . . you hear what I'm saying? That's as far as I can go . . . But you ask me a question about shanking someone I'll tell you all about the fuckin' rush . . .

S: You think, like, uh, maybe you never had anything to lose? Again I don't want to put words in your mouth . . .

H: Anything to lose . . . Uh . . . What can I really lose? Do I have *life*, Shaun? What's life? *You* can tell *me* . . . but can I tell you what life is? Let me sit here and tell you what life is, Shaun, without anything with a rush—I can't do it . . . But you could do that for me, *couldn't* you?

S: I think so . . .

H: Yeah. You could tell me about life, about, uh, atmospheres of Christmas morning, or uh, you know, uh, uh, Christmas Eve when we used to give all those presents away . . . then where was Hawk? Back in the gang and underneath the bridge, you know what I'm saying? Do you hear what I'm saying, Shaun? It was about "Here you go," you know? "I can make you right." And why did I make everything right, Shaun? Because I knew it was right to make right for somebody. But was it right for me to have rightness and everything, I would not know. Do you follow what I'm saying, Shaun?

S: Uh . . .

H: Why do I go out and spend $10,000? Why would I go and do this? You seen me do things around here, Shaun—with my chainsaw and everything.

S: You gave me the frame for my house . . .

H: Because that's *right* to me. But you come and do that for me . . . "Take it the fuck away!" Because, why? Because I don't know what that is. You follow what I'm trying to say, Shaun?

S: I, I . . .

H: You come up to me and say, "Hawk, come on let's go, I'm going to buy you a big something." You ain't buying me fuck all! 'Cause that's what's right to me, eh, Shaun—and it's very very wrong.

S: There's one thing I'm confused about. You had this powerful, strong family. Why—when you were in gangs—were you on the street, rather than living the life that . . . you know, your uncle had?

H: Why? Because, Shaun, when I got into the gangs—and this is where I'm going to straighten out your confusion—when I got into the gangs, Shaun, I went too hard and too fast—so for me to step back and slow down into a family life, I couldn't do it, Shaun. If there was a problem, Shaun, guess what happened? I'd blow the fucker away right there in front of his kids and everybody.

I was so good, Shaun, that I was worser than a hit man. You know what I mean? Okay? You know, hit men screw up and leave things behind—but when it came to that kind of thing it was so *right* to me. You go in and do something, Shaun, at a home or something, well I, I gotta fuckin' take it *all* out. Wouldn't bother me . . .

S: I understand why they were nervous.

H: Riiight . . . And that's what the gangs did to me. 'Cause I got into that rush . . . Punching out fifteen cops? I had no remorse, Shaun, about the law: This man has gone to school, college, training to become an officer of the law to protect the innocent, and I'm out breaking their legs, necks—and that's fucked up, Shaun! My uncle told me—all the old boys told me—you're worser than a hit man . . . And that's just the way it was for me.

S: You, uh, you think you ever want to have a family of your own?

H: (*Pause.*) Good question, Shaun . . . I really don't know, Shaun. I really don't know . . . I, I, uh. That's a heavy question, brother. I think . . . try to follow me here, Shaun—I'm going to try to say this right . . . In the world itself, I think it would be something I'd really like to enjoy and do—you follow what I'm saying? But in the right world of *my* world . . . is it something that I can do? In our society and our world, it is the right thing—to have a wife and babies—you know what I mean? Especially with *my* nationality. But . . . Shaun, have you ever noticed that I . . . I run a real tight life for myself here. Have you noticed that about me?

S: Yeah.

H: I try not to break boundaries, because I don't know about those boundaries. I've been doing that all my life. So you talk about a family? In the world I guess, yeah, I would like to have a family. But in *my* world? Would a family be right? Would it be something I'd be able to understand, and learn about?

S: Is it something that you'd be good at?

H: Exactly, Shaun. Exactly. See, Shaun . . . so speaking to somebody like you—or some other friends I know that, that, have a wife or children or have gone here or done that—you men and you ladies can actually stand there and say, "Yeah, that was a great experience," you know? But *me?* What's it like to hold a baby, Shaun? You know people tell me, by word of mouth, it's the most beautiful thing in the world. I can tell you what it's like to hold a .38 special snub nose and blow someone's brains out—you follow what I'm saying Shaun?

S: Do you think . . . and I might be a bit flaky here . . . that you have that kind of love in you—to have a wife and kids?

H: Uh . . . Love is, uh—for me, Shaun—it's very deep, eh? . . . You talk about knowing love. Yeah, I know love. But love to me is very very very solid. It's like . . . bud says, "Yeah, Hawk, I'm going to be there," then shows up four days later. Whoa-wha-whoa-whoawhao! I will slap you right fuckin' out because of that. The only thing for my excuse, Shaun, is if you're dead. You don't show up, you give me some excuse. That's not good enough for me. So I say to him, "Are you dead? No?" *(Laughs.)* . . . You follow what I'm saying, Shaun? So I have a really big thing about that . . . About love, and loyalty. It's gotta be real real. It's real deep for me . . . So I guess, yeah I guess you could say—

S: I guess why I ask you—if you don't mind me cutting in for a sec . . .

H: Yeah. Yeah, go ahead . . .

S: The way you're talking about, um . . . the love and respect, or whatever, of your brothers and of, of what you feel for people, and bringing people things even though you don't want anything back . . .

H: Well, see that's how much love I have, Shaun. But that's different, because it's love that I have *given*. But you ask me about love for *my receiving of me*, that's totally different, Shaun . . .

S: Okay—but that is what having a child is—is to give and not expect anything in return.

H: So something takes place with the kid and all that, with the school-teachers and all that, and I go in there and break his fuckin' hands . . .

S: That's a problem . . .

H: That's not love, Shaun.

S: Okay, I hear you.

H: So my love for human life, for anything, for a . . . an ant, a worm, a wildlife . . . I love that! You know that, Shaun. I've talked to you before about that. But that's the love that I have *given*, that I have, for love—out in the universe, you know what I mean? But love to *receive?* Wow! Fucking wow! You're talking like a time bomb, brother. Because loving . . . to *receive*—say, if I have a baby or, or a boy or a girl and "I love you, Daddy" and kiss and all that, and that's something I *receive*, and then the schoolteacher does something, I break his fucking hands, wreck the school, punch out the principal . . . You hear what I'm saying, Shaun?

S: I do. I do.

H: So that is a love that I have received, but then that's not a love that I have given back, 'cause I'm stuck on learnin' about the love-receiving . . .

S: And it gets all fucked up.

H: Riiiight. See all my love is really a hundred percent really *giving* the love *out*, eh, Shaun? So . . . yeah, like . . . I'm a big, big lonely wolf. You know that of me, Shaun. I'm a real lonely wolf, and that's the reason. There's a lot of things that I really don't know in life. People always say, Hawk, you're so very intelligent. Yeah, I am intelligent . . . I'm a very intelligent man about all kinds of stuff—but when you want to get down to *love* and *receiving?* Fuck! Yeah, right! I wouldn't even know what to do. You know what I mean? So . . . You know when you got an old lady—a girlfiend, a wife, a fiancée—you give that love so much . . . but to *receive* that love, what is that? . . . What *is* that?

S: Are you asking me straight?

H: Yeah, Shaun. What is that? That *receiving!* What *is* it?

S: Uh . . . to me it's the second part of giving it, but that's . . . not what it is to you.

H: Right, but, receiving it is for, what for you? Shaun?

S: It, uh . . .

H: Like have you ever had a tear come to your eye because of love so strong that came back to you?

S: Absolutely.

H: See, I could not tell you that . . . I'd probably have a fuckin' heart attack if that really happened in my life. All I've ever known is just . . . life, the real life, that's in the real world out there, is just a real *battle* world, eh?

S: Are you happy?

H: I'm very happy, Shaun . . . day by day, minute by minute, second by second. It's just about staying out of everything—the friction, the violence, the action, the roller coaster, the . . . whatever you want to call it. You know what I mean? Business, whatever. You know, I got no charges, no friction, no excitement, I got nothing. All I have is just me, my trailer and my countryside here. That's a great feeling, Shaun, you know what I mean? Nothing to look to, nothing to fall on that I have to have responsibility to take care of. No overhead, over me, no . . . no over *nothing*, Just me and God. That's it. That's all I got. And I am really really happy. Shaun. You can't beat that, brother.

S: Hell, you almost made *me* happy there.

H: Yep.

S: Well, maybe that's a good place to end this.

(I turn off the tape recorder, then have one more beer while Hawk drinks another Coke. Hawk asks if I can bring him a copy of the tapes and I tell him I'll make sure to. He tells me that it was good to talk about these things,

and wishes me luck with my book. He recommends I not interview anyone else down here as they're sure to tell me lies. I thank him for the advice and take my leave. I feel a sense of relief as I walk back to my shack, but also as if these minicassettes are a burden I don't necessarily want.)

April 17

I got some food from the food bank today, and so Bonnie has decided to cook dinner for us over at her place. According to her, there's still a lot to be done to finish her new house—she wants a walk-in closet, the wood panelling inside redone so it all matches, and a latch on the door that looks more Victorian. The captain's bed that she got Calvin to build is too high for him to climb into, and she's marked off an "alcohol-free zone" around her shack with some two-by-fours laid down on the ground.

She starts to prepare the fish fillets with rice and vegetables as I sit just beyond the zone, talking with her until Calvin comes strutting home from a hard day's work. "Hey, little brother!" he calls out, and tries to do a jig in the road.

"Oh, great!" says Bonnie, throwing down the stick she was using to stir the rice. "He's fucking drunk."

It takes Cal so little to get drunk these days, and Bonnie so little to get mad.

She yells at him for a while, grabs her dog and a curiously full bag of clothes, shouting, "I'm leaving you, Cal!" then stomps over to the prefab next to Randy, where Calvin's stuff is still stored.

"Shit," I say. "Guess I'm making dinner."

I start to cook the fish while Calvin gets more and more frantic, pacing and saying, "Aw shit, b'y . . . aw man . . . aw jeez," charging around like he does when there's booze in his blood and trouble in his head—like somebody's wound him all the way up and he's spinning toward the edge of the table, his little legs turning, shoulders bulging.

"Just stay cool. Why don't you eat something?" This isn't going to happen. Even at the best of times he won't eat if he's got a drink in him. "She might come back." I say, and right on cue, here comes Bonnie—stomping back over to the barrel.

"And I'm not coming back!" she says. "I'm not like these other women down here who say, 'I'm leaving you,' then come back the next day. You got it, Cal?"

I nod as if she's talking to me, and she stomps back over to the pre-fab, arms flailing in the air like downed hydro wires. Calvin groans. "I'm going to get water," I say. "Be good. Stir the rice or something."

"Bonnie never fucking lets me stir anything," he slurs, and I go off to get some water. When I get back, Calvin and Spider are rolling around on the ground punching each other—Calvin doing more of the rolling, Spider more of the punching—and it's not easy to get them apart. Finally I pick Cal up in a bear hug, and Spider stands there rocking side to side, fists tight as fisherman's knots. As I tighten my grip on Calvin I growl into his ear, "Stop it, Cal. Or I'll never let you go."

The ridiculousness of this seems to slow him down a bit. Olivia pulls Spider away and I take Calvin back over to the fire barrel

"What was that about?" I say, putting him in a chair. But he is already gone—his eyes squinting into nothing, his body curling toward the ground. And anyway, I know what it's about. It's about trying to beat out the beating inside you—to cover it with bruises and blood. I open the door and help him in before he passes out, then sit there eating fried fish and burned rice with vegetables, in front of the House That Cal Built.

April 18

A week or so ago a girl named Claire, who used to live in Tent City, burned to death in a warehouse across the tracks. There's a service for her today at the Good Shepherd, but since I didn't know her, I walk around downtown instead.

I come back in through the gates at five o'clock, and right away I can tell things are bad. The hood of a wrecked car is smoking from a fire some of the new lost boys have set. There are a lot of crackheads here from outside Tent City. It's a hot evening, and in honour of Claire every-one's getting as drunk, angry and stupid as possible, even those who didn't know her.

Fucked up as he was, I managed to convince Calvin to go to work this morning, so he'd stay out of trouble. I'm just hoping I've made it home before him.

I walk through a crowd of drunken bruisers around Eddie's place, then over to Sluggo who's standing in front of his shack with his arms crossed.

"What's up, Sluggo?"

"Fucking crackheads," he says. "They're going on about tearing people's shacks down, you know? Not mine, though. No, sir."

"Try to get them to avoid mine, too."

"I'll see what I can do."

And now a fire truck has appeared on the main road. I figure someone on the overpass called in the smoke that's rising from the hood of the car in the clearing. But the truck drives all the way down and stops by Randy's prefab. As I approach, I can see Marty behind the fire barrel, crouching over something on the grey hard ground. He stands up and I see that it's a body, curled up like an injured child, shirtless and bleeding. Calvin's body.

"Shit!" I yell as the firemen surround him. I try to get through them, then throw my bag down and start circling the circle of firemen. I look over and see Bonnie standing in front of the house he built. "Shit!" I yell at her.

And now everyone is coming over, trying to talk to the firemen, getting in the way, dogs trying to get at Calvin on the ground. The paramedics arrive as I walk over to Bonnie. "What the hell happened?"

"I'll tell you later, Shaun," she says. Bonnie only refrains from talking when you need her to tell you something. I want to strangle her.

"No," I say. "Tell me now."

"He was up on Randy's roof. And he was drunk . . . I used Julie's cellphone to call the ambulance."

"You mean they knew? Everyone drinking over at Eddie's, all these fucking assholes knew Cal was bleeding on the ground?"

"Can you go to the hospital, Shaun? I can't go."

"That's fine," I say. "Just tell me what happened."

"He came home and he wanted to talk to me, but he was all fucked up. And then, I don't know why, he climbed up on Randy's roof. He was dancing around and he just sort of—you know—let go."

It takes a particular kind of man to work on a roof all day then come home and fall off one. A heartbroken man.

I get in the back of the ambulance and sit on a stool looking upside down at Calvin's face. He is strapped to a board. His neck is in a brace, with two broad strips of tape across his head. His eyes are glassy, but he's conscious.

"Hey, Cal."

"Fuuccck, b'y!"

We roll out of Tent City and with every little bump he lets out a moan and a string of obscenities. Every big one, he yells and writhes against the neck brace. When we cross on to Lakeshore the paramedic starts asking him questions.

"Do you know your name?"

"Fuck! My name's Calvin! It hurts, b'y. Take this fucking thing off!"

"Do you know what day it is, Calvin?"

I have to think about it, but Calvin says, "Fuck! It's Thursday, b'y. It hurts! Take this thing off!"

"How old are you, Calvin?"

This one, I know—since his birthday was just last month.

"I'm fucking 49, b'y. I want to turn over. It hurts!"

"You'll just have to hang tight," says the paramedic. "At least until the doctor sees you. We have to make sure there's no spinal—"

"I don't care, b'y."

"When were you born, Calvin?"

"March 5, 1956, b'y. Fuck!"

The paramedic looks at me, and says, "That makes you 45, Calvin." Calvin doesn't respond. He's thrashing around on the gurney, wailing about how his ears hurt.

"Did you hear that, Cal?" I say. Calvin's told me his birth date a couple of times but I've never bothered to do the math, and apparently neither has Calvin. "You just got yourself another four years! You're only 45!" Looking at his face, even upside down, he looks at least 65. "That's good news, Cal!"

Calvin, though, seems uninterested. He swears and yells and whines, and by the time we get to Mount Sinai his straps are considerably loosened. The paramedic asks me if Calvin's always like this.

In the waiting room it gets worse. Calvin manages to get his arms free, and then this tattooed ex-biker hardcore homeless man is flailing his hands in the air and howling like an infant. I lean over him and say, "Stop it, Cal! Or I'm gonna slap you!" I hear one of the medics say under his breath, "Why don't you just do it?"

I growl into Calvin's ear, "Listen to me! Nobody here gives a damn about you. You're a crazy, drunk bum to them. And you're being a goof, you got it? You could end up paralyzed if you don't lie still!"

"But it hurts, b'y. Get me out of this fucking thing. It hurts, b'y!"

"Of course it hurts!" I snap. "That's what happens when you jump off a roof onto your head. It hurts!"

"I didn't jump!"

And I remember Bonnie quoting the aikido principle, that if you're thrown, the only choice you have is how you land. But Calvin just might keep on falling, even after he hits the ground.

By the time we roll him into the ER, his neck brace is mostly off and I'm trying to pin him down to the gurney, barking at him about his stupid spinal cord. This goes on for another hour or so, with nurses coming in and testing his vital signs, giving him sedatives, grinding their teeth and glaring as he fights against us. The last thing he says is "I hate fucking hospitals, b'y," then he finally passes out.

I've been sitting in this blue plastic chair for hours, just staring at Calvin as he lies unconscious on the gurney. Actually, I'm mostly glaring at him. The nurse comes in every once in a while and shakes her head with disdain, and I change my expression to one of concern and sympathy. It's a bit much to have two people glaring at him as he sleeps.

He stinks of dirty feet, stale sweat, piss and beer. When we took off his shoes and jeans, dirt spilled onto the mattress and all over the floor, and still nobody's cleaned it up. It looks like we scooped up a little piece of Tent City and dropped it behind this pale blue hospital curtain. I could really do with a drink.

x
x
x

We just took Calvin for another CAT scan. I had to wake him up to get him onto the metal table, and he was still acting like an asshole—I could hear him yelling while I waited outside the door. Everybody says the same thing: "Is he always like this?" and I tell them no, usually he's the most charming, cute little guy you'd ever want to meet.

He was mostly conscious when the doctor came around and put seven large staples in the back of Calvin's head. It feels like I've spent an inordinate amount of the past two days restraining Calvin, while he begs and whines for me to let him go.

"Can you staple his mouth shut while you're at it?" I said to the doctor, who smiled and cocked his head like he was considering it. Calvin didn't get the joke and started yelling that we better not fucking staple his mouth! Then he passed out again and the doctor checked the damage to Cal's back once more before leaving.

So now I'm sitting in this damn chair again, glaring at Calvin's unconscious broken body.

I don't know what we'll do if they discharge him tonight. St. Mike's was full so they took us all the way up here to Mount Sinai. Cal's got no shirt, not to mention socks or underwear.

And I doubt he'll be able to make the hike to Tent City—the doctor says he's got a concussion and some small fractures in his lower back.

x   x   x

They discharge Calvin just after 3 a.m. He's sobered up, and all the nurses are amazed by what a nice, charming guy he is. One of them finds a sweater, some underwear and a pair of socks for him. I have enough money to get us halfway to Tent City by cab, and then I help him hobble the rest of the way.

I get him into the prefab next to Randy's, as Bonnie has already reclaimed the House That Cal Built, and I give him a gulp of rye.

"'Night, little brother," he says. He looks morose and exhausted, and can't lift his head.

Then, as I crawl into bed, the thunder hits. I've never heard a storm like this anywhere. It's as if we're inside the thunder—lightning striking through us like missiles, like the harbour exploding, Sodom burning, God's propane tanks blowing all to hell. I wonder what Bonnie makes of the spirits' indiscriminate power, as she lies there with the walls of her new house shaking.

April 19

There is a definite calm after the storm here today. Everyone is hungover, and Claire is put to rest. Jackie came over to tell me that she's leaving Sluggo again and moving into a women's shelter. Bonnie came around to complain that everybody thinks she just used Cal to get her house built.

"Why would they think that?"

"I won't put up with this shit," she said. "I'm not doing it anymore. He's all yours, Shaun."

But I don't want him. He's in a half-comatose depression, washing down Tylenol tablets with cans of Crest, and I don't want to watch. I don't want to follow him around trying to pick up the pieces, and I don't want to fall apart with him either. When I look at Cal I feel like I'm looking at myself in twenty years, and I'm scared for both of us.

April 21

You might be able to avoid the world down here, but you can't hide from Tent City. It's like all eighty of us live in one big house, and nobody's doing the dishes, nobody's mowing the lawn. You can't stand these maniacs with whom you share the kitchen, the bathroom, the river and the sky, but they are your only friends.

Saturday is not a good day to start losing it, with all the soldiers of God and the weekend crackheads from the other side of the fence. Calvin walks around like a zombie, his eyes lifting once in a while like he's asking me to save him. I want to hit him. He thinks just because I'm here it gives him free rein to stir shit up, stepping glassy eyed into every trouble there is.

Eddie's on another binge.

Sluggo's been drinking since Jackie left.

Jane is here all the time now, and it seems she wants me to teach her all about this life down here. Everybody wants something, has questions, thinks I'm Calvin's brother, Jane's boyfriend, everyone's best buddy. They think if they grab on to me I'll keep our heads above water. They're dead wrong.

x   x   x

I've only been asleep for a couple of hours when Eddie pops the latch and comes into my shack. Sluggo and Calvin are behind him.

"What the fuck do you want?" I say, shielding my eyes from the light.

"A bit hungover, buddy?"

"At least close the damn door, it's bright out there!" They close the door and now the four of us are in darkness. "Okay! Open it, get the hell out, and *then* close it!"

They open the door and Eddie sits down in a chair beside the bed, Sluggo leans against the stove, Calvin is hovering in the doorway.

"Morning," says Eddie, grinning like a kid trying to ask his dad for $20.

"What do you want, Eddie?"

"Calvin wants his percs," he says, still smiling too big. Yesterday Jane got Calvin's prescription filled. She paid $12 for twenty-five Percocet and I told her I'd hold on to them for him so he couldn't glug the whole bottle, or sell it.

"If he wants a couple more he can have 'em," I say, sitting up and staring across the shack at Calvin, who can't quite look at me.

"They're *his* pills," says Sluggo.

"Then why doesn't *he* ask me?" I say, still looking at Calvin.

"Just give 'em to us," says Eddie.

"Get out of here," I say. "And then maybe I'll come talk to you."

"No way. Then you'll have clothes on. Can't put up much of a fight like this—can you, kid?" says Eddie, and laughs at his own deviousness.

"Well, you should know right now, Eddie, you're not getting them."

"That's disrespectful to Calvin," says Sluggo. "They're *his* pills."

"Disrespectful!" I growl, glaring around at all three of them. I don't care if I am naked. I'll fight with my balls hanging out. "You come into my shack while I'm sleeping to try to muscle me, and you think *I'm* being disrespectful?"

"Not muscling you," says Sluggo and steps out into the sunlight.

I turn to Eddie. "If I give 'em to you, Eddie, are you gonna babysit Calvin? Eh? You gonna do that?" Eddie shakes his head, smiling. I never see Calvin with Eddie or Sluggo. They don't even like him. "How much can you get?" I say.

"Three bucks each. Comes to $75. And you can have $20."

"Really? Well, thanks. Now you're not getting them on principle—so drift."

Eddie's the one who taught me to say "drift" properly. He shakes his head and gets up to close the door as Calvin joins Sluggo outside. He pulls up the curtain and sits back down.

"You're still here, Eddie."

He looks at me. "I'm sorry, kid." His knee is bouncing. He tries to stop it, and looks down at the floor.

"How much do you need?"

"Ten bucks."

"Okay," I say and reach into my jeans on the floor. I made some money playing pool last night. "You can take it off a 20 piece."

After I get dressed, I go and find Calvin. I tell him to get his shit together and give him three percs.

"If you sell these and get enough for one rock you'll be pain free for half an hour, and when you come out of it you got nothing. Or, you can take one and be pain free all day, and take another tonight, then one when you wake up. If you fuck up, that's your problem."

"Sure, little brother."

"You're pissing me off, Cal."

"Aw, I know."

April 22

She doesn't knock. The latch on the door slides open easily, like she has a key where there is no lock. I can see the silhouette of her face as she slips inside, trying not to make a sound, like she's getting home late from work and doesn't want to disturb me. The light from the harbour illuminates her from behind.

"Hey baby," she whispers as she steps toward me, the door closing behind her. Although it is dark, I can see her wolf eyes shine. I am exhausted, but my heart is racing. She moves to the bed now, and her blue dress is shimmering. It is made of peacock feathers that produce their own light—blue and green and gold, with eyes all over her body.

"I love you," she says as she descends, and I sob into her hair.

In another dream she cuts into my flesh with her teeth, and pours a can of Coke into the long razor-straight cuts.

"What are you doing?" I say.

"I'm doing lines, sweetie," she says, and kisses me gently.

April 24

It is the end of April, and I swear it snowed today. I saw white powder swirling down from the lowest levels of heaven. It has been colder this week than the whole winter put together.

I wrote all night until the sun came up, page after page, and my wrist didn't hurt at all. I remember laughing, so amazed, like I was finally able to see it all, beautiful and wretched—how the air can be so pure here, on the edge of the city and the lake—and then the wind shifts and the stench comes up like bile. I could see angels of vengeance rising, pigeons diving, vagrants stumbling under the weight of their desperate freedom, my thoughts finally flying . . .

When I woke up this afternoon I threw some bread to the gulls. Then I went over and hung out with Sluggo, watching a little duck couple being all cute in the pond that Jackie dug for them. I had a couple Crests with Eddie, checked up on Cal, talked more to Les about his plans for a sports bar, then came back to my shack, sat down with a cup of coffee Bonnie had made for me, and opened my notebook. I looked down at the page, and my stomach lurched.

A dozen full pages and I can't make out any of it. It is all completely illegible—as if I wasn't writing words at all.

Tell your children not to do what I have done.

x
  x
    x

I know this place is swallowing me. Sometimes I can see it happening, like I'm watching myself on a TV screen, out in the sunlight surrounded by trash, the electrical cord hanging off the back, a pigeon perched on the crooked antenna.

April 25

Today we had what is being generously described as a town meeting, organized by the TDRC for the purpose of discussing a cleanup of Tent City—as well as "any other matters that need addressing." In attendance were the president-elect of the Rotary Club of Toronto, Beric, Cathy Crowe and other members of the TDRC, a few of their earnest activist underlings, and a couple dozen of us Tent City residents.

We ate curry and stew, and Eddie got into a fight with the Brothers over a tub of margarine while the Rotary guy looked on in horror. Bonnie kept trying to read from a stack of notes, using terms like "on the table," and "I'd like to speak to that." But everyone just spoke to everything and drowned her right out for most of an hour while the rest of us looked down at the big round table then up at the sky, thinking, *Isn't this supposed to be one of the benefits of anarchy—that we don't have to have meetings?*

The only thing decided was what had already been decided before the meeting—that on May 11 a cleanup crew, financed by the Rotarians, will come down and get as much of the trash out of here as possible.

x
x
x

I bought a bike from Eddie today. He wanted $20 for it, but you never have to haggle with a crack addict. I gave him $5 as a down payment, then half an hour later he came over and said the bike was mine if I could find another $5 right away. I borrowed $5 off Goran, who was here shooting photos, and rode off to play pool.

On the way I stopped at the clinic for my test results, and all of them were negative.

April 27

After winning some money last night, I rode my new bike to the Stone Cutter's Arms to buy a drink and gaze at the cute bartender a while. She didn't seem to mind too much—she let me carry the kegs and give her pointers on pool and even feigned interest when I tried to explain the differences among scotch, rye, whisky and whiskey.

"Is there any kind of booze you *don't* like?" she said, smiling.

"Sherry," I said, and our eyes met. It felt like something was hovering above the bar—because all of a sudden, by accident, I'd spoken her name. A statement, not a question.

"Yes . . . ?" she said, and her eyelids closed like coins flashing as they fall into a hat.

"I don't like sherry," I said. "Not you—the drink. Sorry . . . uh, but I do like you."

"Oh," said Sherry.

"It's too sweet."

"What?"

"Bingo."

"I *hate* Bingo," said Sherry, her eyes squinting. I was about to explain that Bingo is what we call Canadian sherry, but her reaction to the word was so strong that it stopped me. Apparently my bringing up Bingo wasn't the non sequitur it seemed. For Sherry, this game of dabbers and numbers is relevant to everything bad.

"I hate it," she said again. "It eats people, like drugs do."

"Bingo?" I said.

"Yeah. I know it sounds silly. But people can get addicted to anything."

When Sherry was 14, she began dating the son of her mom's best friend. He was 22, and had just got out of prison, and he was a crack addict. Within a year she'd moved in with him, and by then he'd stopped crack—and started playing bingo instead.

"My mama plays, too . . . I mean she plays all the time. These places are open twenty-four hours. I waited days for him to come home. It feels like I did nothing for six years but wait, and then he took up crack again. I just left him a few weeks ago and I'm never going back. I feel like my life's just started. I want to do everything. I've never even been out of Ontario."

I wanted to ask her if she'd like to do something sometime with me—go to a soup kitchen together, bum some change downtown or just stand around a fire barrel.

Before I could come up with the right words, she said, "I'll never be with an addict again. I'm not wasting any more time."

"Yes," I said. My pulse was racing because of her eyes and the silent humming of her body behind the bar, not because of the drugs. But I thought of her wiping away the white residue I'd left in the bathroom, wondering why I left so quickly, so close to last call.

April 28

Chaos is a gentle, thoughtful dog who knows how to have fun. He is in love with Cleo—Sluggo and Jackie's Rottweiler. She prances for him with a car tire around her neck, and he licks at her legs and smiles. He's also tough, and has a strong sense of personal justice. Chaos could fight anyone, or two—but not three.

Today Jimmy D's dogs got together with Karl's, and all three of them went for him. Randy loves Chaos more than anything in the world. But now Chaos is in the hospital and Randy's got his blood all over him.

"He'll be fine," I say. "We all get shit-kicked once in a while."

"Yeah," says Randy.

The two of us stay up drinking all night, talking about Chaos and Cough-X, and pretty girls who make sadnesss move like blood through your veins.

April 30

I have no idea how, but I seem to have thrown my back out. I lie on the floor of my shack, staring up at the shiny silver ceiling. I am sick to my stomach. I feel like this shack has beaten me with brass knuckles. I didn't know you could throw out your back just from drugs and alcohol. I mean, sure, a heart attack, or a drowning, or choking on vomit—those are all good rock 'n' roll repercussions. But throwing out your back—that's just pathetic.

It's the end of the month, so everybody's coming by to bring me drinks. I lie on the floor, raising my head to talk to them and take sips of beer. I guess it would be kind of funny if it didn't hurt so much. Christians come to my door bearing gifts, and I tell them to come back after the sun has gone down. I show them my teeth.

x
x
x

I don't know what is wrong with me. I should not be lying on the floor in a shack by the river, sick and full of self-pity. I'm supposed to be stronger than that. I've got no excuse. I don't know anyone else down here who had a happy peaceful childhood, loving parents, a university education, a good relationship, the opportunity to see the world and a youth free of incarceration and violence. I am young and healthy, and I'm somehow killing myself in a shantytown. I'm supposed to be a tourist here among the tramps. I came here to write about this place and this life, but can barely prop myself up to scribble even this.

Rambo is passed out spread-eagle in front of my shack, and through the open door I can see Jimmy D trying to drag him by his feet toward the underpass where he sleeps. I have to remember who I am.

x   x
x

When I was 4 years old I came home from my first day of preschool to my father sitting on the front steps, all my stuffed animals surrounding him in the bright afternoon sun: an orange tiger, Bert and Ernie, teddy bears, Super Grover, a giant panda . . . all of them waiting there, sitting on the stairs, to welcome me home. "Welcome home, kid," said my dad. And my mum, who had arranged this whole tableau, squeezed my hand.

I wanted to be a baseball player and a Jedi and a cowboy. Then later I wanted to be an ambulance driver and a fireman. I still want to be a fireman. Just last year I sent away for an application form.

x   x
x

When I was 10 I won first prize in the Commonwealth Essay awards. I wrote about seeing my baby sister being born—or almost seeing it. I munched on carrot sticks in the delivery room until they had to rush me out because of complications, in case she died. My sister was okay. They put her in an incubator, and named her Reilley, and later my mum said that all she could remember was the sound of me chomping on carrots.

x   x
x

When I was 16, my dad and I won the Vancouver Press Club doubles eight-ball championship. The trophy is in my parents' dining room. Two of our dogs and two of our cats are buried in the front yard under a cherry blossom tree.

When I was 18, I left home. I've gone back at least once a year, to see the people I love and to remember who I am. But it's been over two years now, and remembering doesn't cut it.

x   x   x

Sherry, who's only 20, asked me how old I am.

"Twenty-seven," I said.

"That's a good age."

"Jim Morrison died at 27. So did Jimi Hendrix, Janis Joplin and Kurt Cobain."

"But they were fucked up," said Sherry, smiling patiently, as if to ease my silly-boy fears. "They drank and drugged themselves to death." I didn't say anything. "I'd like to see where you live," she said.

"I live in Tent City."

"I know."

"It's kind of crazy down there."

May 1

Chaos came home today. He has bare patches all over him where he's been shaved and stitched. The gash on his nose is still bleeding and he moves slowly. Randy walked him around the old town as if Chaos was a show dog working the runway, and Cleo kept circling them, bringing tennis balls, a headless teddy bear, then her favourite tire. Everyone came out to see them, gathering around with cases of Crest.

"Looks fine," says Eddie.

"Just battle scars," says Heartbeat.

"We've all got battle scars," says Sluggo.

"Cleo thinks it's sexy," says Jackie, who's back "just to visit."

We sit around in a circle, drinking and nudging Chaos curled at our feet.

May 2

There are all sorts of stories about Roger: he's a Balkan warlord, he was with the KGB, he was a Yugoslavian sniper and works as a hit man here.

All of this could be true. He walks like a soldier, has hard eyes, and seems fearless.

Roger lives right on the water by the Cherry Street entrance. He built a dock over the edge of the canal, then built a house on top of it. He has three rooms with high ceilings and a garage out back. With the hydro he's tapped from the Cherry Street drawbridge, he runs electric lights, a big-screen TV, VCR and CD player, and is working on an indoor Jacuzzi. He's one of my closest neighbours, though I'd never actually talked to him until today.

I broke my stereo last night, and Roger can fix anything, so Calvin took me over there. When we knocked on his door, Roger was installing programs onto a computer. He took us to see his rabbit hutch.

"The bunnies good, very interesting. Look the bunnies, very good."

We looked at the bunnies for a while, as he tried to coerce them into having sex.

"The bunny screw, very good. Very interesting, the bunny screw."

Roger took apart my stereo and put it back together with a couple of new components. He seems to have parts of everything imaginable. The TV was on, and Calvin asked what he was watching.

"I watch nothing. But maybe bunny show arrive. Very interesting. For me I find very interesting, the bunny show." He barely looked at what he was doing, even while he was soldering. When he'd finished, the stereo worked better than ever.

"What can I give you?" I said.

"Nothing for work. One dollar for parts. I buy bunny food. You see them eat, very interesting." I have no doubt the man is completely lethal.

May 4

Everybody seems to be getting along right now. The gangs of new kids are probably having their own problems, but that's got nothing to do with me. I'm not new anymore.

The Brothers still dislike me. They don't hassle me anymore, but won't talk to me either. Then of course there's Hoyt, who creates in me an uncharacteristic urge to punch him in the head. He got a new puppy last week, but within a day he was taking out his demented aggression on it. The old boys took the puppy away from him and told him to leave Tent City for a while. They won't hit him because he's part of the old crew and has a glass jaw.

Ex-mayor Karl is still around, too. But everyone just ignores him. Except for me—I shout "Boo!" at him whenever he comes near. I'm lucky there's no reason for me to fight now—with my back like this I'd get clobbered.

x
x
x

I'm out by my fire barrel when I hear the *Hockey Night in Canada* anthem like a siren song in the darkness.

I follow the sound along the canal and through the trees toward Les's trailer, homing in on the blue glow of a TV screen. The volume is cranked all the way up but there's no one around. It's kind of eerie: game two of the Eastern Conference semifinal just beginning, the TV glowing out in the open surrounded by darkness. The crowd is cheering, the puck is dropped, cars are going by on the highway, the stars are shining above and no one is watching. I sit in one of the chairs out there, and lean forward to turn down the volume.

"Volume's broken," says Les, materializing out of the darkness to sit down next to me.

"Sounds like it's working too well," I shout over the announcer.

"Yeah-hmm. You could say that."

We pull our seats back about 20 feet so we don't have to yell. I go and get a bottle for us to share, and Les rolls some smokes.

"Toronto's the better team, um-hmm, but it's gotta go seven games, and Ottawa has to win this one—no doubt about it," he says. "The play-offs are fixed, hee-yeah." Les is convinced that everything is fixed.

"Want to put some money on it?"

"Better than that, hey-um—put a beer-can chicken on it."

I told Les about beer-can chicken a while ago, and he's been all jazzed up to try it. It's a pretty simple recipe: all you need is a can of beer and a chicken. You open the beer, drink half of it, then insert it up the chicken's ass. You sit the chicken in a bed of coals so it's perched on the can, and baste the skin in beer. The beer boils and steams, and the chicken cooks from the inside out and the outside in.

"It's a bet, Les," I say, and shake his hand. "One beer-can chicken, on Toronto."

"Let's make it tomorrow," says Les, pulling off the bottle. "You got to teach me how, hmm-hee."

The idea of teaching Les something as simple as how to cook a chicken is a bit ridiculous. After all, this is his TV we're watching—the wires running underground all the way to the drawbridge, where he's tapped into the same source as Roger. The only problem is that the draw mechanism is slightly faulty. When heavy trucks drive over it, the bridge pops up a bit, and the bells start clanging and the hydro shuts off even though the bridge isn't rising. Then the city workers have to come out and reset it. The last time they were here, Les went over and explained to them how to fix the bridge, but they weren't really getting it and it occurred to him that his knowledgeable advice might seem a bit suspicious, so he let it drop.

"Fucking city workers!" he says. "I'm going to go fix it myself tomorrow, hm-yeah. All's I need is the right tools, hey-mmm . . . Who'd I bet on again?"

"Ottawa."

"Shit. Why?"

"Something about a fix."

"It's all fixed, hee-yeah."

Toronto wins, and Les cheers—having once again forgotten who he bet on. I remind him, but he still howls and whistles. "Guess I'm buying the chicken, hmm-yeah!" he yells over the TV. "And the beer!" We get in his big pink truck for a victory lap around Tent City, yelling and honking the horn, and a few people come out of their shacks, thinking the baloney truck is here.

"Toronto!" yells Les. "Beer-can chicken!"

"Baloney!" I shout, and we do another lap.

May 5

Les got a couple of six-packs and two roasting chickens, and we drank the beer and burned our fingers getting them to sit up in the coals. The beer boiled, the skin darkened, and by the time the wings were shaking in the steam, Eddie, Karen, Jackie and Sluggo were all there, too, forks in their hands.

"Hmm-yee!" said Les. "Best damn chicken I ever ate."

"Yeah, it's good," said Karen. "You think we'll get poisoned from the aluminum?"

"Nah," I said.

"We should try a turkey next time," said Les. "King-can turkey, yeah-hmm."

"Vodka pig! . . . Or whisky cow!"

We debated which kinds of booze best suited the asses of which animals until the chicken was all gone, the beer was drunk, and our fingers were sticky as sin.

May 7

At about 3:30 Monday morning Karen wakes up with a sharp pain in her gut. The first thing she thinks is "beer-can chicken." She wriggles around, goes fetal and kicks at Eddie until he wakes up.

"Fucking chicken!" she says.

"What?" says Eddie, still mostly asleep.

"Shaun poisoned us! What the hell's he thinking, sticking a beer up the ass of a chicken?"

"Chicken was good," mumbles Eddie. "Go back to sleep," and he passes out until 4:30 when he gets up jonesing and goes to do a crack run.

Karen is drifting in and out of sleep but her stomach is still hurting. Eddie is smoking rock. He kisses her on the cheek. "Suck it up, darling," he says gently. There are people at the door—there are always people at his door, because he can score any time of night—and he goes out once more. He's still gone when the pain jolts her awake at 6 a.m. It's far worse, and she starts yelling at the walls: "Damn you, Shaun! Damn you and your stupid . . ." And like a blinding flash, a kick from deep inside, something suddenly occurs to her. She stumbles out of bed and over to Sluggo and Jackie's.

Sluggo is also having trouble sleeping, not because of stomach pains, but because of a crackhead who's been knocking on his door. Around 5 a.m., the guy had been banging on my door, yelling for Eddie.

When I told him to drift, he went over to Sluggo and Jackie's, and Sluggo told him the same, but then couldn't get back to sleep.

And now there's someone knocking again. On his feet, with a piece of wood in his hand, Sluggo whips the door open and bellows, "Fuck right off!" his arm cocked to strike.

Karen is standing there, sweating in the cold. "I don't think it's the chicken," she says, and staggers into the shack.

Two crackheads in a white truck drive Karen and Jackie to St. Mike's. By the time she's been admitted, undressed and washed down by a nurse, it's 8:40 a.m., and Karen says, "I think I'm having a baby."

The nurse nods and tells her to push. Before she can say it a second time, however, Karen yells like she's insane with rage at the whole world, her breath catches, and her newborn son appears, held up glistening before her.

Eddie isn't there. The doctor isn't there. Just three exhausted women and a newborn baby boy. When Karen finally holds him to her chest, all she can think is how big he is, how enormous. Although he's barely 5 pounds, she can't believe he fit inside her. She feels so small, like a child.

As she kisses the top of her son's head, Eddie—back at their shack—crashes into consciousness like he's falling from heaven into Tent City. He hits the floor and looks at the clock. It's 8:43 and—as he tells me later—he knows his son has been born. He can feel it.

"Caleb," says Karen, kissing her baby's thin blond hair, though she's never even thought of the name before now. "Caleb . . . How would you spell it?"

x   x
 x

Eddie is coming back from the hospital, through the gates of Tent City, just as I'm heading out for the final in my pool league championships.

"Congratulations," I say, unsure if this is the right thing to offer—I've never talked to him about whether or not he wants this baby.

"God I feel great!" says Eddie, with his charming terror of a smile, and goes rushing off to tell everyone else how great he feels.

On the way up to the bar, I buy a bottle of Canadian Baby Champagne to bring to Eddie and Karen (fitting, I think), and then stop at the library to check my e-mails . . .

x
 x
  x

I'm coming to T.O. and would like to get together next Monday, she writes. *Maybe for dinner or some drinks.*

I stare at the screen for over an hour—far exceeding the library time limit. When somebody asks how much longer I'll be, I growl and show my teeth. And finally I write something—words flashing onto the screen like hands reaching above the waves:

Dear Darlin',
I'm pretty much on the edge right now, and what I told you last time we met still stands: If nothing's changed (for the gooder) concerning us, and you just want to see how I'm doing, please don't bother. If, on the other hand, you have anything in that prickly sweet pineapple heart of yours that would make this life more liveable, I would love to see you. And so I'll leave it up to you. You can just write back with a yes or no.
Love, Shaughnessy

And now, of course, my greatest fear is the word "no." Because I have hope, yes Lord I have hope. I can feel it killing me.

But I can kill, too. I get all hopped up and take down the eight ball again and again. I win every one of my games, but our team still loses. We come in second overall, and I couldn't care less. What is pool when there's hope hanging like an eight ball over the corner pocket? What is eight ball when there are babies being born?

May 8

"I feel great!" says Eddie for the twentieth time, drinking from the bottle of Baby Canadian. "I mean, I really didn't know. I wasn't ready for this, eh? Thought we had a lot more time. But man, I feel great. He's beautiful? Just perfect." Eddie seems calm—a bit too calm—like a man moments before he spontaneously combusts. Nothing moves but the arm passing me the bottle. I drink a quarter of it in one long pull.

"You going to be able to do this?" I say. The Children's Aid Society

(CAS) has already taken the premature baby into custody, though Caleb is still lying in an incubator where Eddie and Karen can touch him through the holes in the Plexiglas.

"No doubt about it!" says Eddie a bit too loudly. "I *have* to do this! Enough fucking around! Gonna get off the crack and get out of here—go through detox, go through rehab. Whole fucking thing! My son Shane's already got a job lined up for me—hell, he's had it open for me for five years. I could have gone any time—and now I've got no choice, right? We're getting that kid no matter what they say! We just got to make an effort, you know, a real effort, for him. For Caleb.

"God, I can't make it real yet, in my head—you know what I mean?" He isn't calm anymore, but hasn't exploded yet either. He's up and moving, like he doesn't know what to do with his body. He takes a glug of champagne, a hit of crack.

"I'm telling all of you right now!" he says, waving his arm around at the four others who are smoking rock in his shack. "I'm quitting! No more runs, no more bullshit! I'm getting out of here. Couple of days— Karen's out of the hospital and we're gone! No way I'm screwing up." None of them say anything. The guy in the corner packs a stem and hands it to Eddie, who lights it and breathes in. "And you!" he says on the exhale, turning to me and laughing. "You're going to have to find your powder somewhere else."

"Sure, Eddie," I say. I see flashes of a computer screen, a heart monitor, a transparent box. I take a shot of someone's rye.

"You want this place?" he says suddenly, looking at me and smiling.

"What?"

"When we leave, you can move in here. It's bigger than your place, got a double bed." There's a dozen of Eddie's crew, friends he's known for twenty years, some of them without even a tent, who'd kill for this place. "You should have it. You're our friend—like a true friend. You should have our place."

"Thanks," I say, honoured but unsure. Unsure of everything.

More crackheads keep coming by to smoke, and they don't seem to want to talk about the baby. When the champagne and rye is gone I give Eddie a hug and a thump on his back. "Congratulations," I say.

"I haven't done nothing yet."

"But you will."

May 9

On the day Caleb was born—and not long after the lady from CAS had left the hospital room—Eddie called the *Toronto Star*. A reporter was there within the hour, and now the story is everywhere and TV crews and journalists keep coming down to Tent City. Eddie tells them he and Karen are going to get their shit together, that Caleb would be better off with his true parents, that they love him with all that's left of their souls. Karen nods and agrees, but she's been pretty quiet since she got out of hospital. You wouldn't believe she just had a baby. You can't see the slightest hint of it, except for her eyes darting like birds for openings in the roof. Eddie is bouncing off the walls.

"You okay, Ed?" I say. It's dark again, and we're back in his shack. I'm trying to get him over to my place so I can do an interview with him.

"What do you think?" he says with a harsh, nervous laugh.

"I think you're bouncing off the walls," I say. I'm bouncing a bit, too. I can't face going to the library.

For two weeks he's been saying he wants to sit down with me and get stuff off his chest, but the time's never been right. Now, of course, there's a lot more stuff to get off. "Time's right," he said a few hours ago. "You bring the booze and I'll bring the drugs."

But time shifts fast for a guy like Eddie, even when it doesn't move at all. Just when we're ready to start, he needs to do one more run. It should take him about ten minutes, but on this—the worst night he could possibly get busted—he ends up sitting for an hour and a half in the back of a cop car with $100 worth of crack cocaine in his underwear.

"That would have been bad," Eddie says, when he finally returns to his shack. "It's hard to get custody when you're in jail."

I've been sitting here with Karen and a bunch of crackheads. I've been waiting and worrying about Eddie, itching to start our interview, and trying not to think about the electronic message waiting for me out in the ether. And now he's come back without any powder for me, and he's talking like a machine gun firing and his bouncing brain seems to ricochet through everything. There are four different crack pipes going, twenty-one empty Crest cans in the doorway and a half-bottle of rye left. "It's not time, young Shaun," he says. "It's not the night to talk."

The taste of a crack pipe is a dirty, metallic, chemical taste, the smell like burnt aluminum and boiled Coca-Cola. If you're using a tube, you pull in very, very slow, controlled, like you're barely breathing, and the smoke flies in through a wind tunnel to your brain. Since Eddie's child has become a physical reality, he is less adamant about fathering me. This is the only time I've done crack since that first time with Eddie, when it made me sick to my stomach. He couldn't get me any powder, and if he's quitting, I figure I'll just go out with him on his last rock 'n' roll. These are my excuses.

I lean over to a woman named Kiwi as she exhales a convex mirror of smoke. "You have nice clothes," I say. "How do you keep 'em so nice?" Kiwi sleeps on a subway grate downtown.

"There's no excuse for not keeping up your appearance," she says. "I just go into Goodwill, and walk out with new clothes. Simple as that—in with the old, out with the new." She cackles and pinches my cheek. "That's why they call 'em *change* rooms."

And suddenly I can see this room waiting for me—this change room, where everything will be different. But I don't know where it is.

"I wasn't jonesing at all in the hospital," says Karen, cleaning out a screen for her pipe. She looks as if she's about to say something else, but doesn't. She doesn't talk about Caleb at all since she got out, except to say how much he looks like Eddie—those grey-blue eyes, that tough Brazil-nut nose, and his feet! His feet are just like Eddie's. It's as if this is how she makes it real, pulls pieces off her man, her life, tries to hold them in her arms. Unlike Eddie, she won't talk about quitting drugs. She just says that she didn't need them when she was in the hospital, as if she can live the rest of her life in there, in that hospital room, with her stormy-eyed sweethearts.

"Well, good," says Eddie, blowing blue smoke into the air. "'Cause I'm quitting, and if you're still going to do it, you'll have to get it some-where else."

She waves her hand in the air and says, "Whatever, Eddie. When they tell us what they want, I'll do it—okay? But not till then."

"I'm gonna stop *before* they tell me," says Eddie. "Then they'll say, 'Look, he did it without us telling him to—he must *really* be serious.' And if I do every goddamn thing and they still take Caleb—you know what I'm going to do? I'll go down to CAS and blow up the whole fucking building—boom!" There are more crackheads coming in the door, and now Eddie's standing over a plate of lit candles in the centre of the shack. "Boom!" he yells. "Kill all those motherfuckers, bring down the whole building! 'Cause if I don't get that kid, that's it for me—I got no reason at all! I gotta step up! I gotta do this! If I don't it's *all* coming down!"

"Ah . . . shut up, Eddie," says Karen, passing a flame over some residue. Eddie is bouncing now. For the past couple of days you can see this part of him, like a hologram of himself, bouncing from one solid object to another even as he's standing still, phantom pieces of him bursting like chemicals on a heated spoon.

"Man, am I scared!" says Eddie, the way somebody might say, "Boy, is it hot in here!" He starts packing a stem with ash. "Just got one last chance," he says. "One last chance . . ."

Eddie says crack lets you feel nothing at all, but I'm not so sure about that. I know it makes you very high very fast and it becomes easier to ignore the future—the fear of tomorrow and big scary words like "No." The sun is coming up. Eddie and I are standing in his open doorway, trying to keep our balance against each other.

"Hey, Shaun," he says. "You want to come to the hospital with me tomorrow—to see the kid? I mean this morning."

"Really?"

"Yeah. Just you and me—we'll go early. Just the men. I won't want to hold him then—I mean I'll be dying to—but not with all the crack on my hands . . . but we can . . ."

"Yeah, that'd be great, Eddie. Why don't we go to the community centre first. You can take a shower there . . . Then you can hold him."

"Then we can hold him."

Our stained and dirty arms cradle air, like we're holding a baby.

x
x
x

We didn't go to the hospital in the morning, just us men, since Eddie kept smoking crack until he finally passed out around noon. At 6 p.m., Eddie, Karen, Jackie and I piled into Jane's car and she drove us to St. Mike's. It seemed like at any moment Eddie was going to throw the door open and start running alongside the car.

One of Jane's endearing qualities is her inability to drive. She insists, as most bad drivers do, that she's good at it. She took up two spots in the hospital parking lot, and when the attendant asked her to move, Eddie went off on him.

"Cool it, Eddie!" I said, holding him back.

"The fucking goof's being ignorant," he said.

"We're taking up two spots."

"I don't care. I'm going to see my baby."

"Well, just cool it, okay."

Eddie's about as good as Calvin when it comes to hospitals. Instead of buzzing us through the nursery door, the nurse came out from behind her desk. Only two people are allowed to the incubator at a time, and she was probably coming to inform us of this, but all Eddie saw was the door, still locked, between him and his baby, and he started to bang on it, shouting to be let in. I grabbed his arm.

"Quit it, Eddie!"

"She's being ig . . ."

The nurse opened the door, glaring at Eddie

"He's *our* baby," said Karen.

Eddie washed his hands for a long time, and they crossed the room to Caleb's Plexiglas box. There were little round windows in two of the sides. He and Karen reached their hands through and touched Caleb gently, like you'd try to hold the best dream you ever had for fear it would disappear. They stayed that way for a long time, and from across the nursery I could see that Eddie had stopped bouncing. They were still and quiet.

When Eddie came back, Jane went over to join Karen. "How is he?" I said.

"He's beautiful," said Eddie, smiling. "I love him." I nodded. "Shouldn't be in here though. I gotta get him out. Go see him, Shaun," he said. "Go see what I mean."

x
  x
    x

His belly is warm, expanding and contracting under my hand, like I'm holding a heart. His grey ocean eyes are open, and though I know he can't yet see, he is looking right at me.

"He's looking at you," says Karen, and I can feel myself about to crack open, insides spilling onto the nursery floor. I try to take a breath.

"Hi, Caleb," I say. My voice sounds like it's underwater. "It's good to meet you."

"Can you believe he was inside me?" says Karen. "All of him?"

"Can I stay here?" I say.

x
  x
    x

Back in Tent City, everybody crowds into my shack. Jane's bought pizza and beer for us.

"Where's everybody keep going?" she asks.

"To smoke crack."

"Oh, right. Are you doing your drugs?"

I don't answer. Calvin comes over and he and Eddie get into a fight about something stupid. Eddie needs to let off some steam, so I let it go on for a while before I tell them to stop. I tell them to get out of my shack. Jane sticks around, however, and she's still here a couple of hours later, when Eddie comes by with a brand-new mountain bike and asks to stash it in the A-frame behind my place.

"Sure," I say, though I want to tell him he's being an idiot. He's supposed to be turning into a father. "How long you leaving it here?"

"Just till morning. I've got a meeting with the CAS lady, and me and Karen have to go to court. Then we'll do the interview, okay?"

"Big day," I say, but I'm not even listening to myself anymore. I want to be alone.

"It's the last day," he says. "Drug-free Eddie after that! But first we'll talk it out, eh. We'll see what's in this head!"

When he's gone, Jane says, "Wow! That's a nice bike. Where'd he get it?"

I shake my head, but when I look at her I see that she's serious. "Uh . . . he just sort of . . . got it," I say.

"Really, what's the story?"

I want to start writing. I want to breathe in deeply, close my eyes and see a newborn baby, gather up some courage and energy for tomorrow—the new day, the last day. I've got to be able to face it all—the library, the incubator, the computer screen, the tape recorder, the chain-link technology connecting this world to that, the garbage on both sides . . . I just need to breathe.

"He stole it, Jane!" I say. "Just now! He stole it from some nice guy who probably had to save his money to buy it! And he's going to trade it for crack! That's the story, Jane. Okay?"

She's quiet for a moment, then says, "I think I need a break from this place."

And finally I'm alone.

x
  x
   x

This is what I want: I want the computer screen to say, *Yes. Yes, I love you.*

Then I want us to adopt little Caleb—she and I together—and take care of him until Eddie and Karen can get clean. I want little Caleb to one day call us Uncle Shaun and Aunt Darling. I want Eddie to find his life, to pick himself up and love this kid, not just for himself—and not just for Caleb and Karen—but for all of us. Tent City could do with a real man right now, especially with all the media attention this birth has brought. I want Eddie to show them all what he can do. And I want Calvin to pick himself up—to stop drinking and beating the crap out of himself. I want Jackie, Terry, Angel, Eddie, Karen and everyone else to stop doing crack. I want them all to jump the fence, or at least look through it once in a while. I want them to be brave, and I want to be proud of them. I want my life back. I want my darling to see that baby's tiny curled-up hands. I want, more than anything, the word "Yes"—like a first star on the darkening night screen.

May 10

No.

An Interview with Eddie and Karen

(I have edited the following down to about 10 percent of its original length, as the tapes are hard to listen to in many different ways. They begin at the end of a day that has been particularly bad for all of us. Eddie showed up late for a preliminary custody hearing, and when they wouldn't let him in he lost it, calling his CAS representative all sorts of nasty things. And ever since the library, I've been bouncing just as bad and high as Eddie. This dialogue begins with the two of us sitting in my shack drinking whisky.)

S: Okay, I'm talking to Eddie. Say hi, Eddie.

E: Hi, Eddie.

S: Yeah, yeah . . . When were you born?

E: December 25, 1948. Truro, Nova Scotia.

S: How many kids you got?

E: *(Edgy laugh. Counts on his fingers.)* Five, yeah.

S: When was the last one born?

E: Uh . . . hoo, just a few days ago . . . Wow. It feels like a month.

S: How you feeling about the kid right now?

E: I just love him. I want to be there. I, I don't know if I have the parts to be there. I left those parts somewhere and I forget about them . . . Like I'm an emotional retard sometimes and I just get so scared and so . . . I know if I just run and hide then I can't help him.

S: I want you to tell me everything that's happened since you had this baby.

E: It's a blur . . . Scary, terrified, running, hiding. And being there with him just ecstatic because he's so gorgeous . . . My daughter showed up yesterday—I hadn't seen her in three years 'cause I called her a fat slob and told her to get the fuck away from me . . .

S: When was that?

E: Three years ago, when I got out of detox and I went to rehab . . . OCI

Guelph, which is full of sex offenders, and everything, and everybody looks down on you if you were in OCI. I lasted there *ten* fucking months, with all that fucking scum that I don't like. I learnt quite a bit actually. And while I was there I called my mom, and she got in touch with my kids. I hadn't seen them in twelve years. They showed up and just, whoa. And I come out, spent six months, never did drugs, did nothing. And I felt *so* fucking good.

(Eddie talks about staying with his son and his grandkids, and the various times he kicked the drugs, then got back into them.)

S: Okay . . . If you don't get the kid, what happens?

E: Wow . . . wow. No, it would destroy me. Guaranteed. If I don't do it then it's because, because . . . I didn't try hard enough and I'm an ass- hole and a jerk-off and I should be done in. I'll disappear, oh yeah . . . It's not going to happen. No. There's no way.

S: Can you tell me about growing up?

(Eddie tells me how he didn't realize his father wasn't his real dad until he was 15, and that his mother never gave him a hug once in his life. He talks about his kids, and his daughter showing up at his shack a few days ago with photos of him from the newspaper in her hands.)

E: They're trying to make me feel again.

(Eddie tells me how, when he got out of jail, instead of going home where everyone was waiting for him, he went out bingeing for four days. He then tells a confusing story about his brother going to jail for something Eddie did.)

E: And then I guess that's why I started beating myself up, to punish myself, right . . . 'cause I was just a dirty rotten piece of shit. Today when I didn't need to flip out, I flipped out. Why? To punish me—to make sure I don't get the kid . . .

S: How many runs do you do a day?

E: I don't know. Some days hardly any. Well, today it's already been five. Yeah, imagine that. Oh, wow . . . Drugs. You don't feel, don't care, don't hurt—nothing matters.

S: And you've also got as addicted to the runs, right? To just doing the . . .

E: Yeah, to the lifestyle. Yeah, 'cause now, like, I used to steal every day. And now I haven't stole in almost three years.

S: Except for last night. (*Silence. Eddie stares at me. I laugh.*) I mean, don't bullshit me, man.

E: No, I'd—I'd forgotten . . .

S: Yeah, how much you get for that bike?

E: What, last night? Twenty bucks. Just a couple tokes . . .

(*We talk over each other for a while.*)

S: You know—you piss me off more than just about everybody down here.

E: That's what friends are supposed to do . . . There's a lot of people who have been really, uh, protective of me—the last day or so. And people I didn't expect it to come from. If I can make it then they can have hope.

S: If you try your hardest on this, and if you fail, then I will still be your man. I'll still be your friend. If you fuck up and you don't even try on this then I don't think I . . .

E: I don't blame you.

S: What do you think fucked you up to begin with? I mean, I know your mother didn't . . .

E: Well that, and being sexually abused in the training school, and then people that you're supposed to trust . . . I don't even really want to get into this part of it, Shaun. Thirty-five years . . . I still can't fucking deal with it, I guess.

S: I'm not saying deal with it, just tell me what happened.

E: I can't tell you what happened.

S: Why were you put in there?

E: Dealing, B&E, trying to get attention. And they asked me in court whether I wanted to go home, and I said no, I'd rather go to jail.

S: What happened to you in the training school?

E: Just . . . well, whatever . . . anyways . . . Well they're supposed to protect you and they abuse you . . . It doesn't matter, it's just fucking fucked . . .

S: You were sexually abused in the training school?

E: Oh, most definitely . . . I came out of there knowing fucking nobody cared and it didn't really matter what the fuck happened. I just kept on doing stupid things and going back to jail. All my friends were in jail— I may as well be there . . . In there I was somebody, out here I was nobody.

S: You were in jail for how long?

E: Altogether? (*Tries to figure it out.*) . . . The sentence second time round was three years, and I worked that into seventeen and a half . . .

S: You want to tell me about that?

E: Yeah. Guy was raping some kid and I just went and stabbed him— well, we had the Kingston riot first. And when we had the riot, we got all the guys who had sexually abused kids, put them in a circle and beat them, cut their legs open and drank their blood.

S: You drank their blood?

E: Yeah—I was fucked up. But I fucking hated them people to death. One guy got up to move, I just took a bar and I just beat him to death. Hole in the head, bit on his face . . .

S: How many did you kill inside?

E: Two. The other one in '75, he was raping this young kid . . . Big fuckin' French guy raping this young 19-year-old kid—used to beat him with beans in a sock, fuckin' raping him . . . My buddies said it was weird, I stabbed him nine or ten times in the stomach, and he almost got past us and he fell down. My buddy said like a sewing machine I jumped on his back and . . . But I don't know—the last few years, the pain that I've caused other people—like look what I've done to his family. Like maybe he was a piece of garbage, but his family wasn't, they didn't deserve it . . .

S: What do you think you would have been doing with your life if you weren't in training school and jail from 14 to 28?

E: Well, you know what? Here's the thing that I think sort of disturbs me a bit. There was a time when I went up for parole and that, and I wasn't that bad of a kid, I didn't think. And they turned me down. I think that one time, if they had given me that, I would have been all right.

(Karen comes to the door. Eddie goes out to do another run, and Karen sits down and picks up the bottle.)

S: How old are you, Karen?

K: Thirty-one.

S: How many kids you got?

K: I have three kids.

S: Three kids . . . When was the last one born?

K: Oh fuck off, Shaun. Let's talk about something normal. *(Laughs.)*

S: Tell me about your family.

K: My dad's a hockey pla—no, not a hockey player, a golfer. I spent a lot of time on a golf course. Well, on weekends . . .

S: You come from a family with a bit of money.

K: Hmm . . . happy.

S: How'd you end up on the street?

K: Um . . . alcohol . . .

S: There's lots of alcoholics out here, and they don't all end up on the street.

K: Switched to crack.

S: When'd you get into the crack?

K: When I came down here.

S: Really? It wasn't till Tent City?

K: Yeah . . . that was a bad time . . . Finally my mom couldn't handle it anymore. She said fuck you. She'd had enough. She was looking after my kids, she didn't need me there. I was too much of a basket case . . . They gave me a list of hostel names . . . Street City, that's where I went (*laughs*).

S: Oh shit.

K: The first place I call out of all the fucking hostels in the city of Toronto—and I pick Street City! Then we moved down to Tent City.

S: What was it like when you moved down to Tent City?

K: Nothing. There wasn't too much here. We used to party here. Dry was here . . . Nancy and Marty . . . Terry . . . That's it more or less. Karl the Mayor was here . . . Then people started showing up, Eddie came down . . .

S: So, how'd he win your heart?

K: I don't know . . . He's a cutey.

S: Tell me about Caleb . . . You guys going to be able to do this?

K: Oh yeah. I just wish it were a dream.

S: Well, it's not.

K: I know . . . it's just, I don't know. Fucking (*smacks tape recorder*) this thing's pissing me off now. Shaun, I don't know, buddy . . .

S: You'll kick the drugs? . . . Who do you think's going to have a bigger problem with that, you or Eddie?

K: Oh, not me . . .

S: It's just when I talk to him, he's all worried about you being able to do this, and when I talk to you, you're worried about him being able to do this. Whereas I think you can both do it . . .

K: I can . . . I can quit . . . The thing is . . .

S: I just feel like you need somebody—I don't know if it's got to be somebody in a suit, and not just me, to sit you down and say if you keep doing this you're going to lose the baby, 100 percent . . . The other day in the hospital all I kept thinking was, man, if I had this—everything would be different . . .

K: Okay then—Shaun, where's *your* family? *(Click.)*

(By the time I turn the tape recorder on again, it's a couple of hours later and we're in Eddie and Karen's shack. I'm pretty messed up. I've been drinking and smoking crack with them, waiting for Eddie to kick out the last of the crackheads so we can get back to it. But now that it's just us they've started playing Yahtzee and the tape recorder can barely pick up our voices over the constant rolling of dice on the table.)

S: You guys got to be playing the loudest fucking game in the world while the tape recorder's on, eh?

E: Can't always bend over when you want.

(The rolling of dice echoes in the shack. They stop only to scrape resin and pack the crack stems. The candles are burning down into the table, the lighters are flicking. Everything smells of burning metal and the air is hazy.)

E: What's up, Shaun?

(I say something that is incoherent.)

E: No, you look fucking more than distressed.

S: I'm distressed over me, and I'm distressed over you.

E: You can't be distressed over me.

S: I can't?

E: Well, you can if you want, but there's no need for it.

S: If you're going to go into this, you got to go into it absolutely 100 percent . . .

E: That's why I have to go to fucking detox . . .

S: Listen to me for a second . . .

E: I am listening to you.

S: It's like at the court today . . . you just got to be your sweet charming self for a while, rather than—

E: I made a mistake. I made a very big mistake. I should have just said, "Sorry, I don't want to talk to the judge," and left, instead of flipping like I did. That was the reaction they wanted, and all in front of witnesses . . .

S: The thing is, they don't realize they're dealing with someone who *is* intelligent, and *is* smart, and *is* charming, and knows how to do all this shit—and you're giving them what they expect. They think you're a couple of fucking crackheads in some shack, and it's going to be easy to take their kid.

(I keep talking, going over this thing again and again. But I'm losing to the dice spilling over the table, louder and louder. I feel like this is what purgatory will be like—sitting strung out and brokenhearted in a crack house with two people who've just had a baby and won't stop playing Yahtzee.)

E: Don't give me that fucking look.

(Pause.)

S: I'm only giving you this look because I'm actually envying you right now. I would love to be in your spot—where you've got a kid and somebody you love, and I don't want you to fuck it up.

K: Two forty-four. *(Karen is counting up her score.)*

S: Can you picture this? You've got some apartment, a bit outside of Toronto . . . And there's the two of you, and your baby. And . . . *(Yahtzee.)*

K: What'd you get?

E: Two eighty-two.

K: How'd you get so much?

S: And you've got some half-decent job . . .

E: I had two-twenty down below.

K: How'd you get two eighty-two?

E: Didn't you hear me? . . . Go ahead, Shaun, we're listening.

S: And I'm going up there once a week maybe to babysit while you guys go on the town, or else just to make you guys dinner . . .

K: Will you let me roll . . . (*Yahtzee.*) . . . What do I have? Twenty-five. Eighteen, a two and a five . . .

(Yahtzee and Yahtzee and Yahtzee, broken up only by crack stems burning. I can hear my voice, and yet it's like I've vanished, like I've left myself in the library . . .)

S: The fact is, if you fuck this up . . . (*roll, roll*) If you fuck this up, I ain't going to be your friend if you fuck this up.

E: You know what, Shaun? You're going to be my friend no matter what happens, as long as I give an honest effort . . . I can have no slack in me anymore.

S: So when does this no slacking start?

E: Well, I'm an addict, I'll tell you that . . . So therefore, I'm going for my last hurrah. In fact if I can sell my percs I can go tomorrow . . .

S: So, tonight's your last night doing drugs?

E: Yeah it is. Tomorrow I don't have no intention of doing drugs what-soever . . . Okay, twenty-eight . . . (*Counting the dice. Rolling again.*) When I'm done tonight I smash my pipe.

K: Eddie! You don't even know what you're saying! (*Yahtzee.*)

S: If you're doing drugs tomorrow I want no part of you.

E: And I want no part of you. 'Cause then you didn't do your job and help me either . . . If my friends let me do drugs tomorrow then there's something wrong with them (*Yahtzee*) . . . and if I want to do drugs then there's something wrong with me . . . It's not about to happen again.

S: This is all about you and your baby, but it's also about everybody, because the media—

E: I don't give a fuck about the media.

S: You guys are either going to be crucified—

E: And if we're crucified, then our friends are crucified with us. Everybody. The whole life down here . . .

(*Karen's still rolling dice, but I'm yelling, and now Eddie's yelling too.*)

S: See, it's a couple of fucking crackheads down by the river who can't fucking take care of themselves—

E: —all the homeless people who are bringing babies into the world that they can't handle!

S: If you fuck it up you're going to fuck you up, you're going to fuck the baby up, you're going to fuck Karen up, you're going to fuck all of us up. And it would be much better if you made us—

E: —proud!

(*We go over everything again, twice as loud, while they keep playing Yahtzee, until Karen wants to go to sleep, but Eddie won't let her. We're all yelling at each other. A crackhead comes to the door, and I yell at him that Eddie's not doing any more runs tonight. Eddie tells me not to speak for him.*)

E: How you feel now? You feel like shit? (*Laughs.*)

S: Can I make a pledge with you? . . . Starting tomorrow, you are not going to do drugs.

E: No, I'm not. I'm done with drugs tonight, right here and now . . .

S: And me, too.

(*Eddie and I shake hands.*)

E: Whether I like it or not. If I do drugs again I'm going to chop my head off—how's that?

K: You can't say that, Eddie!

E: Well, okay—until we have the kid safely, how's that?

K: Can I use your lighter please?

S: Karen, can you do this with us?

E: Nobody's going to make her do anything—

S: I'm talking to Karen. Karen? Karen?

E: You can't fucking force her to say something she doesn't want to say, Shaun!

S: I'm not forcing her, I'm asking her a question.

E: Don't do it that way!

S: Can I ask her a question?

K: You don't have to ask him!

(We all yell over each other for a long while until Karen throws the dice down on the table so hard that they ricochet all over the shack.)

K: What would you like to know, Shaun?

S: Would you be willing to stop doing drugs with me and Eddie tomorrow.

K: I can't say yes or no.

S: Karen, I will spend all day with you tomorrow. We can go out for some hamburgers and take a walk somewhere. I would love to do that.

E: Okay, Shaun. Enough's enough!

S: I'm talking to Karen . . . Karen, do you want this kid?

E: Shaun, leave her alone!

K: It has nothing to do with it. I'm not going to say I'm going to quit drugs and then smoke it tomorrow . . .

S: Well, why would you smoke drugs tomorrow if you know it's going to fuck up your chances with the kid?

E: Shaun, Shaun. Let this go. Right now—

(But I don't let it go, and we all start yelling again. Somebody comes to the door and I yell at him to go away. Then it all starts over again, on and on and on, until the tape runs out.)

May 11

Yesterday is very murky. I remember the computer screen, my throat closing, my brain tumbling through my eyes to the floor. I walked for hours, and finally came back here. I thought if I couldn't help myself, maybe I could at least save Eddie and Karen, and the quiet baby boy. I'm a self-righteous delusional prick. I spent all night getting blasted out of my head and yelling at a couple of new parents on crack who are even more scared than I am—as if Caleb's my baby, my soul in an incubator, premature and up for grabs.

My soul is inside a woman who won't have me. My soul is inside an e-mail account. It is surrounded by chain-link fencing—hooked up to monitors no one bothers to check. My soul may no longer exist.

x   x   x

It is cleanup day. It's the day we all get clean and rise from the ashes like the chickens we are—headless and scorched, full of boiling beer and burnt chemicals.

Everyone's here to help out: the nurses, the TDRC, the Rotary guys, several energetic volunteers, reporters, photographers, churchies and a young dude with a front-loader and a hard hat. Man, he's good with that thing, speeding around like it's a go-cart, scooping up our garbage and shooting it right into those bins, not missing a trick. I could get a job doing that. But I'm not helping one bit.

I couldn't if I wanted to—hell, even if I could, I couldn't. My heart won't let me budge, like it knows if I slip out of neutral I'll spark once and blow up.

In fact, for all the talk at the town meeting, Bonnie's the only one of us who's doing much. Her only vice, after all, is a sense of self-importance. For the rest of us, we can't even *try* to fix the mess we've made.

x   x   x

I've just woken up. The sun's about to go down. I slept for three hours without dreaming. And I feel . . . okay. Something has changed. Something inside me. While I slept, they started carting away 40 tons of trash. There's still that much left, piled in various heaps, but the bins would only hold 40 tons.

Along with the filthy scraps of clothes, the dead batteries, the rotten wood, the broken computers, the wet mattresses, the fractured toilets, the shattered dishes, the splintered chairs, the bent spoons and armless clocks—it seems as though some hard-working volunteers got hold of me while I slept, and pulled the garbage right out of my skull. Something is different inside my head.

There's got to be another dump, some distant landfill where people don't live. And hopefully that's where my dreams of her are headed now. It's hard to let go—even if all you have is toxic crap.

When I woke up, I went outside and lit a fire in the barrel. Eddie came over and stood next to me, watching the smoke.

"How you doing, kid?"

"Surprisingly well rested," I said, but Eddie wasn't listening. "What's up with you, Eddie?"

"I'm doing drugs." He spat it out quickly and sat down. "Right now. I'm doing crack . . . Just thought I should tell you, that's all."

"Good. Thanks."

"We can't get a bed till Monday anyway, so this is just the last of it, you know?"

"Good."

x   x   x

I'm not going to listen to those tapes I made last night. I know I was being an asshole, and I don't want to hear it. But I am going to keep my pledge. I'm going to let the drugs go, let the girl go, and hope that I'll have the strength to be there for whatever comes next.

May 12

I think maybe I was wrong—it's not that we can't clean up our own messes, but that we need some differentiation between our crap and everybody else's before we can start.

Since the big cleanup ended, Sluggo's been sober, and raking the scraps around his shack into one big pile. The Brothers have fenced in their house with plastic orange mesh, and are spreading wood chips across their newly cleaned lawn. Randy has begun to scrape out the storage area next to the prefab, and is preparing to build a new summer house onto the side of it. The large pile of trash between Heartbeat's prefab and my shack was taken away yesterday, and he keeps coming out, hands on his hips, to look at where it used to be.

"Clean, eh, Shaun?" he says.

"Yeah. Nice and clean."

I don't know what to do yet. I want to make sure my first move into this new clean world is a good one.

x   x
x

Along with some of the other guys, I'm trying to keep an eye on Eddie. He's decided to clean up, too, which is much more dangerous than it sounds.

"You seen him?" says Terry as he passes my shack.

"No, why?"

"Some guy staying with Angel has owed him for a while, and he's trying to collect."

"Shit."

We walk side by side up toward Pops's old trailer, where Angel's been crashing.

"Sock full of beans," says Terry.

"What'd you say?"

"Eddie took a sock full of beans with him . . . At least he's being smart."

"Why's that smart?"

"Doesn't leave marks."

"Oh, right."

Nobody's in the trailer, so we cross over and sit with Hawk on his porch.

"Lookin' for Eddie, eh?" says Hawk. "He screwed up yet? It's too bad, you know? It'd be good for all of us if he could step up—with the baby and all."

Eddie comes bouncing over to us, swinging something in his right hand.

"Beans in a sock," says Hawk approvingly, and Eddie grins, cracking the sock down on the stoop next to us.

Eventually we persuade him to abandon the bean-filled retribution.

But as we walk past Karl's place, Eddie remembers he still hasn't gotten revenge for him hitting Karen on Christmas Eve. I'm hardly the right person to dissuade Eddie from beating up Karl, so I leave Terry to figure it out. As I walk away I can hear Eddie saying, "I'll kill him."

"Wouldn't be good for the kid."

"Damnit, Terry. Then I'll just break his legs."

May 13

I wake up in the late afternoon and there's no one around. It's kind of eerie. I can't even hear a dog barking.

Eventually Hawk appears, walking toward me along the road by the river.

"Hey, Shauny," he says.

"Hi, Hawk. Where is everybody?" He just shrugs as though it's always this quiet.

"I got a question for you, Shaun," he says, staring straight into my eyes. "This thing with Eddie, how's it making you . . . you know, feel?" I hesitate. I'm not sure what to say, but Hawk carries on: "It's something I been thinking about—how you and Eddie are so close. Like friends, right? And you know me, Shaun—I'm a real lone wolf. I don't get all tied up in other people like you do—all friends and everything." He says the word "friends" not disdainfully, but like it's an odd taste in his mouth. "And so I was wondering what you think's going to happen with you guys?"

"Well, I don't know, Hawk . . ." I feel like I've been dropped into Bizarro world, where Tent City is a calm sunny place, and Hawk wants to discuss people's feelings. "I guess I'm a bit scared," I say, unsure of what I'm talking about. "I mean, I don't want to see him go—but he's got to. 'Cause if he stays he'll be lost for good. He'd be finished. And me, you know, I guess I'd lose respect for him—if he doesn't step up."

"Yeah," says Hawk. "That's what I'm talking about. That's kind of how I saw it, eh, Shauny? You know it ain't going to happen, eh? They're not going to do it. No way—not going to get off the crack, and not going to leave. You know that, don't you?"

"I hope you're wrong, Hawk."

"Yeah. But I'm not. Mind if I ask you something else?"

"What's that?"

"Hear you been drinking a lot lately."

This doesn't seem like much of a question, but I shrug in answer, anyway. "You don't have to worry," I say.

"Why the fuck not?" Hawk doesn't like being told what he does or doesn't have to do.

"Because I met a girl."

It just comes out, before I even think about it—and we both look surprised.

"A girl?" he says, squinting as though he's trying to decode what I said.

"Yeah. The kind that makes you feel like you just woke up on a different planet. Crazy, eh?"

"Something like that," says Hawk, shaking his mammoth head like a god resigned to the idiocy of mortals. "Good luck, Shauny," he says, then turns and walks away.

x   x   x

At sundown yesterday, I walked into the Stone Cutter's Arms. It was almost empty—just a few regulars sitting at the bar.

"Where you been?" said Sherry, brushing a stray lock of blond hair away from her catlike eyes. "Well?"

"Been short on money," I said and sat down at the bar. She wrinkled her nose like lack of money should never be an excuse for anything, then said, "Well, I'm buying you dinner. So you should decide what you want."

"I think I know. Thank you."

When the food came she topped up the regulars and we sat down at a table in the corner with a plate each of enchiladas and perogies. I couldn't stop smiling.

"So are you going to show me Tent City?" she said, smiling back.

"Okay."

"I'm off on Tuesday. How about then?"

I said okay again, then offered her a single black bean skewered on my fork, and she laughed.

When the place started filling up I told her I'd see her in a few days, and we decided to meet at a bar on Yonge Street. "Wear some crappy shoes," I said, master of the smooth exit line.

May 23

On the Tuesday I was to meet Sherry, I got out of bed before noon. It felt strange to wake up with no alcohol in my system, or at least very little. I took a long shower at the community centre. I still had about $30 left from a good night of pool.

I don't know if it was out of a sense of irony or optimism, but I'd suggested we meet at a bar on Yonge Street that has the same name as my sister. By the time I got there I half wished that Sherry wouldn't show up. I wasn't sure whether this was a date, or a day trip through the slums for a pretty tourist.

She got there four minutes early. I was so nervous, I'd gone through the contents of my backpack twice, and half of it was still strewn across the table: a wet T-shirt I'd used as a towel after my shower, a roll of toilet paper I'd taken from a fast food bathroom, an envelope of Goran's Tent City photos, my writing books, a toothbrush, toothpaste, soap, a knife, a rock, three dead batteries and a KitKat. "Hi there," I said, trying to shove it all back into my bag. "It's starting to rain, huh?"

She sat down, and I remembered why I'd been going through my bag. I dug back in and came up with the KitKat. "Here," I said. "This is for you." From past conversations, I'd gathered that Sherry feels about chocolate the way others do about alcohol or great works of art.

"Oh! That's my favourite!" she said. "Well, one of my favourites." She was wearing a black-and-white sleeveless top, and jeans. Her hair was down, with two thin braids pulled back above her ears. "Thank you," she said, and put the chocolate bar in her purse. I waved away her gratitude like it was nothing, and could feel my palms getting sweaty. *We can't go down to Tent City in the rain,* I thought. *We'll have to do something else, something normal instead . . .*

She ordered a vodka and orange juice, and I said, "Same for me," although usually I only drink that to get rid of a cold. Sherry looked at me sideways—I'd forgotten she was my bartender. "There's no drink I don't like!" I said. "You wanna see some pictures?" And before I knew what I was doing I had Goran's black-and-white photos on the table.

"That's Calvin—he's my brother."

"Really?"

"No, not really."

"Oh."

"That's Eddie—the one who just had the baby. See how his sleeves are always pulled down? That's 'cause he cut his arms all the way up . . . and he lit himself on fire, and hung himself, too—all at the same time. It's kind of confusing . . . he was trying to beat a murder rap."

"Uh-huh."

"He's a great guy."

"Okay."

I think the headless beer-can chickenshit half of me was thinking, *If I show her photos maybe she won't have to see the real thing, and we can just go to a movie instead.*

"This is Spider—he's Calvin's brother."

"Really?" she said suspiciously.

"Yeah, really. And he's also Homeless Dave on the radio . . ."

"Do you want another drink?"

"Sure. Why not? Yeah . . . that'd be good."

When we left the bar, Sherry said, "We don't have to go down there if you don't want to." The rain had turned to a light musical drizzle, singing gently on the roofs of taxicabs. I took off my beat-up raincoat and put it around her shoulders. She looped her arms through the sleeves, small and smiley in this wrinkled mess of dirt and torn black cloth—the cutest little hobo ever.

"Let's just walk," I said. "And see where we end up."

"Perfect," she said, and put her arm through mine, an old mustard stain on our big black sleeve.

x   x   x

The rain had almost stopped by the time we hit Queen Street. I took it as a sign and turned left, toward Tent City. Sherry squeezed my hand, looking up at the skyscrapers.

"Downtown is crazy," she said. "What street is this? I never come downtown."

"Queen Street . . . Aren't you *from* Toronto? Don't you *work* down-town?"

"I live in Scarborough," she said.

"Right . . . Where is that?"

"It's a suburb, I guess. It's basically a bunch of malls and apartment buildings, and housing projects. I just come in for work. I don't know Toronto at all."

"You've never been out of Ontario, and you don't even know Toronto?"

She smiled and shrugged. "And I don't even go to the mall," she said. "I told you, I've been waiting to do something my whole life. So really, anywhere we go is fine." There was a sort of laughing echo in her voice that sounded both awestruck and wise. I got the sense she could have spent her life in a box, with nothing but an Archie comic, and still she'd be brilliant.

"Okay. There's a couple of things you gotta know—first of all, don't call anyone a goof."

"Why would I?"

"I don't know. But just don't, okay?"

"Why not?"

"I'm not exactly sure—but it's the worst thing to call someone. It's a prison thing, and a street thing—it's like a challenge to fight."

"Does this mean we're going down there?"

"I'm not sure yet."

"Okay . . . Damn!"

"What?"

"What if I say goof? I mean, I wouldn't usually, but now the word's in my head. What about goofball? Is goofball bad, too?"

"I think anything with goof in it's bad."

"Shit."

"Don't worry, you'll be fine."

"Okay. What else should I know?"

"If anyone gives you a hard time, just do what you do—you can take care of yourself, I've seen you in the bar. And anyway, I'll be there."

"I'm not worried."

"Good."

I was a bit worried—not necessarily for her, or for me, but for the flow of the universe. I doubted anyone so beautiful, caring and sweet had ever crossed through this fence, and I didn't know what would happen when she did: Tent City would explode, the CN Tower would fall, a wormhole would appear and we'd all be sucked into some limbo where everyone has a bar named after them—skyscraper watering holes made of plywood and tarps, where they served nothing but baloney sandwiches and vodka . . .

"What are you thinking about?" said Sherry.

"Vodka," I said. We stopped at the liquor store, then carried on to Tent City.

"Goose," said Sherry as we crossed over the tracks and through the chain-link fence.

"What?"

"If I start to say goof, by accident, I'll try to change it to goose."

"Like 'you silly goose'?"

"Exactly."

"Uh . . ."

"Don't worry, I'm just kidding. I'll try not to get you beat up."

"Thanks." The rain had stopped altogether and the late-afternoon sun was shining. She dug her elbow into me gently, and we crossed into Tent City.

"That's Hawk," I said as he came lumbering toward us, raising his eyebrows in a question.

"Hey, Shauny," he said, looking at Sherry in that way he saves for young girls—a gentle smile that makes him seem almost sage and soft, like a hairless Santa Claus.

"This is Sherry," I said. "Sherry, Hawk."

"You'll be fine with him," said Hawk, cocking his head toward me. "It's good to meet you, Sherry. You don't worry about a thing, sweetie."

"Okay," said Sherry. "It's good to meet you, too."

As we walked into town, Sherry said, "He seems really nice. But do I have to call him Hawk?"

"Uh, yeah . . . Why?"

"It just, you know, seems so silly. What's his real name?"

"Call him Hawk, okay?"

"Sure thing, buddy."

Tent City looked as good as I'd ever seen it—so much of the garbage gone on cleanup day, the trees covered in leaves, the bushes high and green. The ground raked clean around the shacks looked like crop circles left by misguided aliens.

"Wow!" said Sherry as we walked into the old part of town and the boys came out to surround us.

x
x
x

When they finally left us alone, the sun was setting below the CN Tower, gold streaking the surface of the canal, and we sat in front of my shack drinking vodka and orange juice. "You're still here," I said, grinning in the twilight.

"What'd you expect?" she said.

"You want to help me find some wood?"

We brought back two shopping carts of scrap lumber as darkness fell, and I got the barrel fire going.

"I like it here," she said as the blue flames began to swirl.

"I'm glad. Sorry about Eddie."

Eddie had come over some time after Randy got tired of dancing for us. He sat down and started explaining to me why he hadn't stopped smoking crack yet. Sherry sat off to the side, trying not to intrude, but apparently Eddie took this as snobbery and started mocking her.

"You're being a jackass, Eddie," I said. "She knows more about this shit than I do. Come back later when you're ready to be nice, okay?" He blurted something too fast to be coherent and bounced away.

"Aw, he seems all right," said Sherry as the deep flames began to fill the barrel. "I just don't know why you act so naive with him. I mean, I know you're not naive, but . . ."

"What do you mean?"

"You think he's going to quit crack?" she said. "Why? For the baby?"

"He could . . ."

"I don't want to tell you different, I hope you're right. But really, it doesn't work that way. Not for a crackhead."

I realized who I was talking to—this girl who'd gone through all of high school, then graduated and put herself through two years of university with nothing to trust or hold but the taut, desperate arms of a crackhead.

"It's hard to see it in you," I said. "All that bad stuff, I mean."

"I think I've come out unscathed, or at least my scars don't show. I'm not fucked up by it, and so really I can do anything now. I've just got to start . . ."

As she spoke, her firelit eyes shone with focus, but I wasn't hearing the words. I was too distracted by her mouth, the shadow of her tongue flashing back there like a hidden flame. And still she was talking, her voice soft, laughing between breaths, easily forgiving everyone who should have taken care of her but had done nothing at all. I said something like, "Can you imagine what your life will be like in ten years? God, you'll be amazing . . . ," but I was swallowed by her mouth and the terrifying knowledge that I had to kiss it—like water, when it's finally squeezed from the clouds, has to fall through the sky.

I heard her say, "Hell, I wonder who I'll be a year from now . . ." And I couldn't help but tumble through the dark sky, and kiss her.

"Oh," she said, and kissed me too.

x
  x
    x

We might never have stopped. We may have kept on until Tent City was finally brought down with Tasers and billy clubs and dogs, if it weren't for Karen. She came through the trees hollering. "Okay, Jesus, guys! Enough smooching! Disengage, okay!" then she hung around just long enough to bum a smoke and a couple packets of ketchup.

"God," I said. "I feel happier than I've felt in a long time."

"Me too," said Sherry, and she stroked my lips with her finger.

We were quiet. Finally I said, "Do you like macaroni and cheese?"

"Now that you've said it, there's nothing else I could eat."

I put the grill on the barrel, pulled a box of No Name macaroni and cheese out of an overturned bucket, found some creamers I'd swiped the day before and pulled some dishes out of the dirt and mud. It had been a while since I'd cooked.

When the food was ready, we sat down inside my shack. The room was lit by candlelight. We each had a plate, a fork, a knife and a paper cup. I uncorked the bottle of wine I'd bought, and scooped the macaroni and cheese onto our plates. Sherry had set the radio to an oldies station. "Love Me, Love Me, Love," was playing, and the paper made no sound as our cups pressed together.

"I used to be a germaphobic," said Sherry, lifting the fork I'd found beneath a bush. She scooped the macaroni, cooked in water from a broken hose, off a plate I'd dug out of supposedly toxic earth, and took a bite.

"Really, when?"

"About two hours ago."

"I'm glad you're cured."

We finished the bottle of wine. The radio was playing "Mr. Bojangles."

"Man, this is good!" said Sherry. "And the wine, too. I never really drink."

I leaned over to blow the stove back to life. It wasn't cold, but it was damp, and I could tell Sherry liked the fire. *She's so thin,* I thought. *More than anything, I want to keep her warm and happy . . .* The fire was barely sparking, and yet the shack had filled with the smell of burning . . .

"Your hair is on fire," said Sherry. Her voice was calm, but when I turned toward her I could see how scared she was. I smacked at my head until the fire was out and all that was left was the stench of scorched hair.

"You okay?"

"Yep. Fine."

She put her hand through the burnt patch on my head, and said, "You know, I used to have a fear of fire too?"

"Yeah? When?"

"Until now. A guy lit my dress on fire in grade seven . . ." She was going to say more, but I grabbed her and kissed her until we stumbled over to the bed. "Runaway" was playing and her hair caught fire on a candle. She laughed as I smothered the flame, both our hands flying through her hair as we descended, rain and fire falling together, and I could have burned and drowned on that bed forever.

May 24

On our second date we walked all over downtown, through Chinatown and into Kensington Market. The sun was out and it was warm, but not too hot.

We went to a store where they sold nothing but chocolate, and I watched her try every kind—basil, coconut, strawberry—with her cat eyes closed.

"Hmmmm . . ." she said. "This is one of my favourite things ever."

"What else?" I said, watching her mouth move in soft circles.

"Uh . . . dancing, swimming. And mint chocolate-chip ice cream, and . . . uh, pineapple, and massages, and Patrick Swayze, and cats, and saliva, and making love . . ."

"You're driving me crazy . . ."

"But really I don't know what my favourite things are."

"Why?"

"Because I haven't done them yet."

"Like what?"

"Like going on an airplane . . ."

"You've never been on an airplane?"

"Or seeing the ocean."

"You've never seen the ocean?"

"Would you stop doing that?"

"Sorry. What else?

"Like skinny-dipping. Or going to another country. Or running through a big field of grass naked, yelling as loud as I can—I really want to do that one. Or eating Indian food . . . You've probably done all those things, haven't you?"

"I guess . . . though I'm not sure about the naked yelling thing."

"What are *your* favourite things?" she said, putting a jalapeño chocolate in my mouth.

"God, we're like a hokey musical."

"What are they?"

It had been a long time since I even *had* favourite things. "Dancing," I said. "And swimming. And mint chocolate -chip ice cream."

"What else?"

"And women. And whisky. And wine."

"Lots of Ws."

"And peeing in the shower. And Superman. And Kentucky Fried Chicken. And Bruce Springsteen, and strawberries, and saliva, too."

"Superman?" she said.

"Patrick Swayze?"

"It's a long story."

We had fajitas and margaritas at a restaurant on College Street, then started the long walk back to Tent City. By the time we reached Moss Park, I noticed she was limping.

"It's the shoes," she said. "I just bought them."

"Shit," I said. "I thought I told you to wear crappy ones!"

"That was for our *first* date," she said sheepishly. I sat her down and took off her shoes. Her feet were swollen and red.

"Sorry," she said.

I massaged her bare feet, kneeling before her in the park across from the Salvation Army with all the drunks and junkies stumbling around us. I put my arm around her and she leaned on me as we walked. Finally I found a shopping cart and lifted her in. Then I pushed her the rest of the way, running the last stretch as fast as I could, my own feet lifting off the ground as we flew into Tent City.

May 25

The whole last week has been a sort of blissful haze.

My single bed seems more than large enough for the two of us, and when we do sleep it's deep and quick, with never a dream. She has the ecstatic energy of a 20-year-old girl whose life is just beginning. I have the stunned, bewildered energy of a man waking up after a year-long nightmare, somehow alive and hungry as hell.

We eat whatever we want—peanut butter and apple sandwiches, or steak and fries at the bar. And we go wherever we want. We sneak through the dockyard fence on the other side of the canal and look across the water at Tent City. I've never actually seen it from this vantage point and it looks bizarre. We can hear the yells and laughs rising from the shacks across the water. We watch as Eddie bursts out of his door, thumps on his chest like Tarzan, bounces over to pick the lock on my bike.

"Is he allowed to do that?" says Sherry.

"As long as he brings it back."

Eddie has not stopped smoking crack, but his reasons do make a sort of sense. Apparently Jack Layton—city councillor and long-time friend of Tent City—has taken up Eddie and Karen's cause. Eddie tells me that Layton and their case psychologist have worked out a schedule for them: first they'll be put on the top of the housing list, then—after they've got an apartment—Eddie and Karen will check into detox, coming out only for the first court date. This way they'll have somewhere to go, other than Tent City, when they finish rehab. And Caleb will have a good home with loving parents. Eddie insists that this is a reality, and who am I to doubt his last chance.

Karen, however, has little patience for Eddie's frenetic optimism. The two of them together are like some mythological beast trying to placate and eat itself at the same time.

x
  x
    x

It is a nice warm day and I've got some beer. I put the bottles in a bag, tie it to a rope wrapped around a stump and toss the beer into the canal to chill it.

"God!" says Sherry, looking into the water. "It's filthy in there."

"Yeah," I say. "There isn't much current, so everything sort of gets stuck right here. It's deep, though. When it gets hotter I'm going swimming."

"Not if you want to kiss me you're not," she says, and I kiss her.

We hang out drinking beer and, like a gong show, people come over one after the other to tell their stories, sing their songs and do their drunken dances.

"Guess who I saw today?" says Randy, stumbling out of the bushes.

"Who?" says Sherry.

"Everyone I looked at." I groan as Sherry spits out a laugh.

"Ever done Cough-X?" he says, turning to Sherry with a big blasted Popeye grin.

"Uh . . . pardon me?"

"Cough-X," I say. "He's all hopped up right now. You can tell by the walk, see?"

"Hop, hop!" says Randy, jumping around in front of my shack like a speed-freak bunny, and everyone starts in on all the crazy stuff they do to get high—like they're trying to share all the good parts of this life with Sherry.

"Lysol!" says Spider. "You can hear people singing inside you—like they're living in your tummy!"

"Rubbing alcohol!" says Olivia. "Your ears feel like wings, like your head's trying to fly, and you don't even get a hangover!"

"Mouthwash!" says Karen. "This one time we're up on Queen with our buddy Mitch, and he's just got his cheque, and we're going to the beer store, right? But first we go into Mr. Tasty and order some burgers and beer, but the guy won't give Mitch a drink. I guess he knows him, eh? Well, of course he knows him—everybody knew him back then, especially on Queen.

"So we say, 'Let's just eat the burgers fast and we'll go to the beer store,' but Mitch can't wait. He runs right out of Mr. Tasty, and I mean he actually *runs*—we can see him out the window racing across the road. He goes into that corner store there and buys a bottle of mouthwash— one of those big ones with the big cap—and he comes back out and glugs the whole thing right down?

"He's got $400 in his pocket and he buys a bottle of mouthwash! So anyway he comes back into Mr. Tasty, and his eyes are all fucked up, eh? He can barely walk. And I say, 'Mitch, sit down and have your burger— and then we'll go.' But Mitch just looks at the guy behind the counter, and yells, 'I don't need no fuckin' beer now,' throws about $200 on the table, and goes off stumbling down the street."

"So what'd you do?" I say.

"Oh, we sat there eating hamburgers and drinking beer for quite a while, thanks to Mitch," says Karen. "And then we went to the beer store."

Randy grabs my hands and starts dancing with me. He takes a glug of beer, jumps up on the spool table and bellows, "Do you love me?" with his mouth full of beer—his favourite visual gag—the liquid spurting and drooling from his lips.

"Aw, Randy!" says Marty, who's just shown up. "There's a lady here!"

"Shaun ain't no lady," says Randy. "He just talks that way."

"Fuck off, Randy," I say, laughing and wiping the beer from my face. "And get off my table."

Marty falls into a chair like he's deflating. Randy jumps down off the table, sits in my lap and starts to play footsies with Sherry. "Want to dance?" he says. She giggles, I punch him in the arm, and he turns to Marty. "Why so glum, you bum?"

"Just got out of jail," says Marty, shaking his head.

"What for?"

"That's the thing: I got spot-picked and I don't even know why—something Nancy charged me with a year ago when she was drunk and pissed off. And of course she can't remember what the charge is either, so we both gotta go to court or I'm stuck with another failure to appear—and probably I'm gonna have to do some time for my last one anyway—just 'cause my crazy wife was drunk a year ago and some stupid cop got bored."

"Rough," I say, laughing.

"Real rough," says Randy, and bounces on my knee. I drop my leg and he hits the ground. Sherry gets up and pours Marty a drink.

x   x   x

Spider has somehow come up with a bunch of jumbo hot dogs, and we're cooking them on Sluggo's fire barrel.

"Where's Jackie?" I say as Sluggo hands Sherry a dog. "It's not like her to miss a barbecue."

"Been gone for two days. But I'll still save her a hot dog—Oh honey, you're home from doing crack! I saved you a hot dog. Shit, I forgot to tell you: Hawk came looking for you yesterday. He said something about a bag of apples."

"Apples?" says Sherry.

This is the kind of thing Hawk's been doing lately. I gave him a few smokes last week, then he came to my shack with an apple in each hand, holding them up like a couple of planets he'd just created. "You like apples?" he said. "Me, I can't stand them."

"Sure I like apples, Hawk. Thanks." The next day I brought him a few codeine and a couple of oranges.

"Love oranges," he said.

The Brothers come over, and the barbecue gets rowdier, so Sherry and I go back over to my place, which—although right next to Sluggo's—is now sheltered from sight by spring leaves. Jackie is sitting in a chair in front of my shack.

"Where you been, Jacks?" I say. She looks terrible, her face all red and puffy.

"The hospital," she says, waving at Sherry. "Hey, sweetie."

"Hi, Jackie," says Sherry. "What happened?"

"Had a stroke . . . ," says Jackie, nodding to herself. I don't know whether to believe her, but really it's all the same—whether she was doing crack, had a stroke and ended up in the hospital, or has just been bingeing the whole time instead.

"Careful, Jacks," I say, rolling a cigarette for her. "That stuff's going to kill you soon."

"I know," she says. "What's going on over there?"

"Barbecue."

"Think there's any left?"

"I'm sure Sluggo saved a hot dog for you, Jacks."

"Yeah, good. Thanks, Shauny. See you, Sherry." She lumbers through the trees toward her shack. Watching her move, I get the sense that no heart can really sustain that large a body under these conditions—with the drugs, and the heat of summer just beginning.

"Gimme that dog, you bitch!" she yells through the trees, and starts cackling, then coughing.

Karen, Randy and Marty appear in her wake, carrying hot dogs and beer. "I'm going to tell Sherry the one about the camel," says Randy.

"Have some respect—she's a lady," says Marty.

"I'm sick of that shit!" says Karen. "What the fuck am I?"

"Damned if I know."

Sherry is laughing. "Is it always like this?" she says to me.

"Pretty much, yeah. I gotta go see a man about some apples," I say. "Back soon."

As I walk over toward Hawk's, Olivia is smacking Spider's ass with a spatula and Sluggo is trying to make Jackie beg for a hot dog. It seems everyone's in a good mood today. Except for Hawk.

x   x   x

He is sitting in a wheelchair in front of his shack. Or rather, he seems to be doing all he can *not* to be sitting in a wheelchair, struggling against it like Mussolini with his toe caught in a revolving door.

"Jesus, Hawk, what happened?"

He looks at me and his face is a moving billboard of rage, pain and power-hungry aggression. I decide to keep my distance.

"I want to stand up!" he bellows. "Hold the wheelchair for me!" As he tries to project himself skyward, he yells, "Aaaargh!" and I lunge for the wheelchair. For an instant he is standing, his massive body pressed against mine. "I want to sit down!" he hollers, and tumbles onto the steps.

"What's going on, Hawk?"

"I'm going to kill him." A lot of Hawk's sentences begin this way. I give him a smoke and he lights it, one enormous fist circling all the way around the flame, plunging the cigarette in like dropping a man's soul into Hades. "Son of a bitch ain't gonna live through the night!" he says, wincing as he inhales.

As best I can make out from what Hawk tells me, there are two guys down here who just got out of jail. One of them is Frank—who, last summer, built the shack on the other side of Hawk's—and the other guy is Jeff—who has been staying with his old lady in the place next to Karl's. Frank is a good guy, and Jeff is a goof. Jeff owed Frank some money, and when he went to collect it, Jeff told him to fuck off, so Frank punched him in the head. Nothing out of the ordinary, except by now I realize I do know who Jeff is. While I was getting water this morning, some guy with bruises and cuts all over his face tried to sell Sherry some back bacon.

"The back-bacon guy!" I say, interrupting Hawk. "You're talking about the back-bacon guy!" He looks at me like maybe he should aim some of his wrath at a closer coordinate. "What'd he do, Hawk?" I say, trying to redirect his focus.

"You want to know what he did, this guy? Him and his old lady go up to the 51 and file assault charges, three fucking cruisers come down here, and twenty-four hours after Frank gets out of jail, he's right back in." Hawk's infamous jaw is clenching with every couple of words. "You don't know Frank, Shauny. He's one of us—a brother, like you or me! And this guy goes and screws him like a bitch . . . You hear what I'm saying . . . ?"

By this time I realize Hawk's story has nothing to do with him being in a wheelchair. "Hawk," I say. "What happened to your leg?"

"I fell, Shaun," he says, gritting his teeth. "It was dark last night and I tripped."

Hawk's rheumatism flared up, then he got burned at the bathhouse, and now he's pulled a ligament in his leg from tripping in the dark. "Shit, Hawk," I say. "Looks like someone up there's trying to tell you something."

He erupts like he's been spit in the face. "Who?" he bellows. "Who's trying to tell me something?"

"No, no. I mean up *there*," I say, pointing at the sky, wishing I hadn't opened my mouth but now forced to explain before he wheels off to kill whoever dared to try and tell him something. "Someone up *there* is trying to tell you to take it easy!"

"You tell me who, Shaun!" he says, aiming his finger at me. "Who's talking about me like that?"

"I mean *God,* Hawk!" I say. "I'm just saying that maybe this is God's way of trying to get you to . . . you know, not get so worked up and . . ."

"There he is!" growls Hawk. I turn around, half expecting to see God standing there, a can of Crest in his hand. But it's just Back-Bacon Jeff, picking through a pile of scrap. Hawk's jaw pulses, and he grabs on to the front of his shack to pull himself up, staring at Jeff, who's going about his business, oblivious. "I have to walk!" growls Hawk. "I'm going to kill him, Shaun! But I have to walk!"

"You can't walk, Hawk," I say. "You're injured."

"You watch me, Shauny!" he says, dragging himself up slowly, his whole body shaking as he clings to the side of his shack.

"Be careful, Hawk," I say.

"You watch!" he says, trying to take a step. "I'm going to load my gun right now . . . and tonight I'm going to kill that fucking rat! He's not living through the night, Shaun."

"Hawk," I say.

"What, Shaun?"

"I don't think you should . . . kill him, I mean. You don't want to do life for that rat, am I right?"

Hawk laughs like he's found me out. "I know what it is!" he says, wagging his finger at me, then flailing to catch his balance. "You just don't want me killing people!"

"Er . . . no. I don't."

"Frank was one of us. You would do the same for me." He smiles like I just gave him a gift. "I have to walk!" he shouts.

I leave him a few cigarettes, and head back to my shack. The barbecue has deteriorated into various slurred arguments and people are falling backwards off their chairs.

"Where are the apples?" Sherry asks.

"I think we should get out of here," I say.

May 26

I'm going to try to fix my place up for the summer, to make it nice for Sherry. There's a lot of cleaning up to be done—scraps of lumber and bits of plywood, empty bottles in small mountains, torn blankets, clothes, all kinds of shantytown mayhem strewn around. Whenever it rains, the ground outside my door turns into a quagmire.

Someone left a large rattan fold-out couch on the road in front of Hawk's. I don't know what happened to Back-Bacon Jeff. He's no longer down here, but neither is Hawk in jail. He seems to be walking fine now, and helps drag the couch to my place on a couple of shopping carts. Neither of us mentions guns or killing anyone.

"Thanks, Hawk."

"Don't thank me," he says. "You got to make this place nice for your little lady."

Later on, Mike brings down a truckload of old furniture and I drag most of it over to my shack—a square kitchen table, a couple of chairs, a drink cart, a marble chopping board, a nice long coffee table and a box of tiles. This place could look really good if I work at it. I think I should build a deck. Definitely a deck.

In the afternoon I go to the gym, eat at a soup kitchen, write at the library, make some money playing killer pool at Henry's, then go to the Stone Cutter's Arms to see my girl. I help her close the bar, and she makes me her special Long Islands (a shot each of gin, vodka, tequila, rum, and Drambuie, lime juice and a splash of Coke). We coax the last few barflies out the door by 3 a.m., play all the best songs on the jukebox and dance as we wipe down the tables. We put the chairs up, roll around on the pool table, then finally—like every night so far—we fall asleep in the middle of the morning.

"Don't need sleep," she says as we drift off. "Can't you feel how young we are?"

May 27

Sherry gave me $30 to buy her some pot before she left for work today. She used to smoke a lot, but not since we've been together.

"So how much should I get for this?"

"A half a quarter."

"You mean an eighth?"

"Whatever, you drunk."

"Pothead."

"Cokehead."

"Hey now!"

"Sorry," she said, giggling.

When I'd finally got up the nerve to tell her about the coke she'd said, "I know. It was the only thing I worried about with you—well, there was one other thing—but I'll tell you some other time."

So I go off to find drugs for my sweet little honey.

"Don't call them drugs! It's just pot."

"Okay, okay."

Jackie tells me to go see Jimmy D.

"Really? He's the pot dealer?"

"How long you been down here, Shauny?"

Jimmy D is sitting in front of his shack, shadowboxing to some incoherent radio music, his dogs by his side. The left side of his face is swollen and blue. Word is he had some sort of fit and beat his own head against the ground.

"Hey Jimmy," I say. "Can I buy a half a quarter off you?"

He keeps shadowboxing as he squints at me, "You mean an eighth." Every second time I see him he thinks we've never met before. This seems to be one of those times. "You a cop?"

"No, Jimmy. Not a cop."

"All right. What would you like?"

"Pot. If you got some."

"Yeah . . . but what kind? The Hydro's $25, and the Ses is $20."

"I don't know," I say. "It's not for me. I don't even smoke the stuff."

"Why not?"

"Makes me jumpy, kind of freaks me out, actually."

"What you got to be jumpy about?" I shrug, and he shrugs back at me, then starts shadowboxing again.

"Why don't you give me an eighth of the . . . uh, Ses, and a dime of the Hydro."

He grunts and waves me into his shack, where a couple of lost boys and a girl are passed out on the bed. He locates his bags of pot and a small hand-held scale, then goes rummaging around in the corner of the room. I sit in a chair and he comes back wearing a huge pair of thick glasses like that little old lady on *Golden Girls* wears. "Gotta do this right," he says. I try not to laugh. "Can't see too well . . ." He divides it into two plastic bags and weighs them. "The bags are a gram each." He shows me the scales, and I nod.

I go back over to our side of town and Jackie says, "Sherry won't like that. The Ses is crap. You want all Hydro."

"Oh. I guess I'll ask him to change it."

"Sure you want to do that?"

I shrug and walk back over there. "Hi," I say, and sit back down. Once again he looks at me like he's never seen me before. "Here's the thing: I want to give this stuff back and get Hydro, okay?"

He glares at me as though re-evaluating my status as a cop and points at his own aubergine face. "I didn't get this from a fight," he says. "I don't lose, okay? Wham, bam—I never lose 'em." He stands up, fists pounding at the air, and the lost boys stir themselves from the bed. "Who the fuck are you anyway?"

I stay sitting. "Just a guy like you, Jimmy. I make mistakes. It's $25 for the Hydro, right? I'll give you back all this, and you give me half a quarter, or an eighth—whichever you prefer—and you keep the whole $30. Okay? That's five bucks extra."

"You trying to pull something?" he growls. "What's the fucking catch?"

"Just that you sit down."

"Okay," he says, and his snarl turns into a loopy car-crash grin. He sits down and puts the thick glasses back on. He measures out an eighth, then drops in an extra half gram. As I get up to leave he says, "It's good to see you, buddy," like I'm someone else entirely. The giant octagon glasses make his eyes look like two guppies in a fishbowl trying to see the world outside.

May 28

Sherry comes down in her mom's car, drives right through the front gates and pulls up in front of my shack. "Let's go!" she says. "Get up! Put on some pants."

It's a warm day and the city is already steaming in the midday sun. We drive through downtown and into the suburbs.

"Where are we going?" I say, fiddling with the radio.

"I don't know yet." We crank the windows open, and then suddenly, just like that, we're out of the city.

"Wow! Can you taste the air? It tastes like long grass and . . . air!"

"You want to drive?" She pulls over and we trade places.

"Where to?"

"Anywhere you want."

We pass eight hundred wheat fields, six hundred farmhouses, a couple dozen small towns and an infinite number of churches rimmed with glowing yellow grass. We turn the radio up and Sherry laughs at me singing, all this fresh new air blowing my lungs up like bagpipes.

"I know where we're going," she says all of a sudden. "Turn right here."

She directs us down a few more roads, into a provincial park, and we pull up to the ranger's station as the sun is dipping low. The girl in the office tells us that half the campground is closed for low season, and shows us a map so we can find a site. "It's $28 a night."

"And this here is the part that's closed," I say, pointing at the map.

"Uh, yeah."

"Well, maybe we'll come back in high season. Thanks."

We walk back to the car, and Sherry says, "You're so bad."

At the gate to the closed part of the park, I get out and pull the wooden horse to one side, then back across as Sherry drives the car in. We find a spot with lush grass and overhanging trees, down by the water.

It's our own private world. The birds are singing. The bugs are humming. The waves are licking softly at the shore. Clouds move sparse and quiet across the sky.

Sherry sets up the tent while I gather some wood. We go for a walk, then I put a beer-can chicken in the fire and we lie on our backs in the grass, drinking vodka and looking up at the darkening sky.

"My back doesn't hurt anymore," I say. "Sleeping with you made it better."

"Sleeping with me makes everything better."

"You're right," I laugh. "You're amazing, you know?"

"I'm good at some things."

"It's not just that . . . I really don't understand it, actually. You, I mean." If somebody's in trouble, Sherry's always right there, without a gram of naiveté or false hope. The women in Tent City already trust her more than they do each other. There are some people who, no matter what you bury them in, will transcend it—have souls that hover above the trees. I try to tell Sherry this.

"My soul's got problems too," she says, putting her hand on my chest. "I had this telemarketing job once, and I'd call all these nice people—people on pensions, whoever. Then I found out it was a scam, and I still stayed for another week. I felt sick every night, and couldn't sleep . . . Oh, God, I don't want to think . . ."

Jackie robs Sluggo of every cent she can, for crack. Hoyt beats dogs. Eddie and Karen do crack instead of going to see their newborn son. Sherry's mom takes her money and loses it at bingo, just like Sherry's crackhead boyfriend did.

"There are worse things than telemarketing," I say.

"There's an island in the middle of this lake," says Sherry. "It's called Strawberry Island. Sounds good, eh? There's a monastery over there. I guess the whole island's covered in monks, nuns, strawberries and . . ."

"Come here," I say. The night birds are singing, the stars are falling, coyotes howling, the beer boiling, the chicken shaking, the nuns and priests searching for strawberries in the dark grass, the waves stroking the shore . . .

x x
x

In the morning we leave before the park warden can find us, and drive farther down the beach. I walk out into the lake, halfway to Strawberry Island, and still the water never rises above my stomach. I turn around and can see Sherry like a distant beacon on the shore, the sunlight shining off her sunglasses. She is smoking, the long shadow of her arm moving to her mouth.

"Sherry!" I call out, my voice skimming atop the water. "What was the other thing?"

"You're going to wake up the nuns."

I walk back toward the shore, watching her grow, coming into focus. I wade right up to the waterline.

"What was the other thing you were scared of, about me?"

"I was scared you'd break my heart. But not anymore."

"Why?"

"I think it might be good for me—it's never happened before."

"It's never good. It's the worst thing ever."

She doesn't say anything.

"I'm going to throw you in the lake now," I say. "You're still covered in chicken."

"I love it when you talk like that," says Sherry, and I throw her in the lake.

x   x
x

I know I need sleep. I've been lying out here on my new rattan couch just thinking of what a real night-to-morning sleep would feel like. Sherry and I have seen the sun come up every day for the past week, but tonight she's sleeping in Scarborough.

Les comes over to chat. He's found an adult board game called You Don't Know Dick, and is scouring Tent City for people who want to play.

"But no!" he says, sitting down on the edge of my new couch. "Of course nobody wants to do something fun and normal, hmm-hey, like play a game. Oh no, we just want to beat each other up and smoke crack. It's too much work, hmm-yeah, to play a game—to have some fun!"

"I hear you, Les," I say. "I'd play if I wasn't so tired."

"If Sherry were here, hee-hmm, all four of us could play."

Jo-Jo, who was with Jake before he went to jail, has been staying in Les's trailer for the past couple weeks. Since Jake was busted, she's been coming down for a couple days at a time, like the rest of the prostitutes. But now that the weather's nicer, there's a half-dozen of them living around the rec centre. Les and Jo-Jo seem pretty good for each other. They both talk constantly—whether or not anyone's listening—and laugh a lot, whether or not anything's funny. I believe Les has fallen for Jo-Jo the sweet ho, and wants to be her one and only.

"We should do normal stuff, yeah-hmm," he says. "Like you and Sherry could come over for a drink, ha-hmm and maybe snacks. And we could play a board game, like this one—or some cards, ha-rumm. Or even go to a movie if we got some money. You know, normal things, hee-umm, like people do."

"Normal things."

"Exactly."

May 30

I'm glad Sherry was at work all day. It's the end of the month and every-one has their cheques—except for me, since I get mine on the fif-teenth—so they're all even more messed up than usual.

I was over at Sluggo and Jackie's having some beers in the sun. Hoyt was drunk and he kept trying to grab my Red Wings baseball hat. Detroit is playing Carolina in the Stanley Cup semifinals, and appar-ently Hoyt is a Hurricanes fan. He was getting abusive, and frustrated that he couldn't get the cap off my head.

"Sit down, Hoyt," I said. "Just try to relax."

"Fuck you!" he snarled. "I'm going to beat Detroit—I'll bet you fucking money I beat Detroit."

"But Hoyt," I said, "I don't think you're even playing tonight."

Everyone started laughing, and Hoyt yelled, "I'll fucking bet you!"

"Okay," I said, reaching out my hand. "I'll bet you twenty bucks that you don't beat the Detroit Red Wings—in fact, I'll bet you don't even make it onto the ice."

He grabbed my hand and said, "Twenty bucks! Yer fucked, buddy." He couldn't figure out why everyone was still laughing at him and he wouldn't let go of my hand. He pulled it toward him like he was going to arm-wrestle, squeezing hard to crush my fingers. I leaned back, returning the squeeze, so he pulled harder, then I let go and he fell into his chair.

"Fuck you!" he said, trying to grab my hat again. "I'll kick your fuckin' ass!"

This happened a half-dozen more times until it got really irritating, and everyone was telling him to shut up. He took one more swipe at my head. "I'll fucking kill you!" he growled.

"What'd you say?"

"I'll fucking kill you!"

I pushed my chair away and stood in the clear. No matter how happy I am these days, you can't take "I'll fucking kill you" lightly. And despite the desire for peace, I still haven't lost the urge to hit Hoyt.

"Okay," I said. "Try to kill me."

Hoyt staggered to his feet and faced me, his big moustache drooping like a dead squirrel's tail.

"He'll knock you on your ass," said Sluggo to Hoyt.

"Oh yeah?" said Hoyt, and tried to shuffle like a boxer.

"You better believe it," said Jackie. I was surprised they were so sure of this. A few people came to Eddie's open door, crack pipes in their hands, to see what was going on. Lenny came over and stood behind a chair.

"I'll tell you what, Hoyt," I said. "Not only will I let you take the first swing, but I'll put my hands in my pockets." I dug my fists into my cargo pants. "How's that? Go ahead, Hoyt."

Lenny started saying, "Right on, Shaun. Right on . . . ," and Sluggo said, "What you waiting for, Hoyt? Scared he'll beat you without his hands?"

I had no idea what I was doing. I'm a bluffer, not a fighter, but it seemed the audience had taken my boast to mean I'd fight with my hands in my pockets—rather than just take the first punch like this—and it felt contrary to the spirit of the moment to clarify. Hoyt was rocking from one leg to another, probably more confused than scared, but I decided to push the bluff.

"This is your last chance, or you never open your mouth to me again, except to offer me a beer. Now, take a fucking swing."

He rocked back on his heels and, for a moment, I thought he would. But then his eyes darted around, to Sluggo, to Jackie, to Lenny.

"No?" I said, waited another few seconds, then sat down in my chair and Jackie handed me my beer.

"I-I'll . . . ," stammered Hoyt.

"Shut up, Hoyt," said Sluggo. "It's not like he didn't give you a chance."

"Yeah!" said Lenny, the more hapless—and therefore more forgivable—of the Brothers. "That was funny!" he said, slapping me on the back.

"Uh, thanks."

Everyone was laughing as Hoyt stumbled away. Strangely enough, I felt both sorry for him and disappointed that I hadn't hit him. It had gone as well as it could, though. Now everyone would be trying to figure out what lethal, skilful move I'd have employed to beat Hoyt without my hands. I tried to visualize it myself; it looked awkward and fairly impossible. I laughed.

"Yeah, you showed him," said Lenny. "It was funny, eh?"

May 31

Everyone's going down, dropping, trying to stay up but out of fuel, out of breath, out of crack and booze. The day after cheque day is the most depressing down here—people's eyes half-open, people vomiting on their shoes, cursing and growling at each other without enough energy to yell or fight.

My bike is gone. Apparently it's been gone for a couple of days, but I hadn't noticed. I told Eddie he can grab it whenever he wants. Terry throws me a buck or two to take it to work when he's got some roofing, and Eddie's buddy, Norm, brings me smokes, a coffee or a beer when he or his girlfriend, Sandy, need it for a run. The bike has always come back—until now.

"Was wondering when you'd notice," says Eddie. "Jackie wanted to use it and you weren't here, so I picked the lock for her—which I shouldn't have done. But I knew you'd lend it to her if . . ."

"Sure. Of course."

"But then she let Sandy use it for a minute, and that was two days ago. She hasn't come back, and Norm's not around either. But don't worry, eh? You don't do a thing—it's my responsibility, I got it covered."

x
x
x

By dark, anyone who's not crashed right out is scrounging for enough to get up again. I was over at the rec centre, trying to drag Calvin out of trouble. He and Bonnie are sort of on again, and sort of off. When they're off he's all messed up on booze and crack, and tonight they were definitely not on. I had to grab him by the throat before finally he noticed I was there.

I punched a guy to get out the door, and once outside, a hooker heft-ed a full 5-litre keg of Molson Canadian against my chest. I thought she was going for us, then realized she just wanted to sell it. Some of the deals I'm getting these days are amazing. Last week I bought two bottles of vodka for $5. I gave the hooker $10—the magic number for a crack-head—then carried Calvin and the keg away.

"Where's my angel, little brother?"

"Not here, Cal."

x   x   x

I'm in the middle of writing when Jackie comes to the door.

"God, Jackie," I say, looking at her face.

"Do you mind . . . if I just . . . sit here," she says, sitting down in the chair by the door. She isn't slurring, stumbling or vomiting, but this is far scarier. It's as if she has turned into a translucent rock of crack, burn-ing to ash. Her eyes are like glass, like a doll's eyes, and her skin is so hot I can see the heat rising through the air.

"Jesus, Jackie. How much did you smoke?"

She doesn't answer, but she looks at me like an infant trying to fig-ure something out. Her clothes are soaked right through with sweat. I wet a towel and put it around her neck, then I talk for the sake of filling the empty space, saying mindless things like, "You got to stop this, Jacks. You're gonna kill yourself." Or, "What can I do for you? Can I help?"

Jackie gets paranoid when she's on crack. Sometimes I see her emerging from the rec centre, or Heartbeat's, or out from under a tarp somewhere, looking around like a hunted animal before diving back in.

She stares at the floor. Finally she says, "Shaun. Can I borrow $10 till tomorrow?"

"I don't have any money," I say. "And anyway, I wouldn't give it to you like this."

"Five dollars? I just . . . need one more . . . before . . ."

"You got any booze in your house, Jackie?" I realize this is my answer for everything—but at least it's better than crack.

"Yeah, Sluggo's . . . passed out . . . but there's still some left . . ." Which surprises me. Usually she'd have sold it for crack the moment he started to fade. I see her realize this, too.

"No, Jackie," I say. "That's not what I mean. Go and drink the beers—it'll take a bit of the edge off, and maybe you can pass out."

She sits here a while longer, as though she's forgotten who she is. I'm not sure either. Finally I stand up and take her by the hand. We walk over to her shack. In the dark, I find three bottles of beer and pull off the caps so she won't be able to sell them so easily.

"Drink them, Jacks," I say. I light a candle, and see that she's already staring at me, as if she could see me in the dark. When I move to the door she's still looking at the dark space where my face was. I put a beer in her hand. "Good night, sweetie," I say, and close the door behind me.

x
x
x

It's taken me a while to realize the change that's happened down here. I guess I didn't see it because I've been so preoccupied with Sherry, and because I'm not a crackhead. Until recently someone—usually Eddie—would have to leave this place to buy crack at Street City, then bring it back here to smoke. But now the crack is here. Two big black guys are selling it out of the rec centre. They don't live here, just park their cars and set up shop, and now nobody has to leave to get a fix. A lot of the hookers from Street City have followed the dealers here. Pimps, after all, are a myth of seventies B movies, or they run escort agencies and strip clubs. There are no pimps on the street. There are crack dealers who sell crack to the hookers. They take no cut and offer no protection. They don't have to: crack is the pimp. It makes the money, and it keeps the girls coming back.

So now everyone's strung out and screwed up even more than before, scrounging and sucking and selling, then rushing over to the rec. I can't ignore how much of this world is made of white, translucent rock. I don't know when Eddie and Karen last saw little Caleb. I don't know whether Caleb is hooked on drugs. I don't ask. Jackie. Calvin. Randy. Terry. Heartbeat. Sherry's ex-boyfriend. Eddie. Karen. Caleb?

I wouldn't say people end up here because of crack cocaine, but it definitely keeps them around and around and around and around. And it's making me nervous—things are getting rougher just as I'm losing my guard, and have something to lose.

June 2

I finally did my part of the big cleanup, and everyone came out to watch—even Hawk. "Don't you lift a finger, sweetheart," he said to Sherry. "Just sit back and tell him what to do."

"Sure, Hawk," she said. Whenever she says his name I can see her stifling a giggle.

So everyone just sat back and told me what to do, while I tried to clean up, build a deck, and rearrange all my new outdoor furniture. Eventually I brought out the keg of beer to keep them occupied. Les found some glasses, and they all started pouring drinks, but then Jackie pulled me aside and said, "Don't let Sluggo see the keg."

"Sluggo can have some beer."

"No, really. He might recognize it."

"Aw, Jackie." I shook my head. For the hooker to have made any profit by selling me the keg, Jackie would have got no more than a $5 rock. "So you're saying he can't even get a sip of his own keg!" She shrugged and poured a beer.

Lenny came walking over with a six-pack.

"How you doing, man!" he said. Derek was nowhere around.

"Uh, okay . . ."

"Any more trouble with Hoyt? Ha-ha! That sure was funny! I'll go get our wheelbarrow and shovel, okay? So you can move all this trash better."

"Okay," I said, and he walked back over to his place.

"What's with that?" said Sherry.

"I guess we're friends now."

I built the deck out of skids and a large platform that Calvin helped me carry over from behind Randy's. I put the spool table on the deck with a few folding chairs, then tucked the couch beneath the trees on the west perimeter of the yard for afternoon shade. It's been hovering around 30 degrees the past few days. I put the coffee table in front of the couch, with the drink cart on one side and the serving table on the other. I put up a backless, standing bookshelf and placed a plush white chair behind it. I laid down some planks as a walkway from the road to my deck, then pulled the fire barrel back into the middle of my new outdoor lounge.

"Still something wrong," I said, standing back to look. I'd been working all day and the sun was starting to drop. Calvin, Randy and Les had already claimed the couch, and Jackie, Karen and Sherry were sitting on the deck. Lenny was still trying to figure out how to use the wheelbarrow.

"I know what it is," said Hawk. "You got to get rid of all these bums . . . I don't mean you, of course, Sherry—excuse me, sweetheart."

"No problem, Hawk," said Sherry.

"A fence!" I said. "I'll build a nice little . . ."

"Barbed wire on top, or razor wire," he said, and walked off down the shore.

June 3

Today Eddie comes soaring down the road and skids my crappy white bicycle right into the deck.

"I told you, kid! What I tell you?" The way he tells it, he went to some crack house uptown, smashed a window and came out with my bike. Who knows how many people he had to knock out in the process.

"Thanks, Eddie. But wouldn't it have been easier just to get another one?"

"It's the principle of the thing. You've got your bike back now."

"I do."

"It's good to have you like this," he says, flopping down on my couch.

"Like what?"

"You're happy now. You're more relaxed, and easygoing—you know? You're smiling now. It's a better way to be down here."

"Smiling?"

"Smiling."

It's a funny thing: I've been practising my Yul Brynner glare for so long and now Eddie tells me it's better to be smiling. I guess it's just a question of reaching another level. Sure, with the right look in your eye you might keep the wolves at bay and the jerks off your back. But to play things a bit, you've got to be confident and relaxed enough to smile.

"Like cleaning up your place, making it nice," he says. "It shows you're more comfortable down here, eh? That's 'cause of Bingo, right?" Eddie calls Sherry Bingo, which only he can get away with.

"Yeah, sure. I cleaned up for her."

"And you don't have to be running all over the place now. You can settle down a bit. I'm happy about that, it's good."

This from a guy who's bounced his way out of every good chance he ever got. The name Caleb hangs between us and, even though I want to, I won't be the one to reach for it. If Eddie and Karen's life-schedule still existed, they'd be in rehab by now. But instead she's still wandering back and forth from their shack to the outhouse, to the crack houses. And he aims his energy into things like "Operation Bike Retrieval," directs his thoughts into a study of my comfort level in Tent City as reflected in my smile and newfound domesticity. He puts his heart into a crack pipe and buries his soul in the toxic ground.

"Yeah, I'm happy." I pour him a drink. "And I'm going to build a fence. But I got to say, Eddie, you're . . ."

"Just don't build it too high," he says, smiling. "Don't build that fence too high."

June 4

"You want to adopt a kid, Shauny?"

I look up from stoking the barrel fire as Jackie comes through the trees, waving her big meaty arms. For an instant my heart rises to the base of my throat. I see myself wrapping little Caleb in a soft blue blanket and walking with him into the afternoon sun, his tiny body in my arms . . .

"This kid's been hanging around all day, and he's driving me nuts. He's stunned, you know—doesn't know the first thing about the first thing . . . I'm thinking maybe you can talk to him."

"What kid?" I say, and follow Jackie back through the trees. A skinny, bare-chested guy—about 18 years old, with tattoos and a loopy grin—is sitting by their barrel, shovelling handfuls of Lucky Charms into his mouth. Sluggo is staring at the kid's masticating jaw, as if imagining it fractured.

"Those things are better with milk," I say.

"Uh-huh," says the kid, his mouth hanging open. "Hey! You got some milk?"

"No."

"You got *any* food—I *really* got the munchies, eh? Like *always!*"

"This is Shaun," says Jackie, like I was the evening's keynote speaker. "You listen to what he's got to say, okay?"

"Uh . . . ," I say.

"I'm Tom," says the kid, and crams some more Lucky Charms into his mouth. "You can call me Thomas, though."

"Sure thing, Thomas."

Jackie starts to peel some potatoes, watching us out of the corner of her eye. Sluggo is still glaring at the destruction of purple horseshoes and four-leaf clovers.

"You got something to eat, dude?"

"Where are you staying, Thomas?" I ask.

"I was back there, but I got sick of those guys, eh? They're like fags," he says. When he laughs, his mouth is full of rainbow saliva.

By "those guys" he means a group of ten or so teenage boys and a few of their girlfriends who pitched some tents in the bush when summer arrived. Bonnie's taken a few of the boys under her wing. She says they work as prostitutes uptown, although she thinks only one of them is actually gay. I don't know what would happen if the old crew found out. Homophobia's about as prevalent as crack down here. In fact, other than Bonnie, Les is the only one who doesn't exhibit an aggressive fear of homosexuals. ("Gays are great, hmm-yeah!" he told me. "I've had lots of friends who are gay. They know how to party, you know? And the best thing, all right, yes'm, about gays is the more of them, the more babes for us!")

Thomas is staring at a little yellow dollar sign in the palm of his hand.

"Where are you staying now?" I ask him.

"Oh, some guy gave me his shed. No problem, dude."

I look at Jackie. She says, "Crazy Chris let him stay in his place."

"Okay, Thomas," I say. "Here's the deal. Don't call me dude. And don't call anyone else a fag, okay? You should call people by their names, unless you haven't been introduced. The guy's name is Chris, and it's not a shed, it's a prefab. And he hasn't *given* it to you. You got it?"

"Okay. Whatever, dude . . . uh, *Shaun.*"

"You got to remember this stuff."

Jackie nods and Sluggo emits a short grunt.

"If you're on your own you've got to be careful—you've got to be smart, okay?"

Thomas looks at me like it never occurred to him to be smart.

"Like right now. Jackie's making dinner. You don't want to overstay your welcome—you understand?"

"Yeah, sure, man," he says, leaning in to slap Sluggo playfully on the arm. Sluggo growls.

"And you don't want to do that."

"I sure am hungry!" says Thomas.

I'm surprised they've put up with him this long. Although he seems hopeless, I'm still kind of moved by the idea of adoption. "Come on, and I'll find you some food," I say. We walk over to my place and I dig through a bucket of cans. "Here's some Zoodles. And some ravioli, and some beets."

"I don't think I like beets . . . What are beets?"

"Take 'em."

He nods, turns and walks a few steps, then stops. "Hey, man, how do I open them?"

I go into my shack and find one of those one-handed, wedging can openers. He stares at it. "You'll figure it out," I say. "You find a good place to make a fire, and cook 'em up."

"How do you make a fire?" says Thomas, grinning.

"Jesus, Thomas. How long have you been on the street?"

"Four years."

"Uh-huh. Tell you what: My barrel's already going, but tomorrow you got to make your own fire, okay?" I hand him a pot. "Make sure you wash it first though." He nods, holding the pot like it's a big remote control. "You know where to get water?"

"Sure, dude . . . Shaun . . . uh, *no*."

I grab a bar of soap and walk him over to the water hose where I show him how to wash a pot. "The important thing," I say as we head back, "is that you . . . Hey, where's the can opener?" Thomas stops and looks at his empty hand.

"Go back to the water hose and get it, then cook the stuff on my barrel. But don't go in my shack. I'll be at Eddie's—that one over there, okay?"

"Sure . . . ," says Thomas, turning around. "Where's the water hose again?"

"Fuck, Thomas! This isn't cute." I point back from where we've just come.

"I'll try to find it," says Thomas, and heads off.

I go over to Eddie's, and he hands me a can of Crest.

"What's up?" he says. "You look kind of in pain."

"I just adopted a moron," I say, nodding to Terry and Heartbeat. "Here, I'll show you." We step outside and I point through the trees toward my fire barrel.

"What the hell's he doing?" says Heartbeat. Thomas is bashing one of the cans with a rock.

"Making dinner," I say, and we go back into Eddie's.

After ten minutes or so, Thomas walks up to the open door. He has a dented can in one hand and the opener in the other. "Hey, man! Can I come in?" he says, stepping into Eddie's shack.

Karen shouts, "Hey, buddy!" I wince, and Eddie rocks back on his chair to block the doorway.

"Whatcha think you're doing, kid?" says Eddie.

"Don't walk into someone's house without asking," I say. "Okay, Thomas?"

"But I did ask," he says. "I said, can I . . ."

"Are you retarded?" says Eddie. "Asking doesn't mean a thing if you don't wait for an answer."

"You're going to get yourself killed," says Karen. "We're just trying to help you."

Thomas steps back out the door. "I can't open my can, dude! What the *fuck?*"

June 6

I swam for a while at the community centre, ate some tuna casserole in a church, brought a chocolate bar to Sherry at work, then returned to Tent City to find Thomas sitting inside the gates.

"Hey, Shaun! Hey, man!" he said. "I got some more *cans!*"

"Way to go, Thomas. You build yourself a fire yet?"

"No. That's what I wanted to talk to you about. Can I cook them at your place?"

"Guess so. But make it quick. We're going to use the barrel for dinner."

"You and who?"

"Don't worry about that, Thomas."

I walked down to my shack. Les was lying on the couch, talking to himself.

"Hey, Les."

"Hm-hm, the love of my life is out sucking cock. Yessir. That's what she's doing."

"She's a prostitute, Les."

"Yeah. All right. Uh-huh. Yes. But she's *my* prostitute. Ha-ha!"

"You want to adopt a little moron? Might take your mind off things. He's very dumb."

"Really?" He sat up smiling, his whimsical silver eyebrows rising like two sunlit birds. "How dumb *is* he?"

Right on cue, Thomas came through the bushes, a can in each hand. "You know how to work these things, dude?" he said to Les, holding up the can opener like he'd been meditating on it all day.

"I'll take him!"

"They're not like the normal ones," said Thomas. "They're a *lot* harder!"

"That, my boy," said Les, springing off the couch, "is an *exceptional* can opener! Mm-hmm! Simple design! One-handed! Basic rocking motion—all in the wrist. It's an original—hmm-hey—nothing better!" He took the can and the opener from Thomas, who gazed in awe as Les cut the rim and folded back the lid.

"Wow!" whispered Thomas.

"Hey, guys," said Sherry, coming through the trees.

Thomas turned and looked at her. "Wow!" he said again.

"Behave yourself, Thomas," I said, and Sherry put a small cooler down on the spool table. "Hello, Lester," she said. "What are you boys doing?" I kissed her.

"We're opening cans," said Thomas and Les at the same time.

"That's nice," she said.

Les showed Thomas how to get a barrel fire going while Sherry and I poured some drinks and started to prepare the steaks she'd brought.

"Don't be scared of it, hmm-na," said Les, dipping a hand in and out of the flaming barrel. "It won't burn you if you don't let it."

"Oh," said Thomas.

"You know what a pyromaniac is, Thomas? Hey-yum. That's me—and a pyromaniac knows his pyro as well as his mania. You got to practise at fire like you practise at sex . . ." Thomas was staring at him through the fire like he'd just seen God. "I was 7 years old, hmm-hey, and I burnt down a golf course clubhouse—right to the ground . . ."

Les rambled on about his history of firebugging and promiscuous sex until Sherry said, "Your spaghetti's burning," and Thomas started dancing around the barrel, trying to grab the pot's handle.

"It's hot!" he squealed. "It's really hot!"

"How long's he been on the street?" said Les.

"Four years," said Thomas. "Ow! Fuck! How're you supposed to do this? It's sparking!"

Les picked up the pot up by the rubber handle and put it on the table.

I started cooking the steaks while Thomas ate his burned spaghetti out of the pot. When he was done, Les said, "C'mon, kid, I'll teach you how to tap into the hydro—then you won't need fire!"

"Later, dudes," said Thomas, and followed Les down the road, a can in each pocket and the opener in his hand. "What's hydro?" he said, and Les started to sing.

x x x

As we're finishing dinner and a bottle of wine, Calvin comes stumbling up to the deck. I offer him some steak, but he's too far gone to eat.

"Aw, b'y!" he says, falling into a chair. I give him the heel of the bottle. "Aw, darling!" he says, turning to Sherry. "How you doing?"

"How are you, Calvin?" says Sherry, rolling a cigarette.

"I'm . . . okay," he slurs, "but the old lady's killing me . . . eating my fucking heart."

"Where you staying, Cal?"

"That's what I'm saying, b'y. I'm not staying anywheres—she won't let me in the house, you know, and I can't stay in the prefab either. You know why, b'y? That's where we were together for the first time—too many fucking memories . . . Fuck!"

Sherry glances my way, but I don't look up. I don't want to think that four plastic walls and a filthy floor are too full of memories for him to sleep there anymore.

"Where are you then, Cal?"

"I don't know," he says, getting to his feet. "Under the bridges."

I want to grab him. "Don't do that, Cal. That's going too far back."

He stumbles over to Sherry and hugs her. "You take care of him," he says. Then turns to me. "Don't worry 'bout me. I'll be all right, little brother."

"Aw, Jesus! Quit it Cal."

"Bye, sweetie," he says to Sherry.

"Bye, Cal."

"You're an asshole, Calvin," I say, but he's already gone.

June 8

Today I built a fence. I got the design from studying the one Les built around his trailer. He stood up short rounds of logs about 10 feet apart, then laid out longer logs across the tops and tied them together with twine. Unfortunately the only logs here now are all the way over by Karl's place, and they're about twice the thickness of the ones Les used. They're so big I could only fit three at a time into a shopping cart and it took half the day just to drag them over.

Sherry helped for the first while, but it was scorching hot and I figured the least I could do is build a fence for my girl. "Just sit back and relax," I said. "Have some drinks and chili dogs." For the first time since Steve was run out of town, the Purple People Eaters were here, with the same songs, handing out bags of the same pale blue underwear.

"They're kind of creepy, eh?" said Sherry.

"Yeah. But who knows—they might mean well."

The young girl Steve had scared so badly came over while I was working and gave me a hug. "I was hoping to see you," she said.

I told her I was proud of her for coming back, and I wanted to tell her she was strong enough to do without her crew, but the Purple People quickly surrounded her.

"I like your fence," she said, and they coaxed her away.

x   x   x

In the late afternoon Calvin shows up with a tiny kitten in his arms.

"Oh, shit!" says Sherry. "Don't let me see that!" She has a soft spot for cats. "Let me hold him . . . Don't let me hold him! Look at him—he's got your eyes!"

"You noticed that too, eh, sweetheart?" says Calvin, handing over the kitten and grinning ear to ear. He's a bit drunk already, but not too far gone. "Got him from Les's litter. There's one more left, if you want it."

"Don't tell me that!" says Sherry, the kitten snuggling into her breast.

"You want one?" I say, rolling yet another log across the yard.

"Of course I do!" she says. "But I don't even have a place! You have to take care of them . . . don't you, sweetie," she says to the kitten, tickling its ears. "Like they're your baby." There are a couple dozen cats in Tent City now, over half of them kittens.

"You going to be able to take care of him, Cal?" I say.

"Oh yeah, b'y." Then he turns to Sherry. "I've had every kind of animal you could think of. Lots of kittens, too."

"And where are they now, Cal?" I ask, but he ignores me. The kitten is climbing on Sherry's shoulders. "Well, just keep him away from Cleo," I say. Jackie and Sluggo's Rottweiler has a thing for kittens. She's already killed two of them.

By the time it's dark I've finished the fence. It's only a couple of feet high, but circles my whole yard. At nine o'clock Sherry and I go up to the gates to wait for Sister H. She's a wonderful, smiling church lady who comes down once a week with hot meals of curry, dumplings and spicy meat. She used to come around to every shack, but now there are so many people down here—about a hundred by my count—you have to meet her at the road if you want to get a meal. The Street Help and Street Patrol have stopped bringing sandwiches since—according to Hawk—they got ambushed down here.

"But they've got nothing but baloney and soup!"

"Crackheads, Shaun," said Hawk. "Crackheads."

A dozen or so of us stand in the middle of the road for about an hour until finally Hawk says, "Looks like she's not coming."

Sherry and I go back to my shack, back to rusty cans of pasta and dirty dishes somewhere in the dark. I'm too tired to manufacture a dinner and I collapse on the couch as Sherry starts gathering wood for a fire. Then, as she lights the kindling, we hear Sister H's horn honking at the gates. By the time we get out to the road, however, Marty is walking toward us, holding up his empty hands. "Already gone," he says.

I look at Sherry, and she shrugs. I feel exhausted, and hungry, and kind of ashamed. What's the point of spending all day building a fence if you can't even put food on the table? When Sherry wants us to go out, she pays. But right now she doesn't have any money either. She doesn't make much at the bar and, even if she were rich, I wouldn't feel any better about this.

Sherry insists it isn't a problem. "You don't need money," she says. "Most of what we do is free. And if there's one thing I've learned from my mama, it's that the whole idea of money is ridiculous."

Sherry's mom spends money on two things: bingo and jewellery. She takes Sherry's tips and loses them at bingo. Or, if she wins, she comes back with $1,000 worth of gold trinkets. She never mentions the money she took, just shows off her new rings. "One day you'll appreciate jewellery," she tells Sherry. "Just wait—one day you'll appreciate it."

I look up and see Hawk coming down the road toward us.

"Here, Shauny," he says, and hands us two meals, two containers of soup and two drinks. "I just told all those punks that Shaun and his old lady need some dinner."

Sherry and I walk back to my shack and sit down on the deck to eat.

"Shaun's old lady, eh?" says Sherry.

"Yeah, sorry about that."

"There are worse things to be."

"Thanks."

The fire is going and the stars are out, and when we're finished eating, a shower of meteors falls through the sky. There's no one around, but then a girl appears out of the shadows. She walks through the front entrance of my yard, up to the table, and sits down in a chair.

"Hi," she says. She is very pretty, with long blond hair and bare feet. There are tattoos snaking up both her arms. She is wet, like she walked right out of the canal, a skid-row mermaid who's grown legs. "That fire's all right," she says, and stares into the barrel for a while. Then she jumps up and heads back into the shadows toward the other side of town. Jimmy D's dogs don't even bark.

"That was weird," says Sherry. A couple of swans drift by, glowing white on the dark water. Sherry rolls a joint, and I take a couple of small tokes. "This place can be kind of beautiful," she says. "And I like the fence you made."

We start to fade in the dark early morning, when a police cruiser drives up and stops in front of my shack. They turn a spotlight on us, blinding white light, and they don't move.

"Hey!" I shout, shielding the light with my hand as I stand up. But Sherry pulls me back down, leans in and begins to kiss me. We stay like that, in spotlight, until the cruiser finally pulls away, and then we can see the stars again.

June 10

Today Jackie and Sluggo came over to invite me to the Brothers' place for steaks.

"Really?" I said. "You sure?"

"It was their idea," said Jackie.

Derek did scowl when he saw me, but then his old lady, Donna, got up to give me a tour. No matter what I think of them, I've got to give the Brothers this: They sure can build. Their shack is the size of a large one-bedroom suite, with a living room, kitchen and even a bathroom. In the living room there's a big couch where Lenny sleeps, and a parakeet in a copper cage. The kitchen counters are made of hardwood. The bedroom has a king-size bed and skylights in the ceiling. The bathroom is a bath-tub behind an orange curtain. There's even a tool shed out back with tools in it. The perimeter of the yard is fenced with orange mesh tied to upright logs. In the yard, they've built a smoker out of pipes and a fire barrel, as well as a picnic table with a plastic canopy for when it rains.

We had steak with potatoes and beer, and Lenny kept getting up to re-create the infamous standoff between Hoyt and I.

"He just left his hands in his pockets," said Lenny. "Like this! It was funny!"

"Yeah, I get it already," said Derek, but he did stop glaring at me.

"These are some good steaks," I said. "Thank you."

"Someday," said Derek, "you and that little lady should come over for perogies."

"Perogies?"

"Oh yeah, we make the best perogies," he said, nodding seriously.

"You guys Eastern European?"

Lenny squinted at me like he wasn't sure what I meant, and Derek said, "We're from Idaho."

"Oh. Where'd you learn to make perogies?"

"Halfway house. The old woman there taught us. We make 'em right from scratch—best fuckin' perogies ever. You come over and try 'em."

"All right. Thanks, guys." When I left they gave me a beer for the road, as if we were friends now. Which is fine with me. You keep your enemies closest, especially when you're running out of them.

My bike, on the other hand, has gotten away from me once more. Apparently Terry borrowed it to go scam some percs with a phony pre-scription, and got caught. So now he's in jail and my bike is sitting in front of some drugstore, but no one knows which one.

June 11

I think even to himself, Les is a mystery. And a comedy, and a tragedy. Intelligent and self-aware, he sits there laughing and cringing at the movie of his own life—this epic adventure in self-destruction. He could stop the projector but, like the rest of us, he wants to see what stupid thing he'll do next.

And maybe it's for the sake of this movie—the Fear Les, Hope Les, Love Les Show—that he's fallen in love with Jo-Jo. She chews up his heart—but it makes for great cinema.

"I threw her out again last night, yeah-hmm. I lit her clothes on fire, too."

"Oh yeah?"

We were walking down to the park at Harbourfront. Les had heard that there were free outdoor movies there every Wednesday night. "Guy said he went there last week for some Schwarzenegger flick and they gave him free popcorn, hmm-hee. Said he ate his weight in popcorn!"

"Why'd you throw her out this time?"

"I'm out roofing all day, hmm-yeah, trying to make a living. So I come home with stuff for my baby, right? I got food and beer and smokes and cupcakes, too, hey-ymm. She likes 'em, right? She's smiling! She's happy, hey-yeah! She cracks a beer, puts two cupcakes in her mouth and says, 'Just a second, I'll be back in a sec!'"

Les laughed like he was getting to the best part. He held up his hands. "So I sit there, um-hmm, waiting for her . . . for three hours! Three hours go by, and finally I see her getting out of some asshole's truck—right in front of the trailer! You know what I did?"

"You kicked her out and lit her clothes on fire?"

"Not just that, hmm-nuh," said Les, shaking his head with a sort of melancholy whimsy. "I stomped on the cupcakes, too."

"Good thinking, Les."

This is the essence of our man Les. Sure, he used to have his own roofing business, and lots of money and a wife. Sure, he can tap into hydro, and build fences and design windmills. But when it comes to an immediate emotional problem, Les lights things on fire and starts stomping on cupcakes.

"You know what my mmm-problem is?"

"Crack . . . Booze and crack . . . Booze and crack, and you're insane?"

"No, no, no . . . It's just, hmm-nuh, that I'm overly susceptible to crazy, drug-addicted women."

Even here Les is deluding himself. It's not crazy women in general—it's Jo-Jo. He truly believes that if she would just stop whoring, they could be happy together. So he spends his days scheming about ways to get her out of here and, when none of them work, starts dragging her toward the gates—as if all he has to do is get her to the other side, and suddenly her eyes will fill with love and fidelity.

"I mean, hmm-yeah," he continued, "I could have a nice lady. But the crack hos are way more interesting! Maybe we should talk about that at our next session. She sure opens up to you, eh?" Every couple of days, Les and Jo-Jo come over and sit on my couch because—for some reason—they think I can help with their love life.

"I barely understand a word she's saying, Les."

"Nobody does. It's not *what* she says, hmm-hee, but *how* she says it—so fast and like a song."

"Right."

We searched Harbourfront for an hour or so, but couldn't find a movie screen anywhere. We did, however, find an info booth.

"Where are the movies, hmm-yeah?" said Les. "Free popcorn!"

"Excuse me, sir?"

But no matter how Les tried, the guy behind the desk couldn't find the right info.

"He ate his weight in popcorn!" said Les. "He told me so."

"Who did, sir?" asked the info guy, still trying to be helpful.

"Some gimpy dude! I forget his name, hmm-hey—some drug dealer with a weird eye!"

"I'm sorry, sir. Is it possible he was mistaken?"

"His weight in popcorn! He said so!"

On the way back to Tent City, I asked Les what had become of Thomas.

"Who, the dumb kid?" Les's face lit up as if he was remembering a puppy he used to have. "I took him to the Good Shepherd for lunch, right? And this girl walks in, hmm-umm. She's strung out, she's got no shoes . . . and boom! It's like two magnets—they're joined at the lips. Turns out she's his girlfriend, and they've been looking for each other for like a week, hmm-nuhh. I mean, these two don't have half a brain between them. They've been wandering around the city looking for each other, trying to remember who was in charge of the quarter of a brain. It would be kind of sweet, hmm-hey, if it wasn't so pathetic. She was down here looking for him, too."

"What'd she look like?'

"Pretty—long blond hair, a bit too skinny, but sexy, with tattoos on her arms."

"The mermaid."

"Exactly!" With Les, the less sense you make, the more he understands you. "The strung-out siren with no shoes. She leaves you wandering around the city, hmm-hee, looking for your last bit of brain. And you can't help but love her."

We both nodded, and looked up at the sky as we crossed over Lakeshore.

"See the silos?" said Les, as if you could miss them, standing next to Tent City like God's cigarettes still in the pack. From my shack they block out half the downtown skyline. "You need money, right?" said Les. "You see that trim around the top? I'll bet that's copper." When Les isn't roofing, or tearing his heart out over Jo-Jo, or setting something on fire, he's usually looking for scrap metal. Like other industrious addicts down here, he does about a round a day with a shopping cart, searching the junk piles of Tent City for aluminum, steel or, ideally, copper.

"You want to go up there tomorrow?" he said, pointing to the roof, about fourteen storeys off the ground. "If that's copper, it's about six grand."

"How do we get up?"

"Hawk says he's done it. And Crazy Chris, too. And Marty . . ."

"Then how come the copper's still there?"

Les shrugged. "I'll wake you at eight. In the *morning*, hmm-hey."

June 12

At 7:45 Les was banging on my door and singing incoherently. I pushed it open to tell him to shut up, and Roger the Yugoslavian hit man was standing there next to him.

"Oh, great!" I said. "I got to deal with him too? He makes even less sense than *you* do."

"We go copper now," said Roger.

"A copper-us now!" shouted Les. "I love the smell of crack hos in the morning!"

"Oh, Jesus!"

I'd been in the silos about six months before, just to check them out. If you're looking for somewhere to film the climax of a horror movie, it's a perfect place. These abandoned grain silos have got everything: a precarious busted-in entrance, shadows that fold into utter blackness, bizarre monster-like pieces of machinery, scurrying animals, graffiti, echoes and even some creepy human inhabitants.

When I went in there before, I assumed I was alone. Eventually my eyes started to adjust to the dark, and as I turned a corner I saw a woman lying on a mattress. There was just enough light to see her mole eyes squinting at me. "I'm sorry," I said, and she pulled a plastic tarp over her head. I'd thought of going back since then, though why exactly I wasn't sure. To bring her some muffins? To film a movie? That's about all I've come up with.

One thing the silos don't have is a way to the top. The metal stairs on the outside have been broken off halfway, so they now start about seven storeys above the ground. "How we getting up?" I said as we slipped through the fence that separates Tent City from the silos.

"Hawk says you can get up into one of the silos, hmm-huh, and there's a ladder there."

"Why isn't he with us, then?"

"Big bottles," said Roger.

"Yep, they look like bottles, Roger," I said as we climbed through a hole in the wall.

"Gonna buy lots of bottles tonight, hm-yeah," said Les, and we dropped down into the darkness with a splash.

"Ahhh!" "Shit!" "Fuck bottles!"

Our yells echoed off the walls, and Les switched on the flashlight. The place was flooded, dark dubious water rising to our thighs. Roger swore about bottles. Les began to sing as we waded through the dark, stinking sludge. I could hear things moving in the water—not just us, other things.

"At least there won't be anyone here," I said.

"*You're* here," said a voice, and Les and I both shrieked. He waved the light ahead, and we could see the figure of a tall, thin man rising from the water. It moved toward us, and I half expected to see a disembodied head tucked under an arm, the beam of light passing through a translucent, floating body.

"I'm Les," said Les, for no apparent reason.

"Uh . . . I'm Shaun," I said.

"Greg," said the figure before us.

As he waded into the light he looked surprisingly normal—a baseball hat on his head, a sparse beard and a jean jacket. He lifted his hand in a bored little wave and let out a sigh.

"You don't live down here, do you?" I said.

"The water's only been here a month or so. I *am* getting a cough, though." He coughed as if to prove it, then shrugged, like someone trying to make the best of a slight mould problem in his apartment.

"Uh, Greg . . . ," I paused, trying to figure out how to explain to him that he lived below the earth in an airless, lightless, flooded, rat-infested grain elevator, and his cough was probably a symptom of the Black Death.

"It's been raining a lot," he said, nodding apathetically. "But my bed's above the waterline . . ."

"Big bottle!" bellowed Roger, obviously anxious to get on with our mission. "We copper now, okay?"

"There's no way up," said Greg, as if Roger had made sense. "I'd have found it by now." Then he shrugged once more and said, "But be my guest."

We searched for an hour and came up with nothing. We were able to get the hatch to one of the silos open, like Hawk had suggested, but there was no ladder inside.

"There's got to be a way, hm-nuhhh." said Les. "They all say there's a way."

"They're all pathological liars, Les."

"That *is* true."

"Fuck big bottle," said Roger, and we waded back through the water once more. As we were leaving, I went over to Greg, who was standing in front of a hanging plastic tarp.

"This can't be good for you. You should come live in Tent City." Greg just shrugged. "Is that where you sleep?" I said and reached for the tarp.

"Please don't." I pulled my hand back, nodded, then waded off toward the light.

By the time I got outside, they had a new plan.

"Robber Hood!" said Roger, nodding seriously.

"What?"

"Robin Hood!" said Les, smiling and nodding. "We're going to get a crossbow . . ."

"I have crossbow."

"Oh. Roger *has* a crossbow. So all we need is a really long rope, um-hhh," said Les. He pointed seven floors up at the metal stairs. "We shoot it through, climb up the rope, tear off the copper, drive it to the yard in my truck and, hee-yim-haa, we'll all be drunk by nightfall."

"Sure, Les," I said. "Sounds foolproof."

"Good then, uh-humm. I'll come over when we've got the rope."

"Roger Hood," said Roger, squinting at the horizon as if aiming an arrow.

x   x   x

I am sitting on my deck, writing some stuff down, when Les comes over. But instead of rope, he has a case of beer—and instead of Roger, Jo-Jo is with him.

He puts the beer on the table and sits on my couch. Jo-Jo sits down too, then stands back up. She wiggles her butt and touches her toes. Jo-Jo never stops moving.

"Tell him what you did, Les," she says.

"I got some beer, hm-hmm," says Les. "Told you we'd be drinking!"

"Where'd you get the money?" I say, pulling the caps off three bottles.

"Brought some a-loo-*min*ium over to the yard. Yeh-a-hmm . . . A-loo-*min*ium!"

"Jesus! You must have had tons of the stuff!"

"Tell him what you did, Les," says Jo-Jo again, dancing around the couch.

"Left the truck there, uh-hmm." Les glugs his beer. "Guy gave me $80."

"You sold your truck?"

"Yepsir."

"For eighty bucks!"

"For beer!" says Les. "For beer!"

"What happened to our summer job? What happened to roofing, and doing runs to the yard? What about the copper? What about Robin Hood? You sold your truck!"

Les shrugs and cracks another beer. Jo-Jo punches him lightly in the ribs.

Terry comes flying into the yard on my crappy white bike. "Sorry about that," he says. "I was in jail."

"Yeah."

"Have a beer?" says Les.

Roger is walking down the river toward us, carrying a crossbow.

"Want to buy some percs?" says Terry, snapping a beer cap into the air.

June 13

We have a goldfish now, named Dude.

I got my $195 early this month and took Sherry out on the town. We ate a lot and drank a lot and walked a long way home.

It was 4 a.m. by the time we got to the Esplanade, where they've set up a small summer carnival—a fairground, with rides and a boardwalk. We were nicely drunk, there was no wind and the night was quiet. We walked into the dark carnival without even glancing at each other, as if we'd been headed here all along. There were no security guards in sight. As we crossed the fairground, it felt as if we were the only people left on Earth. Without saying a word, we climbed over a small barricade and pushed through a door that read, "House of Haunted Hell!!!"

We walked down a narrow hall of warped and scratched mirrors, looking at each other's reflection—fat then thin, short then tall, then finally splintered into pieces. I pushed her along a track in a red cart with flames on the side, ducking through a tunnel of tinfoil. We crossed one of those playground suspension bridges, slid down a pole, then stood on a circular floor that turned beneath our feet.

As we exited through a door of plastic streamers, Sherry finally spoke. "Hell wasn't so bad," she said, and even her voice sounded like a dream. I nodded, and we walked over to the booths on the boardwalk. There were already balloons pinned to the wall for tomorrow, the darts laid out. As I reached for one, I noticed a large blanket covering something like a tent in the next booth over. I leaned in and pulled it back.

"Oh!" said Sherry.

And there, shining in the dim street light, was a pyramid of small glass bowls, stacked one on top of the other, a golden fish in each.

"They're asleep."

"Do you want one?" I said. "Do you want all of them?"

"One."

I picked the one off the top and covered them up again. As we walked out of the fairground, a couple of security guards were crossing the street toward us, doughnuts and coffee in their hands. I tucked the fishbowl under my jacket, and we made it safely past.

As I pulled the goldfish into the light, Sherry linked her arm through mine and said, "What should we call him, dude?"

"Dude," I said.

Sherry laughed in the quiet street and I passed the bowl into her hands as Dude began to swim.

x   x
x   x

Life is funny. One day you've got nothing but a gut full of sorrow and a tent full of rats—and the next you have a little house by the water, a fence, a deck, a rattan couch, a girlfriend and a goldfish.

We changed his water this morning, as well as his bowl. So now Dude lives in a beer pitcher. I was watching him swim in slow circles while I wrote, when Jackie came over.

"Nice fish," she said, and sat down. "That's what Eddie should do, get a fuckin' fish instead. I'll fucking cut *his* head off."

"What are you talking about?"

"He took Les's last kitten, eh? I mean he lives right next to us, and he *knows* what Cleo's like with cats. He says he'll chop Cleo's head off if she touches his cat. You don't fucking threaten my dog!" She was wringing her big red hands like she does when she's nervous or jonesing.

"What's going on, Jackie?"

She breathed out, and relaxed a bit. "I'm leaving on Monday," she said. "I'm going back to Kingston, back to my family . . . I have to get away from this stuff, Shauny. It's killing me, eh?"

"Yeah."

"I'm going to stay with my mom, then I'm going to move in with my sister, and get clean. So I can be with my kids again."

"That's good, Jackie." I put my hand on hers so she'd stop wringing them. "I'll miss you, but I'm glad you're going. You think you'll make it?"

"Oh yeah, I have to. I *have* to, you know."

That's what everybody says—I *have* to. It's what Eddie says about getting his baby back, what Les says about getting Jo-Jo out of here, what Calvin says about going into detox, but when I get him a bed he still doesn't go. I *have* to, they all say, and it sounds like a threat to themselves—or a last prayer to an absent god.

x
x
x

When Jackie left I took Dude in his 50-ounce Moosehead beer jug over to Eddie's shack. Karen was sitting on the floor playing with the kitten, singing to it and lifting it up to dance.

"Nice fish," she said, peering into the pitcher. "You know what you should do? When Eddie comes back, tell him if his cat touches your goldfish you'll chop its fucking head off." She laughed, and lifted the kitten up to look at Dude.

"Yeah, Jackie told me about that. You named him yet?"

She shook her head. "You want to hold him?"

I held the kitten. He scratched at my wrist and tried to bite my arm.

"Can I ask you a question, Karen?" I said, passing him back to her. "You seen Caleb lately?"

"Not really," she said, and cradled the kitten in her arms.

"When was the last time?"

"I *dunno*, Shaun," she said. "I don't fucking know—okay?"

"Okay, I just wanted to ask."

"Well, now you know."

When I left, she was spinning the kitten like a furry top on the floor.

"Don't forget to tell Eddie my joke about cutting his head off," she said. "That'd be fuckin' funny."

"Yeah, Karen," I said. "I'll be sure to remember."

x
x
x

I hope Jackie makes it. Everybody laughs, and says she'll be right back here within two weeks. Everybody laughs, because they're all like her, and they're all going down. They've been treading water too long, and are finally cramping up, finally sinking. "She'll be back," they say.

"Hey, young Shaun," says Eddie as I'm walking over to my shack. I haven't talked with Eddie in a long time. He's always too busy bouncing, and I don't know what to say anyway. He looks worse now—kind of transparent, like a ghost.

"You been hitting it hard, eh, Eds?"

He laughs and shrugs, like we're in it together—waves curling over both our heads. I start to tell him Karen's little joke, about keeping his kitten away from my fish, but he cuts me off. "I guess I've given up," he says.

"On what?" I say, though I know what he means.

"I'm not going to get the kid. It's too late now. Maybe at one point, if I'd got the housing, but . . ."

"Why didn't you?"

"It's all talk, Shaun. It's all crap. Jack Layton says he'll do something. Homes First says they'll do something. The workers say they'll do something. Everybody talks a good game, but nobody does a god-damn thing."

"Maybe there's still time," I say. "If you—"

"It's not that, Shaun," he says, shaking his head like I should just shut up and let him drown. "I say it's that, but I'm full of shit, right? I just got to finally do what's best for Caleb. I wanted him because it would have been good for me, not for him. I've got to stop being selfish, is all. I'm just a fuck-up. The kid deserves better than that. I can't help anybody. What do you think of that?" He smiles at me, like he's hoping to piss me off. "I'm giving up and going down. What do think of that, young Shaun?"

"I think you're right, Eddie," I say. "The kid deserves better. You had a chance, and you couldn't step up, and now it's easier to just throw it all away. And now you're really going to be fucked up, Eddie—'cause you know this was your last chance. That's what I think of that."

"Yeah," he says, smiling like a man cut free from Earth—helpless and resigned to the terror of infinite space. "I'm sure fucked now. Just waiting to die, eh?"

"Yeah. It's too bad," I say, then walk over to my shack. At the fence I turn around, point my finger at Eddie and shout, "And if your kitten even *touches* my goldfish, I'm chopping his head off!" Karen starts laughing loudly from inside their shack. Jackie comes to her door and yells, "Yeah, Eddie!" And Eddie gives me the finger. I walk through the fence, sit down on my couch and stare at the grass sprouting up between my feet.

I get up to go look for Calvin. I tell myself it's because he owes me $5, but he's owed me $5 for a long time. Like with Eddie, I haven't talked to him much lately. Like Eddie, he seems to be trying to make himself disappear.

I go over to the rec, wander through the bushes, visit a couple of barrel fires. And finally I find him behind Roger's house, in Pops's old trailer. Apparently Roger bought it off Hawk for $50 and plans to turn it into a deluxe rabbit hutch.

"I thought this was for the bunnies, Cal," I say, and step inside.

"Not till they start the breedin', b'y," he says.

"How you been doing?" It's a rhetorical question. His eyes are so red there's no twinkle left. Half the trailer is full of empties.

"You want a sip?" he says, lifting up a can of Crest.

I wave it away, then take a gulp. "You got my five bucks, Cal?"

"Nah, b'y."

"Where'd you get the money for all this?" I say, pointing at the beer cans.

"If I get five bucks, it goes straight to the beer store, b'y."

"Don't b'y me, Calvin. You're being an asshole. Drink yourself to death on somebody else's cash."

"I'll get it to you tomorrow," he says. He's been saying this for a month. I feel so cold inside I can't explain to him that it's got nothing to do with the money. It's got to do with everybody giving up and going down.

I sit down and look around. "Where's the kitten, Cal?"

He stares into the can of Crest. "Sold it to one of the girls, b'y . . ."

I'm up. I've got the collar of his shirt in my hand. I'm yelling in his face. "You stupid little shit! What are you doing? That was your kitten! You were supposed to take care of it! I told you I would, if you couldn't. I told you we'd look after it if you went to detox—remember? It had your eyes, Calvin! It had your fuckin' eyes!" I let go of his shirt and walk out of the trailer.

"I didn't sell her!" shouts Calvin, coming out after me. "I was just kidding! The girl's just borrowing her—she's just playing with her! I was kidding, little brother!"

I walk over to the rec. One of the girls says, "Yeah, he sold it for a $5 rock." But she doesn't know where the kitten is now.

June 15

An Interview with Jackie

(On the night before she leaves, Jackie and I sit in my shack. We drink some rye and Coke, but other than that, Jackie is straight. The interview is drastically edited for length and clarity. Just before I turn on the tape recorder, I ask her what her plans are.)

J: I wanna stay here and smoke my brains out, but I think there's another plan for me in life.

S: Oh, I thought you said another planet.

J: Ha-ha. Yeah, there's another planet for me in life . . . It's right up there somewhere.

S: How old are you, Jackie?

J: Thirty-two.

S: Where are you from?

J: Kingston, Ontario.

S: Can you tell me what it was like growing up there?

J: I guess it was like . . . a lot of ups and downs. I mean, I didn't come from a rich family, and I didn't come from a poor family. I mean, my stepdad drank a lot . . . We had to go to church every Saturday—it was the Worldwide Church of God—was started by Ted Armstrong and . . .

S: What's that all about?

J: Well, we didn't believe in Christmas, we didn't believe in birthdays . . . none of the pagan holidays . . . And it was rough for the most part because I wasn't allowed to go to any dances, and they wondered why I was rebellious. 'Cause I didn't have any freedom. And when I went to the roller rink, my dad had to be there . . . I didn't always wear the best clothes because my mom always had to make my clothes . . . I'm glad those years are over. But when I was 17 I left home and the first time I had sex was the first time I got pregnant.

S: That's some bad luck, Jackie. Who was it? What happened?

J: He was over at a place I was staying at. Somebody told him there was a new girl on the loose, so he decided to come over. And things happened.

S: So you'd moved . . .

J: . . . out of my house.

S: And how did that happen?

J: I just ran away from home at the age of 17, I was putting up drywall in our basement . . . And, uh, I didn't do it right. So my stepdad kicked me in the thigh, and I went to the police about it.

S: Was that the first time he hit you?

J: No. It happened all through my life, and he used to beat my mom.

S: So why this time did you go to the police?

J: Because he left an outside bruise on me. Well, actually, it wasn't me that went to the police, because I was in gym and the teacher saw the bruise on my leg.

S: Have you talked to your mom about this since?

J: Yes. Oh yeah. But my mom . . . I mean, even my stepdad sexually assaulted me and stuff when I was a kid.

S: Did you ever come to peace with him, or talk to him?

J: Yup. Before he died he apologized for everything he did to me. And I . . . I can learn to forgive and forget. I've done mistakes in my life and I'm hoping people have forgiven and forgotten.

(Jackie tells me about everything that happened after she left home—about having her first baby, and then her second at 19.)

S: Why did you come to Toronto?

J: Well, really I had come to Toronto to sell flowers.

S: Sell flowers? Oh, sweetie . . .

J: For Mother's Day.

S: And you stayed.

J: Yeah. I got paid one day and that was it, I stayed in Toronto. I met up with the wrong crowd and ended up in Queen Street Mental Health Centre . . . I actually got pregnant while I was in there.

S: You've been pregnant six times? Five times?

J: Six times . . . but one passed away . . . He was the one murdered . . .

S: What happened?

J: I was out playing bingo and . . . and I left the father there, and he got a babysitter and he went out himself. Don't know where he went—and that still isn't clear today if he even went out. But, anyways, when I came home there was a dent in the back of my son's head about the size of a golf ball. And his head was swollen to about this size . . .

S: So, twice the size it should have been.

J: Yeah. The next day I took the baby to the doctor and the doctor admitted the baby into the hospital. And they put a shunt in to . . . drain the water off the brain into the stomach. The guy, James, was already charged . . . and was already doing thirty-six months.

S: This is the babysitter?

J: The babysitter. Thirty-six months for injuring my child . . . The shunts weren't working, so we let him go into a coma and eventually we had to pull the plug on him. And that was very hard . . . he was 6 when he died.

S: So this happened pretty recently. He died only a couple of years ago, eh? Is that when you started going hardcore?

J: Yeah . . . I used to work the streets, and up three, four fucking days and . . .

S: When did you start hooking?

J: That was in '97.

S: Why'd you start?

J: Actually, I was forced out onto the street. I was with this guy and we were smoking crack. And I just didn't have . . . I don't know why I started, actually.

S: So your family's been taking care of five of your kids?

J: Yeah. My mom had Ryan when he passed away.

S: You weren't there when he died?

J: No. I couldn't . . . And then I moved to Street City.

S: Why did you move to Street City? . . . Weren't there other shelters then?

J: Street City is for hard-to-house people . . . So it was the only option I had at the time . . . Street City is a government-run crack house . . . Just took in all the hookers and all the crack dealers and all the crack-heads, knowing full well what they were and what they're doing and they let it go on for so long that now the place is being closed down because of it.

S: What's the worst thing about being a prostitute? What was?

J: What was? Um. What was the worst thing? Guys mauling you all the time. Like as if you'd been going out for years, you know what I mean?

You can never have a steady relationship . . . I don't know . . . Out on the street . . . it was rough. But when you brought in good money every night and stuff . . .

S: Do you know why crack? I mean, it's everywhere. What does it do for you?

J: It makes you jones.

S: When was the last time it made you feel good?

J: The very first hit.

S: So when did you move down here?

J: A year ago . . . with Sluggo.

S: Where'd you meet him?

J: I was living at Street City and we were all drinking up at Trinity Park and I liked him from the first time I seen him. And I just went up to him and I lifted my top and I got my first date. (*Giggles.*)

S: That's how you get the men, eh?

J: And then I seen him a little while later, I was sitting in the Bismark—a few weeks later—sitting in the Bismark. I'd left Street City and did my own thing. But I was sitting in the Bismark. He had a few bucks in his pocket and he sat down and bought a couple of drinks . . . I said I didn't have anyplace to go, and he said he didn't have anyplace to go. So we went down to St. James's Park and slept on a picnic table, and I kept him from falling off the picnic table all night.

S: And that was love . . . ?

J: That was love. Love is grand.

S: What do you think of Tent City?

J: It'd be a nice place, but too many crack dealers down here now. Too many crackheads. It's time for me to go home . . . I want to get my soft side back again.

S: You shouldn't be worrying about not being able to find your sweetness, 'cause I know you're sweet . . . You just need to be around people who are nice to you too.

J: That's the thing.

S: Anything you're going to miss about this place?

J: A few people, not everybody, but a few of them . . . Sluggo thinks I'm coming back in a week or so to get the rest of my clothes.

S: Don't come back for the clothes . . . I have to say that I'm happy you're the first person I met here . . . You've always been good to me.

J: I try. Too bad Sherry can't come back tonight. I'd like to have said goodbye to her.

S: Anything you want to add for the record?

J: (*Long pause.*) I just hope you're well, Shaun, and . . . You should feed your fish.

S: I already fed him today. You don't want to overfeed them. Maybe we'll give him a little bit. You want to feed him a little bit?

J: Sure.

S: Sherry showed me how to do it very specifically. I'm scared of killing the damn thing. I'm not going to give him too much. See, just crumble that up real small—like tiny. But don't put all that in, I think. Cute, eh?

J: Yeah. Here you go, buddy.

S: He is a little hungry, isn't he?

J: No. He's not.

S: He's not? Okay, 'cause I already fed him. I fed him quite a bit.

J: If he's not hungry, he won't eat it.

S: Good. Smarter than me . . . I just don't want to kill him while he's in my care, 'cause that's not going to look good for me. Sherry won't be happy with that. He's a cute bugger . . . You're taking the bus? . . . Who's paying for it?

J: Sanctuary.

S: Oh, good. That's good.

J: Plus Sluggo gets a few dollars tomorrow, so he's going to give me $50 to go down with . . . But I gotta get a dime of weed before I get on that bus.

S: Don't buy anything else.

J: Oh God no. If I did that I'd . . . that would be it . . . I leave here tomorrow and I live. Or I stay here tomorrow and I die . . . I better get to bed.

S: It's going to be a good life, don't worry.

J: Oh yeah.

June 16

It's late, Sherry's already in bed, and I'm walking back from the water hose with a jug for the morning coffee. As I pass Sluggo's shack I hear a rustling in the bushes. It sounds bigger than a rat or a raccoon, so I go over to see if Cleo's got herself caught in something. And there, in the middle of the bush, is Sluggo, moaning on his belly, half-conscious and covered in mud.

I get him up on his hands and knees as he growls and scratches at the earth. I lock my arms around him and pull him to his feet. "Aw . . . ," he says, his chin dropping to his chest. "I'm out."

"What?" But then I look down, and I see what he means.

"I's takin' a pish."

"Well, do it if you have to." I try to let go of him but he starts to fall. So I stand there, holding him up from behind as he pisses into the bushes. "Shake and put it away," I say when he's done. "I'm not helping with that."

"You know what?"

"What, Sluggo?"

"You know what? . . . My baby's gone . . . And you know what . . . ?" I stagger him over to the door of his shack and let him fall forward onto the bed.

"What?"

"You know what? . . . I saw her get on the bus. I watched her get on the bus. I took the bike over to . . . where the bus goes. And you know what? . . . The bus went the other way so I couldn't wave to her . . . so I rode after the bus, eh? For, like twenty blocks . . . or twenty-three! But I couldn't catch it . . . I couldn't catch it!" he yells, and thumps his chest. He picks up a bottle of beer and tries to open it, then hands it to me. "You know what? . . ."

"What, Sluggo?"

"She was a . . . bitch! She yelled at me! She called me a fucking drunk! She hit me . . . But you know what? . . . You know what? . . ."

"You love her."

"I *love* her! . . . That's the thing! . . . I *love* her!"

I leave him there crying. As I walk back to my shack, it begins to rain. My roof is leaking. I lie down and hold Sherry tight as she sleeps, water dripping gently on our blankets.

June 17

Eddie came over between crack runs today, to help me fix the roof. We didn't talk about Caleb, or drugs, or anything. We wedged some plywood and plastic in between the ceiling and the attic roof while the sound of Sluggo's moaning and crying travelled through the trees.

"I wish to hell he'd shut up," said Eddie. "What's he saying anyway?"

"I don't know." But it did sound like he was trying to say something—one drunken, moaning word, over and over again. Finally I went over and asked him. "Say it more carefully, Sluggo," I said, and he moaned even slower. "Say it clearer."

He moaned again, and this time I could hear it.

"Without!" I said, calling over to Eddie. "He's saying 'without.' Over and over again."

"Why?"

"I don't know."

"I . . . am . . . *without!*" moaned Sluggo, and he bashed his head against the door.

"Jesus, Sluggo," I said. "You got to pull yourself together."

He looked up at me, as if he was evaluating this advice, and said, "You know how I feel?"

"How do you feel, Sluggo?"

"I feel like . . . I just lost 280 pounds!" He laughed and punched the ground, then repeated the joke louder, and began to cry. "You *get* it? You *get* it, man?"

"I get it, Sluggo," I said. "It's funny."

"It's fuckin' funny!" said Sluggo, and sobbed into his beard.

x   x   x

Hawk came and knocked on my door this evening. "I have something for you, Shauny," he said, waving me out to sit on the deck with him. He put his leather tool belt on the table. "It's yours," he said. I picked it up, pulling out a hammer, a staple gun, a tape measure . . .

"You sure?" I said.

"Yeah. I'm leaving this place." He says this every couple of weeks, but this time it sounded real. Hawk's not the kind of guy who gives his tools away on a whim. "There's nothing we can do anymore—people like you and me. They're little fucking children, Shauny, you understand?"

And suddenly I got this image in my head—dozens of little kids living together in these dollhouses and homemade forts by the water. I haven't met anybody here who wasn't abused as a kid. I looked at Hawk and thought of what he told me, about his head going through the wall.

"You'll put 'em to good use," he said, pointing at the tool belt in my hands like he'd just given me his holster and six-gun.

"Thanks, Hawk. When are you leaving?"

"Tomorrow morning . . . Unless I decide to kill everybody tonight— then I'd probably stay."

"I'll miss you, Hawk."

He reached out his arms and pulled me into a bear hug. "You be good, Shauny," he said. "Keep using that head of yours."

"All right, Hawk. You too."

"Your roof's been leaking, right?"

"Uh . . . yeah."

"You need a new tarp, that's all."

"Me and Eddie tried to fix it today, we'll see . . ."

"It'll leak," said Hawk, "until you get a new tarp. Trust me."

After Hawk left, I came into the shack and hung the belt on a nail above the wood stove. I sat on my bed for a while, then picked up the black metal bar that was sitting on the bookshelf. I flicked my wrist, and the steel baton telescoped out. Hawk liked this thing when he first saw it—he kept nodding while he flipped it out, his big hands testing the weight. I closed it up and walked to his shack.

"Here, Hawk. A going-away present."

"What do you mean?" he said. And for a moment I thought I'd made a mistake. I remembered what he'd said about Christmas—how he didn't know what it was to receive things. He took it from my hand, and the bar shot out like a bullwhip cracking. He nodded. "These things are good. Thanks."

On the way back to my shack, I decided it was a good omen—this urge to give away my weapon. I hadn't used it, and now I never would. But of course with Hawk gone anything could happen. I guess now we'll see if he was a peacekeeper or a warlord, the sheriff or just another gunslinger.

June 18

"A Shantytown is swelling on the shores of Lake Ontario, practically in the shadow of Canada's richest banks. The 80 residents have squatted on five acres of undeveloped land [*sic*]that is soaking in mercury and lead. Dogs rummage through garbage. Outhouses donated by charities have a stench . . ." Thus begins the *New York Times*'s recent exposé on Toronto's Tent City. It also states that "the emergence of Tent City and growing homelessness suggests that the quality of life in Toronto, as in many other Canadian cities, is beginning to fray." This has created a good dose of Canadian self-consciousness, as well as a new round of debate over Tent City. The fact that our destitution has become newsworthy in the States is making news all over Canada—and you get the sense that we're the ones who will bear the brunt of our country's embarrassment.

June 20

I spent the last two days working for a roofing company with Terry. The two hottest days of the year so far, and we spent them uptown on a black pitch roof, so that now my body's burned and my brain is boiled to mush.

On the first day, four of us went out—me, Terry, Brother Lenny and a skinny guy named Butch who lives in a shack by the Lakeshore fence. By noon the heat had got to Butch and we had to carry him down the ladder. Lenny started puking in the late afternoon, and when we were finally finished—around 9 p.m.—Terry said he and I were the only ones hired back the next day. "That's great," I said. I couldn't feel my legs.

Terry grew up on a reservation but can't go back there because of a lot of stolen cars and a police chief with a broken nose. Everybody says Terry is the best scrapper around. Even Hawk's voice fills with awe when he talks about how Terry fights. Hawk may be a killer, Jimmy D a boxer, and Eddie a berserker—but everyone agrees that Terry is the best scrapper around. Only Frizz comes close, but that's another story.

Terry—although he does his share of crack—is the only one down here who actually looks *younger* than his years. He's got plenty of scars and broken teeth, and fading tattoos on every inch of his torso, but he still looks no older than 35.

"I'm older than Eddie!" he says, which would make him at least 50. Eddie—who looks about 65—is hovering somewhere in his late 40s. They have been running together for almost twenty years.

"We've lived in four different cities together," says Terry. "I don't know why, but I keep following him around. That's my problem in life, eh? I'm a follower. Eddie follows the devil, I follow Eddie—something like that. He lived in my closet for two years."

"What?"

"I had this place in Ottawa. And him and this girl stayed in my fuckin' closet. There wasn't even room for a mattress in there—and they never left. For two years! He had the crack delivered to the fuckin' closet!"

"What'd you do before this?"

"I used to be a carny."

"You serious?"

"I had my own carnival—rides and clowns and everything. All summer, going from place to place. That was a good gig, man! Lots of money. Different girls in every town."

"So what happened?"

"I don't fuckin' know . . . Started following Eddie around instead. Different kind of circus, you know? I guess I became a mark, like everyone else. The crack gets you. Least I keep workin' though, eh—not like those other bums. You gotta work to stay sane."

Terry works hard all day. He climbs the ladder with a 90-pound roll on his shoulder, and even when it's 42 degrees with the humidex he keeps his head and his sense of humour.

You can't wear sunscreen up on that roof—the pitch dust sticks to it, and then the sun burns even worse. When I got back to Tent City last night, sunburned and black from pitch, I drank four beers straight down at Eddie's, then stumbled over to my place. And there was Sherry, sitting on my porch with a bucket of Kentucky Fried Chicken.

"Are you real?" I said, and fell to my knees.

"It's one of your favourite things," said Sherry.

"Yeah it is . . . I love you . . . I mean, I adore you."

"I know. Just eat your chicken."

x   x   x

There was no work today, and when I finally woke up I went over to Eddie's. "Hey, young Shaun," he said. "Terry came by to say he'll have your pay tomorrow."

"Good. If I'm not here just ask him to hold on to it." Eddie laughed. "Shit. Forget that. Don't do a thing," I said, but Eddie was still grinning.

"I'm going to get it," he said. "You *know* I'm going to get it. Oh, Terry'll try to do the right thing at first, but I'll wear him down—I'm good at that. He'll feel bad about it, sure. But he'll smoke your pay with me anyway. Ha-ha!"

"Fuck off, Eddie. I'm serious." But Eddie just laughed. Sure, I'd trust him with my life—but not with my money in a grey area like Terry's pocket. So when Terry came back this afternoon, I went over to his trailer.

"Eddie says he'll get my money off you. He's turning it into one of his stupid mind-game things. Don't let him, okay?"

"Your money'll be here," said Terry. "Don't worry."

"You sure? Remember what you were saying—about being a follower?"

He thought about it for a second, then shook his head. "Your cash'll be here anyway," he said. It didn't exactly inspire confidence, but there wasn't much more I could do. As I was coming out of Terry's trailer Eddie saw me and let out a laugh.

"It's already mine," he called out, then turned around and mooned me.

I went over to Les's trailer to see what he was up to. Ever since he sold his truck, he's been flying around on crack, and Jo-Jo's been coming by for their little therapy sessions alone. He wasn't at the trailer, and Big G—one of the crack dealers—was there instead, with a few of his henchmen. "Not his no more, mon," said Big G, flipping his hand in the air.

"What do you mean?" I said, and they shut the door in my face.

"Oh, yeah," said Les when he finally turned up this evening. "I sold the trailer, hmm-hah."

"You did what?"

"Oh, you know—hee-hmm—we're leaving anyway, so I made a few bucks."

"By selling us out? By turning this place into a crack house? Are you nuts?"

"They were moving in anyway," he said, and grinned.

"But you made it so easy for them, Les! They didn't have a place down here, and now they've got the whole corner!"

"Ahh, fuck 'em all," said Les, still smiling. "It's time to move on."

"So where you staying now? Since you don't have your truck or trailer."

"Over in that dollhouse I bought off Eddie, hmm-yeah."

"So what—you kick her out of your trailer 'cause she's a hooker and you can't deal with that, and then you buy her a little plastic box too small for one person 'cause you still love her, and then you sell your trailer to the crack dealers she hooks for, and move into the plastic box with her? Have I got it right?"

"I guess so, but—"

"Boy, Les—you're really moving up in the world."

"I just got to get some money from my last job, hmm-yeah, then we're out of here. I already found a place for us to move into, hmm-hee. And if she isn't ready I'm going anyway, oooh-hey—I'm out of here if she comes or not . . ."

Nothing changes, nothing changes, and then everything does. Jackie is gone. And Hawk is gone. Nobody believed either of them would ever leave. And as soon as Hawk left, the dealers moved right in. And Les, who says he's leaving too, has given them the keys to the whole goddamn kingdom. But still, you can never tell. Is it an exodus, a changing of the guard, an end, or just another day in Tent City?

June 21

I hang out with Sherry at the bar, winning drinks at pool until closing. We wipe down the tables, stack the chairs, then put some music on the jukebox and smoke a joint.

When we get to Tent City, we pour some drinks and smoke another joint—not a smart idea for me, but I'm feeling good and decide I can handle it. Except for some traffic over at Crack Corner everything seems quiet—nothing to deal with but the moon, the water and a few rats.

So I'm sitting there, looking into the barrel fire, glancing up at the stars, talking to Sherry about life, and all the changes going on down here, and I'm thinking, *See, I can smoke pot—why not? I'm fine. Nothing to worry about* . . . when Penny appears out of the darkness and walks into my yard, a lost boy at her side.

"Hey," she growls. "What's going on?"

Penny lives in one of the shacks across from where Hawk used to be, and she doesn't come down to this end much. Even when I'm not stoned, I find it hard to deal with Penny. She is tough, aggressive, muscular as a heavyweight, covered in crude tattoos and blessed with a voice like Dr. John on Lysol. I never know how to take her. Mostly, I try to be nice.

"Hey, Penny."

"So this is your place, huh? It looks good."

"Sherry, this is Penny and . . . I don't know who that is." The lost boy grunts.

"Kevin," says Penny, grabbing a 2-litre bottle of beer out of his hand and taking a swig. "Man, she's pretty!" She circles back behind Sherry and touches her hair. "God, aren't you the purtiest little thing. Look at you—you're just like an angel, eh?"

"Yeah, thanks," says Sherry, and coughs out a laugh. I'm not sure what to do. If it were a guy I could tell him to keep his hands off her, but . . .

"No, really, she's *pretty,* ain't she *so pretty?*" says Penny, looking at me. She's all dressed up like she's been out causing trouble downtown—leather pants and a long leather coat, with her black hair greased straight back.

"Yeah, she's pretty," I say, and Penny starts rubbing Sherry's neck. "You're looking all right yourself, Penny," I say, then think, *Oh, Jesus— I'm way too stoned for whatever's going on here.* "So," I try again. "What can I do for you?"

Kevin says something under his breath. "What's he saying?" I say. "Tell him not to mumble."

"Hey!" says Kevin, taking a step forward. Penny blocks him with her arm.

"Oh yeah . . . she's a pretty one . . . ," says Penny. And now we're all just staring at each other, on and on, with the firelight flashing across our faces. I don't know what to say, or do. I feel like I can't move, like I'm sinking in molasses.

Finally Penny says, "Hey, man. Can I talk to you a minute?"

"Go ahead," I say.

"Nah, man," she says, and nods her head toward the water. "Just you and me." I have no idea what we could possibly have to talk about.

"Well, he's not staying here," I say, pointing at Kevin.

"Hey!" says Kevin again.

"Shut up, bitch!" Penny says to Kevin. "Go down the road a bit, I'll catch up to you." Kevin glares at me, then turns and walks away.

"Back in a second," I say to Sherry, trying to sound casual. Penny and I walk out of the yard and over to the waterline.

When I turn to face her, Penny growls. "You're bad . . . You're a fuck- ing dog!"

"What are you talking about?" I say, and see that she's smiling.

"What about your old lady?" she says. "That little chicky I seen you with?"

"That's her," I say.

"Don't fuck with me," she says, grinning. "That one had glasses . . ."

"She took her glasses off . . ."

"And red hair . . ."

"That was just a rinse, it washes out . . . ," I say.

"You think I'm stupid?" says Penny. I feel like I'm lost in some disturbing dream where people speak in codes, hair changes colour and faces morph.

"What do you want?" I say.

Penny squints at me and squares her shoulders. Her hands are buried in her long leather coat and she's shifting from foot to foot. I want to see if Kevin's behind me, but I want to keep my eyes on Penny. *What's she got in her coat?* Penny's the only person I know who's sucker-punched Crazy Chris. And she's a woman, and I'm covered in tar.

"Listen," she says finally. "You got five bucks you can lend me—just till tomorrow?" Suddenly I'm relieved. This at least is familiar territory, and I know how to answer. I've vowed not to lend any more money. And anyway, I have none to give. "Sorry," I say.

"What about the pretty one?" says Penny. "Didn't she just come from work?"

"I'm not asking her. And neither are you." But it's too late. When someone's jonesing for crack and they smell cash, there's not much you can do short of swinging a stick.

"You think I'm not good for it?" she says, grabbing my arm. "You think I'm no good. I told you I'll get it for you tomorrow!"

We argue back and forth, until I feel my sinking brain just wanting to quit—Penny staring straight through me at pretty Sherry behind us. I can't deal with this . . . "Okay," I say finally. "It's worth the $5 to see what you're made of."

"I swear. I'll pay you back tomorrow."

I leave Penny at the fence, and go ask Sherry for $5. I feel bad doing it, and the pot makes it feel even worse.

When Penny is finally gone, I turn to Sherry. "Sorry," I say. "I don't know how to deal with that . . . I'm stoned, and she's a . . . girl."

Sherry lets out a little laugh. "It's okay. But you have to treat her like she's another guy. That's how she acts. Any other way, you'll tie yourself up."

"I just got muscled by a girl, didn't I?" I say. Sherry laughs and kisses me.

We have a last drink, then Sherry gets undressed and crawls beneath the sheets. It's about 5:30 by now, the dark outside turning to grey. I pull off my shirt and my shoes. Then I hear something out on the deck. It sounds like there's at least two of them, talking loudly and kicking my stuff around.

"Stay here," I say. "And don't make a sound."

I open the door. Two black guys are sitting in the chairs on my deck.

"You want a drag?" says one of them, holding up the butt of a cigarette.

Still standing, I put one of my feet up on the low table in front of them and lean in. "Get out of my yard," I say. I'm still stoned, but I finally feel like myself—like I know what I'm doing.

"This your yard?" says the guy with the butt. "You pay for this place, man? You got something says we can't be here?"

"Didn't pay for it with money," I say. "But it's mine, and you gotta leave."

"You saying we can't be here?"

I want to be so careful, I want to stand my ground, but keep us safe. I feel the weight of the naked girl in the bed behind me.

"You can't be here," I say, slow and deliberate.

They look at me. Butt Boy throws the cigarette on the ground and gets up. They walk out of my yard. "That's the way you want it?" he calls over his shoulder.

"Yep."

"We'll be back."

I let out a laugh. I couldn't stand up to a girl from down the road, and now there's a couple of gangbangers here with me half-naked, and all they can do is say they'll be back.

"Now's good a time as any!" I call out, then shut myself up quickly. But it doesn't matter. They keep walking.

"What was that all about?" says Sherry as I finally take off my jeans and slide into bed. My head is spinning a bit, but I feel okay.

"Just more of the neighbours," I say and I kiss her pretty throat.

June 22

Sherry headed back to Scarborough yesterday and I was hanging out in the sunlight, waiting for Terry to come by with my pay, or maybe even

Penny with my $5. Heartbeat walked out of his prefab and over to my fence just as Sluggo was passing by, taking Cleo for a walk.

"How's it going?" said Heartbeat. His moving into Nancy's old place has been a good thing for me. I couldn't ask for a better next-door neighbour if I lived in the suburbs. Heartbeat isn't your usual crackhead. He is thoughtful, dependable, respectful, quietly intelligent, and always there to lend a hand.

"Hey, Heartbeat," I said, and told him about my early-morning visitors.

"No fucking way," he said, shaking his head. "That shit's not going to happen here. You should have called me." Heartbeat is known for beating people with shovels, and such, which I find hard to reconcile with his calm and constant neighbourliness. "We got Frizz here, too," he said. "And Terry in the trailer, right? You have any trouble, just yell or throw a rock at the door. You won't have to do a thing, Shaun . . ."

"Or just give a whistle," said Sluggo. "I'll let Cleo go at them—she's got a thing about nig-nogs."

They were being so nice to me I figured this wasn't the time to get picky about racist slurs, so I just nodded at Sluggo.

"Seriously!" said Heartbeat. "Hey, have you met Curly? Just a minute." Before I could answer, Heartbeat left and came back with a huge guy who's staying in a tent behind the pink prefab. Curly has a big drooping moustache and a gentle respectful manner. I'd met him the day before, when I gave him a T-shirt that was too big for me.

"Yeah," said Curly. "He gave me a smoke. And this shirt. Not bad, eh!"

"Hey, Curly," I said, shaking his hand.

"Professional heavyweight. Fifteen years," said Heartbeat. "You got no worries."

"Don't box anymore," said Curly, but he was smiling.

x   x   x

It's hard to figure out the cause and effect—what to attribute to what. It could be that everybody's coming down here because it's summer, or because Street City is being phased out, or, more specifically, because of the crack dealers. And the crack dealers could be down here because

Street City is going down, or because Hawk is gone. And Hawk could be gone because of the crack dealers—because he saw his control slipping away and didn't want to fight them. It could be a coincidence that those guys were at my door last night—the first Friday after Hawk left, and the day after Les sold the corner. Maybe they were just high and itchy, and weren't actually trying to drive me off my land like railway thugs in a cowboy movie. Who knows?

It's only been a few days since Hawk left, and already Jimmy D has moved into his place—that Spartan checkpoint right by the front entrance. Apparently Hawk sold it to three different buyers, but Jimmy D boxed his way to the door. Big G bought Pops's old trailer off Roger, and moved it over next to Les's old place. So now Calvin's out of luck, along with the rabbits and the rest of us. People are trading everything they have for rock, Crack Corner is expanding, and I live right on the edge of it. Thankfully, my neighbours are looking out for me—of that, at least, I'm almost sure.

x   x
x
x

I waited around for Terry or Penny until the community centre was about to close, then headed out the gates for a swim and a shower. Just as I was crossing Parliament, Sluggo caught up to me on his bike.

"Here." He handed me a wad of twenties. "That's from Terry."

"Thanks, Sluggo," I said. Around here this is not a regular kind of occurrence.

"He says there's $25 missing—some, uh, discrepancy with the pay. He said to tell you he didn't trust himself after all, and asked me to hold on to it for you. I said sure—but then I see everyone heading over to his trailer, eh? Like a swarm of fucking flies? So I think, hmm . . . maybe I shouldn't have this around. I mean, I'll hold it for you, man, but I don't want to deal with that, you know? So I tried to catch up to you."

Sluggo doesn't usually go out of his way for anyone, not even for one of his crew. "Thanks, Sluggo. I'll bring you a beer later."

"That'd be good," he said, then turned and rode back toward Tent City.

With the money, I bought a twelve-by-six blue tarp, some candles, a case of beer, a bottle of vodka, a pouch of tobacco and three strawberry tarts from Tim Hortons for Sherry. Then I picked her up at work, and we headed home.

There were still a few hours of daylight left and the forecast called for overnight showers—so I started on the roof. "What do you think?" I said.

"Well, what's the problem with the old one?" said Sherry.

"I guess it's worn too thin, it's got holes . . . and it's too loose . . . and it's not sloped enough . . . and there's gaps around the stovepipe, and . . ."

It was a hot, hot day, and you could feel the pressure in the evening air. With Sherry patiently directing my every move, I finally got the new tarp over the roof, tight and perfectly sloped, just as the sky was turning to twilight. The clouds rolled in, the wind blew high above the trees, the air crackled slightly, and I kissed her. It began to rain.

June 25

In jail, as the story goes, Les's alter ego was Captain Amazing. At opportune moments he would slip into his costume—a green muscle shirt, red tights, bedspread cape and large pink sunglasses—and he would escape. Or at least he would run, howling, through the whole jail, leading the guards on a ridiculous chase that would end in lockdown—and Captain Amazing's inevitable disappearance. He did this kind of thing for one reason and one reason alone—to be amazing.

When, many years later, his oldest son ended up in the same jail, he went around telling everybody he was the offspring of Captain Amazing. And he quickly got the shit kicked out of him.

"Well, of course you did, kid," said Les when he went to visit. "You're not supposed to divulge Captain Amazing's true identity! You're lucky you didn't get killed, hmm-hey, you little moron!"

The problem, of course, is that there's a fine line between amazing and crazy, super and stupid. You could say that trading your generator for crack, selling your truck for beer, giving your trailer to a drug dealer and moving into a small plastic box is amazing, but it's also a lot of other things.

When he's particularly fried, Les still wears the big pink sunglasses, and no doubt he was wearing them when he made good on his threats to escape Tent City—with or without the fickle, infamous Jo-Jo. Apparently he piled everything he had (as well as some of Jo-Jo's stuff) into two shopping carts (which, incidentally, belonged to me), doused them in gasoline, set them on fire and pushed them burning into the canal. Then he made his escape. This time, however, no one ran after him.

Terry isn't working anymore. He says it's because of the heat but I think it's because of the crack. Apparently he forgot what he told Sluggo about a discrepancy in pay, and now says that the contractor just ran out of cash, but assures me I'll get the rest soon.

Even the Toronto outside workers are out of work right now. They've gone on strike, which means no garbage pickups for those who live in the city, and no showers at the community centre for those who live in shacks. Coincidentally, Beric and Cathy came down today and handed out solar-heated shower bags donated to the TDRC—the kind you take camping and hang from a tree. Like the wood stoves they got for us in the winter, these should make living down here a lot more manageable. Most people, however, just sort of shrugged, and Terry gave me his, so now I've got a shower bag each for Sherry and me. I just have to build a stall.

There's been a stronger police presence over the past little while. They're coming by in boats and filming us from the canal, and a police cruiser drives in and does the rounds at least once a day. This could be a result of the *New York Times* piece, or it might be something else.

"Gonna be this weekend," says Sluggo, "'cause of the Pope." This is the latest theory in Tent City: The Pope is coming to Toronto next month for World Youth Day, and a lot of people think the city might try to clear us out well before that. All the signs are pointing that way—and now, with the booming crack trade, they've got a good excuse—come in and wipe it out before things get worse. Whatever the case, everyone's on edge. Except for those who've already given up.

"Just sitting back," says Sluggo. "Just sitting here, all alone. Just waiting for it all to end . . . waiting for the big finish, waiting on the big man, waiting for the Popemobile . . . Want a beer while we wait, Shaun?"

June 28

Well, the shit came down, and things blew up—but not the way anybody expected.

As usual, since it involved explosions, brimstone and fire, I was absent. I was at the bar into the early morning, getting carried away with Sherry. When we finally got back to Tent City, the dark sky was turning light, the day emerging before our eyes. It was quiet. You could hear the birds chirping in the air. But what made it so strange was the number of people awake, just standing around.

Frizz, Terry and Marty were in the middle of the road.

"What's going on?"

Frizz shook his head and smiled, "Look," he said, and pointed toward the river.

"Jesus! What the hell happened?"

x   x
x
x

This, apparently, is what happened:

It is just after 9 p.m. Donna, who is living with the Brothers, is arguing with Julie over which one of them is the bigger bitch, and it's turning ugly. Donna gives Julie a shove and Julie comes at Donna with an axe handle. Eddie's out there, and he yells at Julie to drop the weapon.

"Make it a fair fight!" he says, and because it's Eddie, she tosses the axe handle aside and starts swinging. Donna outweighs her by at least 40 pounds, and takes her down first. But Julie's got a lot of practice with this sort of thing. She and Patrick, who just recently got out of jail again, are always beating each other up.

Pretty soon she's got Donna beneath her, and then she just doesn't stop, bashing away with both fists. Finally Eddie steps in and tells Julie she's proved her point, so she gets up and walks back to her shack.

The door is open and Patrick grunts, "I thought the dog was with you." So Julie goes back out, looking for their puppy—and that's when the Brothers jump her.

Now things get a bit confusing. Julie manages to get away before they beat her too badly, but the damage is already done. Everybody's out there, crowding around, so that Patrick can't get at the Brothers right away, and Derek is smart enough to realize they'll be killed if they stick around. It's fine to beat up your own darling—but not anybody else's. Derek throws a few things in a shopping cart and tells Donna and Lenny to head for the gates. By the time he catches up to them, there are flames coming out the windows of their palatial shack by the river. Donna tries to turn back, but Derek grabs her and laughs. "If we ain't living there, no one is," he says.

Instead of going after the Brothers, people start running toward the burning house with buckets of water. And then there's an explosion, like a bomb has gone off. The whole compound blows up. Frizz's prefab is incinerated, and the Brothers' propane tank shoots skyward, finally coming down like a burning meteorite all the way over by Randy's place. People pick themselves up, stunned, making sure they're still intact, then begin to douse the nearby shacks with water so the fire doesn't spread. The air is hot and black with smoke. There are another two dozen propane tanks in Tent City, and at any moment the whole place could go up like Rangoon. The fire is still raging when the sirens sound.

x x x

And now Tent City is like some surreal study of entropy—everything's blown apart, broken down, and coming together again in the form of chaos.

x x x

Jo-Jo is standing outside what's left of her plastic dollhouse. The front wall has melted away, so there's just the frame. It is grotesque, like a half-baked skull.

"Shaun, please do me a favour," she says. "If you see him, ask him to come back."

"Who, Les?" I say. "You want him back?"

"I love him."

"But . . ."

"Don't you think he's heard about this? Why hasn't he come back?"

x x x

Sluggo is sitting on the bed in his shack. Beside him, there's a brand-new eighteen-speed mountain bike with a price tag still hanging off the handlebar. There are twelve cans of Crest on the floor.

"She's back," he says.

"Who?"

"Jackie. Her dad died. She bought me a bike, and twelve cans of Crest . . ."

"Uh . . . good, I guess?"

"Guess so."

"Well, where is she?"

"She's out right now."

"Oh."

x
x
x

Julie is striding down the road, yelling and sobbing.

"You're a dumb prick," she shouts over her shoulder.

Patrick bursts out of Jimmy D's, yelling back at her: "Come here! Come here now! I'm going to punch you in the head."

"I just wanted to go to the beach today! That's all! It would be a fucking good day to go to the beach."

x
x
x

"The Brothers are dead," says Terry, grinning.

"I'm going to kill them," says Frizz.

"You'd be dead right now," says Randy. "If you'd been in your shack."

"I'll kill 'em myself," growls Jimmy D.

The radio news stations report that suspects are wanted in connection with the fire in Tent City—on counts of arson and endangering human life.

"I'm going to chop them up," says Eddie.

"They hit Julie," says Patrick.

If the Brothers are lucky the cops will pick them up soon.

x
x
x

Somehow, the Brothers' picnic table is still intact, and Eddie and I are sitting on it, looking at the black charred remains. Eddie is totally wired.

"I haven't slept for five days," he says, and he's not exaggerating. "If I can, later, I might crash on your couch. I don't want to be near her. I just want to smash her when I see her."

"Karen?" I say. "Things are that bad?"

"She's in there, smoking," he says, waving at his shack, not really answering me. "I haven't smoked all day. It's not about the crack." I don't really believe either of these things, but I nod nonetheless. "We hate each other now, eh? We despise each other. Because I blame her for not being strong enough. And she blames me. And now we're stuck with each other. With this . . ." He waves his hands at the wreckage, but he means all of it—Tent City. "We traded it for what? We traded our son for what? Eh? That's the joke. For this. And there's nothing here."

"So what are you going to do?"

"Nothing. It's over now, or almost, I guess. I'm just waiting for it to be over. I'll kill her if it doesn't end soon. It's like we don't want either of us to get out of this, the hate's that big. I want the ground to open up and swallow us both."

"So, that's it?"

"I don't know. Nothing's ever it. I haven't signed the papers yet."

"What do you mean?"

"I haven't signed the paper—about letting Caleb go."

I'm not sure such papers exist, but I guess I know what he's saying.

x
x
x

I'm walking past Eddie and Karen's shack when their kitten squeezes through the door and comes running out. I pick him up and knock at the open door.

"Leave her alone!" says Karen, then she sees that it's me. I drop the kitten on the floor and look up. The room is dark, except for a single candle, but I can see Jackie there. She seems to have grown to twice her size, like she's taking up half the room. She pulls from a pipe, exhales with a cough, and looks at me.

I will never forget those eyes. The doll's glass eyes have shattered inside her smooth plastic head.

"Hey, Jacks," I say. But she can't answer. The broken blue eyes look right through me.

"Get out of here," says Karen. Then she follows me out and punches me on the shoulder like a sister would. She laughs too loud, looks down at the ground and says, "Do you think I'm couth?"

"What?"

"Can you use it like that—like instead of *un*couth? I never hear that."

"Sure, you're couth, Karen."

"Your brain's like a record player, Shaun. All those different speeds."

"I'd say yours is too, Karen."

"Mine is too Karen what?"

"What?"

"You heard me!"

I turn and walk back to my shack.

x   x
 x

"Jackie's over there," I say to Sherry, still shaking my head. "She's been in there the whole time. Terry says she's smoked $2,500 so far. Her dad died yesterday, and they gave her $5,000. And she took a cab right here."

"From Kingston?"

"All the way. Must have cost a grand. She's been in there with Karen for eight hours. When it's gone she'll sell the bike she bought for Sluggo. He hasn't even bothered taking off the price tag. And he'd better drink that beer fast. Jesus, you should have seen her eyes."

"I've seen enough of them," says Sherry.

x   x
 x

I need to do something constructive. It is still unbearably hot, so Sherry and I decide to build a shower. I choose the tree-shaded corner behind my shack, past the outdoor kitchen I've made. I lay down a skid for the floor of the shower stall, and find three large pieces of plywood for walls. Sherry holds them straight as I hammer it all together, with a thin crossbeam/shower-curtain rod across the top of the doorway.

It takes me a while to decide the best way to hang the shower bags, but finally I hammer a small plank diagonally across a top corner. I sit a chair on it and pile rocks onto the seat as a counterweight. I bend a spoon into the shape of an S-hook, then hang one of the full shower bags off the back of the chair.

Sherry and I take off our clothes and get into the stall. I pull a fourth piece of plywood up as a door. The water is the perfect temperature on our hot, sticky skin. And suddenly there is nothing but these four walls, the leaves on branches and blue sky above our heads, the soft sound of water falling, rolling down our chests and bellies, into the earth.

"We have a shower," sings Sherry.

And just like that, in the middle of this heat wave, this filthy place of arson and scorched earth, we've got our own bag of sweet summer rain.

x   x   x

It's late in the afternoon, and Sherry's gone to work. I've refilled the water bags, and I walk around Tent City, inviting people over for a shower. I'm the only one so far who's built a stall. They come one at a time, still covered in ash from the fire, in dirt and sweat from the day. I don't know, but I think it might help if we all get clean.

While my friends are bathing, I strip down to my underwear and walk to the edge of the canal. I look across at the giant tanker full of concrete, I look down into the water, and I dive off the edge.

I dive deep and keep my eyes open, but my mouth closed tight. The water is thick and billowing green. I know it's full of toxins and oil, but it's cold and deep, and I swim through it before I rise to the surface. I swim down along the bank until I come alongside the outhouse and the burnt wreckage of the Brothers' compound. I pull myself up the concrete wall, back to land, and walk to my shack in dripping underwear with bare feet—over broken glass, nails, charred wood, gravel and dirt. I have the wimpiest feet in the world, but I don't feel a thing. I want to do good. I want to make the world clean. I walk through the front entrance into my yard, then up onto my deck. I look over, and Eddie is lying on my couch with his mouth open. I don't know if he's asleep or if he's dead. I don't know if he knows the couch folds into a bed. I walk through my outdoor kitchen to the shower, and wash the grime from my skin. I towel off, put on some jeans, and watch Eddie breathe as I wait for the sunset.

July 1

It's a new month, a new day, people are scraping up the residue and getting on with their lives. And Les is back, too.

You might expect someone who, two days earlier, pushed a shopping cart filled with his earthly belongings flaming into the river, calling out, "Adios, assholes! I'm outta here!" to be a bit sheepish upon his return. But not our man Les. Not Captain Amazing. Instead, he walks right into my yard and starts strutting around like he just won the Stanley Cup.

"What's the matter, Les? Didn't go out with enough of a bang? Your big exit overshadowed by the Brothers'?"

"I was just, hmm-mm, trying to burn my bridges, literally. You know?"

"Well, you missed your literal bridges and got my shopping carts, Les."

He shrugs and laughs at himself, and Jo-Jo says, "He's back now, Shaun!" in case I didn't see the bottom line.

"Well, welcome back, buddy," I say. "What you going to do now?"

"I want to move the prefab, hmm-hmm, to where the Brothers used to be."

"Of course you do, Les."

So we round up a half-dozen guys and start struggling the one-ton prefab through the rubble into the charred remains of the Brothers' yard. While we work, Jo-Jo babbles on to me about what a healthy move this is, symbolically, for them as a couple, how it's like they're making a new start, together. "Don't you think, Shaun? Don't you think this'll be good for us?"

"Oh yeah, Jo-Jo. You guys are doing great. There's no stopping you now."

We finally get the prefab to where they want it, but as we clear away the rubble there's a strong putrid smell that just gets worse. Finally Terry discovers two dead rats under the front wall of Les and Jo-Jo's plastic, half-melted home.

"Look," he says, scooping them up in a shovel. "It's Derek and Lenny!"

x
  x
    x

Apparently the TDRC has issued a press release explaining that the fire was a result of arson by individuals who were not, in fact, homeless, nor full-time residents of Tent City. Since the Brothers share an apartment with Donna, it's a valid statement, and will hopefully make us look a bit better. According to Bonnie, the TDRC has also made a suggestion regarding punishment of this crime, putting together a petition for recompense rather than jail time. They want the Brothers to come back and build shacks to replace the ones that were destroyed. They don't realize that the only reason people down here would allow the Brothers in would be to implement the sort of justice that's not too good for public relations.

The more I get to know the members of the TDRC the more baffled I become. Sometimes it seems that in trying to open people's eyes to their cause they blind themselves to what's going on down here. In order to make their struggle a valiant one, they tend to turn people here into victims—not of their lives, but of politics and the status quo. They are sure it's about housing, but I'm just not convinced. Tent City is a place of drug addicts, alcoholics and criminals. And unfortunately, by presenting us to the public as hapless simple-hearted hobos, the TDRC tends to lose the respect of those they're trying to help. Sure, people are glad to get the wood stoves and shower bags, and they're happy that someone is lobbying for them—because they get stuff out of it—but when their saviours are gone, they just laugh, roll their eyes and go about their day.

I wish this wasn't the case. I like Beric, Cathy and the others, and I respect what they're trying to do. I'm truly thankful for my stove and my shower, and I'm in awe of their energy and conviction. I believe they're doing this because they want to make a difference, and because they want to believe in something. I just think it's too bad that they cut themselves off from the reality of this place. People down here have been mangled and beaten throughout their lives, but that doesn't mean they're just victims. They are also aggressors and fighters. They mangle. They beat themselves and beat others for reasons far more complex than a lack of housing and rights. If you don't acknowledge that the flock you're trying to lead is made up of thieves, liars, drug dealers, pimps and addicts, then you can't tell when they're being kind or generous or brave, or superheroes.

But I guess that doesn't matter when it comes to the cause. Beric and the others have to blinker themselves to focus on the fight. I'm glad there's somebody who can do that; it's just too bad that by doing so they can never really know the people they're trying to help.

x
    x
        x

Eddie came over in the early evening, while Sherry and I were changing Dude's water in the Moosehead jug. "You should give him more room to swim," he said. "How'd you like to live in a beer pitcher?"

"I'd like it just fine," I said, and Sherry snorted.

"Just a second," said Eddie, then came back with a large plastic basin. "Try this. But make sure you wash it out first. I'll be back in a minute."

"Perfect," said Sherry. "A wider, more shallow world."

I laughed and washed out the basin. "We should find some things to put in it—like castles and mermaids and stuff."

Eddie came back through the trees. "These'll be good," he said, placing three black soapstone figurines on the table. There was a large squirrel, an owl with huge planetary eyes and a small walrus with one broken tusk. "And goldfish have no memory, so they'll always be new, every time he sees them." He bounced away before I could thank him.

I filled the basin and Sherry placed the animals in the water, then she reached into the Moosehead jug and dropped Dude into his new wide world.

"He does look happy."

"He's a goldfish," said Sherry, as if that's the answer to life.

x   x   x

So now Les and Jo-Jo have a view of the lake, and Dude is swimming large circles around these giant black creatures. I'm watching him while I write, and I can almost feel his constant wonder: "Look! A walrus! . . . Look! A squirrel! . . . Look! An owl! . . . Look! A walrus! . . . Look! A squirrel! . . ." The sky is enormous above him.

July 2

Dude is dead.

Sherry doesn't know yet. It was the first night she left me alone with him. And worst of all, I think he died of a drug overdose.

"What the hell'd you do?" said Eddie.

"I don't know! He was fine when I went to bed! And then I woke up this morning and . . . and . . ."

"Did you feed him? Did you feed him too much? Was the water too hot? Was . . ."

"Yes, no! No! I don't know! Maybe the walrus kept scaring him, and . . ."

"How well did you wash them?"

"What? I washed the basin out with soap! Like you said!"

"No, the carvings. They've been in my shack for months. People pick 'em up all the time, with their hands all covered in resin. That's why you gotta—"

"Are you saying my goldfish died of a crack overdose?"

"I'm saying it's a possibility," said Eddie, hanging his head for just a moment. "They don't have much tolerance, you know."

We threw Dude in the river, and Karen suggested I get another goldfish before Sherry comes back.

"I don't think I could do that."

Eddie laughed and Karen said, "Way to go, Eddie! Leave it to you to kill a fucking goldfish with crack. Yeah, you'd make a great father!"

She was laughing about it, but Eddie said, "Fuck you, Karen!" and punched a hole in the wall of their shack.

I went back to my place to wait for Sherry.

x   x
x

"Goldfish die," said Sherry when I told her. "It's part of what they do."

"But so soon?"

"They've got no memory. For all he knows, he lived to be 100."

July 3

I ran into Calvin on the street today. He hasn't been in Tent City for a while now. He says he's leaving for B.C. tomorrow. Ever since I met him, Calvin's been talking about his land out west. For a long while we were making plans about going out there together, hitchhiking or getting a car, or just riding the rails, and going to see his kids. He's told me a dozen stories about his kids, his land and his horses—which his kids may or may not have sold—galloping across the land that may or may not be there. "We could have our own place up there, little brother. We could ride horses and drink whisky. And my kids would love you." I believed him for a while.

When I ran into Calvin today there was a plump young girl with him, and a tall thin man with a long beard. "This is my little brother!" he shouted, and wrapped his arms around me. The girl didn't say anything. Neither did the guy with the beard.

Calvin said that his son had sent money for a bus ticket, but that he had to stop in Sudbury to get it, so that he wouldn't just drink the money away in Toronto. He said the three of them were leaving tomorrow, on the 4:30 bus.

"You really going to go?" I said.

"We're going—ask her!"

"Are you really going?" I said, turning to the girl, but she didn't say anything. Neither did the guy with the beard. *Who the hell are these people?* I thought. It was like they were silent figures in both our imaginations. I turned to Calvin.

"She's my girlfriend," he said, but didn't mention the tall guy. *Maybe he's the new little brother,* I thought. "You want to meet for a beer before I go?" said Calvin.

"Yeah, Cal," I said, though I felt like he was receding into our imaginations too.

"I'll meet you in the park where we were on my birthday, at three o'clock."

"Okay, brother," I said. "I'll see you tomorrow."

x   x   x

I think Bonnie's going to be leaving Tent City too. Something happened with her the other night that I haven't had a chance to write about yet.

Bonnie, like me, came down here heartbroken and lost, and way underweight. She's become a little less idealistic and has some muscle tone now. She tried to change this place. She's got her alcohol-free zone. She posts notices about housing rallies and squatting protests, and has been trying to start what she calls a harm-reduction centre, which is mostly a post with a bag of condoms nailed to it, where the hookers can come for coffee and a bit of rhetoric.

Anyway, I was sitting in front of the House That Cal Built the other night, listening to her talk about the TDRC and OCAP and a bunch of other acronyms, when this tall and handsome man came walking down the busted-up road. And then something miraculous happened—Bonnie stopped talking. She looked at him, and launched herself into his arms.

She'd never admit it, but I'll bet every day since she moved into this squalor she had visualized this moment—her man walking through the rubble toward her, wrapping his long arms around her, asking her to come on home. And as it turned out, I was there to witness it.

"This is *him,*" Bonnie told me when she'd caught her breath, and after shaking his hand I left them to their life.

I thought my bitterness toward Bonnie was due to her treatment of Calvin. But maybe part of me was just reacting to how similar our situations were. Like me, Bonnie doesn't really "belong" down here. She hit a particularly bad patch, and lost her man, her job and her happiness. She came down here out of a sense of loss, intrigue, desperation and investigation—to see if she could learn something and teach something, too—or at least distract herself enough to survive this part of her life.

Since her ex showed up, Bonnie has changed. She is witty, sweet, sincere and good-natured. I guess she was hurting so much before that it suffocated all her best qualities. She is still self-involved, and she still talks too much, but it's nice to see her happy.

"Are you going back to him?" I ask.

"I don't know," she says, smiling and blushing. "I told him I'm not quite finished here. I'll know when I'm ready to go—because I'll dream it."

I get the feeling she'll have that dream pretty soon.

"I saw Calvin," I tell her. "He says he's leaving tomorrow."

"I hope he'll be okay."

"Me too." And we sit in front of the House That Cal Built, hoping.

July 4

As I was heading out of Tent City to go meet Calvin, Eddie was in front of his shack trying to build a shower stall. It didn't seem to be going well.

He was holding a nail, but didn't have a hammer. His whole body was vibrating and his eyes were staring through a sheet of plywood like he could drive that nail into anything with his bare hands.

"You okay, Eddie?" I said, and he turned to look at me.

"Just trying to stay busy . . . ," he said. "There's no edge, you know. You can look as long as you fucking want, but there's no edge to this whole thing . . ."

"There's no bottom."

"Exactly! No edge, no bottom . . ."

"You could go down forever . . ."

"That's what I'm saying! You can fall forever, Shaun. You build a shower on the way down . . ."

"Yeah, I know."

"I could get out of it if . . ."

"If what?"

"If I had a hammer!" he said.

I went to my shack and got him Hawk's hammer, then headed off to say goodbye to Calvin.

x
x
x

It's getting hotter every day, and walking through downtown you can already see the effect of the city workers' strike. The streets are piling up with garbage, and it's starting to stink. Tent City is probably the cleanest part of Toronto now, since we're used to living without garbage pickup.

I got to Bay and Dundas just before three o'clock. I bought some cans of Crest, then went and sat in the park, on a small shaded hill. Calvin wasn't there yet, but Nancy was. I could see her lying next to her wheelchair, wasted and topless. There was some drunk guy next to her, moaning into a bottle, and a strung-out woman laughing. I watched them as I waited.

By 3:15, Calvin hadn't shown up. Nancy was still without a shirt, rolling around on the ground as though she was in pain. I got up, walked down the hill, and over to her wheelchair.

"Hey, Nance," I said, crouching over her half-naked body. "You okay, honey?"

"Get the fuck away from her," the strung-out woman screeched. Her long greasy hair had caught in her mouth, and she was choking on it as she shouted.

"Nance," I said again, and she opened her eyes. "You should put your clothes on."

"Get away from my sister! I'll kick your ass!" yelled the woman. I could see why she and Nancy would get along. "Get the fuck out of here!"

"Would you shut up," I said, and turned back to Nancy. "Where are your clothes, Nancy?" I lifted my eyes to scan the grass for a shirt or even a bra, and the yelling woman punched me hard in the side of the head.

I stood up and took a step toward her. "I'll fucking hit you," I said. She spat at me, then stomped off, saying she'd be back with some guys to kick my ass.

"Oh, Shaun's all right," said Nancy, slow and garbled, like she was just waking up. "He's my friend." But the woman who'd hit me was long gone, and the drunk guy was moaning into his own lap.

"Thanks, Nance," I said. "You doing okay?"

"I'm hungry. I'm really hungry, Shaun."

"Okay, tell you what," I said. "You put your clothes on, and I'll get you a hamburger—all right?"

"All right."

I found her T-shirt tucked into the wheelchair, and helped her pull it over flat gin-blossomed breasts.

"If your friend comes back, tell her to stay away from me, okay? Or I'll slap the bitch."

"Oh sure. All right."

I don't know when it became so easy for me to talk like this, but my head was aching where she'd hit me and I decided not to think about it. I went into the mall and bought a cheeseburger at McDonald's. The smell of the place made me realize how hungry I was. When I got back outside, Nancy was on the corner in her wheelchair, begging for change. I pushed the chair into some shade beneath a tree and handed her the burger.

"You seen Calvin?" I said.

"Nope."

"You been down to Tent City lately?"

"I was there for the fire, eh?" She shook her head. "Derek's a goof—what he did. And poor Lenny. He's a sweet guy, you know? Just dumb. Me and him were together, eh?" She smiled at me like it was a naughty little secret. "When the place started blowing up, he came back to see if I was okay. Bet you didn't know that."

I shook my head. Despite the unappealing image of Lenny and Nancy "together," there *was* something sweet about it.

"Now they'll probably kill him along with Derek. It's too bad, eh?" she said. I nodded, and we shared a can of Crest while she finished the cheeseburger. I stayed there until 4:15, then walked over to the bus station. The guy in the booth said there was no such thing as a 4:30 to Sudbury.

July 5

While I'm waiting for Sherry to get off work, it seems like a war is brewing. One of Big G's guys is trying to corner Frizz with a knife in his hand, and then I see Eddie bouncing toward Crack Corner with a machete in the gym bag he uses as a sheath. As I'm walking to the gates to cut her off, Sherry comes driving up in her mother's Sunfire. "Hey, dude!" she says, rolling down her window. "I got the car for a couple of days."

"That's great." I can hear yelling. I open the door and get into the passenger seat.

"Want to get out of here?" she says, driving toward the old town.

"Yeah, if we can."

"What do you mean?"

"Nothing. Just stop here and wait a minute, okay?" She pulls in behind Randy's, and I get out and walk over to Crack Corner. There's a lot of people, but it seems quiet now—strangely so. They're just standing there like the undead waiting for shovels to dig their own graves.

"What's going on?" I say.

"Nothing now," says Heartbeat. "The boat just came in. You know how it is—that's all that matters." I guess the dealers ran out of crack for a while there, but they've restocked and everyone's calmed down—they're in that limbo, waiting on a fix.

I walk back over and get in the car. "It's okay now," I say. "We can go through."

Spider and Olivia's shack is so close to the rec centre that you can barely fit a car on the road between them. So you always have to drive slow around Crack Corner. As we make the turn, a dozen expressionless faces stare at us through the windows.

"Spooky," Sherry whispers. And then they are gone.

July 9

Sherry's boss closed down the Stone Cutter's Arms without paying her, and now she's out of a job. When we got back to my shack, someone had busted down the front part of my fence. It wasn't a good night.

x
  x
    x

Apparently Calvin did leave town after all. Randy says he saw him just before he got on the 5:30 bus for Sudbury.

"He said you were supposed to meet him at City Hall. He said to say hi."

"You sure it wasn't bye?"

"Yeah . . . I guess you're right. He was with some skinny guy and a girl with zits."

So 5:30 and City Hall, not 4:30 and the park. I guess it'll always be that way with Calvin—a little bit off, a little too short, too sweet, too drunk. It made me sad to think of my big brother getting on a bus with this creepy mute couple, the three of them heading west, to God's country.

I don't know why, but I feel like I should go and tell Bonnie that he's gone.

She responds in typical fashion: "Yeah, I guess I'll be going too—once I have the dream . . . but there's no way in hell I'm leaving it to Jackie! I mean, can you believe that, the nerve of her!" Despite the fact that she and Bonnie have never gotten past their argument over condensed milk, Jackie has apparently asked Bonnie for her place when she leaves. "It'd be the same as giving it to the dealers! Yeah right—I did all this work so you can have your own crack house, I mean . . ."

One of the hookers from Crack Corner comes strutting over, looks at the post on the edge of Bonnie's booze-free perimeter and says, "Bon-Bon, yer out of domes. Ya got any domes?"

"Oh yeah," says Bonnie, getting up. "Some idiot threw them all over the road, so I've got them inside now. You want flavours?"

"Nah, don't need no flavours . . . thanks, Bon." The girl takes about twenty condoms, says, "Should do for now," and goes strutting off again.

"I'm starting to worry about these girls," says Bonnie. "Things are changing. You talk to Jo-Jo today? She's scared, you know? That guy, Les . . ."

But I don't want to hear Bonnie's take on Jo-Jo and Les. I nod, get up and walk over to the half-melted prefab by the water.

Jo-Jo is completely wired—her body stretching out in all directions like her constant buzzing voice. Her tongue is flashing through the blue-sky spaces in her teeth. I concentrate, and try to comprehend.

"He scares me, eh, Shaun?" Apparently this is the topic for today. "He's in the hospital now—with pneumonia—or so he says. I don't want anything to do with him, eh, Shaun? He scares me! He throws everything in the lake. All of it, Shaun. Don't you think that's odd? I have no food 'cause he throws it in the lake. He used to just burn things. Ha-ha. He comes down last night and says he's got pneumonia and he escaped from the hospital. He's still got the IV thing—what's it called?—hanging out of his arm, and he's not wearing shoes. Which maybe is good since he's been wearing those stupid cowboy boots. I hope he lost them.

"And what's he coming *here* for? So he can take me *away* from all this. *Please!* Gimme a break. Oh yeah—Les the big hero with pneumonia and no shoes. He told me he head-butted his wife once, and they *both* got a concussion—like that's a good story to tell! Like I don't already *know* he's crazy: Hello! Where's my food? Gotta go fishing for a can of corn! He really scares me, Shaun. And Bonnie agrees too, eh? She says he might be dangerous. She thinks I should be scared. I mean, really, I've known *you* longer than I've known Les, and I know you're his friend and all—and he says you don't understand anything I say 'cause I talk too fast, but do you understand what I'm saying?"

"Les is in the hospital?"

July 12

It was my birthday yesterday, and the old crew lined up to punch me in the arm. Randy gave me the money he owed, Eddie gave me a stack of classic rock 'n' roll records, Sherry gave me tickets to see Billy Idol, and the city legislated the striking workers back—so we've got our showers, gyms and swimming pools again, and the streets are being cleared of garbage. From my publisher I got a Superman T-shirt and a bottle of scotch. Sherry got a job at the first bar we went to and we played three songs on every jukebox this side of town.

So this morning I woke up in a shack by the river, hungover and sweating and 28 years old—surrounded by rats and trash and burnt-out lighters. And still, I feel like this could be a very good year. I could become a man with a record collection again—a guy who walks through clean streets and sips single-malt Scotch, who exercises, bathes and goes to concerts, who holds his head up, smiles at the sky and does the right thing more often than not. If I can just survive Tent City.

July 14

I left early to go to the library, where it's air-conditioned. You can barely think in this heat. You move like you're trudging through a lake of warm beer. As I was making my way toward the gates there were some guys coming in. I didn't recognize three of them, but the fourth one was glaring at me, trying to stare right through me with his doglike Idaho eyes.

"Hi Derek," I said. He didn't answer, and before they reached me, I turned around and walked back into Tent City. I could hear their footsteps slowing down behind me, and they started arguing with each other. I rushed over to Eddie's shack to tell him that Derek was coming with backup.

By the time they showed up—walking down the river road— Randy, Terry, Heartbeat, Hoyt and I were standing outside Eddie's shack. There were a couple of two-by-fours and half of a pool cue leaning against the wall beside us. Eddie was sitting in a chair with his machete lying flat across his lap. Hoyt was holding a yellow X-Acto knife in his pale sweaty fist.

"That's them," I said as the men walked around Les's dollhouse and through the rubble of the Brothers' yard, but Derek was nowhere to be seen.

The biggest of the three yelled out "Bastard!" as they moved toward us. Eddie stood up and hollered back. "Bastard!" He and Eddie advanced on each other. They came right up, face to face and eye to eye, and then Eddie started to laugh. The big guy dropped the machete, and they embraced.

"Ollie!" said Eddie. "We were ready to kill you guys!"

"Eddie!" said the big guy. "You'd need more than this, you little fuck nuts!"

It was like a clichéd movie scene, but it still took a moment for the rest of us to relax. The big guy, Ollie, pulled some six-packs from his bag and handed them over.

"What happened to Derek?" said Eddie, passing the cans around.

Ollie shrugged. "He turned back when we got through the gates . . . The fuck's going on here anyway? What's with the blades?"

Eddie pointed to the scorched earth behind them and told Ollie about the Brothers' dramatic departure.

"Fucker!" said Ollie. "Never said nothing 'bout this. He bought the beer, though."

As we stood in the sunlight, drinking beer and looking across the ruins to the river, Les stepped out of the dollhouse in front of us. He rubbed his eyes and waved, then pissed on the burnt black ground. I walked over and handed him a beer.

"'Morning, Les. How's it going?"

He murmured something unintelligible, stepped over to the picnic table and pulled back a blue plastic tarp. The table was piled with groceries—raw corn on the cob, potatoes, ribs, steak and chicken—all still wrapped in cellophane. "Gonna make a feast, hm-yeah," he said. "For me and Jo-Jo."

"Where'd you get all the food?"

"The food store."

"Right . . . Where you been the past few days?"

"The island."

"What island?"

"Don't know. But this *one* guy—he wakes me up so I can go to bed. I *hate* it when people do that, mm-hmm, so I left the island."

"I thought you were in the hospital."

"No, nah-hmm—that was *before*."

"Before the island . . . and the food store."

"Exactly! We shall have corn—hmm-yeah!—and meat and potatoes!"

"Welcome back, Les," I said, and headed off for the library.

July 15

This place is swelling up fast in the heat. Even while I write this, there are another half-dozen shacks being built, each one bigger than the last. If this keeps up we're going to run out of room down here.

The traffic into Crack Corner is constant now, all day and all night. The dealers have added two more trailers to their crack empire, and with so many people coming to buy and get high it's hard to tell who really lives here. Every day I see a dozen I've never met.

Obviously the dynamics of Tent City are changing—and the colour, too. Until about a month ago everyone down here was white, Native or a mixture of the two. But the crack dealers are pretty well all black, mostly from Jamaica. So this one corner of Tent City—getting bigger every day—is now inhabited entirely by white hookers and black dealers, and they have control over most of Tent City.

In some ways it seems impossible that the old crew and Jimmy D's crew, and all the others, would let themselves be subjugated so easily. These guys are fighters. They're independent and resilient, and for the most part racist. But since they're crack addicts, and becoming more so every day, they're at the mercy of their new neighbours—who aren't crack addicts, and therefore control the crack.

I have no idea how this will all work out. We'll have to wait and see. One thing I *do* know is that while the old boys are treating the dealers like their oldest friends, some of them start muttering the N-word as soon as they're out of earshot, that white rock clutched safely in their dirty white hands.

x
x
x

On days like this it's hard to tell which is worse—the suffocating, yet shaded, interior of my little shack, or the blazing air outside. This morning we've chosen the former, and are lying on my bed under damp, clinging sheets, listening to the distinctively familiar sound of ambling, out-turned feet and wordless singing coming down the road.

"Hey, Lester!" calls out Sherry. We wait a minute, until he appears in the open door.

"How'd you know it was me?"

"You sound different from everyone else. Like some people have a distinctive smell—even from far away, even if you're not talking," says Sherry.

"Are you saying I sound like other people stink?"

"Maybe." Sherry giggles.

"What's up, Les?"

"I finally realized something."

"What did you realize, Les?"

"She's crazy!" There was no need to ask who. "She's completely insane!"

"This just occurred to you now?"

"I was at work all day, hm-hey. I brought her back two wheels of cheese from the monastery, and she says—"

"Whoaa, whoa, Les—since when do you work in a monastery?"

"I'm putting a roof on the thing . . . Anyway, I come home from work and she says, 'Where have you been?' uh-hm, like I haven't been at work."

"Well, why would she think that?" says Sherry.

"I told you, she's crazy!"

"No other reason that you can think of?"

"Well, I guess 'cause I was wearing shorts and flip-flops . . . and my cowboy hat, yum-huh, you like my new flip-flops? But it was hot! I changed on the way home!"

"And also you were carrying a couple wheels of cheese . . ."

"Exactly!"

"Well, you can kind of see her point, Les. Can't you? Most roofers don't come home in beach wear, bearing fresh cheese. You see what I mean?"

"But I got it from the monastery! I stole it right out of their—whatchamacallit?"

"Cheese drawer?"

"No. Like, a *whole room*. Like an old word."

"Larder?" says Sherry.

"Yeah! I stole it right out of the monks' larder."

"*I* believe you, Les."

"But it's like once food has touched my hands it's unclean or something—she won't take a bite! It's like that big feast I made the other night. She says it's all burned and goes out for burgers! It was *blackened!* Yeah-hmm! It was *supposed* to be blackened! I tell you—everybody *else* seemed to enjoy it. I mean, I come home with two big wheels of monk cheese—mozzarella and cheddar, and what does she do? Hmm-hey? She goes straight up to the store and buys a pack of Velveeta. Seriously, is that not the mark of a crazy woman?"

"I guess so, Les."

"You guys want some cheese?" he says. "I'll trade you for a cigarette."

July 17

If you happen to live among crack addicts, many of the hassles you deal with tend to be about money. Most people are under the mistaken impression that Tent City is an impoverished place. In many ways it is, but not necessarily economically. Especially now, hundreds—maybe thousands—of dollars exchange hands on this side of the fence every day. That is not to say that people (other than the dealers) *have* money down here. A crackhead never has money. A crackhead only ever has crack—and only for a moment.

Unfortunately it seems that Sluggo and I are the only ones left down here who aren't hooked. He came over this afternoon with some tobacco.

"Here," he said. "For all the smokes you've given me." A while ago, Sherry gave me a cigarette-rolling machine. Since the new tobacco tax came into effect last month I've been making a bit of change selling smokes for a quarter. But I also give them away to neighbours. Like me, Sluggo gets his $195 halfway through the month and was now on his way to the beer store, and then to the bridge to drink with his "bridge club." Apparently he'd managed to squirrel some of the money away, where Jackie hadn't found it. "Do I owe you any cash, Shaun?"

"Not a cent, Sluggo."

"Good thing. Can you do me a favour? I owe this guy some money, and I'm sort of on a payment plan. Can I leave $30 with you, in case he comes down while I'm gone? I don't want to hang around here. All these crackheads make me edgy."

"Sure, Sluggo."

He handed me $30, then thought for a moment. "Actually, can you hold another $20? Then even if Jackie gets it all, I'll still have some left." He gave me another $20, and turned to Sherry. "He's the only guy I can trust—'cause he doesn't do crack . . . You ever done crack?"

"No," said Sherry.

"Neither have I," he said, then turned back to me and squinted. "How 'bout you?"

"I've done it twice, but . . ."

"Give me back the money! There could always be a third time!" He laughed, then turned to Sherry. "Just keep your eye on him, okay?"

"Hey, Sluggo," I said. "Can I ask you a personal question?"

"That depends."

"How long you been clean?"

"Nine years!" He smiled and held up his bare arms like he was performing a magic trick. "And check it out: No tracks! . . . I did it right . . . in . . . here," he said, miming the careful insertion of a needle into his groin. "That's why you'll never see me in Speedos!"

x   x   x

Karen found a book of lateral-thinking puzzles in a garbage heap and is becoming obsessed with them. She tries them out on me a few times a day.

"How do you make seven into eight?" she says.

"You add one, Karen."

"No, no! That's not it! It's how do you make seven into . . . shit!"

As opposed to linear problems, which screw me every time, I have a knack for the lateral ones. But Karen thinks I've been sneaking into her shack to peek at the answers. So she keeps hiding the book, but she forgets where she hid it, then tries to stump me with brainteasers she can't remember right.

"How do you make seven even?" I suggest.

"What?"

"You take off the S . . ."

"That's it! That's it! How'd you know?"

"Guess I've got a lateral mind, is all."

"You cheater! Okay, okay! Here's another one: There's six and a half baskets of apples . . . No, wait! There's six and a half apple *trees* . . . No, that can't be right . . ."

This goes on for a while, and Jackie shows up to have a drink with us. Karen is drawing apple trees, or bushes, on a piece of cardboard, and Jackie is pretending to pay attention, but I can tell she's distracted.

"So," she says. "Sluggo give you that thing for that guy?"

"Yep."

"Good, good," she says, nodding seriously, and I turn my attention back to the surreal orchard that's growing on Karen's piece of cardboard. "Yeah . . . ," says Jackie. "I just gotta wait till seven o'clock, eh? My friend's bringing me down some money."

"Uh-huh."

"You got the time, sweetie?" she says to Sherry.

"It's six."

"No! Six and a half!" says Karen in frustration, referring, I assume, to apple baskets or trees.

"Yep. Only an hour to wait—" says Jackie.

I don't say anything. In fact, I try not to look at her. She's sweating hard, and her eyes have that unearthly blue glow to them. I figure it's been at least an hour since her last toke. Three more times Jackie mentions—in what she seems to think is an offhand manner—her friend coming down with the money. I still don't respond.

"Shaun . . . ," she says finally.

"No," I say, and look at her once, straight on, hoping it'll stop there. But it doesn't.

"Please, just $10! I'll give it to you at seven o'clock!"

I tell her no. But it doesn't stop.

"Please, Shaun."

I try everything I can. I look into her eyes. I lower my voice.

"You don't understand, Shaun! I *need* that money now! Just $10."

I use logic. I explain things. I tell her politely. I am firm. I make it final.

"Please . . . please . . . ," she begs. "It's Sluggo's money . . . not yours! You *have* to do this for me, Shaun. You *have* to . . ."

It gets worse and worse until Karen—who's long since given up on her lateral apples—gets up and leaves. And then it really gets ugly.

Jackie begins to howl my name. "Shaun!" she howls. "Give it to me! Give it to me!" She is yelling, and her whole face is wet. I feel my resolve wearing down, and can't look over at Sherry. Jackie's brilliant blue eyes are glaring at me as she howls. I know she's full of fury, but tomorrow she will be my friend again. I tell her this, but she doesn't seem to hear. I tell it to myself too, that I've got to do what I said I would, even as she begs and howls just inches from my face.

"Why, Shaun?! Why!?" she yells.

It makes me sick and sad that she knows my name, because this isn't Jackie. It's not her.

"Please! Please! Please! Please! Please . . ."

It goes on and on, until I can see that she's turned my face into a piece of white rock. She is staring at me as she pleads, willing me to burn so that she can suck me into her lungs. Her hands are curling and grasping the air, like an infant reaching for . . . for anything.

"Jackie . . . ," I say. I don't want to tell her to leave, to get off my land. I don't want to say the words. But I stand up. "Jackie . . ."

And then, just in time, some wise and inspired part of her brain—buried somewhere back there—says, "Shaun, do you want to buy a bale of tobacco? Five dollars for a bale!"

"Okay," I say. "Sure, Jacks." And suddenly it's like she can see me again. She glances over at Sherry and smiles, the fluorescent storm receding in her eyes. I've managed to keep my word to Sluggo. And to not lend her any money either. It's as fair a deal as you can make down here, even if Sluggo bought the tobacco, and even if I'm still giving her money for crack.

"That was hard," I say once Jackie's gone to get the tobacco.

"Jesus!" says Sherry. "I can't believe you held out for so long. I was about to give her the money myself." And I realize that somehow Jackie kept herself from crossing that line. Even while grovelling and howling, she hadn't looked to Sherry once.

x   x   x

Karen comes back over while Jackie's filling up a pouch from a tobacco canister. I hand her five bucks, and Jackie says, "You want to buy another?"

"Don't do it, Shaun," says Karen, grinning a blasted, loopy smile. "That's Sluggo's tobacco."

Jackie turns to Karen, but before she can do anything, Sherry says, "I'll buy it!"

Once Jackie has the $10 in her hand, she's gone, and Karen lets out a short laugh. "I don't know why I try to help Sluggo," she says. "I mean, I feel bad for the guy—how much she takes him for. But you know once she's got the rock, I'll be over there smoking it with her . . . That's sort of a brainteaser too, eh?"

"I think that one's more ethical than lateral, Karen."

"I guess so, eh?" She takes a pill from where it's rolled up in the ankle of her sock. "Anyone want a codeine?" she says. "Man! I used to take a hundred of these a day."

"One hundred!" says Sherry.

"Oh, yeah. Fucked up my life pretty good. But man, I had the cleanest apartment you ever seen. Used to clean for hours! Whoa! Is that a crumb? That looks like a crumb? Those were the days, ha, ha, ha! Cleanest apartment in the whole wide world . . ."

x
x
x

Sluggo comes back along the river road, weebling and wobbling into my yard.

"*I,*" he announces, "have . . . given *you* . . . $50!" He's saying it slowly so he can get it straight in his own brain. "Thirty dollars . . . for the man . . . $20 for me!"

"That is correct."

He nods vigorously and heads off toward his shack. But then, a moment later, he stumbles back in through the side entrance. "Do you or do you *not,*" he says, holding up a finger in dramatic query, "smoke crack cocaine?!"

"I do not," I say, and he nods.

"And *will* you give that money to Jackie—even if she begs you?" he says.

"I will not." I see no reason to tell Sluggo I've already passed that test.

"Good," he says. "Thank you." And he staggers away.

For half an hour we listen to Sluggo and Jackie going at it, until finally he comes back into my yard and holds out his hand.

"Better you than me," I say, and give him the $50.

July 19

Yesterday, on the way up Parliament Street, Dirty Willy pulled his bike to the side of the road and waved me over. Willy owns a bicycle-repair shop and gets drunk every night at Henry's. His shop is a garage behind a church, with a sign that reads "Willy's Basically Bicycles."

Dirty Willy is always trying to buy or sell something—right now it's back rims. He heard there's a lot of bike parts in Tent City, and offered me $10 for every suitable rim I could get. So when I got up today, I went out looking.

Eddie had already been going at it for a while, and he was on an aluminum kick.

"I don't care where I find it, I'm getting all of it! Pots! Pans! There was a door over there with a magnetic lock—some guy just put it up, and it's already down!"

"Well, just stay away from my place, Eddie."

"Why? You got aluminum?"

"You're pretty whacked out, eh?"

"Me? No! I don't do that shit anymore. I'm *selling* now! I'm going to sell crack—like a smart fucking person, and then you know what I'm going to do? I'm going to buy a PlayStation! No more crack for Eddie. I'm drunk now, though. How do you like me drunk?"

I found eight back rims, and as I was carting them over to my place, Eddie was standing in front of a stack of plate-glass windows he'd taken right out of Dry's front yard—and he was smashing them with a hammer. The shards of glass were showering over him like a thousand shooting stars.

"Aluminum!" he said, his eyes like broken windows.

July 20

It might be a while before I can get any money out of Dirty Willy. I went up to Henry's with Sherry last night, but by the time we got there, Willy was already drunk and said he'd got all the rims he needed. I told him he was going to pay me anyway, but then he started pawing at Sherry with his dirty little hands and things got ugly.

x   x
 x

When I went out for some water this evening, Jackie was pushing a stroller down the main road. "Come here, Shauny!" she said. "Come and see Jessie!"

I walked over and, sure enough, there was a baby in there.

"Jessie, meet Shaun," she said, brushing her large fingers against the girl's tiny cheeks. "Mommy's letting me take care of her *all* night, *isn't* she? . . . Yes she *is!*" she said, and the baby let out a gurgling laugh. "Isn't she an angel, Shaun?"

"Hi there, Jessie," I said.

"That's Jessie's mom," said Jackie, pointing over to Randy's barrel, where a woman was sitting in the firelight, drinking beer with the boys. "She used to be bad too, eh?" By this she means she used to be like us. "She had to fight *real* hard to get this little cutie back." Jackie was tickling the girl's tummy, touching her nose, her little toes. "But you *sure* are worth it—*aren't* you? Yes you *are.*"

Jackie mothers every young thing who comes near her—baby or beast or fowl. You give her a little Jessie and she suddenly seems like the Madonna—this large lumbering unfit mother who bore six children and lost them all, one of them shaken to death when she wasn't there. This gentle, crackhead, loving mother.

"How about you, Jackie? You doing okay?"

"Oh, sure . . . Sluggo tried to hit me with a chair earlier, and I knocked him down pretty hard. But I'm not smoking right now. Being with Jessie makes me calm. She's really nice, eh? I'd be with her *always* if I could . . . *Wouldn't* I now? *Wouldn't* I . . . Yes I *would!*" As I left to get water, Jackie was lifting Jessie from the stroller into her soft giant arms.

July 21

I woke this morning to what sounded like a particularly bad fight. I pulled on clothes and went over to see, but when I got there everyone was just standing around not saying much. Except for Randy.

It looked like he'd lost his mind. He kept throwing himself against the outside walls of his prefab, screaming and breaking anything he could get his hands on.

"What's going on?"

Before anyone could answer, Randy turned on us, "Friends! *Friends?*" he shouted. "Some fucking *friends* you are! A man's got *one* thing in the world and you just sit and laugh as it gets . . . ripped away from him! You're fucking *useless!* Every one of you! You're not worth a thing—*anything!*"

"Chaos is gone," Jackie said to me. "Someone took him."

"Who? Who took him?"

Jackie sighed, and Randy started tearing apart a bag of dog food with his hands.

"That woman who was down here," she said.

"Jessie's mom? Why? Why would she take him?"

Jackie looked at the ground, then lifted her head and yelled at Randy to shut the fuck up.

"Does anyone know where she lives?"

"Scarborough. But Scarborough's a big place."

"Poor Randy," I said as he spat an angry stream of abuse at us.

"Fuck Randy," said Jackie. "Poor Jessie—having a mother like that, who'd steal a man's dog."

When Randy's fury seemed to have abated a bit, I approached him slowly.

"We'll find him, Randy," I said.

"*Who?* Who'll find him—nobody *here's* going to help, that's for sure! And *where?* Where are we going to find him?"

"I don't know—Scarborough."

"Why Scarborough?"

I told him what Jackie had said.

"Well, why the hell didn't anybody say anything? Why didn't they stop her? Does anybody know her last name?" he yelled. Nobody said anything. "You're all *useless!*" he shouted, then howled "Chaos" a couple more times, grabbed his backpack and headed for the gates. "I'll find him without you!" he shouted back over his shoulder. "You *son of a bitches!*"

x   x   x

It was still early. Sluggo, Les and I decided to go to the Sunday brunch at Osgoode, and we picked up Jimmy D on the way out of Tent City. "Yeah, why not?" he growled. "Got another two hours to kill." On Sunday the beer store doesn't open until noon.

We each got a copy of the *Sun* from the nearest box, and flipped through it as we headed downtown. "All crap," growled Jimmy D, and we had to agree. He threw his paper into a trash can and said, "Who'd steal another man's dog? That's just not right. Poor son of a bitch." Seeing as he and Randy claim to hate each other, and hate each other's dogs even more, it was nice to hear such a sentiment from Jimmy.

But then, while we were waiting in front of the law courts to be let in for brunch, Randy showed up. When he saw Jimmy D, he came right at us. "You *happy*?" he shouted. "Now your mangy dogs don't have to bother killing him! You *happy* about that?"

Jimmy D stepped out of line. "I'll knock you out!" he growled.

"Come on—right now!" yelled Randy, and whipped his own backpack onto the ground, like he was body-slamming some dog-thieving dwarf.

I learned a long time ago not to get in the middle of these things. But this was just too stupid: three hundred hungry people watching two confused dog lovers fight at the door of the law courts for no reason whatsoever. It was the kind of thing that gives Tent City a bad name. So I stepped between them. They kept trying to go for each other, but I didn't move and we danced around in this awkward volatile threesome until Sluggo and Les reached the lunch-room doors and called to us. Jimmy D followed them in, I handed Randy's backpack to him, and said, "I'll see you soon. Try to calm down, okay?"

At our table over brunch, Jimmy D kept growling into his tuna melt: "He called me a goof! The guy called me a goof! I'm going to kill him!"

"Don't bother," I said to Jimmy D. "If he doesn't find Chaos he's already dead." The others grumbled in agreement.

"Yeah, I guess . . . ," growled Jimmy D. "He sure loves that stupid dog."

x   x   x

In the late afternoon I picked up Sherry at work, and we went to a free barbecue at Trinity Church on King Street. A lot of the guys from Tent City were there, and so was Dirty Willy. I went over to have some words with him. He's that sleazy kind of character who makes Dostoevsky novels and Scorsese films so colourful—the kind of guy that people grab by the collar. I grabbed him by the collar, and he said he'd come look at the rims tomorrow, then he went over and apologized to Sherry for being "annoying, disrespectful and creepy" the night before.

"Those sound like *your* words," said Sherry when he'd gone.

"Yeah. He's really quite eloquent," I said.

Before we left, I overheard Randy asking the priest to pray for the return of Chaos. "Chaos?" said the priest.

"He's a very good dog," said Randy.

x
x
x

Sherry and I are sitting out on my deck playing gin rummy by the light of the full moon, listening to glass breaking, people fighting each other, sirens coming in through the gates and Randy's occasional howl of "Chaos."

A storm blows in. As I'm laying down a five-card run, the thunder cracks and Karen comes through the trees into the yard with a bundle in her arms. "You guys want a kitten?" she says. Sherry's up faster than the flash of lightning across the water, and the kitten's in her arms before the thunder cracks again.

"Oh my God!" she says. "He's the cutest thing that ever lived!"

"It's yours if you want it," says Karen. "Those guys don't deserve it."

Apparently Dan's and Donny's girlfriends were put in charge of Roger's rabbits while he's on vacation in Eastern Europe, and tonight they were fighting over who was responsible for one of the bunnies, which apparently died by jumping into the canal. Dan's girlfriend beat up Donny's and then she and Donny left without their kitten. When Karen went over, it was just sitting there, surrounded by broken glass, hungry dogs and drunk people still trying to beat each other up.

"That's Peaches's sister," says Karen as Sherry sits down with the kitten in her lap and starts to rub its belly.

"Who's Peaches?"

"My kitten," says Karen defensively, as if I should know she's named him Peaches. "She's one of Les's litter. Her name's Strawberry. They can live next to each other!"

"Peaches and Strawberry?"

"Are you sure it's a girl?" says Sherry as the kitten stretches across her thighs. "He seems like a boy. *Don't* you, baby. Yes you *do*." The kitten reaches up and paws gently at her nose.

"Well, I don't think we can keep her, Karen," I say. "But we'll look after her tonight." Sherry isn't listening. She's lost somewhere in the cuteness of Strawberry's skinny belly.

Jackie comes through the trees and sits down. "It's going to be a bad night," she says. Every time the thunder cracks she starts to shake. There was a storm a few nights ago, and Sluggo found her crouched and sobbing in the cubby house behind their shack.

Randy drags himself in through the fence and sits down on the couch. He looks like a little boy who's been lost in the woods for days.

"What's that?" he says.

"It's just the cutest kitten in the whole wide world!" says Sherry, lifting one of its paws to wave at Randy.

"Chaos would have liked her," says Randy, his eyes red in the candlelight. "He was good with kittens." The lightning bursts above our heads, the ground shakes with exploding thunder and finally it begins to rain orphaned cats and stolen dogs.

July 22

The storm kept up all night, beating down on the roof so that Sherry and I could barely hear each other. One bolt of lightning hit the tree in front of Eddie and Karen's shack, and cut a huge branch down onto their new shower stall.

That darn kitten, however, seemed completely unfazed. It was as if she knew she only had one night to win us over. She purred and meowed until it sounded like singing. She chased her tail, played with Sherry's hair, did backflips off a chair and kept stretching herself out for lengthy belly rubs. She ate the tuna and water I gave her, very politely, and cleaned herself afterwards. You could see the difference that one good meal made, her tiny ribs receding just a touch. She kissed our faces with her coarse little tongue and curled at our feet as we slept.

"You've got to admit," said Sherry in the morning, "she's the best little cat ever."

"Yeah."

"And she's got no one to take care of her."

"Uh-huh."

"And look at that—she's standing on your foot!"

"Okay, okay! We can keep her!" I said. "But I'm not calling her Strawberry."

So now Sherry's taken our new kitten to Scarborough for a few days—to fatten her up, get her shots and clean her ears. Mostly, though, I think she just didn't want to leave her here.

"And I'll keep an eye out for Chaos," she says, though Scarborough's the size of a city.

x   x   x

On the way to the library today, I ran into Lenny and Donna. I hadn't seen them since their summer house was detonated. They said they haven't seen Derek in a couple of weeks.

"That prick!" said Donna. "He better hope I don't find him. Look what he did to his own brother!"

Lenny's straggly hair was gone and his lips were puffier than usual. He glared at the ground and said, "Aw, sit!"

"He can't even talk right!" said Donna. "Derek broke his teeth. And he shaved his head! His own brother! The guy's dangerous, you know?"

"Well, yeah."

"That was bad, what happened down there," said Donna. "I didn't know he torched the place. I really didn't! But I turned him in, eh? I called the cops to tell 'em who it was who done it. Just a matter of time before they pick him up." Lenny was looking at the ground and nodding slowly.

"You're better without him, Lenny," I said. "He gets you in too much trouble."

"Es, I nuh," he said, and shook my hand. "See uh aroun."

x   x   x

When I came back to Tent City this afternoon, there was a crowd of people at Randy's. I went over to see what was going on. And there, sitting in the middle of them, was Chaos.

"He's back, Shaun!" said Randy. "Chaos is back!" He handed me a can of Crest, then tried to pick me up in a bear hug, the beer spilling all over us. Jessie's mom was sitting in a chair off to the side. While I was standing there, Eddie went over to her and said, "I should slap you in the head, you bitch. You don't take a man's dog."

She shrugged, and handed him a bottle.

"Chaos is back!" said Randy again, and he started to dance.

July 23

Karen and I spent a lot of time today trying to draw four straight fences through a field of eleven apple trees so that no two trees are enclosed together.

"It's impossible, Karen!" I said, and she just frowned. She had found the book again, but had torn the answers out of the back and hidden them, and of course she didn't remember where. "You *gotta* get off the crack, girl."

"I'm going to look for them again," she said, and stomped back into her shack.

I dropped in on her later, and she was sitting on the floor with her kitten in her lap. There was a piece of paper in front of her, and she was writing so furiously that she didn't even notice I was there. I watched her for a while. Finally she looked up and said, "I don't know what to do with this."

"What, Karen?"

"*You* write stuff, eh, Shaun? Do you think you can . . . No, forget it. Forget it! . . . Okay, just read it fast!" She handed me the paper.

"What is this, Karen?" I said.

"It's nothing . . . it's just writing. Don't read it!" She grabbed it back out of my hands. She held it in the air and said, "It's just writing. Like, how I'm feeling. Do you think that's okay?"

"Is what okay?" I said, watching the piece of paper hovering between us.

"I'm just writing this stuff—not for any reason. Do you think there's something wrong with me?"

"No . . . not because of the writing." She'd told me to read it fast, and now I was mad at myself for hesitating. "In fact," I said, "the writing might help."

"It feels good. It makes me more relaxed after . . . but you don't think I'm crazy—for writing?"

"No, Karen. Keep doing it," I said, and reached for the piece of paper. She pulled it away.

"Maybe I'll write a book," she said, then began to tear the paper into long, thin strips, popping them into her mouth and chewing them slowly.

July 24

Today was a bad day. I'm still trying to understand what happened. Or what happens, down here. This place is full of love and aggression, violence and fear and sometimes desperate hopefulness. It is also full of animals. People put their fearfulness, hope and hunger into their pets, who've replaced their children. And it's almost like the animals are left to carry on the struggle, like confused kids running on their parents' leftover energy. I'm probably projecting and personifying too much, but down here rabbits drown themselves, goldfish die from crack, and a dog will stab a kitten in the gut.

By the time the sun reaches the top of the sky today, Sluggo and Jackie are fighting as usual. As the heat gets worse, so do they. Sluggo is drunk, and you can hardly hear him, but Jackie keeps screaming: "You call me a *crackhead!* You fucking call me a *crackhead!* Why you gotta throw that in my face? *Why?* I've been clean for three days! How long *you* been clean, you fucking *goof?* Hey? *Hey?*"

I don't want to listen, but they drown out the sounds of the whole city, and the wind, and the thousands of cars going by on the highway. They go on and on, and although Sluggo is barely audible, she's yelling at him to shut up, like a child in tantrum. "Shut *up,* shut *up, shut up!*" I can hear Sluggo's drunken voice counting the times she punches him. "Okay . . . Thatsh three . . . Thatsh jusht great . . . Thatsh four."

It's not funny, but I laugh because there's nothing else to do. Cleo is barking like a frantic child trying to get between her fighting parents, to stop them. And the barking, yelling and counting goes on and on.

Suddenly the barking stops.

At this moment, I can feel a shift. I'm standing in my yard, on the other side of the trees, and I can feel a change in Cleo—a growl too low to hear, or just a space in the air when the dog turns her head. And even as the screaming continues, I know that Cleo is gone—galloping over the ground.

I run through the trees, out of my yard. I can see her charging toward Eddie's shack. At the same moment I see Paul—a friend of Eddie's who lives downtown—coming from the opposite direction. I see that Eddie's door is open, and that Eddie is over by Randy's barrel. I see Cleo pouncing through the door.

Jackie is still yelling. Sluggo is still counting forlornly. Paul shouts Cleo's name and I shout at Eddie. The three of us reach his shack as Cleo comes running back out, her teeth glistening in the sun.

We're standing in the doorway. Before our eyes can adjust, we hear the sound—a sort of high-pitched, breathless whimpering. Karen is rising out of bed and rubbing her eyes as we step through the door. She swings her feet to the floor and looks down. "Oh . . . no, God," she says. The kitten's stomach is open, and there's something coming out of it. His paws flutter in the air.

Karen begins to moan and Paul drops down on his knees, covering the kitten with his body. "Maybe we can still . . . ," he says. I move toward them, then see Eddie's eyes flashing next to me in the dim light. And I remember his dumb threat that we turned into an even stupider joke: "If your kitten . . ."

"Eddie!" I say, but he's already got the machete in his hands. He pushes past me out the door.

Jackie and Sluggo are inside their shack now, but you can still hear her yelling. And Cleo is trotting back toward us, as if to see what happened.

"I'm going to cut your head off!" growls Eddie. I get between him and Cleo. Eddie's holding the blade up in the air, but I've got my hand on Cleo's collar. And I run—all the way to Jackie and Sluggo's door without looking back.

Inside the shack, Jackie is sitting on Sluggo's chest, and her arms are streaked with blood. They're both yelling and striking at each other with their open hands. "Keep her here!" I shout as I pull Cleo inside. "Eddie's going to kill her! She got his kitten!" But as I slam the door behind me, they're still going at it, like they haven't heard a word I said.

By the time I get back, Eddie is inside his shack, beating at the walls with the butt of a pool cue. Paul is still on the floor, and he's wrapping a torn cloth around the kitten's abdomen, trying to hold in the guts.

"He's still alive . . . ," he says. Karen is just staring at the floor.

I begin to patch up the kitten with some cloth, gauze and a roll of scotch tape. Paul is trying to tie the kitten's back legs together to stop him struggling. Jackie and Sluggo are still yelling from inside their shack. Eddie is shouting at them and banging on his open door, Karen is moaning. Suddenly, from inside Jackie and Sluggo's shack, Cleo jumps out the window, taking the window frame with her.

There's a crash. I see Jackie turning to look at us through the hole in the wall as Cleo runs into the bushes. "Mind your own fucking business!" she yells.

"I'll kill you!" says Eddie. And now everybody's moving, except for me and Paul, still trying to wrap the kitten's guts, his little stomach rising and falling beneath the bandages.

From outside I hear Sluggo say, "Without the wood, Eddie." And as I look up, Eddie drops the cue from his hand and hammers Sluggo in the jaw with his fist. Sluggo falls to the ground.

"This first, Eddie!" I yell. "He's still alive! Fucking deal with this first!" Eddie turns around and comes back inside. Karen stops moaning and starts to shout. "Don't let him die! Don't let him die, Eddie! He's *ours!*" The kitten's eyes are closed.

We decide to put him in Eddie's grey gym bag, so Eddie can take him on his bike to the vet at the humane society. I run over to my shack to get a clean shirt to wrap him in, and then we zip the kitten into the bag, leaving it open just a bit. Eddie puts the strap over his shoulder and cycles away like his life is after him.

We wait for a while.

"He'll be okay, right? Do you think he's okay?" says Karen. She asks this a few more times, and then I walk outside.

Although Sluggo's jaw has no doubt been cracked, if not broken, he and Jackie are still going at it. I walk over and get Cleo, who is running circles around their shack. Jackie is beating on the wall with an iron bar. I put a rope through Cleo's collar and bring him over to my place.

I sit in front of my shack, patting Cleo. I turn on the radio to try and drown out the noise of his parents fighting. Curly comes out of the pink prefab and throws some pieces of bread onto the water for the seagulls and pigeons. A police boat comes up along shore, a man in uniform looks at us through binoculars for a while, and the boat leaves. The horn sounds from across the canal, which means the Essroc tanker is returning to port. Eddie comes riding by on his bike, but I don't call out to him.

Ten minutes later, Karen walks through the trees and onto my deck. She looks down at us sitting there, and says, "Fuck you, Cleo!" then begins to cry.

I stand up and hold her against me. Then she kneels down and puts her arms around Cleo. She holds her and hugs her while Cleo's big Rottweiler tongue slobbers all over her shoulder. "It's not your fault, Cleo," she says. "It's not your fault, baby."

July 25

Although we're still in the middle of a heat wave, everyone's cooled down a lot since yesterday. When Eddie brought my shirt back, holding it out to me like a funeral shroud, he said, "I don't blame any one person, you know? There were a lot of . . . what do you call it? . . . contributing circumstances. Probably my fault, too, as much as anything." He doesn't want to kill Cleo or slug Sluggo anymore, and has even reconsidered his decision to take Cleo to the humane society. For now at least—as long as she wears a muzzle when she's off her chain—Cleo can stay. And I've decided that, for the time being, our new kitten should remain in Scarborough.

When I finally took Cleo home last night Jackie was long gone and Sluggo had started to sober up.

"Shanks," he said, but he wasn't slurring because he was drunk. His jaw was swollen to twice its size, his cheek was blue, and I could see in his blurry eyes that he finally understood. "I'm shorry 'bout the cat."

Karen came over this morning with what appeared to be a large picture frame wrapped in a pink bedsheet. "Is Sherry here?" she said.

"No, she's staying with her mom . . ."

"You got a pen—like a Magic Marker?"

I gave her a black pen and she wrote *For Bingo* across the sheet, then handed it to me and said. "Make sure you give her this, okay?"

"Can't you just write *For Sherry?*" I said.

"It's not for her!" said Karen. "It's for the *kitten*—I think you should call it Bingo." It's actually not a bad name for a brave and lucky little cat, and might help exorcise Sherry's bingo demons. But even before she'd come over, I was thinking we should offer the kitten to Karen, now that hers is gone.

"Karen, do you want . . . ?"

"No! No way. She's yours! Just look at the present, okay?"

I unravelled the sheet and held the frame at arm's length. It was a blown-up photo of an orange kitten with a very worried face. The kitten was dangling in the air, hanging on to a tree branch with only one paw. Underneath, in big black letters, were the words "OH SHIT!!"

"Doesn't it look like Bingo?" she said. I coughed out a nervous laugh. The thought of Karen walking around with this picture in a wrapped-up bedsheet was just a bit too heavy. And none of it was lost on Karen. "Look," she said, pointing at the spiderweb glass. "The glass is broken. It's kind of fitting, eh? . . . You know what I mean, like the symbolism and . . ." She trailed off, still staring at the picture, then said, "Eddie found it this morning. I thought Sherry would like it . . ."

"Yeah. Thanks, Karen." I put the picture down and leaned it against the wall.

"So make sure you give it to her, eh?" said Karen, still looking at the kitten in the frame. "Do you think she'll get it? Like all the . . . uh, implications, or whatever . . . with the broken glass?"

"If she doesn't, I'll point it out to her."

Karen nodded. "Oh shit!" she whispered, reading the caption on the poster. "Oh *shit!*" she said again, then hurried away before I could see her cry.

July 27

For the past week or so, Les and I have been discussing a new money-making scheme that would take advantage of our current heat wave, as well as our location. Every day, hundreds of yuppies and tourists on Rollerblades and bikes pass Tent City on the Trans-Canada bicycle path. They are hot and dehydrated, and no doubt they could do with a nice refreshing pop. Enter Shaun and Lester's Cold Drink Emporium: ice-cold drinks, for only $1!!

It is, of course, illegal to set up a roadside stand without a vendor's licence. Unless, however, you remain on private property (or at least this is what we assume), which is why we'll be selling from inside Tent City, passing cold drinks over the fence to all the rich and thirsty people on the other side.

Our main obstacle so far has been a lack of start-up: both the financial and the get-up-and-go kind. Les may be a man of action, but he is also a man of falling-down-confused-not-really-remembering-what-the-heck-he's-supposed-to-be-doing. And then there are the delusions.

Every day for about a week now, he has promised that our grand opening will take place the following day—because that's when his boss will finally pay him, and then his friend will come down and pick us up in a truck, and he'll take us somewhere that sells cans of pop for a dime apiece. The problem is, I'm not sure that Les actually *has* a boss (or, for that matter, a job). I'm not sure that Les has a friend with a truck (let alone one who is intending to drive us anywhere). And I'm almost completely certain that Les hasn't bought a pop for a dime since about 1958.

But I always want to believe. So I went over to his place again yesterday morning in order to get everything set up by noon and be selling like crazy in the heat of the day. When I knocked on the melted front wall of his dollhouse, Kelly, one of the rec centre girls, whipped it open and began throwing stuff out.

"No, Les don't fuckin' live here!" she informed me. "And he better not fuckin' come near here, you hear! And also, you know what? He can go fuck himself, yeah!"

Eventually I discovered Les way back in the brush, lying in a dollhouse with no roof. He was unconscious, but still babbling, and both his hands were in his pants. When I shook him he looked at me and said, "Shaun and Lester's Cold Drink Emporium." Then he giggled and passed out again. This is the kind of thing that makes Les a somewhat difficult business partner.

x   x   x

Eddie, meanwhile, has become an errand boy for the crack dealers. Most of the old crew now spend their days tripping over themselves as Big G sits there snapping his fingers in the air. It's embarrassing to watch: all these tough, smart warriors—some of them legends on the street—being sent to get pizza, sweeping the concrete in front of a trailer, doing the laundry, fetching water, all day at the dealers' beck and call.

Yesterday, as I sat under the shade of my new patio umbrella, Eddie went by pushing a huge septic tank on a dolly, going to clean out Big G's shit . . . Eddie, who could have run this place, who could have been the philosopher king of the bums . . . Frizz, who is one of the most famous street fighters around, and studied creative writing for two years on a college scholarship before he went to the pen . . . Randy, who's been sleeping under the stars every summer for a decade, dancing with Chaos on Cough-X . . . all these good fucking guys have sold themselves to the Big Man for a bit of his crack.

x
x
x

"We pray for you—that you may stand up to the devil, even as you stand at the gates of hell. We have hope for you, and you are in our prayers."

Sister H looked at us, or rather, looked *upon* us, and smiled gently.

"I don't look at you as people I have to help. I look at you as my family and friends. If I could, I would have you all to my home, but for the problems of transportation. I do love you. And God loves you, too."

There were three tables of food in the centre of the old town, and people kept filling up their plates. Bonnie, who's had her dream and is moving back to Hamilton with the tall guy, was apparently under the impression that we'd gathered in her honour. So when Sister H was finished talking, she got up to make a speech.

"I would first like to thank Sister H for this barbecue," she began. "Unlike all the other church people who come down here, she has never talked down to us, and never preached." (Apparently she hadn't been listening that closely to the Gates of Hell speech.) "I, as you may know, will be leaving Tent City soon. I will be leaving this land, which is Indian land. And *our* land. But I will not be leaving the struggle!"

In her new life, Bonnie intends to set up a "squatters' rights group." Tomorrow she is giving a speech at a squatting rally on the west side of the city. A few days ago some protestors took over a vacant building as a demonstration against the housing crisis in Toronto. The action is known as the Pope Squat, in reference to His Holiness's coinciding visit. She is perfect for this kind of thing. For Bonnie, even a born-again barbecue is a political soapbox.

x
x
x

Sherry and I went to the drive-in tonight, although we don't have a car. The theatre is just over the bridge and down the road, at The Docks—

an adult amusement park and disco. We brought two fold-up chairs, a bottle of booze, some food and my radio.

A few days ago, Les, Spider and I did the same. We sat outside the fence, set the radio to the station that gets the movie soundtrack and stared up at the giant screen waiting for the show to begin. We sat there for almost an hour, until I turned to Les and said, "Are you sure there's a movie tonight?"

"Yeah, yeah-hmm! This guy told me . . ."

"The gimpy one-eyed drug-dealer guy?"

"No. No, this . . ."

"But a crackhead, right?"

"Well . . . *yeah*."

I walked to the fence and climbed up. There wasn't a single car on the other side.

So this time I checked the movie listings myself, and we left Spider and Les at home. Les still hasn't come through with the cold drinks.

"I can lend you the money to get you started," offered Sherry as the cars drove by us through the drive-in gates.

"Nah," I said. "I'll figure something out. You spent enough this week." She's paid for all of Bingo's shots and some stuff for ear mites, and food and toys, too. The vet said the kitten's healthy, all things considered, but that she isn't a she.

"I told you," said Sherry. "He's a boy—you can tell by the way he gets when you rub his tummy. He purrs the same as you . . . and his name is *not* Bingo!" Then she curled against me as Austin Powers took to the screen, over the fence and under the stars.

July 29

I asked Bonnie how her speech at the Pope Squat went, and her long arms shot up in exasperation. "It's a big circle jerk!" she said. "I had a speech written, but when I realized the intelligence level I was dealing with I diverted from it pretty fast. I told them to shove their agenda up their ass—I mean, squatting rights wasn't even *on* the agenda!" For Bonnie, an agenda is like body odour—it's fine as long as it's your own. "I mean, they've got flowers planted and it's all clean and everything, but it's like a game. I told 'em to try living in Tent City full-time, thinking every time you see a cop your home's about to be bulldozed, freezing your ass off all winter . . ."

"So you're leaving, eh, Bonnie?"

"Yeah. I had a sit-down with Eddie, and I wanted to talk to you, too. I'm leaving my place to Hazel." Hazel is a friend of Bonnie's who's been camping here the past week or so. "I just don't want Crack Corner to get it, you know, Shaun. I mean, Eddie says he'll look out for her, but I'm starting to think he doesn't have enough muscle anymore." And of course she's right.

"It's all slipping away, Shaun. I mean, they're really fucking away any burgeoning sense of community down here. The dealers are going to grab it all. I mean, they already tried to muscle you."

"Well, I don't know, it was a pretty pathetic example of—"

"Well, the next one might be a lot less pathetic, you know? You got to remember, Shaun—you're not a crack smoker, so you're not really worth anything to them. You're expendable. This place could have been great, it's too bad. It's just sad, you know?"

"It could just be summer, Bonnie. It might just be that."

"Perhaps," said Bonnie. "But probably not."

July 30

I finally got sick of waiting for Les to get our business started, and decided to go ahead without him. I went up to the No Frills grocery store on Parliament and priced out their pop and water. I figured I needed almost $40—enough for twenty-four cans each of No Name cola, ginger ale and diet cola, twenty-four bottles of water and two bags of ice. So last night I borrowed $10 from Sherry and went to play pool. It took me nearly six hours, but finally I managed to squeeze $34 from a few tired drunks. Then this morning Sherry and I went and got the supplies. I made four large signs with felt marker on plywood: two that read, "Cold Drinks Ahead! Only $1!" And two that read, "Cold Drinks Right Here! Only $1!"

I set up the signs at appropriate spots along the bike path. We rolled a spool table to the inside of the fence, put out two chairs, my patio umbrella, the radio and four buckets full of ice, pop and water. Sherry blew up some balloons, and by one o'clock Shaun and Sherry's Cold Drink Emporium was open for business. "I don't know about the name," said Sherry. "It sounds like a puppet show."

By five o'clock, we'd smoked eighteen cigarettes, listened to four dozen songs on the radio, drunk six cans of pop and one bottle of vodka, watched three hundred people go by on the bike path, changed the company name five times, and sold a total of three cold drinks.

"Kind of slow today, isn't it?" I said for the twentieth time, as a dozen more cyclists pedalled on by. "You think we should make the signs bigger?"

"I don't think the signs are the problem," said Sherry, ever patient. "I think people are intimidated."

"By us? Look how sweet we are!"

"Well, more by the fence—stuffing their money through a fence, into a shantytown—buying a pop from some bums. I don't know. I guess it just seems weird."

"But you don't look like a bum!"

"Which is even weirder, I guess."

"It'll pick up," I said for the thirtieth time. "It's just slow today."

Strangely enough, we had more customers from this side of the fence than the other. They kept coming over on their way in or out of Tent City to see what we were doing.

"W-w-w-what are you d-d-doing?" said Jerry. He's been out of jail for about three weeks now. I gave him a free ginger ale and told him how we'd ended up adopting his brother's kitten, but he seemed preoccupied with some recent disagreement the two of them had. "I gonna cut his th-th-throat, from ear t-t-to ear. I gonna m-m-make him another m-m-mouth, eh eh, he, he. I gonna k-k-kill Donny." He managed to drag this one sentiment out into a forty-five-minute monologue, until I finally offered him another complimentary pop just to leave.

"Charming fellow," said Sherry once he'd gone.

Finally, as the shadow of the overpass began to stretch across the bike path, and the insufferable dehydrating heat—which people were apparently suffering through nonetheless—began to abate a bit, Les came riding up on a bicycle.

"Hey! How's it going?" he said. "You guys must be making a killing—yeah, hmm! How 'bout a drink on the house?"

July 31

I went to Osgoode for dinner with Les this evening. While we ate he came up with a mental list of ways to improve the cold drink business. In six hours Sherry and I had made a total of $15 and that was thanks to a particularly generous Rollerblader who told us to keep the change from a $5 bill. "That's about a dollar and a quarter each per hour, Les."

"Don't you worry. I got lots of ideas . . . Hey, missy," he said, calling out to one of the young girls who was volunteering. "Would you buy a pop from a couple of bums? On a really hot day."

"Y'all don't look like bums," she said. She had a West Virginia accent and a friendly little smile. "Where y'all living now?"

"I just sold my trailer to a crack dealer!" said Les, smiling proudly. "And now, hmm-hey, I've moved into a plastic box with my girlfriend—she's a hooker!" I told Les to shut up, but the girl just said "Oh" and giggled. Then she started talking about herself—how the church-group leader split up her and her friends because they talk too much, and she got put in a group with a couple of younger girls and a boy who's a geek, which made her really mad at first, but she's been with them for almost a week now, and she likes to talk, right—she'll talk to *anyone*—and now they're her friends! She pointed them out across the lunchroom. "It's weird," she said. "Being friends with grade eights and geeks. But they're actually really nice!"

On the way back to Tent City, Les said, "That girl was something, eh?"

"Yeah, I guess."

"No, really. Think how lucky she is—hmm-hey—to have learned that already, that you got to be open-minded and give people a chance. That's the kind of thing that can change your whole life."

It's always hard to tell when Les is being sincere. And yet when it came to the subtle epiphanies of a chatty 16-year-old Samaritan, I could see he was serious.

"It's like a blessing," he said. And I didn't even laugh, because I think he might be right.

x
x
x

Bonnie was crying when she moved out last night, as if she'd dreamt what I'm seeing—friends killing themselves in the middle of summer, more quickly now than slowly.

August:
A Few Dozen Different Mixed-up Dreams

August 1

The last of their monthly cheques, like their minds, are already gone, and more little bits of Tent City are blowing up in the heat like pop rocks in a mouth full of saliva. Luckily Sherry is at her mom's for a couple of days.

Curly, the ex-heavyweight, walks up to my porch.

"Excuse me, Shaun," he says. "I'm sorry to bother you." Curly is always very polite. We have short friendly conversations over my fence. Last week Les told me that Curly's wife and child were killed by a drunk driver.

"What can I do for you, Curly?"

"I'd like to ask your advice on something, Shaun," he says, offering me the can of beer in his hand. "I've been walking back and forth for an hour just thinking about this . . . I've known Randy for ten years, okay?"

"What'd he do now?"

"Well, I don't want to bring you into this shit about crack and all that, but a few days ago he's got some money, so he buys a 20 piece and shares it with me, right? And so this morning I've got a bit of cash left, so I figure I'll do the same for him . . ." He says Randy took his $20 to Crack Corner but, instead of coming back, went to Heartbeat's and did it with him.

"It would be one thing to sneak off and do it by himself—but to skip right over me, and do it with my best friend! I was too upset to do anything, eh? So Lisa went over to ask him, and he told her to fuck off—he actually *said* that!" Lisa is Curly's girlfriend. Between the two of them they represent more than half my cigarette sales, coming over with quarters all times of the night. "I mean sure, I could just go over there and break his jaw, and really I should. I'm really angry, but more I'm hurt. I mean, he hurt my feelings. And I . . . I just . . ."

"You don't know what to do."

"No."

I tell Curly my latest theory—that the combination of the heat, the constant availability of drugs and the basic stress of being addicted and homeless is scooping out people's brains and turning them against themselves. "And I guess like a lot of people down here now, Randy's lost himself. He doesn't care anymore."

"He's got a death wish?" says Curly, like this is something he knows a lot about.

"Yeah, I guess so."

"So what should I do?" I'm about to answer him when Lisa calls out that Randy is coming.

"Well, that's good," I say. "Now you two can talk . . ."

Before I can finish, Randy appears on the road and Curly yells out, "You lookin' for me?" And then he is over the fence, going right at him. Randy is backing up fast, saying, "Curly! Curly! Don't get mad," and Curly is throwing punches, saying, "I'm more than mad—I'm *hurt!* You hurt my feelings! I'm *hurt!* You know that?"

For some reason Curly's punches aren't really landing (maybe evidence of his subconscious affection for Randy—or why Curly never got a shot at the title). Whatever the case, Randy has time to shout out, "No, I didn't know that! I'll get you the money!" before he finally trips backwards into the bushes. Curly drops down on Randy's chest with his knees.

"You'll get me the money!" he yells. "You think I care about the *money?* You . . . hurt . . . my . . . *feelings!* It was worth the $20—to see what kind of man you are now—what kind of *friend!*" He stands up and walks away, Randy still lying in the bushes.

I leave and go to the library, where there's air-conditioning, and less distraction.

x
x
x

After the library, I go to Henry's and nurse a couple of beers as long as I can. I figure by the time I get back, things will have cooled off, people will be asleep. But it's too hot to sleep. It's like God took off and left the devil in charge of the thermostat. It's after midnight and over 30 degrees. And even if it weren't, it appears nobody's got time for sleep—they're all too busy going insane.

I put down my bag and sit in front of my shack. The air is buzzing like water just before a boil. I hear some loud banging coming from Eddie's, and walk over. Part of a wall is missing and he's trying to cover it with a piece of plywood. "Hey, Eddie," I say. "Just checking on you."

"I'm always all right, kid," he says (which, when it comes down to it, might be Eddie's biggest problem). "But that bitch comes around here again and *she* won't be all right. No *siree!*"

"Karen?" Eddie gets me to hold the flashlight while he hammers at the broken wall. "What'd you bust it with?"

"Just my fist . . . had to, so I wouldn't punch her in the face. If she comes back here and starts up with me again, I tell you, the whole house is coming down . . . And either way I'm leaving . . . Oh yeah, I'm leaving in the morning—quitting all of it. I'm going to see if my kids'll help me. That's right, young Shaun. Eddie the asshole is finally asking for help. Going into detox . . . Who knows? Maybe I'll even get Caleb . . ."

"Eddie," I say, shining the flashlight into his eyes. "This the drugs talking?"

"It's me," he says, waving away the light. "I'm not stoned, not even drunk. I'm stopping tonight, Shaun. And I'm not going to sleep . . . I've got to keep my wits. It's all happening now, right now! You understand?"

"You're not high?"

"Haven't smoked for two or three hours . . . haven't slept for three days. I'm going to go lie down." Eddie drops the hammer on the ground and opens the door.

I walk back over to my shack, sit down on the couch and think about Eddie leaving. There's still yelling and fighting from both directions down the shore, and then the garbled pleasant sound of Les's perpetual song. He walks into my yard and over to the barrel.

"Can I ask you a question, Les?"

"Shoot," he says, handing me a cigarette.

"You're always singing, but I . . ."

"Aha! You can never tell what song it is—right? Am I right?"

"Yeah . . . exactly."

"Well, hmm-mmm, you know *why* that is? It's because I don't know the *words* to any songs. I never—"

Eddie interrupts this revelation, however, calling out my name as he bounces into my yard. "Shaun!" he says. "That sound like Karen to you?" We stop and listen. One of the things about living here is that you begin to tune out the superfluous yelling, so that sometimes the voices don't get through at all. At this moment there are at least two different fights going on, as far as I can tell.

"I'm not sure . . ."

"That *is* Karen!" he says. As I follow him through the dark trees, I notice that he's wearing nothing but boxers, and they're inside out.

Since Cleo killed the kitten, Jackie's been sleeping in her tent back in the bush. And although she's not there now, a half-dozen women are around the tent shouting and shoving over God knows what. Eddie pulls Karen out of it and we holler at them to shut up, which they do for a moment. But then Eddie and Karen start pushing each other, and Eddie storms off. Karen follows me to my place. I sit back down on the couch. Les has disappeared.

"Can I ask you something?" says Karen, shifting side to side like she does when she's really wired. "Do you know John Daly—the golfer?" This is the kind of question Karen comes out with a lot. Yesterday she asked me, in a serious tone, which peanut butter has the peanut on top—then went into a long tirade about the cheap people who buy themselves Skippy or Jiffy, then toss a No Name jar into the food-bank box.

"John Daly? Isn't he the fat one who drinks a lot?"

"Yeah, yeah, he's an alcoholic. But can I ask you, Shaun, do you think that makes him a worse golfer?"

"I'm not sure," I say. I've learned to answer these questions carefully.

"I mean, the guy's a professional, right? He can golf, right? And fuckin' Eddie says the guy can't play as good as he should, *because he's an alcoholic!*"

"Just wait," I say, holding up my hand. "That's what this is all about—this thing with you and Eddie—it's about John Daly!"

"Yeah, but you see what I'm saying, right? I mean . . ."

"I'm not getting into this, Karen! Not if it's what you two are fighting about."

"If I'm a golfer—like Greg Norman or someone, I get up there and I try to put it in the hole, right? Or am I wrong? Do I try to miss? Eh? Do I try to *miss?*"

"No. I guess not. But I told you, Karen—I'm not getting into this . . ."

"Right! So John Daly's different just because he drinks? You think he *plays* drunk? He gets pissed and tries to miss the hole for fun!? He's a professional athlete!"

"Karen . . . !"

"Okay, something different—let's say it's tennis. It's 30-love and . . ." One of Eddie's complaints about Karen is that when she's high she'll argue about anything.

"I am *not* getting into this," I say once more. "In *any* sport. You're *both* wrong. That's it. Whatever it's about, you're both wrong, okay?"

"No way! If I'm wrong then John Daly—"

But Curly saves me from the next level of Karen's argument, calling out my name as he enters the yard.

"What's up, Curly?" I say, and just like that Karen disappears. That's how it is with crack addicts—always vanishing into the next thing, but never going anywhere.

"I just wanted to apologize for earlier," says Curly. "I was worried you might think I was crazy or something."

"Not at all."

"I don't know if I did right . . . But I didn't hit him, you know."

"You okay?" I say. I seem to be asking this a lot lately, collecting answers like dental records.

"Not really, Shaun . . . Smoking too much crack. Cuz, you know, the old lady smokes it all the time . . . Yeah, I'm fine." This is a common answer.

It sounds like a vicious fight is gearing up near Jimmy D's old place, and Curly and I walk down to check it out. Les comes out of the bushes and stands next to us. He's another guy who's fine, not really, and for whom smoking too much crack is due to his old lady's habit rather than his.

"I'm leaving here tomorrow," Les says.

"Hey, Les," I say. "You know John Daly?"

x   x   x

When it starts, it sounds like nothing I can identify. It sounds like a man taking apart his own life.

I walk out of my yard and into the clearing, and there is Eddie. I stand and watch as he tears his walls down, one after another. It sounds terrible—the windows shattering, the door torn off the hinges, the wood splintering and ripping as it falls. He has nothing but a hammer and his two hands, but he is persistent. Karen is trying to stop him, begging and yelling and grabbing at his arms. No one else does a thing. They take one look and go into their shacks. There's nothing they can do. It's like his heart is more set on this than on anything ever before. All you can see is his dark shadow in the bright moonlight, the silhouette moving on the last remaining wall as he beats against it, tearing at the roof. I stay and watch in case it falls on him.

"You're going to hurt yourself!" Karen shouts.

"Already done!" says Eddie. Then he yells at her again to go away.

"You're going to hurt *me!*"

"Then *go away!*"

The storage shelf above the bed comes crashing down on Karen. I move toward them, but she is already back up and yelling again.

The roof, however, won't come down. There's one wall still standing and, no matter how he tries, Eddie can't bring that roof down.

At one point he stops for ten minutes, until finally I hear him swearing in the darkness, and Karen begins singing like a 6-year-old, "Eddie lost a 10 piece! Eddie lost a 10 piece . . . Eddie wrecked his stupid shack, and now he can't even find his crack!" She laughs and laughs, until he starts to pull on the broken, swaying roof.

"The roof'll come down!" she yells.

"No . . . it . . . won't!" he shouts, tugging at it like he's trying to pull down heaven itself. "That's the problem!"

"Okay," yells Karen. "Destroy our home! Kill yourself! I don't care!" Eddie lets go all of a sudden, and for the first time I can see his silhouette turn to face hers.

"No, you don't care about anything!" says his shadow.

"Me!" says hers. "What about you? You got any photos of Caleb? You got any photos of him!?" I turn away from their ruined home.

x
 x
  x

It's been almost two hours since he started, and still their roof is standing. I feel like my insides are busted up and broken down. I can't listen to this anymore. I can't sleep with all the noise. I don't know why that fucking roof won't fall. The air is so full of heat and pain it's hard to breathe. That bitch of a sun will be up again soon.

August 2

It looks like a missile hit their shack. In the middle of the rubble, against the last remaining wall, beneath the precarious (yet apparently indestructible) roof, Karen and Eddie lie in each other's arms, asleep on a mattress in the morning sun.

There was no way I was going to fall back asleep, so I decided to go to Dixon Hall for breakfast. I set up one of the shower bags and took off my clothes. All of Tent City seemed to still be passed out, and finally sleeping well. The birds were making those echoing sunlit sounds that only last until people start barking and growling into the day. And there was something else. I could . . . *breathe.* The humidity had finally broken just a bit and a slight breeze was blowing.

I stood beneath the cool umbrella of falling water, concentrating on the quiet singing sounds around me, trying to think of Karen and Eddie without becoming hopeful or depressed. I knew why he'd done it. Eddie could only get out of this place and not come back if there was nowhere

here for him to live. And Karen, too. If he wrecked her shack she might go with him.

I suddenly realized a voice was calling out to me. "Hey, dude . . . dude!" it was saying. I lifted my head to look out over the shower door.

"Hi, Thomas," I said.

But he was too busy saying, "Hey, dude!" to hear me. "Dude, it's Thomas! You remember?!" I pulled a towel around me and stepped out.

"Yeah, I remember. I just said, 'Hi, Thomas.'"

"Really?" He grinned. "I didn't think you'd remember me! I just got out of jail, man! . . . I'm really hungry!" This was not actually a non sequitur. While we were walking up to Dixon Hall, Thomas told me he'd been in jail six days and hadn't eaten the whole time. "You never eat when you're in jail, dude!"

"Really, Thomas? Why is that?"

"The guards all piss in your food, man."

"Is that right?"

"Yeah, that's what my friend told me."

"What about guys who spend ten years inside. They must *really* get hungry."

He appeared to think about this for a moment. "I dunno, dude," he said. "I guess they just eat piss food."

We sat at a table with Sluggo and Randy. I could tell neither of them remembered Thomas. After the meal, I volunteered us to help clean up.

"What happened to the mermaid?" I said as we stacked the chairs.

"What?"

"That girlfriend of yours."

"Oh, that bitch! She's the one who got me popped!"

"What were you arrested for?"

"Failure." This is the rather revealing way people say "failure to appear," and this is what they all say if you ask—as if the original charges had nothing to do with it. For all his idiocy, or maybe because of it, Thomas is a natural with the lingo.

"Well, what was it originally?"

"Uh . . . ," he said, thinking about it a moment. "Assault with a weapon, and uh . . . uttering threats. It's a long story."

"A long story, eh? How'd it start?"

"It started with, uh . . . pushing."

I laughed, and Thomas looked at me quizzically. "Do I have something on my face?" he said.

"No, Thomas," I said. "There's nothing on your face."

On the way back to Tent City, he told me that he wanted to build his own place. I said I'd lend him some tools but he'd have to do the work himself and bring me back the tools every night. "And you gotta be smart," I said.

"Yeah, sure."

As we were walking over to my shack I said hi to Frizz, who was unwrapping a pack of cigarettes. Thomas turned to me and said, "You think he'd give me a smoke?"

"Who, Frizz?" I grinned. "Don't know—you can ask if you—"

"Hey, Frizz!" he yelled out. "You got a smoke for me?"

I winced and turned around, expecting to see Thomas hit the ground. But Frizz just looked past him, to me. I shrugged, meaning I had no vested interest and it was up to him—not whether or not he wanted to give him a cigarette, but whether or not he wanted to teach him a lesson. Frizz just turned and walked away.

"Hey, man . . . !" started Thomas, and I hollered at him to get his ass over here. Randy and Heartbeat were standing at the barrel laughing.

"What? Wha'd I do?" said Thomas.

"You don't talk to someone you don't know as if you *do* know him—especially Frizz. You don't grab his handle and shout at him like that. Remember about being smart?"

But Thomas just shrugged and said, "What do you expect? I'm Thomas!" I looked into his eyes, trying to figure out how much was show and how much plain stupid, and then I noticed there was a bit of food stuck to his cheek.

"Thomas," I said. "There *is* something on your face."

x   x   x

When the sun is high in the sky, Eddie and I sit down on a couple of milk crates and stare at the destruction.

"Wow," I say. "You sure did a number on that one." Eddie just nods, then lets out a laugh. "You going to leave, Eddie?"

"Going to leave or go to prison, for something *really* bad. I'm just going to take down that tent first." He points to the tent behind the wreckage, where some of his crack buddies sleep, "so there's no place for Karen to stay—then maybe she'll go home." I'm surprised by how conscious he is about all this.

"I feel like I'm just waking up," he says. "Like it's all been a dream, you know?"

"Yeah . . . Go to detox instead of prison, okay, Eddie? In six weeks you'll be okay, and then you can walk out of rehab alive. If you go to the pen you'll never wake up."

"I've been dying a long time," says Eddie. "Living is the hard part." Eddie's got two modes of speech. One is completely wiseass, and the other is wrapped up in these truthful clichés. "You were dying for a while, too," he says.

"Yeah . . ."

"You might be slipping into a hole."

"I'm doing okay, Eddie."

"That's not what I said."

"Let's get you out of here, okay?"

"Sure . . . Hey, isn't that the retarded kid who was here last year?" Thomas is walking toward us.

"That was two months ago, Eddie."

"Jesus, are you sure? Two months, really? . . . When was Caleb born?"

Thomas sits down on a piece of wall, looks at Eddie and says, "Aren't *you* a pretty sight."

"Watch your mouth, Thomas," I tell him, but Eddie just laughs.

x
x
x

Sluggo, Heartbeat and Hoyt are drinking beer with Randy by the barrel. Sluggo hands me the can as I sit down.

"Can I have some, too?" says Thomas, and we all snort out a laugh of disbelief.

"Jesus!" says Sluggo. "You're really starting to bug me. I just met you today and you've already asked me for two smokes and a slug of beer."

"You met him before," I say, and remind Sluggo that he and Jackie pawned him off on me.

"*That* kid?" says Sluggo, as if Thomas isn't there, and I tell him about Eddie thinking the last two months were a year. They all nod in understanding.

"How long you been here now?" says Hoyt to Sluggo.

"Fourteen months," says Sluggo. "And Eddie was here four months before that."

"Two years this October for me," says Randy. I can imagine them having the same conversation back in the pen, but without the beer. "How long for you now, Shaun?"

"About nine months," I say.

"Really?" says Randy. "Seems like you've always been here."

x
x
x

Eddie asked me to do him a favour. He said he wanted his son to come down and take him to a detox centre in Hamilton.

"Can you call him for me, Shaun? Can you ask him to come and get me?"

It was still early when I went to the pay phone, but I kept getting an unidentifiable voice mail. I left a message something like this: "Hi, it's Shaun here—from Tent City. Eddie asked me to call you. He's got to get out of here. He's ready to go now, but it's got to be today. If it's possible, he'd like you to come down and get him—as soon as possible. Thanks . . . I, uh . . . thanks. Please come and get him, he's ready to go . . . thank you."

After a couple of hours, I got through to a real live person who had no idea what I was talking about. So now I've left messages on answering machines for Goran, Julie and Jane as well, all of whom I think have access to Eddie's son, but none of whom appear to be home. Finally, I called Bonnie in Hamilton. I'd run out of quarters, and only had enough for three minutes of long distance. Someone else answered and it took two minutes for Bonnie to get to the phone.

"Don't start talking, Bonnie," I said. "Please just keep phoning Jane until you get her, and tell her to call Eddie's son and tell him to come and get him, today. And if she can't, please ask her to come herself—if she can, as soon as possible—" and then the operator cut me off.

Now it's getting late and nobody's shown up. Eddie's off drinking beer in someone's shack, and I just hope to God he's not smoking crack yet. I know he's ready, at this moment—but that window could be closed in an instant. The roof, after all, is still there. Sure, if he were strong, he could walk out of here on his own two feet, and never come back. But he needs help. He needs to tear his house down with his own hands, then get into someone else's car and fly out of here at 100 kilometres an hour.

Karen came over a while ago, obviously high.

"Lookit this," she said, handing me a small scrap of newspaper. "I cut this out a while ago. And I just found it in the . . . house," she laughed.

It was a one-panelled Ziggy cartoon, with Ziggy and his dumb little dog climbing a hill or something. The bubble over their heads read, "If you feel like you're falling behind in trying to follow your dreams . . . just remember—they can't get far without you."

"It's cool, eh?" said Karen.

"Are you going to leave if Eddie does?"

"Oh, Shaun . . . ," said Karen, as if I still didn't understand a thing.

August 3

Les was whacked out, singing and telling us ridiculous stories beside the fire barrel last night, when Eddie came over to say he was going to bed.

"G'night, Eddie," said Sherry.

"I'm sorry I couldn't get anybody down here for you," I said. "I left messages. Jane'll probably be here tomorrow. Will you go with her?"

"Yeah," said Eddie. "I'm gone tomorrow, kid." I couldn't tell if he was high. He waved his hand in the air and went off to bed. But then, a little while later, we could hear banging over at his shack—like someone trying to rebuild broken walls.

"Gggggreat!" said Les. "One night he keeps us awake tearing it down, hmm-nuh, the next he's building it up again! Can't he do this shit in the daytime?"

But Eddie's hollow hammering was like soft water falling in a Buddhist garden compared to what started up as we lay down to sleep. Apparently the boys over at Crack Corner found the soundtrack to hell, and decided to blast it through giant speakers all night. This was *not* music, no matter how open a mind you have. It was a garbled pounding beat with a couple of aggressive repetitive men yelling vicious threats over it. It was loud as an air-raid siren, and it went on for hours and hours fed at volume 10 across Tent City into our heads like the goddamn victory song of the Fourth Reich.

"Jesus!" shouted Sherry, pulling more blankets over her head. "What *is* this?"

"The end of the world," I yelled.

x x x

I've just got back from walking Sherry to work and I'm sitting outside my shack, staring at the sun on the filthy mouth of the river, when Jane, Julie and Goran come by. I've barely slept, and I'm in a real bad mood. They tell me they've already been over to see Eddie.

"And . . . ?"

"He's coming with us, to detox."

Jane sits down and asks me questions I don't want to answer—about Eddie and Karen, about their shack, about me, about everything.

"His son isn't coming down," she says. "But Eddie's going to phone him from the café. Come on—we're all going out for coffee . . ."

I'm thankful they've come to help, but none of this makes any sense to me—going out for a cappuccino and a cellphone chat with his son.

"No coffee," I say, as if in a position to be deciding things. Just then Eddie comes into my yard. I point at him. "If he's ready to go, then he's ready to go. Get him to detox and don't bring him back for anything."

"What's the rush?" he says, flipping out his fingers like we're all just here to have fun. "Everything's fine, so just cool out, okay? We'll go have coffee and come back, I got to get some stuff together and . . ."

I can see it in his eyes, squirming back there. And it makes me sick.

"*What* stuff?" I say. "Yesterday you said all you need is the shirt on your back."

"Well . . . that was yesterday . . ."

"C'mon, Eddie! What's the problem?" I should just give up now. But I don't. "You wanted your hand held, you wanted to go to Hamilton, and now your friends are here! So why don't you just—"

"I can't go to Hamilton."

"What?"

"It's a different jurisdiction. I've been working toward getting my pension, and if I go out there I got to file the whole thing again and . . . and that's why I have to come back here—to get my claim, to get the sheet for the pension . . ."

"What the hell are you talking about?"

"I don't have to explain to you . . . We're going for coffee, and then . . ." He looks at Jane and walks back through the trees out of my yard. I follow him into the clear.

"Get it now!" I say.

"What?"

"Whatever the fuck you need—whatever stupid piece of paper you're talking about, go and get it now. And then get the hell out of here!"

"Don't you talk to me like that! I can't find it right now."

"Well look for it . . . This is bullshit, Eddie, and you know it . . ."

"What's bullshit? You think I'm lying? You think I'm lying? I'll show you the card for the . . . claim, the . . . thing!" He has a wallet out, and is digging through it, pulling out business cards and pennies and bits of pipe screen. It's probably not even his wallet.

"They're here, Eddie!" I say. "Just go with them now!"

"What's the fucking rush, eh? What's it to you?" he says, pulling out a small rubber hose—some crack-pipe accessory. "*You* don't fucking care."

"You're full of shit!" I say, and he whips the piece of rubber at my face. My hand goes up to hit him, but he just stands there grinning.

"Go ahead," he says. "Come on, you little shit."

I drop my fist and take a step back. "I'm bigger than *you*," I say, then walk away.

Jane, Julie and Goran come out of the trees, but don't say anything as I walk by. I sit back down in front of my shack and stare at the sunlight on the surface of the water.

x x x

When they came back from coffee, Jane said that Eddie told them he needs this afternoon to get his stuff together and he wants to finish making the shack safe enough for Karen to stay in. He said he'll be ready to go tomorrow, and so Jane's coming back in the morning.

I didn't tell her not to bother. But of course she shouldn't. Eddie just went by my shack pushing Big G's septic tank. He didn't look at me, but I could see his cracked eyes reflecting the big blue sky.

August 5

It was Sherry's birthday yesterday, and I woke up in a bit of a panic. I'd managed to get together some silly little presents, mostly from the dollar store, but I told her a while ago I'd take her out dining and dancing. This was back when the success of all my business ventures seemed inevitable. Now, however, all I had was $9.50 in change, a pile of rear bike rims and three flats of warm cheap pop.

Dirty Willy has been avoiding me when he can, and whining and sliding out of coming down to check out the rims whenever I catch up to him. I told him if he didn't make good by Sherry's birthday I'd make good on him—but even I don't know what that means.

As far as the Now-Not-Very-Cold Drink Emporium goes, Les has been far too occupied with tearing out his own heart over Jo-Jo to implement any of his new business models, and I've been too dismayed by our sales record to try again.

In one shameless moment, I did manage to convince young Thomas to buy the business from me.

"You mean I'd be my own boss?" he said, his eyes widening with possibility.

"Sure would."

"And I could hire other people—and be their boss too?"

"You could . . . but you'd probably want to start small, you know. And that way you don't have to share the profits."

"Yeah, that's a good point!"

We decided on $50 for everything—the inventory, as well as the signs, location and the name.

"The name?"

"Sure—Shaun's Cold Drink Emporium, but you can change it if you like—to Tom's Cold Drink Emporium."

"Thomas's," he said, correcting me, and didn't even ask what "emporium" means.

Unfortunately he didn't have the money just then, and that night he disappeared, and I haven't seen him since. He could be starving himself in a jail cell right now.

So I loaded the bicycle rims I'd found into a shopping cart and went out to look for Dirty Willy. I finally found him in front of a church on Queen Street, trying to sell rebuilt bikes at a weekend bazaar.

"This is your last chance for a great deal, Mr. Willy," I said, trying to mix some menace into my voice, and finally we decided on four rims for forty bucks. I dumped the rest in a back alley and headed back down to Tent City, still without enough for dinner and drinks. Jackie brought over some balloons and I blew them up as I told her about my money problem.

"Well, you damn well better come up with it," she said. "Sherry deserves a nice birthday, you bum!"

"I know, I know, but—"

"Go ask Big G," she said. "He's loaded. He'll probably buy that pop off you."

"You think so?" The thought of doing any sort of business at Crack Corner made me a bit uneasy. But the idea of taking cash from a crack dealer did have a certain appeal.

Big G is very big—or rather, he is very fat. He walks down a road like it's his alone. He sits in a chair like he owns every chair in the world. His eyes look out of his wide black face like he just bought you, thinks maybe he paid too much, and is deciding whether to eat you now or later. He is enormously calm, and everyone around him always looks small and nervous.

When I went over, he was sitting in a large white chair, between two trailers. Crack Corner now consists of the rec centre (a tiny, rat-infested plywood room), Les's old trailer, Pops's old trailer, two other small trailers, an enormous grey one like you'd find on a construction site (for which Big G supposedly paid a thousand cash) and a large multi-roomed shack that Eddie and the boys have been building for him.

Eddie was there now, along with Karen and a few others, flitting around Big G like crack concubines. There was a small digital scale at Big G's feet. He was breaking bits of white rock in his hands and dropping them down. They all leaned over the scale, staring at the shards of white, trying to read the shifting magic numbers.

I stood behind Eddie, watching, until he turned around. I hadn't spoken to him since he threw that piece of rubber in my face.

"Not now, Shaun," he said. "I'll talk to you later," as if I would be so audacious as to interrupt him while he's scrounging for crack.

"I'm not here to see you, Eddie," I said. I didn't mean it to sound as dismissive as that, but Karen let out a laugh.

"Who are you here to—" said Eddie.

"The Big Man," I said, and Eddie kind of twitched. I saw what might be going through his head—that maybe I'd lost all sense, and was here to confront Big G like some fed-up parent coming to tell the bully to stay away from his kids. I didn't care to ease Eddie's discomfort and right then I felt that I'd made a split—from Eddie. I wasn't going to be looking out for him anymore, and I didn't care if he was looking out for me. I was here on my own silly business, and he could damn well build his walls back up by himself if he wanted to.

Finally Big G and the others finished playing around with their little white crumbs, and I stepped forward to make my soda-pop deal.

"Ginger ale, too? You got ginger ale?" said Big G, his eyes flickering over me with a bored kind of suspicion.

"Sure do," I said. "About twenty-two cans of it."

"It's a good deal," said Eddie. All the others had scurried off, except for one woman whom Big G was directing with a series of grunts and nods to take care of something inside the trailer. She kept apologizing, over and over, until he turned and looked at her, and then she was gone too.

"You could sell 'em for a buck apiece," added Eddie. "And there's water too."

"*How* much?" said Big G.

I'd paid about $30 for seventy-two cans of pop and twenty-four bottles of water, and had something like sixty cans and eighteen bottles left.

"Thirty bucks," I said.

"Yeah, okay," he said, then flicked his fingers at Eddie and told him to move along. I couldn't comprehend anyone talking to Eddie like that, but he left nonetheless.

"I'll bring them over," I said.

When I returned with the cases in a shopping cart, Big G scanned them with his eyes, then selected a bottle of water and unscrewed the cap. He sniffed it then took a slow sip as I tried not to laugh out loud. I guess a drug dealer's habits die hard, but they look pretty silly when it's pop and bottled water. Big G nodded, screwed the cap back on and fished into his big pockets for fifteen toonies.

Everyone came over to wish Sherry a happy birthday. Jackie brought her a bouquet of wildflowers she'd picked, and Karen gave her a photo of me taken by Eddie with a disposable camera the night after Caleb was born, as well as a couple of percs she took out of her sock. We drank a bottle of vodka with lemonade. The girls all smoked a joint and started giggling in the twilight. And when the sun had finally set, Sherry and I floated off for some dinner and dancing.

August 8

Jackie's been sick for a few days. She's having more trouble breathing than usual, her left eye is red and swollen, she's nauseous and can't keep liquids down.

Sherry finally persuaded her to go to the doctor, who supposedly diagnosed bronchitis and Lyme disease. "It's bad!" she said. "You gotta be careful, eh, if you're eating limes—even if you're just getting them in a drink in a bar or what-have-you. It's real possible they could be diseased! Just look at me! I'm living proof!"

"Uh, Jackie . . . ," I said. "I don't think you get Lyme disease from limes."

"What do you think, then? You get it from acorns?! Since when are you a doctor?"

She says she's supposed to go for follow-ups, but seems certain that as long as she doesn't consume any citrus she'll be okay.

x
x
x

Eddie, meanwhile, has turned into some sort of bionic anti-hero: *Crackman!* Able to build shanties for three dealers at the same time! Able to stay awake for days without food, rest or introspection! To steal bikes, tools, jewellery and sell it all uptown for practically nothing! To push cart after cart of steel, aluminum and copper to the junkyard! To make fences, shingle roofs, get pizzas—all for other people, while his own shack is barely standing! Able to bounce all day and steal all night—in one hand a machete, the other a pipe! Look over there—flying by on someone else's bike! No shirt, no shoes, a grin on his face! Is he a lunatic? A demon? A Horseman of the Apocalypse! No, he's a crackhead! The hardest-working addict in the world! Defender of all delusions! The dude of the white rock! Your friendly neighbourhood *Crackman!!*

August 10

Around 3 a.m., I was awoken by an unidentifiable noise in front of my shack—sort of like the bowels of a whale being purged. I pulled on my jeans, opened the door, and there was Big G—his rotund silhouette lit by the Essroc ship in dock—emptying his septic tank onto the river road in front of my shack. He looked rather undignified, and I could only assume he hadn't been able to wake any of his crack lackeys to do the job for him. There is a broken drain on the road in front of my shack. God knows if it actually leads anywhere. Mostly it just sprains people's ankles and pops their tires.

"Shit or shower?" I said.

Big G lifted his big head as whatever was inside the plastic barrel sloshed around the drain, spilling over the concrete.

"What say, mon?" said Big G.

"Shit or shower?" I said again, as if it were a common question—like *Heads or tails?* "Are you dumping your shit in my front yard? Or is it merely your bathing water?"

"Yeah, shower water," he said, and I was happy I'd given him this out. But then he seemed to remember he was the purchaser of souls, the owner of all, and stepped toward me. "Where be dis fron' yard, mon?"

"Uh . . . what?"

"You say I's puttin' de shit in yuh fron' yard. Where yuh fron' yard, mon?"

"Right here," I said, gesturing at the land inside the fence.

"And where I be standin'?"

"Uh, the road. You're standing on the road . . . yeah, I see your point . . . but . . ."

"But whot?"

"It's just . . . let's say it *was* shit: Well, you should probably dump your shit at *your* place—don't you think?" It was too dark for Big G to see me cringing at my own words. I heard him breathe in, like one might do before one says something important, or shoots someone. "Fortunately," I said, "it's shower, not shit."

Big G held up his hand in the dark and said, "You don' worry, mon. An' I don' worry neither." It's funny how, given the right tone, even the most reassuring message can sound like a threat.

"Oh, I'm not worried," I said.

"Uh-huh," said Big G.

But still I wanted to leave him with something, so I said, "Just so long as it ain't shit," then added, "G'night, Big G," and walked back into my shack.

I lay awake for an hour, wondering if he'd come back with guns, or dynamite, or a whole truckload of his own feces. But he didn't.

x
x
x

About four months ago, a weird little Frenchman came down here. He was a friend of Roger's, and started building a shack right on the water next to the rabbit hutch, just down and across the road from me.

The first day, he walked into the old town and started picking through Terry's pile of building wood without saying a thing. When we went over and asked what he was doing he held a piece of plywood above his head and announced, "Tonight, this become a roof!"—like he was the first to ever think of this. We tried to explain to him the importance of being a respectful neighbour, but he just threw down the wood and stomped off.

Over the next week, people tried to engage him in conversation as they passed his place. "I do *not* have de time!" he'd snap from atop the roof. "Do *not* talk to me! I must finish de roof today . . . No! No! I do *not* wish to talk!"

One of the prison rules that holds—or at least used to—down here, is that you never go uninvited into another man's space. And so I was surprised to see Eddie inside the Frenchman's house today. He was ripping apart the floor and interior walls for building materials.

"What you doing, Ed?"

"Guy's been gone a week and a half," said Eddie, as if referring to some well-known Tent City bylaw.

"So?"

"Roger says the guy pulled a knife on him . . . says he's crazy."

"So?"

"So I'm getting stuff to rebuild my house."

But he took the Frenchman's floorboards and plywood over to Crack Corner instead, and Eddie's shack is still the same as it was—four shaky walls propped up against the roof that won't fall. I don't want to think of Eddie, who got Steve safely out of town, then made sure Nancy's house wouldn't be touched; who tried to make every fight fair; who stood with his hand on little Caleb's tummy, his eyes closed, as he barely breathed, who always fought for the little guy, until he had one of his own, then gave up altogether. I don't want to think of Eddie tearing up some poor schmuck's house, just because the guy's got no one to back him up. I don't want to think of Eddie at all.

x   x   x

While I was sitting here writing, some guy came running through the trees, over my fence and onto my porch like a devil was chasing him. He tried to get by me, into my shack, saying, "Let me in, let me in and we'll do a toke!" I told him to drift and he kept grunting, "A toke, a toke," as he took off through the trees.

I've seen people walking around this place with their backs hunched, heads down, searching the ground for pieces of crack—walking around like this for hours, getting more and more frantic, trying to go over every inch—27 acres of dirt, bushes, scrap lumber, garbage, trash, mud, grass, concrete and gravel—in the hopes that somebody, at some point, dropped something. You can see them downtown, too, scouring the ground as if crack grows out of the sidewalk. It's as if once, a long time ago, some crackhead stumbled across a 10 piece just lying there and since that day they've all been staggering around picking up bits of plastic and chalk and gravel, licking them to see, searching for that elusive white rock.

I've seen people crawl around trying to look at the soles of people's shoes, in case there's a piece of crack stuck in the treads.

I've seen people rubbing ash all over their faces, hoping that a bit of resin might soak through their pores in miraculous crack osmosis.

I've seen the bravest bums—the greatest vagrants of my generation—turned into lousy crackheads.

August 13

Les sees Jo-Jo as karma, the lesson he's being taught for a lifetime of cheating on, lying to, laughing at and lusting after women. According to him she is the first person he's ever been true to. And she is a hooker. The irony overwhelms him—he paces back and forth in front of my shack, mumbling and laughing to himself, waiting for her to get home. He believes that all he has to do is get her out of Tent City and everything will be okay. Every Wednesday, like clockwork, he tells me they're leaving Friday morning and never coming back. Come Friday night she's still on the stroll, and he's waiting for her to come home to their half-melted dollhouse, so he can explain to her once more how she's the cosmic punishment for all his past sins, and then beg her to be his and his alone.

Les has trouble with cause and effect. In the hopes of winning Jo-Jo's devotion, he lights their clothes on fire, chucks their food in the canal or—as most recently—leaves home to become a pimp.

He's been gone five days so far, and this evening Jo-Jo comes over to my place full of finger-snapping, head-weaving, ass-shaking anger. Like Les, her rage always seems more comical than caustic, and it takes me a good five minutes to figure out what she's talking about. Apparently Les has resurfaced on the stroll, where he is looking out for a young prostitute from Vancouver.

"What the hell's he think he's doing?" says Jo-Jo. "After all his sermons and speeches about how I shouldn't be a whore, he goes out and becomes a pimp! On *my* stroll! With some ugly bitch! I mean, I'm sorry, Shaun, but this girl is *nasty!* How does that make me look?!"

"Uh . . ."

"I mean, he's just making a fool of himself! And anyway, there's no such thing as a pimp anymore—not like that, all standing in the shadows and watching over some tramp! No such thing! Except for Lester the Molester, of course. You should see him! You know how he's got to always dress up in some stupid outfit? So now he's got this ugly yellow suit with a chain around his neck and a big dumb hat, like he's the Big

Daddy in some crap movie! And every time a car comes by he just jumps into the bushes. I told him, eh? I went right up to him and told him how stupid he's being—I mean, you don't mess around with that. The bitch'll only get a night, but he could do serious time, eh? I mean, what's he thinking—parading around with this slut like some retarded peacock?"

"I don't think he *is* thinking," I say. "He's all messed up over you, Jo-Jo, and guys'll do anything when they're like that. We make fools of ourselves—it's what we do."

"But why's he got to do it on *my* stroll, honey? I swear, I'll slit that girl's throat if I see her again."

"Well, that's why, eh? It's your stroll. I guess he wants to make you jealous."

"It's pretty fucking dumb—it's *dangerous.*"

"Of course it is. It's *Les*—he's a pyromaniac. He *likes* playing with fire."

"What an idiot!" said Jo-Jo. "I miss him though, eh, Shaun?"

x x x

Eddie has now sold what's left of the Frenchman's shack to Spider and Olivia. I'm glad that they've finally got out of Crack Corner, but it was hardly Eddie's to sell. So now the dealers have expanded their empire a bit more, Spider and Olivia have waterfront property, and I have new neighbours. I just hope—for their sake—that Eddie's around to explain his little one-and-a-half-week clause when the irritable Frenchman shows up.

August 14

When I came in through the gates at five o'clock this evening, Sherry was standing in the road next to a police van.

I walked over and put my hand on her back. They were writing down her vital statistics. "What's going on?" I said.

"I got off work early—" she was about to offer some further explanation, but the cops cut her off.

"Is that him?" said one of them. And the other said, "We're talking to the lady—step away from the van."

"I'm staying right here," I said.

"They want to give me a ticket for trespassing," said Sherry.

"What? You guys got a warrant?"

"You want to go to jail?"

"Why are you bugging her?"

"Why are you being so defensive?"

"Why are you being so aggressive?"

"You ready to go back to jail?"

"You ready to—"

Sherry put her hand on my arm to stop me. The cops were still seated inside the van, but one of them was holding his handcuffs like a warning, and the other was barking at me to come around to his side of the van.

"Be nice," said Sherry—to me, not the cops—and I told her to meet me down at the shack.

"Hey!" they said as she left. But Sherry kept walking, and they turned to me instead. "What's your problem?" said one of them, at the same time as the other said, "What's your name?"

"Shaun," I said. "My name, not my problem."

"Think you're smart, don't you?"

"Why were you harassing her?" I said.

"You want us to arrest you? This is private property."

"Well, I live here," I said. "And you can't do anything without a warrant." As I said it, however, I realized I wasn't sure about this. It could just be a myth we keep telling each other.

"We can arrest you," said the cop holding up the handcuffs, obviously preoccupied with this part of his job. The one without the handcuffs had a pen and notepad in his hands. "What's your full name?" he said. I gave him one. "Date of birth?" I recited some numbers. "That's January seventh?" he said. I nodded. "About five foot ten . . ." I was about to protest, but managed to keep my mouth shut. "A hundred seventy-five pounds . . . You ever been arrested?" I shook my head. He repeated the question with a bit more menace in his voice.

"I've never been arrested," I said. "I graduated university. I even paid taxes once."

The cop with the pen stopped writing. "Can I ask what you're doing down here?"

"What—why I live here?"

"Answer the question."

"It's interesting," I said. "It's an interesting place to live."

They both stared at me. The cop closed his notebook and said, "Well, you better watch yourself once it gets dark—these boys get pretty wild when they start drinking."

"Thanks for the warning," I said. "I'll keep it in mind."

x   x   x

"Man!" said Sherry when I got down to the shack. "Those guys really *hate* this place. They really hate the people here."

She said they stopped her coming in the gates, and told her she didn't belong here. She told them she was going to see her boyfriend. They looked surprised, then laughed and one of them said, "You should get a better boyfriend. They're all scum down here, you know, and all the women are prostitutes."

"And a lot of them," Sherry had said, "are my friends."

That did it. I guess they figured there was no saving her, and threatened her with a trespassing ticket instead.

They never did get a chance to ticket her, but she's nervous because she gave them her real address and birth date. I asked around, and no one else had been hassled. I guess they all looked like they belong. It would be kind of funny, though, if Sherry were the only one to get busted for trespassing.

x   x   x

Les, meanwhile, has given up his dreams of becoming a pimp, and returned to life in Tent City.

"Just one of those things," he says, and laughs. "Jo-Jo says she's going to kill the girl if she sees her again."

"So I guess your stupid plan worked."

"It wasn't a plan exactly, hmm-huh . . . Really I was just trying to help out the poor girl. But you know how it is. Things have a way of getting twisted around. It's all good now, though. No more crack. No more hooking. We're getting serious now. We'll be out of here next Friday for sure, hmm-hey."

August 16

The cops were down again yesterday and stopped Jackie on her way to the outhouse.

"Oh, no. I don't live here," she said, a roll of toilet paper in her hands. "I'm just cutting through to Cherry Beach."

Today Beric from the TDRC knocked on my door. It was rumoured that I'd been ticketed for trespassing, and he wanted to know everything that happened with the police.

"I think I know those two," he said, based on my description of them as "short-haired and, you know, cop-looking." "They harass the homeless and we've had reports of one of them beating up women on the street."

Beric seems to distrust and dislike the police more than most criminals do. He's mad as hell that they're coming down here and "harassing" us, while most people who live here recognize it for what it is—something inevitable, brought on by the transformation of this place into a 27-acre crack house. Meanwhile Beric is concerning himself with getting stoves for the new guys down in the corner.

"Crack Corner?" I say, but he doesn't seem to hear me.

"It'll be winter again before you know it," he says, as if the dealers can't afford a luxury apartment, let alone a stove. "It's too bad you didn't get a ticket. 'Cause then we'd have something to fight."

What he means, I guess, is something outside this fence, something outside ourselves—bigger than us, and smaller than the world.

August 17

It's still hotter than hell, and also more humid. Eddie is running day and night like a penned-in chicken with his head full of drugs. Jackie is still sick, and still smoking, her eye swelling and bloodshot. Sometimes she sleeps with Sluggo in their shack, sometimes in the tent, and sometimes on my couch. She listens when Sherry tells her to go to the doctor—listens, but doesn't go.

The last couple of mornings, the irritable Frenchman has been back to the shack he built, threatening to burn it down, and Spider keeps chasing him away with a two-by-four.

"Well he *did* build the place," I say, but suddenly that doesn't matter.

August 20

Today a dozen cops showed up with a team of Toronto Hydro inspectors and went shack to shack with video cameras looking—according to them—for hydro hookups.

As far as I know, the only ones who have tapped into the hydro are Karl, Roger and the dealers. But the police went all over the place. They went into Randy's prefab while he wasn't there. Julie says that when they pushed their way into her shack, one of the cops said he'd shoot their puppy if it didn't stop barking.

Eventually the inspectors found a line leading from Crack Corner to one of the Lakeshore advertising billboards, and they cut it. But that was it. Why they didn't find the others, I have no idea. I find it hard to believe the guys down here have methods too sophisticated for Toronto Hydro—well, maybe Roger, but not Karl. It appeared as if the cops were there to protect the Hydro guys, but when I asked one of the inspectors why they'd come down, he said the Toronto police had called them.

Nobody was charged with anything. But by the time the cops were rolling out, Beric had arrived (along with a couple of Street Help vans and a Citytv cameraman) and was treating the police action as a declaration of war. He went around getting reports from all of us, then called an emergency meeting for August 22, two days from now.

August 22

Although as frustrating and chaotic as the first Tent City meeting, the one today was quite different. The most vocal participants at the last one—Bonnie, Hawk and the Brothers—have now been replaced by a bunch of summer bums who have no idea what's going on.

Beric did most of the talking, backed by a number of TDRC people. Although there was much lively argument, most of it pertained to divvying up the Kentucky Fried Chicken they'd brought down. When the food was gone so were most of the people, and it became easier to get down to business.

Beric asked me describe my run-in with the cops in the van, and then Patrick got up and spoke about the police going into his shack without a warrant and threatening his dog. It was important to Beric that we recognized these events as part of a systematic attack on the homeless. He gave the sense—which may be true—that the eviction of Tent City residents is imminent, unless we take action right away.

Somebody brought up the problem with the shitters. Like the wood stoves and the shower bags, the donation of the porta-potties was originally orchestrated by the TDRC. The problem is that the shit is going in, but it's not coming out, and things are getting stinky. Beric cited this, too, as evidence that the municipal noose is tightening. When I ran into one of the guys who works for the porta-potty company, however, he said it has nothing to do with politics—they just don't want to deal with the needles. Also, the clothes that people have been using in lieu of toilet paper are clogging up their hoses.

Whatever the case, it's obvious that Beric and the TDRC have found something to fight. The point of this meeting, it turns out, was to propose that we hold a press conference in Tent City. And so a week from now, we will try to be news.

August 23

Jackie has lost one of her eyes. Or rather, it's still in her head but she says she's lost sight in it and it's going to have to be removed. She says that it's something called iritis, and is associated with the Lyme disease. It all seems pretty strange to me, but she won't talk about it much, except to say that she's going to get a pirate patch and a parrot, and that we'll have to call her One-eyed Jacks. The pupil is entirely dilated, so that she's got one brilliant blue eye, and one that's all black.

She doesn't seem too bothered by it, though. I don't know if that's just because it hasn't hit her yet, or because—in the grand upsetting scheme of Jackie's life—it doesn't mean that much to lose an eye.

x   x   x

Tickets for Bruce Springsteen go on sale tomorrow. Ever since Ticketmaster implemented a per person limit to dissuade scalping, the scalpers have been paying bums to line up for big-selling shows. Most of the old crew's going up there tomorrow, but even if there was a spot for me I don't think I could relinquish a Springsteen ticket once I had it in my hand, so I gave Sluggo the bus fare, and he's going to buy us some beer on the way home.

While Sluggo's out doing tickets, and Sherry's at work, Jackie and I are going to try to make a bit of money, too. I uncovered a large pile of scrap iron over near Spider and Olivia's new place, and we're going to cart it over to the scrapyard. Jerry says they'll pay 10 cents a pound. Although he's a less than reliable source, I don't want to let on to anyone else. Between Springsteen and scrap iron, we might be rich by tomorrow night, or at least be having a few drinks.

x x x

At the meeting yesterday there was a small black boy hanging around the edges of the crowd, and I assumed he was with one of the activists. But when I went to fill up at the water hose today, there he was—diving a Buzz Lightyear action figure through a puddle by the drain. I said hi, but he didn't look up until I asked his name. "Leo," he said, and then told me he was 6.

I talked to him for a while and he seemed extraordinarily polite. When I asked if he was living in Tent City, he didn't answer. Then a white guy came through the trees and grabbed his hand.

"Just down for the day," the guy said. "Just visitin' his dad." And he pointed to one of the new shacks by Penny's place.

"He was here yesterday, too," I said, but they'd already left.

When I first came down here, I was told that there were only two rules: One, no kids allowed. And two, there are no other rules. At the time it just sounded like a catchphrase from a bad Kurt Russell movie. But if Leo's still here tomorrow it's going to cause some trouble in Shantytown.

August 24

Jackie and I were out early. It took us an hour to load up two shopping carts with what we thought would be about $80 of scrap iron, and then another half-hour over rough terrain to the scrapyard. When we finally got there they gave us $16.

One-eyed Jacks was too dejected to face the long walk back, so we left one of the carts at the scrapyard and I pushed her in the other one, running fast over the old trolley tracks to make her squeal. She doesn't have her eye patch yet, but as we went over the bridge to Tent City she was shouting like we were walking the gangplank, waving to the traffic like a giant pirate queen. It was good to see her smiling.

By 10 a.m. it was too hot again, and I headed for the library. On the way out of town I saw little Leo, his black hair bobbing as he weaved through the tall grass. I walked over to Patrick, who was standing in the road. "You see that, Pat?"

"What?"

"There's a kid in there," I said, and we peered into the brush like shark hunters scanning the waves.

My take on Patrick has changed over the months since he helped kick me around for Christmas. And since he got out of prison this last time, it's become obvious to me that he, more than Jimmy D, is the leader of the lost boys. Patrick, after all, is level-headed, charismatic and forceful, whereas Jimmy D is merely insane. Since his release from prison, he cuts an impressive figure—weight-room muscles, jailhouse tattoos, and even his shaved skull is more Yul Brynner than skinhead.

Patrick has been living down here as long as anybody, and seems more interested in the pride and politics of Tent City than the crack. I don't hold that beating against him. He was never as enthusiastic about killing me as Dan and Karl were.

"This is no place for a kid," said Patrick. We found Leo playing with a crushed toy car in front of one of the new shacks near the water hose.

"Hi, Leo," I said. "Is your dad around?" He nodded and looked at the shack.

"What's your dad's name, Leo?"

"Donald," he said. I knocked on the door. The place was full of crackheads, who kept poking their heads out to look at us. Eventually Leo's dad came to the door.

"You Donald?" I said.

"Call me D."

I told him our names, and asked if we could talk somewhere away from Leo.

"He's okay," said D, as if I was worried his polite little son was a narc. "It's all good."

"Well, it's not all good," I said. "We've only got one rule down here. And that's no kids. The cops and CAS would be here in no time if they found out."

"And it's no place for a kid," said Patrick. "*You* know what goes on down here." I was happy to let badass Pat say what I felt. At the moment I didn't give a damn about Tent City—all I wanted to do was get Leo out of here.

"Don't worry," said D. "There's somebody coming down to pick him up today."

"So we understand each other?" I said, and D nodded. Leo was still on his knees, looking down at his miniature crushed car. "Bye, Leo," I said, but he didn't look up.

x   x
x

On the way up to the library I ran into Greg—the guy who lives in the dark and flooded silos. It was weird to see him outside, in the sunlight. He was pulling a little laundry cart full of empties and sucking on a Crest.

"Hey, Greg," I said. "Remember me? I live in Tent City. We—"

"Yeah, man. I remember."

"How things going? You still flooded in there?"

"Oh, yeah," he shrugged. "Man, today I was walking out and I stepped in a dead raccoon. Big one too, eh? . . . Totally rotted."

"You're going to get sick living in there, Greg."

"Oh, yeah . . . I'm already sick."

"You should come and live in Tent City—it's got to be better than—"

"Yeah, I know."

For someone living in 2 feet of dead-rodent water in a dark abandoned silo, he's exceptionally lucid and personable. Yet talking to him about moving into Tent City is like talking to my friends about getting out of there. "Yeah, I know—" they say, eyes darting up like a bat just flew by. You feel like it's beyond their control.

x   x
x

There are these *things* just inside the front gates, across from Hawk's old place, that I've wanted to write about since the first day I saw them. I've tried, but haven't been able to do them justice. They're that crazy. They're that . . .

There are three of them. These *things*. And they look like . . . like giant musical vehicles from a Dr. Seuss parade. It's as if someone took a bike, a trike, a Big Wheel, a dozen drum kits, a collection of Kandinsky oil paintings, some fairy dust, acid and 200 pounds of rebar, and put it all in a giant cosmic blender—then built something out of the remains.

They have wheels and seats and gears, they are painted in a dozen different colours, they are made of twisted iron and steel, they involve cages and umbrellas, but also a dozen different drums, cymbals, chimes, triangles and bells. They could never fit under the warning bar of a parking garage. They have platforms on which you can stand, and pedals that you can pedal, to turn the wheels.

The man who made them is called Phil. He lives in one of the shacks along the Lakeshore fence. I've never had a conversation with him but we always say hi to each other, and sometimes I see him and a few other guys loading these *things* onto a flatbed to take them somewhere—a parade on Mulberry Street perhaps. And sometimes in the evenings you can hear him practicing, banging away at the steel and buckskin like it's Mardi Gras on Mars. The drumming seems to make Tent City both kinder and crazier.

When I came back from the library this afternoon, Phil was standing in one, up on a platform, drumming a deep and steady beat, and little Leo was beside him, playing on some pipes and cymbals. It sounded beautiful. The twilight was making the hot sky shift colours, and as the beat kept building, an airplane growled overhead. Watching Leo's concentration I loved this place again for a moment and wondered if it was really best for him to leave. I mean, who knows who's coming to pick him up, or where he's going to go? Where the hell can anyone go?

x   x
x

I drank some beer with Jackie and Sluggo until Sluggo fell off his chair for the third time, then I went over to tell Eddie about little Leo.

"Not right now," he said, intercepting Jerry who was coming down the river road in a car he'd just stolen. Eddie went through the trunk before he'd let him pass, taking out a set of golf clubs and a giant box of diapers.

"What the hell are you going to do with that?" I said.

"Go golfing, have another baby—what the fuck is it to you?"

As he dragged the stuff over to his shack, I tried to tell him about Leo.

"What's it to you?" he said again. "The guy can't be down here 'cause he's got a kid?"

"He's 6 years old . . . ," I said.

"Not enough room here, is that it? You the fucking sheriff now?"

"I got this from you, Eddie—you're the one who was always talking about the rule. He's a kid!"

"You're a kid. There *are* no fucking rules."

"You're talking out your ass, Eddie," I said. He chucked the diapers into his partially demolished shack then grinned at me, and I walked away.

On my way to pick up Sherry from work I went back to the crack shack where D is staying.

"The kid's still here," I said.

"Yeah, yeah, they're coming to pick him up tonight. Don't worry."

"I'm going to come back tomorrow morning and make sure he's gone. Okay?" D's shirt was off. I stared him in the eye, hoping he wouldn't notice how much bigger he was than me. There was a scar running all the way down his right cheek. "Okay?" I said again.

"No problem, man."

"He's too good for this fucking place," I said. We both nodded, and then I left.

August 26

When I came home today Leo was nowhere to be found, and the TDRC's press release was taped to my door:

Media Release

August 27, 2002   For Immediate Release

"We will not be moved...
Until there is housing"

Tent City under Duress -- Threats of eviction, police harassment and lack of basic health standards

Rally and Press Conference
10am, Wednesday August 28, 2002
Tent City -- south of Lakeshore Boulevard, between Cherry & Parliament St.

Tent City, the village that Canada's homeless disaster built is being threatened with evictions, police harassment and inadequate facilities. Police entered Tent City last week, ostensibly to investigate the "stealing of electricity." Police entered homes saying they "did not need a search warrant". When a resident protested and his dog barked at them, witnesses heard police threaten to kill the dog.

Police spoke to Beric German of the Toronto Disaster Relief Committee (TDRC) and separately to a Tent City resident and said "soon people will be out of here". The reality is that Tent City residents need more aid including electricity, toilets, and food. They need the simple necessities for the site to meet international refugee camp standards and to fulfill basic public health criteria. As one resident put it, referring to police actions and lack of health standards, "we are not animals."

It has been over one year since the City agreed to a plan to house Tent City residents. No land has materialized to fulfill that task. In the meantime, there have been hostel closings, and numerous police sweeps of homeless people from parks and alleys, even during the Pope's visit. The result has been that Tent City has swelled to over 100 people. Not incidentally, the village of Tent City is saving the hostel system at least $10,000 a month and a million dollars a year. This would be a substantial down-payment to house all the people on a new site.

Tent City residents and supporters will gather on Wednesday August 28, at 10am to speak out about these matters. They will also sing a resounding old and appropriate song **"We shall not be moved."**

It's not that I don't support the cause. I think there should be squatting rights in Canada, and a "use it or lose it" law in our cities, as well as a lot more affordable housing. I don't think shelters and jails are a solution to homelessness or poverty. I don't think the police have any right to enter someone else's home just because they are curious. And I believe these are our homes, at least for now.

But I don't believe in whining. Beric assures everyone here that hydro is our right, as is running water, sanitary toilets and a daily life free of police harassment. But who says? And really, I'd be happy if the cops came in here and dragged out everyone who's pilfering the hydro. Then the dealers would be gone, and this place might be worth fighting for again. As it is, it's a bit ridiculous to chastise the police for their increased interest; after all, there *are* six or seven different crack dealers down here now, which means there could be a gang war any day. The dealers have brought most of the heat to Tent City, and heat's the only thing (other than the cold of winter) that's going to encourage them to leave. So it may be that Tent City's salvation is actually in the hands of the cops, as long as they bust the right people.

Although most of us understand the situation down here, there are some people who seem to be buying into this dream of our rights. They seem to have forgotten that we're squatting here, that we built here knowing that it's survival of the fittest, that you have to fight for your space, and that one day the Man from the other side might show up at your door—with his guns, dogs and pieces of law—and you'll have to fight him, too. I respect and appreciate Beric for trying to take this fight to them before it comes to us, but the sense of indignation just seems ridiculous to me—this shock that the police are shining light in our eyes, that the porta-potties are overflowing, that the power's been cut off. It's sad to say, but some of the "hardcore homeless" suddenly sound more like disgruntled campers in a poorly maintained RV park.

Not Les, though. "You do what you got to do. You fight, you steal, you cheat," he says. "But you never, ever, whine." He wants to hang on to that shitty plastic dollhouse in case one of the many "relocation proposals" actually goes through, at which point he figures those of us with shacks in Tent City will get first dibs on whatever housing may materialize. Unfortunately, the dealers probably have the same idea, so that any relocation of Tent City could just turn into a second Street City—another government-funded crack house.

Meanwhile, if things go according to Beric's plan, we will all come together a hundred strong. We will join hands, smile for the cameras, then break into song like the Whos down in Whoville.

August 28

Although dozens of reporters and photographers showed up—as well as a bunch of bicycle cops—the press conference was actually quite boring. Bonnie came back for the event, but since nobody brought food or coffee, not many residents bothered to hang around.

The only interesting moments occurred on the periphery of the rally, each due to typical Tent City–style errors in judgment. An eccentric Hungarian named Ishmael, for example, was under the impression that it was the media presence rather than that of the police we were protesting, so he shovelled a wheelbarrow full of fresh cow manure into one of the TV news vans.

Then there was Spider, who—for the sake of public relations—was going by his professional name, Homeless Dave. He wanted to make a speech to the press, but Beric intercepted the microphone and announced that due to time constraints, Homeless Dave would be leading us on a marching tour of Tent City instead. No doubt Beric thought this would be safer than letting him speak, but Spider is not what you'd call a born leader.

So our rally of consolidation ended with dozens of reporters and activists wandering aimlessly into the bush, stumbling around trying to find their way through the trees and piles of garbage. Homeless Dave, insulted by their inability to follow him, returned to the centre of Tent City and began ranting loudly about the lack of respect.

The final error in judgment took place after the reporters and cameramen had gone. As the cops were finally heading toward the gates, Jimmy D stepped out of his shack and called out in his booze-burned voice, "See ya later, assholes!"—at which point they got off their bicycles, walked over to Jimmy D and punched him in the head.

"You can't do that," he growled. "That's police brutality—I'm calling a press conference!" And then he started to laugh.

x
x
x

For me, the high point of the press conference itself was the speech that Bonnie made. She said that when she found herself unemployed and homeless, the system never did a damn thing for her—but the people down here did. They went out of their way to help her, took her in, tried to keep her clothed and fed, helped her build a house, looked out for her and became her friends. She said that it was thanks to the people down here—the caring and kindness so seldom recognized—that she was finally able to move on to another stage of her life, redeemed and dreaming.

Bonnie looked right at me a few times during her speech, as if to make sure I understood. After all, she is right, that *is* part of the story— mine too: the goodness of this place, of these people, of us. I just wish I didn't feel like that part is already over.

August 29

There was a guy living down here named Ron. I never did write about him. It's not that he wasn't interesting—he was actually fascinating. And it's not that I didn't like him—I did. But as with many others down here, I wasn't going to write about him until something *happened*—because of him, to him—to make him part of the story. And he stayed out of reach, hard to pin down.

When I first saw him, he was doing pirouettes in front of his shack in the cold morning sun. His place is right on the water, but it's well hidden, surrounded by heavy foliage and an elaborate fence of bicycle parts, twisted tree branches and bits of old furniture. Leaning against the outside walls of his low bungalow are a number of large paintings, a sign that reads "Walden III" and some planters full of bright plastic flowers. I was looking for a place to build my shack, and the spot behind his looked pretty good. When I asked him, however, he shook his head and said, "We're trying to keep it clear." I didn't know what he meant. I shrugged and moved on.

Since then I've talked with Ron a lot. I'd see him riding his antique black bike—a wicker basket and bell on the front—in and out of Tent City, and we'd say hi. Or he'd be going through piles of trash and donations, searching for treasures, and we'd have a short conversation about what he'd found.

It wasn't just the morning ballet and plastic flowers that made Ron different. For one, he had all his teeth—the only guy down here, other than myself, who could make such a claim. He kept his clothes clean and seemed in good health. He didn't appear to drink too much and he wasn't a crackhead. He was smart and well educated. But more than all that, he was *into* things—he had interests, and they were similar to mine.

Like me, Ron went to the community centre for a swim—or at least a shower—almost every day, so we often ended up talking in the change room. He liked to read and play pool, and we'd talk about different authors or a particular pool shot. One day I used a brick on the shower-room wall to represent a standard eight-ball table, and divided it up to demonstrate how you could see certain angles. A week later he brought me back over to the same yellow brick to ask about a bank shot I'd shown him.

"Oh, back *left* spin!" he said, like he'd finally be able to get a good night's sleep.

He'd go out dancing up in the Annex, where all the cool college kids live. I can't be sure, but I think he was probably bisexual. He'd talk about "going out to play with the boys and girls," then complain that he never got anyone home to frolic on his floor: "I've even carpeted my shack for such an occasion." He was open and he was always trying to learn things. He'd ask my advice on getting a date and we'd trade gambling stories and books.

Ron wasn't the only avid reader down here. Street people spend a lot of time reading because they don't have TVs. But Ron was into everything about books—from the rare-book business to the effects of Oprah's Book Club—although his favourite genre was peculiar.

I have stacks of books on the floor of my shack, a trunkful of them on the deck and a whole shopping cart of paperbacks in the yard. Whenever a box of books is left as a donation, someone lets me know—because I'll bother to get them out of the rain—so people come to me when they need something to read. Of course, everyone's got their own taste: Jackie only reads romance novels, particularly Danielle Steele. Sluggo likes spy thrillers. Randy is into courtroom dramas. And Eddie will read anything to do with serial killers.

Ron, however, would come over and search my collection for books about "manly men, doing manly things." Although he was just about the opposite of a manly man, I could never tell how much irony was involved between him and all that pulp fiction—those cowboys, detectives, soldiers and race-car drivers. The first book I lent him was an old dime-store paperback edition of *The Adventures of Studs Lonigan.* The last book he lent me was *The Great Escape.*

When they found him, Ron was sitting in his shack with a smile on his face, and a book in his lap.

Ishmael is the one who found him there early this morning. Ishmael lived next to Ron and was his only close friend down here. But he didn't know what to do. Who would? He knocked on Patrick and Julie's door and said, in his thick Hungarian accent, "Do you know something about dead people?"

I went over just as the police and ambulances were showing up. Jimmy D came and cut the chain on Ron's old bike, but nobody else would get too close.

"He just died," they all said, standing around and shrugging, like men die for no reason all the time. "I guess he was sitting there for a while, eh?" A lot of them didn't even know who Ron was.

"The tall guy with the nice smile," I said. But they shrugged. "He always rode his bike . . ." They shrugged. "He liked to dance . . . He lived right *here!*" But they just shrugged, even some who've been down here longer than me. Eventually I was the only one left standing there, as the police and paramedics worked around me. I found myself stepping closer and closer until I was looking through the door at Ron. He'd tipped over sideways on the couch. His eyes were open and his skin was yellow.

"What happened?" I asked a few times, until one of the policemen directed me away from the door. He said he couldn't tell me anything. Then I started telling him about Ron, and he said, "Okay, okay . . . you were a friend, and so I'll give you this: There *won't* be a criminal investigation."

"I'm not worried about that," I said. "Nobody would have hurt him." I realized what I meant was nobody would have bothered—they barely even knew he was here.

"What I'm saying," said the cop, "is he was ready to go."

"Was he sick?" I said, still not getting it. "He seemed healthy. He—"

"Listen to me!" said the policeman, no doubt regretting having confided in me. "He *chose* to go. He *chose* it. Do you hear what I'm saying?" And he glared into my eyes until he was sure I understood.

August 30

Why was Ron the one to kill himself?

I don't even know how he did it, and nobody else here seems to know either. Supposedly there was a note left for Ishmael, but when I went over there today he wasn't around and somebody else was already moving into Ron's shack. Everything had been cleared out except for a box of his books. There was a leather-bound King James Bible, a world atlas, a recent edition of *Webster's* dictionary, a book on gambling strategies, one on alchemy, an encyclopedia of birds, a field guide to planets and stars, a book on mutual funds, a Lonely Planet guide to the Bahamas and several old cowboy books. I left them all there.

I just don't get it. Out of everyone down here, Ron, at least, wasn't being consumed by this place. He was fascinated by the world that stretches outside these fences, past the birds and the stars. He loved things, he danced, and he didn't seem to be hooked on drugs. But maybe that's why.

I've come to think that drugs—although they may get you to a point where life's barely worth living—also postpone suicide. If you put all your energy into drugs—stuff your soul down into them—they will hold you afloat enough so that you keep breathing and you don't have to face other things. Eddie describes his crack high as a place where he feels nothing, is not anyone, is not alive. And that is the only place he can be—otherwise he might kill himself. Ron didn't have that, because he still had the world.

Although I know nothing about his life, I can't help but feel that Ron went down because this place is going down. What I mean is this: At one point, Tent City was a place where a man like Ron could live. It was a place not only of desperation but also of guts and will and a few dozen different mixed-up dreams. That's where he built, here on this lawless land on the outskirts, yet the centre, of the world—where the highways, waterways, airways, smog and rats all converge. He said to me a few times, while pulling some obscure relic from a pile of junk, or brushing his teeth at the community centre, "You have to be resourceful." He seemed to love that idea—that you have to negotiate this fucked-up, sprawling world the best you can, and make something out of it, quietly, on your own. But this place went the other way.

I have no idea what finally did it for Ron, who chose to let himself go the day of the big press conference while his closest friend was out shovelling manure in a confused act of protest.

September 1

On my way home from Henry's last night I came across Crazy Chris doing figure eights on a BMX in the middle of the street. I'd been drinking, but he was smashed.

"Where you headed?" I said, watching as he made a drunken infinity sign with the cars swerving around him.

"Going to find some trouble!" he said. This is never too hard for Chris. Just two days ago, he and Jerry rolled Mike's junk truck on the highway, and almost right off the overpass. The truck flipped three times, and when they crawled out the windshield, the wheels were still spinning in the air, like it was trying to drive on the sky.

"Well, just watch yourself," I said. As if these were the words that released him, he quit the looping figure eight, saluted me and started riding toward Queen Street. I walked another block before I heard a screech of brakes, followed by a crash. I ran back to the corner of Parliament and Richmond, and there, of course, was Crazy Chris. His bike lay mangled under the front wheels of a white Le Baron, the windshield of which Crazy Chris was banging with his fist. He jumped off the hood and started circling the car and yelling at the four guys inside, showing them his scraped side and his bleeding knees. He made a big show of reading the licence plate aloud, and finally the driver opened his window. Chris grabbed whatever the guy was holding in his hand. He pulled the broken bike out from under the car, still yelling, swearing and clutching his ribs, and the car drove off.

"You see that!?" said Chris, dragging the bike toward me. And then his face broke into a grin. "Right over the fucking hood! That was beautiful, man!"

"Lucky you didn't go under the wheels."

"Fuckin' right! That's as close as it gets, man . . . You saw it, right?""

"Just heard the crash."

"But you saw enough! Did they stay? Did you see the driver get out?"

"No, didn't see that."

"Hit and run, right? That's all you gotta say . . . I'll phone it in right now . . . We'll go fifty-fifty. Come on!"

"Chris . . . ," I said, then followed him into the gas station on the corner. A car was backing away from one of the pumps. "Watch yourself there—" But before I could finish, Chris threw the bike at the rear bumper of the car and slammed his hands onto the trunk. The brakes screeched and he dived to the ground, rolling around and shouting like he was in terrible pain. The driver got out of the car.

"Fuck!" yelled Crazy Chris, still on the ground. "You hit me, man! You fucking hit me!" He reached out a hand dramatically and I helped him to his feet. The driver was apologizing and Chris was yelling, "Sorry!? You're *sorry?!* You fucking hit me with your *car,* man!" I pulled the bike off to the side so I wouldn't have to stand there with the two of them. The same bystanders who'd gathered for the first collision had already regrouped for this one. No one was calling him on it, though. One of the benefits of being a guy like Crazy Chris is that people tend to avoid confrontation.

When he'd finally finished berating the poor driver, showing him his ribs and his knees and shouting the licence plate number, he pocketed the guy's money, then began yelling again as the car pulled away. "You're leaving?" he shouted. "You just hit me and you're *leaving!* That's hit and run, you piece of shit!" but he was already grinning. He showed me the $20 bill in his hand, then went into the gas station and bought two packs of smokes from the cashier, who'd been watching it all through the window.

Back outside, he unwrapped one pack and handed me the other, along with a pack of matches. There was still a small crowd of people watching us.

"Thanks," I said. "But I'm getting out of here. And you should, too."

"Just have a smoke with me."

"Well, at least get away from the pumps," I said, and we walked over to where I'd dumped the bike.

One of the bystanders called out, "Hell of a way to make a living, buddy."

Chris fortunately took this as praise. "Fuckin' A, man!" he shouted, did a few hip thrusts and let out a laugh.

"Maybe a lower profile at this point . . . ," I started, but he was already howling at a passing car, shouting, "I *love* the scene of the crime! I love it, lovit, lovit! I *am* the scene of the crime, baby!" Then he turned to me, his voice suddenly low, and said, "We should work together, man. We should be partners!"

"I don't think so, Chris . . ."

"No, really! I see you around all the time. You're solid, you're smart, you're doing your own thing—you know how much I made from claims in the past two months? You know how much?"

"How much?"

"A *lot!* I trip over an apple in IGA—boom! I slip in my own spit going into Dominion—boom! They all want to give me money, man! I'm getting paid for crashing Mike's truck and the thing didn't even have plates, and I was drunk! Figure that out! I got thousands rolling in, man! Hell, I'd break my face for a grand. Why not? What do I need a pretty face for?"

"Uh . . . nothing, I guess."

"Exactly!" A cop car drove by and Chris howled with laughter. "So, what do you think? Partners?"

"No way, Chris," I said, dragging hard on the cigarette so I could get it finished and be on my way. "I'm better working alone. You be careful tonight, eh?" I threw the butt on the ground and stepped on it.

"Yeah, yeah," said Chris. "But think about it, man," and he twirled around, pointing his finger at the few bystanders who were still there. "Blam-blam-blam!" he shouted. "You're all dead! Just like me, mother-fuckers!"

September 2

The stench is unbearable. For about a week now, nobody's dared use the porta-potties. Even the least discriminating crackheads wouldn't open the doors for the smell and flies swarming out like a Hitchcock horror movie. So they've just fermented there, buzzing and bubbling, untouched by everyone.

Probably as a result of pressure from the TDRC and a bit of awkward publicity during the press conference, the porta-potty guys finally came down here. Although they pumped out the septic tanks, they neglected to wash anything down and they piled the clothes people have been using for toilet paper outside the outhouse doors. So now a foul and profound smell is hovering over this place, as though something sick and festering has been unearthed.

Beric has been down here almost every day since organizing the press conference and insists that this is part of the plan to drive us out of here. "But we're going to clean it up ourselves!" he says. He means that he's paying one of the new kids $10 an outhouse to scrub them all down.

The TDRC has also come up with money for another mass cleanup of Tent City, scheduled for three weeks from now. They'll be paying us this time—$30 for three hours' work, for each of thirty Tent City residents. When I asked him where the money was coming from he said it was a big company I should know well, but he wouldn't say who.

"Home Depot?" said Sherry, who's a lot swifter than I am about these things, and Beric smiled and nodded like she'd got it exactly.

After the press conference, the *Toronto Star* reported that, in response to "homeless advocates and squatters worried they will be kicked out of their downtown shantytown . . . Home Depot, the company that owns and controls the site, says it's actually pushing a plan to move residents into manufactured homes—on its land—until a permanent location for them can be found." Apparently this plan would involve all of us leaving for a week or so, while Home Depot demolishes Tent City as we know it, paves the ground so as to restrict the supposed contamination, then drops dozens of prefab houses onto the concrete. And just like that we will have brand-new healthy homes complete with water and electrical hookups.

When I asked Beric if this was actually feasible, he said, "There's been a hundred plans—this is a new one. We try to use it to our advantage." I wasn't sure what he meant, and when I asked why Home Depot should feel obliged to help us he seemed to suggest it was some dubious ploy. He spoke as if he's a player, too, in this game of Home Depot, Homes First, the police, the city and the homeless who live in homes we built ourselves.

When I suggested to Beric that it's a pretty sad thing when you've got to pay people to clean their own shit, then pay them more to clean their front yards, he finally changed the subject to something I could understand. "Petra's in trouble," he said. "I'm worried about her—she's not doing so well."

Petra, Jimmy D's old lady, is rarely doing well. Her crack binges gather around her like wind funnelling into a cyclone, until she blows away, tearing through anything in her path. I've seen her ripping apart bags of donated clothes, yelling at every shirt and skirt as she tears them to bits and throws them into the dirt. "She's often in trouble," I said.

"No, really. She's having a tough go of it. I want to get her some food—and some food for the dogs." It occurred to me that it might not be a case of Petra doing any worse than usual, just Beric being down here more—especially since he seemed to think her problems could be tempered with food. "But the dogs," he said. "They're out of control. Do you think . . ."

"Don't worry. I'm fine with the dogs. If you want to bring some food I'll help you out."

Beric bought some hamburgers and a bag of dog food, and once I got the dogs under control, he presented the food to Petra, who actually seemed to be doing okay.

"Uh . . . how have things been? A little bit difficult?" he asked, like a lawyer leading a witness. And then, as if she'd been waiting for someone to ask, Petra bounded out of her shack and started yelling about how Jo-Jo is a thief.

"I'm going to kill her! I'm going to kill that *fucking bitch!*" she yelled, waving her hands toward where she thought Jo-Jo might be. And I remembered Les this morning laughing about how he threw Jo-Jo's crack pipe in the canal again, and about how Petra had then caught Jo-Jo trying to steal hers.

I said bye to Petra, who was now filling her pockets with rocks to throw at Jo-Jo, and left Beric to try to sort it all out.

x   x   x

The sun is going down and a skinny rat-haired guy is ravaging the outhouse with a mop and a bucket that Beric gave him. And finally the stench is drifting off with the day.

Les just went by on his hourly search for Jo-Jo. He has one of the best walks I've ever seen—shoulders swaying, legs bowed, leading with his tough little belly, like the most relaxed, ambling buccaneer on the whole high seas. "Door's gone, hmm-yeah," he says with his calm ironic smile.

"What'd he say?" asks Sherry from inside the shack.

"Said his door is gone."

And now Jo-Jo just walked by, going the same way. They do this a lot—follow each other around in circles, acting like they're just out for a stroll. Jo-Jo's walk is even better than Les's. Although every part of her moves perpetually, her little butt swaying and limbs stretching in all directions, her knees never bend. And yet somehow she is still graceful, with a manic sort of ease.

"Fuckin' Petra ripped my door off!" she blathers with an incredulous laugh, so that I'd surely mishear her if it wasn't for Les's prior complaint.

"What's that?" says Sherry.

"Door's still gone," I say.

Jimmy D's been losing a lot of doors lately, too—and ones that are much more difficult to rip off than the one on Les and Jo-Jo's dollhouse.

Although he moved into Hawk's shack, Jimmy D hasn't quite managed to take his place. Every time he leaves, it seems, someone tears the door off and steals his dope—so that Jimmy D standing in his doorless doorway, growling and spitting bloody murder, has become a recurring

sight. Apparently the only thing that had been stopping people from ripping him off before was the threat of his crazy dogs. But Petra's got the
dogs now, and she's ripped the door off the dollhouse because Jo-Jo
needed a crack pipe, because hers was thrown in the river by Les, because
Les is jealous of the men she does to take the drugs, and resentful of the
drugs it takes to do the men.

It's late now, and Les just ambled by once more. His smile in the
moonlight is more desperate than usual, but he's still laughing. "They're
coming to the house now," he says, by which he means that the johns
have been showing up at his doorless little dollhouse, looking for the
love of his life.

"Shit, Les," I say, but he's already swaggering away.

"What was that?" calls out Sherry, curled up in bed.

"They're coming to the house now," I say.

"Oh shit."

A few nights ago we went with Les to see *Moulin Rouge*. (It turns out
there *are* free outdoor movies at Harbourfront—they just didn't start
showing them until mid-July.) He'd already seen it twice, and was hoping Jo-Jo would come with us. He says it's his favourite movie of all
time—a musical about a tortured and hapless poet in love with a prostitute. He sang the words wrong to every song and laughed so much that
we did too, until I thought we'd cry.

"See that!" he said when it was over. "There's nothing like being in
love with a whore! Everything's as it should be, hee-yeah! It's going to be
just fine!" Then we walked home along the railroad tracks beneath the
stars, singing "Roxanne" all the way to our proud and shabby shacks that
smelled of smoke and shit.

September 4

There are a dozen strange signs that something's about to change.

For one, Hoyt—easily the most racist homophobe in a place full of
confused rednecks—has fallen in love with a black lesbian he met
uptown.

"And she likes me, too!" he says. "She thinks I'm comical! She really
does! She sees the . . . you know . . . the *real* me!"

"What? You're really a woman?"

"Shut up! You don't understand," says Hoyt, blushing. "I'm just say-ing I can be different."

"The black lesbian made you want to be a better man, is that it?"

"Maybe it is! And she's a *Canadian* black, okay? She's a classy black lady. And I like her. Maybe some of us got open minds, okay? You watch, you just watch! I'm not going to be an asshole anymore! What d'ya think of that?"

"That's great, Hoyt," I say. "I'm glad to hear it."

Randy's new romance also seems fortuitous, although much less inspiring. A bunch of us were drinking in my front yard today, when he came in and shouted, like announcing royalty, "Shaun, dear Shaun! Let me introduce you to my new girlfriend . . . Perky Patty!" And then he stood aside to reveal the woman who'd punched me in the head while I was trying to get Nancy to put some clothes on—surely another sign that things are reaching some sort of cosmic breaking point.

And then there's the narcs and their week-long barbecue. Four days ago, Les pointed them out to me, sitting between a smoking Hibachi and a black SUV on the other side of the canal. "Strange place for a picnic, don't you think?" he said, grinning. At the time I just marked this down to Les's paranoia, but they're still over there, and you can see the sun shining off their binoculars.

"They've got cameras up on the silos, too," says Les. I'm inclined to believe him. The cruisers are coming through town a couple times a day now. The police boats slow down along the shore to take photos.

Then Petra brought me plastic flowers and hash. She came into my yard dancing and singing in her spastic way, and put her presents down on the table. I haven't seen hash for years and, as opposed to pot, I feel good when I smoke it. The worst that happens is I tend to see things as more meaningful than perhaps they are. So I've been smoking it all afternoon with Sherry and Jackie. We raise our beers and wave to the narcs barbecuing across the water as the sun is going down.

Eddie just went spinning by for the tenth time this hour. He's still building houses for the dealers during the day and has taken to breaking into cars at The Docks nightclub. You can see the trail of his soul spread-ing out behind him, like slug slime, or angel dust.

These plastic flowers remind me of Ron. Maybe that's where Petra got them from. Nobody talks about him. I can't help but think that his death was the beginning of the end of Tent City—this place that changes every day, but never really does, this deep and vagrant earth.

September 6

Jo-Jo still insists that she's really scared of Les. No matter how I try, I just can't see him as a scary guy—or, for that matter, Jo-Jo as a woman who gets scared. Even Sherry, who'd be the first person to go to bat for a woman in trouble, finds it hard to see Les as controlling or abusive.

"Look at them!" she says. "I don't know how he hasn't strangled her yet—I would! It's like she's torturing him. But then I guess he sort of likes it somehow. Does she sleep with the johns, do you know? Or is it all blowjobs and stuff?"

"I don't know. It's sort of a tricky thing to ask."

Of one thing I *am* certain: if Les ever hurt her, I would know. He tells me everything, or at least everything the way *he* sees it. He said to me yesterday, "Well, I tried hitting her, umm-ha. Thought that might work—but it didn't."

"What happened?"

"I slapped her once. And then I grabbed her throat and she pulled her groin muscle when she kicked me in the stomach. At least it's slowed her down a bit."

"You can't do that, Les. Don't hit her."

"Oh, I know. I think she kind of liked it, too, which defeats the purpose."

"Tell me, Les, does she sleep with them? Or is it all blowjobs and stuff?"

"Oh, she says she doesn't. But sometimes, you know, she's gone like half, hmm-hee, an hour, right? And comes back with $80. You got to do a lot, oh-yee, for $80. But then she rips them off sometimes, too, right? I know that 'cause I get guys coming around looking for the money she stole, and she's going all squirrelly, and I gotta be the big man and chase them away, hmm-yeah."

Then this evening Jo-Jo came over for her turn at therapy, with an even stranger strut than usual because of the groin pull. She stretched herself out on my leaf-strewn couch.

"How're you doing, Jo-Jo?"

"Aw, jeez. Okay, I guess. Heard from Jake, eh?"

"Jake? Really?"

"Yeah, my sister's husband went and visited him. He said, 'Tell her I love her. Tell Jo-Jo I love her.' That's nice, eh?"

"Uh . . ."

"I mean, this guy Les, he's so tough and everything, right? Always strutting around, big man on campus—ain't *no* one tougher than Les! I mean, c'mon honey, *you* know Jake. He'd walk right through big Les. He'd chew him up and spit him out. You know what I'm saying?"

"Uh yeah . . . Jo-Jo, can I ask you something? Does Jake think you're still, uh, his . . . girlfriend?"

"I don't know."

"Well, have you talked to him?"

"No, Shauny—he's in *jail.*"

"All right then . . . I guess . . ."

"But Les, eh! He's like a little kid! It's *all* about Les. Can't do anything wrong, knows everything. Oh, he's a deep-sea diver now—did you know that? Goes on about sharks and underwater plant life. I'm like, 'I don't got time for this, Diver Dan' . . . Hey, what you writing?"

"What?"

"What are you writing, Shaun?"

I've gotten so used to sitting out here and writing—with people coming over and interrupting me like I'm not busy at all—that I've subconsciously started to feel that what I'm doing is invisible to everyone but me. And in some way, it is. It's such a strange thing to be doing here that people can't compute it, so usually they just go on like I'm not doing anything.

"I've told you, Jo—I'm writing a book about this place."

"Am I in it?"

"Sure you are. You're one of the heroes."

"Yeah, right! The freaky hooker that never bends her legs." She jumped off the couch and touched her toes to illustrate her own character.

"Exactly. Why do you do that anyway? Even when you pick something off the ground you don't bend 'em—isn't that hard?"

"It's easier! It's immediate! It's right there, so I pick it up!" She scooped up a cigarette butt, folding her body in half and straight again, then lit the filter in the candle flame. "You should write that down—it's right there, so she picks it up!"

"I will, I'll write it later."

"I don't cheat on him, you know? I mean, I do this because it's what I do. It's work—but I don't lay, you know. I don't do lays." This often happens—I get an answer from one of them to a question I've asked the other. Apparently they confer between sessions. "But he's just so jealous! I mean, he threw my Coochie in the canal!"

"Your Coochie?"

"My teddy bear," she said, her hands buzzing around her like bees, landing on the couch cushions, lifting off. She got up, sat back down. "I was hugging Coochie and dancing with him, right?" she said, acting it all out for me. "And Les goes," she dropped her voice into a dopey low mumble, "'You spend more time with that teddy bear than with me.' And then I said, 'Well, he's cuter than you . . . ' And wham! Coochie's in the river. But don't write about that."

"Why not?"

"I don't know. It reminds me of my Tiny Tears doll."

"Your Tiny Tears doll?"

"Oh my God! My brother, when I was a kid, gets all this hockey equipment for Christmas, right?" She was up again, putting on the pads, banging her stick on the ice. "He gets every little thing—except they forget the pucks. And all I get is this Tiny Tears doll. I mean, it's better than the one I had before—like, I had one that just said 'Mommy' when you'd press its tummy, but this one cries, like, real tears, and says 'Mommy,' too—double action, right! So, after Christmas dinner I go down to the basement, and there's my brother in all his stupid gear. And he's playing hockey with the head—with the head of my new Tiny Tears doll! He ripped the head right off! I mean, it's eyes are *walled*—looking out both ways, and the hair is just freaked, you know—the face all pushed in! These fucking dickhead men!" She laughed. "What do you think I should do?"

"Uh . . . about Les? Well, you just got to figure out what you want, Jo."

"What do you mean?"

"You gotta decide if you want to be with him or not, if you love him—to be with just him, you know? If not, it's not going to work out." I said this with a straight face, actually believing for a moment that such things could ever work out.

"I told him, it'll change when we get out of here—but not before, you know?"

"But is that what you want? I mean, there's a reason he's trying to drag you out of here, right, Jo-Jo?"

"Oh yeah, I want to go . . . I mean, this isn't *it*." She spread both arms out like a disco dancer presenting Tent City. "This can't be *it*. But he's like, 'I'm getting a bed for you—you're going into detox! I mean seriously! It's like, take a look at yourself, Don Juan! But no! Everyone's a drug addict except for good ol' Les! I mean, Jesus—*I'm* not the one who needs detox! That's not what I need!"

"What do you need, Jo-Jo?"

"I mean, he's just so ridiculous. He comes spilling out of the dollhouse yesterday in these leather pants. And he's got these pointy cowboy boots on! I mean, these things could kick the eyes out of a snake! And this stupid tie, right? And that black Juan Valdez hat he's got! And you know what he says—you know what he says? 'We're going to the football game, baby!' And he wonders why I never do anything with him. I mean, seriously! Look at the way he dresses! And do you think he has any idea where the football stadium is? Or if there's even a game on—any *real* idea?"

"Uh . . . I asked you what *you* need, Jo-Jo."

"Well, I sure as hell don't need *that* . . . I don't know, Shaun. I just don't know. I think I gotta see my mom," she said, and laughed, touching her toes.

"So I guess you didn't go to the football game?"

"Nah. We had a fight instead—and then he threw my Coochie in the river."

x
x
x

They come over once more just before midnight. And this time they're together, straight-legging and strutting, groin-pulled and glassy-eyed.

"Lester, Jo-Jo, how you doing this evening?"

"You still writing, honey?"

"He's writing a book, baby."

"I know what he's doing, Les."

"It's all about what an evil, unscrupulous woman you are. Hmm-hey."

"Can you talk to him, honey?" says Jo-Jo, turning back to me.

"What about, Jo-Jo?"

"About what we were talking about earlier, about not being so jeal-ous—it sounds better coming from—"

"Jealous!" says Les, slamming his hand on the table and falling to one knee. I can see by his eyes that the drugs have got the best of him tonight. "I'm not the only one who's jealous! You girls are nuts, you hookers! You go off with whatever dick'll pay you, but God help, ha-hee, if I look at another woman . . ."

"I don't care who you look at, Les."

"And you can go out shakin' your booty, but if I take my shirt off in public it's all—"

"You could walk around naked for all I care, Les. Especially if you're going to wear clothes like those."

"You saying you're not jealous of me?! Yeah-huh!?"

"Uh-huh . . ."

"You're, hum-hee, saying you don't get jealous when I walk around all sexy!"

"All sexy! What planet are you on? I told you—walk around naked, I don't care."

"You don't care, eh? You don't care? You won't be jealous if I get naked?"

"No."

"All right," says Les, pulling his shirt awkwardly over his head, "all right then," working at his belt and kicking off his shoes at the same time, "if it's all the same to you," until finally he's standing in front of us barefoot and naked, his clothes bunched up in his arms. And for a moment it seems he has nothing to say. He turns around and struts out of my yard, his white butt shining in the moonlight. He drops a shoe, but either doesn't notice or chooses not to.

"Uh, Les," I call out as he crosses through the fence. His perpetual need to talk gets the best of him and he shouts, "There you go! I'm naked now! Hm-hee, whatya think of that?" Then he disappears behind the trees, heading down the road.

A few seconds pass, and then we hear Karen yelling and cursing from down the river. Presumably she's run into Lester. And now we hear Eddie growling, and Les's strange heroic war cry. "I am naked! Heee-haw! I am naked!"

"Perhaps I should bring him his shoe," says Jo-Jo.

"Good idea," I say. She crosses the yard to where his lone Hush Puppy is lying on the ground. She reaches down without bending her legs. It's right there, so she picks it up.

September 7

Randy came over this afternoon with a miniature, battery-operated fan. He was looking a little worse for wear—a wrapped wrist from a fight with Jimmy D and a bruise on his forehead from one of the lesser drug dealers.

"I'll give you ten minutes with my fan for a cigarette," he said to Sherry.

"Sounds kind of kinky, but okay. As long as you hold it."

"What, the cigarette or the fan?"

"Both."

So he sat next to Sherry, looking strangely forlorn for a man with smoke and wind in his hands. "God, it's hot!"

"For September, yeah . . . Where's your girlfriend?"

"Who?"

"Perky Patty."

"Ah, we broke up. Don't know what I was thinking there. I gotta get out of here." He moved the fan around Sherry's head like he was tracing a halo. "I got some people looking for an apartment for me—I just need one with Chaos is all. I'd die without him, you know? I'm not leaving him. I'm not!"

"You okay, Randy?"

"I'm hoping maybe my daughter'll come down here to visit. Well, the older one at least. I've got two, eh? Both live in Timmins. The older one's 32—I had her when I was 16, I've got grandkids, eh? The other one's 13. I took her to the Ex when she was 7. That was a really good day. She went on all the rides."

"What's up, Randy—you sure you're okay?"

"Oh, yeah. Pretty good. I think things are going to be good. I quit crack, eh?"

"Yeah, how long?"

"Three days now. I hate it. I really do." He turned to Sherry, lowering the fan to make sure she understood. "It's just not me."

"How about the street fighting," I said, trying to make him smile. Randy after all is one of the least violent drunks down here. "You quitting that, too?"

"Aw, fuckin' Jimmy D . . ." He lifted up his bandaged hand to take a drag on the cigarette. "I don't know why—when he gets drunk he just picks on me, like a bully almost. You know what I mean?" He looked at Sherry again. "At least this time I got the better of him. This wasn't from him," he said, touching the bruise on his head. "Popeye did that one."

"I thought *you* were Popeye," said Sherry, taking the fan from his hand and directing it back at his bruised, sweating brow.

"Yeah, but he's called Popeye, too. Maybe that's what the fight was about. I don't know. I don't understand it. I mean, I just like to make people laugh, you know—that's what makes me happy. Even if they're laughing at my expense, I don't care. As long as they're laughing . . ."

"You're funny as hell, Randy," I said. But hell's no joke, and Randy hasn't been funny for a while.

"It's the crack," he said. "With the crack, something else happens— I'm not me. I'm glad I quit. The last time I quit I became a really good person. I just gotta stick to the booze and Cough-X. And I gotta get out of here."

But since Hawk and Bonnie left, the only long-time residents who've managed to get out of here are Heartbeat—who's disappeared amid rumours that he owed Big G a lot of money—and this kid Jerry, who people say won a million dollars in the lottery and bought a condo.

September 8

I'm sitting here writing, sometime after midnight, and suddenly there's a screeching of tires like a car is spinning out of control on the main road. I figure Crazy Chris is drunk and has got hold of a new ride, but then the horn starts in and I can hear yelling, and the tires are still screeching. So I put down my pen, blow out the candle and go over to take a look.

As I walk toward Randy's shack, the air is thick with dust swirling off the road. I can see a car tearing from one side to the other, up into the garbage heap, against the back of Dry's house, spinning around in circles. The horn is still blaring, someone's still yelling, and then I notice there's a pair of legs jutting out of the driver's-side window.

I don't know it right then, but the legs belong to Frizz. Frizz, after all, is the quickest man around. He would make a great special-ops agent, provided he didn't have to play by any rules and could do a lot of drugs. He's not a leader and not a follower. He's dangerous the same way Wolverine is, and in fact he looks and acts remarkably like him.

This is the kind of thing you should know if you're a young rich kid with a nice car coming down to Tent City to rip off a crack dealer—especially if he's Frizz's dealer. That way, when you pocket the drugs, jump in your car and hit the gas, you're ready for Frizz to come sprinting alongside the car and dive through the window. If you're not ready for it, you have no chance. Which brings us to where we are—Frizz's legs calmly jutting from the speeding car like he's accustomed to flying as he hammers the kid's head with his fist.

And now, in an inspired—or merely desperate—move, the kid throws open his door in the hopes of sending Frizz flying in the other direction. But as the door swings open, Frizz somehow pushes off with his stomach muscles and soars into the speeding car, so that his feet are on the open door and both his hands are on the wheel, his body above the kid like a bomb about to drop. As Frizz smacks an elbow into his jaw, the driver's foot comes off the gas, and Frizz yanks at the wheel. The car spins around a couple times and finally comes to a stop down by the trailer where some of the lost boys live. And now the kid is really screwed.

By the time I get there, Frizz has him out of the car and is going through his pockets. The kid is trying to pull free to look for his car keys, which Frizz has tossed into the brush. "Let me go!" says the kid, then, appealing to the group of lost boys that's starting to form, "He's crazy, man! He's crazy! He hit me!"

And now Eddie is there, and Norm and Curly too. "You're lucky he just hit you once!" says Eddie.

"He didn't!" whines the kid. "He hit me lots of times!" Frizz has all four car doors open and is systematically searching the seats and the floor. It's a nice car, a 2001 Lexus, probably his parents', and now there's a few of them going through it, grabbing stuff from the glove box, trying to find the lever to open the trunk.

"Where is it?" says Frizz, standing up again. He's found some of the drugs, but not all of it. "Where's the rest of it?!"

"That's all, th-that's all of it!" stammers the kid. "Please just let me go!" Frizz punches him once, quick, just under the eye. "Ahhh!" yells the kid. "Jesus! Jesus! What're you doing?" The lost boys surge forward at the fresh violence. It's like a scene from a movie where someone turns down the wrong alleyway and is suddenly surrounded by street thugs. One of them has a stick in his hand and cracks it across the back of the kid's head. Eddie grabs the stick away from him. "What are you doing, ripping off homeless people?" the lost boy says. It's a ridiculous thing to say, but the rich kid blubbers an answer.

"I've been ripped off three times down here!" he whines.

"Then why do you keep coming back?" says Eddie. "You come down, you address it head-on—that's fine. You bring some boys with you and sort it out. But you don't try to rip someone off 'cause they ripped you."

I don't know where Eddie gets this stuff, but all this talk isn't calming the kid down. His whole body is shaking. "Can I go now?"

"Now you're pissing me off," says Eddie. "You don't want to do that. Just give us the drugs."

"I did, I did . . . ," blubbers the kid. He's so scared, he can't speak anymore. He's not offering any resistance as they go through his pockets again, and he's making a strange whiny noise, like a wounded rabbit. The only understandable sound coming from his quivering, crying mouth is "Please." When Frizz finds another small rock and goes to shake him down once more, the kid just falls apart in his hands.

Then, like a scythe through the tall grass, Big G comes riding out of the shadows—bare-bellied on a bicycle—and everyone inhales at once.

He throws down the bike and circles the car toward the kid. You can't understand a word he's saying—his Jamaican accent has become like some swirling, earthbound wind. He's standing in front of the kid, breathing fire, and still no one else has exhaled. The kid whimpers a soft sob and Big G belts him across the side of the head with the heel of his big black hand.

We've all been struck by the same quick thought—he's going to kill him! We stand back as the kid's flight instinct finally kicks in and he bolts. We watch as Big G chases him around the car, then—thanks to a bizarre and panicked move on the kid's part—in through the open passenger door. Big G has him by the shirt and you can hear it tearing, the kid screaming as Big G pulls him back across the front seats. Somehow he kicks free. He dives out the driver's door and breaks into a run.

Frizz is right on his heels. Even if you're young and fast, running for your life, you can't outrun Wolverine.

"Leave him, Frizz!" I yell, my shout echoed by that of Eddie and Curly. It seems none of us want to see the poor little rich kid torn apart by Big G. Hearing our yells, Frizz stops just long enough for the kid to escape down the road, sprinting toward the gates.

"Let him go?" bellows Big G, rageful and mocking. "Whatta yas mean, let him go?! Let him go, why?" But nobody'll look at Big G, nobody will answer him. "You stealin' from me, I lettin' you go? I show you! I show you!" And with that, Big G grabs his bicycle and pedals madly toward Crack Corner.

A few guys stand around, debating whether or not to pop out the car stereo. I try to point out that the kid, no matter how scared he is right now, is not going to just leave his parents' Lexus down here—so sooner or later the cops will show up. Curly and Eddie agree, and slowly everyone drifts back to whatever they were doing before. I'm the only one still outside when Big G comes back on his bike, a thick lead pipe in his hand. I stand in the shadows and watch as he smashes every window, headlight, tail light and mirror. Then he starts on the hood and roof, glass showering over him as he swings his pipe in the moonlight.

x   x   x

This morning the car was gone. All that remained was a large circle of shattered glass cubes reflecting the sunlight in a dozen different colours, like a ring of fire burning out.

"Holy shit, that kid was scared!" said Frizz, laughing, as he showed me the long welts where the car door had cut into his stomach. "When you think about it, we did him a good turn."

"How's that?" I said.

"You can bet that kid won't get so much as a jaywalking ticket for the rest of his life, if mom and dad ever let him out of the house again. And he's not going to do crack again any time soon, no way. We scared him straight."

What concerns me more than some frat boy's questionable salvation, however, is Big G. How he dealt with the kid's car wasn't exactly good business sense. The man with the drugs and the power, and no doubt the police's attention, has proved to be as unpredictable and crazy as any of us. So really, nobody's in control of anything down here. I guess it's just luck that we haven't yet killed each other, let alone some misguided kid who thought he was smarter and faster than the bums of Tent City.

September 13

For the past few days there's been a work crew on the other side of the fence. Yesterday I went over there and they told me the silos are tagged for demolition. They didn't know there was anyone living in there, so I went in to find Greg, but came out with nothing but soaked jeans.

Later in the evening, Randy and I ran into him as we were heading downtown. Goran was showing some of his Tent City photos in an art exhibition, and I'd managed to coerce Randy into coming to the opening with the promise of free wine and cheese.

When I told Greg what the construction guys had said, he nodded his head. "Yeah . . . I saw them out there, thought it might be something . . . ," he said.

"What are you going to do, Greg?"

"Leave, I guess," he said, shrugging. And I thought: *Eeyore! That's who he reminds me of!*

Randy and I were the only bums at the vernissage and we got pretty loaded, so as not to disappoint. Randy stood in front of a photo of himself and Hoyt, to make sure people recognized him as he told dirty jokes.

"I didn't used to be so funny," I heard him explaining to the gallery owner. "But that was when I was doing crack."

x
x
x

Today I dragged myself up to the welfare office and there again, getting off the elevator, was Greg.

"Hello," he said, like he'd just lost his tail.

"Hey, Greg, how goes it? You still in the silos?"

"Yeah, I talked to those guys . . . They were all right . . . Said I could stay a few more days. Then I gotta go."

"Come over to our side, Greg. I'll help you get settled."

"I know. I know. I've been meaning to come over and see about that, and I will. I'm just really busy the next few days."

I didn't ask what a guy who lives in an abandoned, flooded grain silo could be so busy with. I know how it can be—people who don't live on the street always laugh if I say I'm too busy. "I thought you were a bum!" they say, but I can't see the irony of it anymore—everybody becomes consumed with their lives eventually, everyone gets busy.

"Well, come over when you can," I said. "And we'll find you a good spot."

"Yeah . . . the thing of it is . . . I got some worries . . . I got some . . . worries . . ."

"What is it?"

"It's pretty rough over there, eh?"

"Yeah, but it doesn't have to be, Greg. I'll help you out."

"You know that guy Jimmy D?" he said carefully, weighing the words like he might not be able to carry them.

"Sure—you don't have to worry about him."

"The guy's got problems or something. He throws rocks at my place . . ."

"At the silos?"

"Sure. And he's always yelling about his door or something, and throwing more rocks. The guy's insane. And he's right at the front gates . . ."

"Yes, he's a bit unbalanced, but that's no problem, Greg. Really, I could get that sorted out in a second. I'll talk to Jimmy D, and I'll give you some tools to build with, okay?"

"Okay," said Greg. "Probably time to move anyway."

September 14

Last night Karen came over saying Eddie had broken her ribs and cracked her jaw. They've been getting a lot rougher with each other lately. I gave her some whisky and a painkiller, and asked if she wanted to go to the hospital, though she looked to be more jonesing than injured. She said maybe later, but I guess later she found some crack.

Early this evening she was back again. "My ribs are broken and my jaw is cracked," she said. "I can't breathe properly." She was crying.

"Then you have to go to the hospital, Karen," I said. "I'll go with you."

"Eddie's taking down my shack," she cried. "I don't want him to."

I walked out through the side and into the clear. She was right. Eddie was destroying their shack again. But it was a careful destruction. He was systematically taking the walls apart and stacking the wood on the ground. Once in a while he'd stop and load some of their belongings into a shopping cart. Then he'd push the cart over to the mountain of garbage across the main road and dump it.

I came back into the yard, and now Jo-Jo, Olivia and Sandy were there, too. "I'm sorry, honey," Jo-Jo was saying, "but you're whining, all right? And you won't do anything about it. Go to the hospital, already— or don't. But if you won't go, I don't want to hear you whining anymore."

"I'm not whining!" Karen whined.

"We're going to the hospital," I said.

"Do you have Jane's phone number? I want Jane to go with me."

"Why do you have to bring Jane into this? Why can't I just go with you?" I wrote down the number for her.

"It's not the same!" she said, by which she meant I don't have a car. Karen, after all, never leaves this place—never even walks outside the gates. I don't think she's been out of Tent City once since Jane drove her to see Caleb in his little glass box.

"Just come with me over there, Shaun," she said, waving a hand toward their quickly disappearing shack, letting out small frantic sobs. "I'm scared to go alone. I gotta get something."

I didn't want to go with her. Not for any particular reason, I realized, but just because that will to help, the desire to make things better, was suddenly gone—or rather, I finally noticed it was gone. I didn't actually want to go to the hospital with her, either, and maybe she'd picked that up in my voice. I didn't want to help her get Jane down here. I didn't want to get myself between her and Eddie. What was the point? Nothing I'd tried had worked at all—not with Karen or Eddie or Calvin or Nancy or Jackie or any of them.

And yet it's Karen. When I was on the ground, being kicked, and couldn't get up, she came out and yelled at them to stop, yelled that I was her friend.

"Yeah, sure," I said. "C'mon." And I walked ahead of her, over to where Eddie was disassembling what was left of their shack. The roof was still standing.

"Hey, asshole," he said when he saw me.

"Hey, Eddie."

Karen kicked around in the rubble, whimpering and getting in his way. He told her to get the fuck out of there and she started to yell at him. I stood there and watched. It was so hot and humid, almost as hot as the first time Eddie tore down his walls. It felt like it should rain, should pour—like the air had been holding back a sob for too long.

Randy came weebling and wobbling down the road behind Dry's place, but there was something wrong—he was weebling more, wobbling worse, his famous drunk balance disappeared, hands grabbing slow yet frantic for something to support him, something that wasn't there.

Karen threw a lighter at Eddie's face, then sobbed.

I reached Randy just as he was falling forward in slow motion.

"Shauny . . . Shauny . . . you asshole . . . ," he said as he staggered back to his feet, now giggling madly, like it hurt to laugh.

"What'd you do, Randy?" I said. "What'd you do to yourself?"

He giggled, gasped, then said, "Twelve ounces . . . 12 ounces . . . of Cough-X."

"Have you ever done that much?"

"No ... no ... just 8 ... once 10 ... not 12!" he wheezed, then laughed and laughed. As the giggling started to subside he began to pass out. I pulled his arm over my shoulders and walked him around until his legs seemed to work again.

Karen stumbled off into the dark. Sluggo walked out of his shack. Eddie stood back from the demolition of his home. Randy took a couple of steps on his own and turned around. And now the four of us were facing each other—Randy, Sluggo, Eddie and I, in the grey moonlit clearing, in the middle of our four shacks, and nobody said a thing.

I can't explain why this strange moment among a thousand of them stood out. An airplane growled overhead, then another. It felt as if we'd just materialized here, transported to the outskirts of the city, the edge of the water. I felt like the others knew this, too. But rather than bringing us together, the sensation seemed ... meaningless.

Then the party boat arrived.

Almost every night now, a big cruise ship blaring Latin dance music and crappy pop—people dancing and drinking under spinning disco balls on the deck—comes sailing across the lake, down the canal and right over to Tent City. Then it turns around slowly so that the people all over the boat can get a look, watching us as we open a can of beer, wash our hair in a bucket, weeble-wobble home or tear down our own shacks. Every night there are different people on the party boat, but we're always the same. Somebody yells at them to fuck off, somebody gets up and grooves to the music, somebody moons them. I usually just wave, then try to stare them down until the boat has finished its slow scenic turn.

This time, as the coloured lights and disco stars shone upon us, the macarena thumping through the air, none of us did a thing. And when the party boat finished its turn, sailing back onto the open lake, we were left once more in this strange grey silence.

Eddie turned back to his shack, pushed at the last remaining wall, and the roof came crashing down.

"Oh no!" he yelled, "I'm homeless!" and he began to laugh. Nobody else did, though, not even Randy.

x
x
x

I went looking for Karen. When I couldn't find her I walked back over to where their shack used to be. Eddie was stacking plywood on a dolly.

"Well, that's done!" he said.

"Yeah. Where should I forward your mail to?"

"Wilf's place. I'm going over there, just till I move out." Wilf was a guy who built a shack back in the bush, then left a couple weeks later.

"Did you hit her, Eddie?"

"Yeah ... yeah. With my elbow. I shouldn't have hit her. I know that. I just can't be around her. That's why I'm moving. If she comes and bothers me now ..."

I went back over to my place and sat down. There were leaves all over the couch, and I lay on them. Fall is not coming. The leaves are not changing colour. But still, some of them are falling. They fall green, and turn brown on the ground, or on my couch. There are earwigs on the couch, too. And spiders. I finished a bottle of whisky, and Eddie came over.

"Here," he said, holding out a dreamcatcher. "Do me a favour and hold on to this until I get a lock for my new place."

I was about to say that I doubted anyone would want to steal his dreams.

"I should have done this a long time ago, eh?" he said, shaking his head.

When he'd gone I sat there and stared at the dreamcatcher—a twine web encircled by a leather-covered hoop, feathers and beads hanging down like tired leaves and coloured tears. The first flashes of lightning pulsed and shimmered in the sky, and now I could hear Karen yelling— over where their shack used to be. "I want my blanket, Eddie!" she yelled. "I can't *do* this!"

I thought of what Karen had brought over the last time Eddie had torn down their house—stupid simple Ziggy with his idiotic bubble thoughts: "If you feel like you're falling behind in trying to follow your dreams, just remember—they can't get far without you." I sat here with Eddie's fucked-up dreams caught in my hands.

"I can't *do* this!" she yelled. "My ribs are broken, Eddie! ... It's going to rain!"

But it didn't. The sky kept flashing, the thunder cracked, but it didn't rain.

x
x
x

I'd been sitting on my bed for almost an hour, looking at the dream-catcher hanging in the corner, when Jane knocked once and burst into my shack.

"Where is she? Where is Karen? What's going on?"

"I don't know, Jane," I said. "But I'll find her for you."

"What did Eddie do? I was having dinner . . . Is Karen okay?"

We looked everywhere for her. It was awkward going to all these crack shacks with Jane tagging along, but she refused to wait at my place. She wanted to come to Crack Corner with me, too, but I persuaded her not to. Big G and a couple of his knockaround guys were sitting on lawn chairs between the trailers. I asked if they'd seen Karen.

"Karen, yeah—bitch be in da lake," he said. "Go you look in da lake, mon."

"Thanks a lot."

"We drowned her, mon."

"Yeah. I get it."

I looked around some more, and then saw Jackie sitting behind one of the trailers.

"Hey, Jacks," I said. "I need to find Karen. Have you seen her?" She looked up, but it was like she didn't see me. I looked into her eyes, and through to her dark frozen brain, then gave her a quick hug.

"Shauny?" she said.

Jane came with me to the crack shacks on the other side of town, but everywhere it was the same—stoned jackasses shaking their crack heads and shrugging. Then, as we turned away from D's place, where little Leo had been staying, I said, "She's in there. Karen's in that one."

"How do you know?" said Jane.

I shrugged, and Karen appeared in the doorway.

"Hey, Jane," she said. Jane rushed over and hugged her.

"Come on," Jane said. "I'm taking you to the hospital."

"Yeah . . . no, that's all right. I feel fine now . . . Maybe we can go tomorrow instead."

"Fuck, Karen," I said, and she looked at me with eyes the same as all of them. Lightning flashed and the thunder cracked, but still it didn't rain.

"What's it to you, Shaun?" said Karen. And I turned and walked away.

x
x
x

She's right. What's it to me? Nothing. I don't care to help any of them anymore. Not Karen—except that she took a two-by-four on the side, and maybe saved my life. Not Randy—except that he gave me my roof and my bed. Not Jackie—except that she calls me her big brother and calls Sherry her best friend. Not Jo-Jo and Les—except that they've told me all their secrets. Not Eddie—except that on my first day here he said, "Shaun's all right," and watched my back for a long, long time.

Finally the flashing sky burst open and it began to rain. And I realized that to look out for people when you yourself need to do so, when you have a desire to help, is no great feat. But going out there when you don't want to, when you don't care anymore, that might just mean something. So I went looking for Karen once more in the deafening rain, to see if she needed to come inside.

But she was already in Wilf's old shack with Eddie, both wrapped in their drug dreams, out of the storm. I came back drenched and sat on my bed in the candlelight, listening to the rain.

September 16

Curly came over to get a cigarette tonight. It was late, but I have insomnia again, so I asked him to stay for a drink.

I've always been intrigued by Curly. It's as if he's got a thoughtful rage working the heavy bag behind his eyes. "You know what happened?" he said, taking a careful and appreciative sip of whisky. "To my . . . family?"

We had been talking about the regular things—crack and the cops, and the events of the day. (Frizz had had his cheek cut open with an X-Acto knife. One of the dealers had been busted trying to sell a stolen van to an undercover cop. Karen, having finally gone to the hospital with Jane, had been escorted out of the waiting room by security. She'd called the nurse a stupid cunt for saying there was nothing wrong with her. A typical day.) We'd been shaking our heads and smiling, when Curly said, "To my . . . family."

"I'm not sure," I answered.

"I can tell you," he said. "I started talking about it five months ago. I can tell you."

Ten years before Curly started talking about it, he lived just outside Kamloops, B.C., maybe close to where Calvin is now. It's an area I know well—the roads are dangerous and beautiful, and you can go forever in almost any direction.

He owned a home and two roadside restaurants. He had a wife and three children.

Both the restaurants were a long way from their house. One night the snow piled up too high for his little car to make the drive home, and he'd had a few drinks. He called his wife and asked her to pick him up in the four-by-four. She didn't want to leave the kids alone, so she piled them into the car, all three of them.

He didn't go to the funeral, but on the night after they were buried he took a sleeping bag and slept on their graves. The next day, he left. He went in every direction. His only plan was to get into the same prison as the drunk driver who'd been on the road that night. But he kept getting thrown into the wrong jail. Then he ended up here.

"You seem . . . okay," I said. "I mean, you're still . . . here, at least."

"Yeah," he said, actually understanding what I was trying to say. "You know when my life started again? When I wrote the guy a letter in jail— and told him I forgave him. That's when I realized it was me I couldn't forgive, who I wanted to kill, you know? So now I'm doing okay. The only thing is, I haven't worked a day since they died. And then there's the crack, too."

"Yeah."

"But we've all got stuff to figure out," he said.

September 17

I've been drinking a lot—more than usual, in the hope that I'll pass out for a full night's sleep, but it's not happening. The weird thing, as Sherry keeps pointing out, is that my insomnia started when I hung up Eddie's dreamcatcher. But what if I take down the aboriginal web in which my once-closest friend and doppelgänger's crack dreams are supposedly caught, and suddenly I can sleep? I don't want to deal with that. So I'm just not sleeping, and my mind is getting muddy.

If I *had* been sleeping, I would have been woken this morning to

Spider yelling at the whole damn world. Apparently someone broke into his and Olivia's shack and stole all the food they'd just got from the food bank. As it was, his anger merely got me out of bed, and I hung out with Olivia while he went to do his Homeless Dave radio show.

I like Olivia. She puts up with a lot from everyone, not just Spider. She sees how this place is being choked into something cold and submissive by the crack and the dealers. She talks fondly about the old days, when there were just a few dozen of us here—the Dirty Thirty, she calls us. She talks about that time as if it were our salad days.

"Things were good down here then, eh? It was real nice—we were like a family, everyone looking out for each other. They stole my food, Shaun. My food!"

At least she didn't have to go hungry, though. Jackie made a large stew with lamb and chicken and potatoes, and we all went over to eat. Jackie was issued two cheques this month, since her last month's cheque was sent to Kingston by mistake—where it was cashed by her sister. She asked me yesterday if I'd go to welfare with her this morning to hold on to some of the money. But she heard I was drinking all night, and decided to let me sleep (or not), and got Norm, who doesn't do crack either, to go with her. Everything went all right and she came home with $100 worth of booze, some food and pot, and we were eating and drinking all afternoon.

But it's always just a matter of time. When Sluggo passed out, she gave me a bottle of whisky and disappeared. Olivia and I were sitting on my deck, talking about the glory days, listening to the yelling and watching the moonlight on the water when Jackie came back, her eyes full of crack and her arms full of half-empty bottles to sell.

"Oh sweetie . . . ," said Olivia. "It's gone already?"

"I don't have to explain myself . . . to you," said Jackie, staggering toward Crack Corner.

"Take care of her tonight, eh, Shaun?" said Olivia.

And so now I'm out on the deck alone, writing by candlelight, looking through the window at Jackie smoking crack in my shack.

She's been in there, sitting on my bed, for almost an hour. It is a slow, steady process. Precise. Every flake, every grain, every speck of residue is tracked laboriously—on her fingernails, on the large thigh of her pants. She runs the lighter again and again over the surface of my bed even though there is still a fair-sized rock on the bedside table. Sometimes she gets lost staring at a still point on the floor, on the palm of her hand, or the stem of the pipe. And her huge round doll's eyes glaze over, unblinking, on and on. It's as if she's looking at the last crumb of crack in the whole world, or at the whole world itself, or at nothing at all. Until finally, something happens and she moves. She starts the slow steady process of packing the ash once more, heating the rock and smoking—tracking every speck like tiny shards of her life.

This is not an easy thing to watch. I want to go in there and scream at her.

She knew it was a lot to ask, to use my shack. I've said no to her before. Because of . . . principle, I guess. My shack has become sort of a sanctuary. People come here, inside my curving log fence, and sit and drink instead of going to the crack houses. Nobody ever fights here, not really. And nobody does crack here—they would never ask, wouldn't even think to. Not because I'm opposed to it—I've never said such a thing—but because I don't do it, and they are respectful, for the most part.

But Jackie asked because she's getting scared. And she knows how much I'd do for her. I want to say no, but the night is full of wolves, and I love her—would rather have her here where I can watch her, where she's safe to kill herself slow and carefully.

"Just this once, Jacks," I say, as if on principle. But I'm not sure I care anymore, about principle.

She stares at her hands for the longest time, as if each skin cell might be a bit of the drug. When I'm ready to try to sleep, I come inside and sit in a chair by the window, watching her. At one point she forces herself to talk to me.

"Where's my Share Bear?" she says. This is what she calls Sherry.

"At her mum's place, Jackie."

"I really . . . love her, you know?"

"I know."

She looks at her hands holding the pipe. And then she's gone again.

When I can't watch any longer I tell her I want my bed and she can sleep outside on the couch. She runs the lighter, lit, over every inch of the bed, then the bedside table, then the floor, then her lap, her hands, the floor again, the bed. She gets down and looks under the bookcase, then under the stove. Then she tries the bed again, her hands . . .

"Jackie," I say. "Jacks." I hold her hands. "You've got it all. You've got all of it." I lead her outside and lay her down on the couch, her eyes as bright and round as the moon.

September 18

I was going to try not to drink too much today, but Sluggo got his $195. Although Jackie spent twice that amount yesterday, Sluggo still bought $100 worth of booze and called me over. I don't for the life of me know why he does that. He knows that even on his best days he can't drink more than $15 of cheap beer and whisky, and that Jackie will pawn anything that's left and they'll fight each other in the morning. But still he blows it all on one cheap, expensive, fast drunk day—unless he can hide some cash somewhere she can't find it, in which case they'll fight another day, too.

So I went over and drank with Sluggo, Jackie and the boys.

"Where's Share Bear?" said Jackie, her voice alive and laughing and full of warmth, totally unlike the night before. She coughed and held her hand to her mouth. I'm scared that she's dying.

"I told her I'd meet her at Osgoode," I said. "For dinner."

"You guys are good, a good couple," said Sluggo, slugging on a beer.

"We were just talking about that," said Jackie. "That you guys are the best couple down here."

"You were talking about that?" I said.

"Yeah! It's too bad *more* people can't be like that," said Jackie, grinning malevolently at Sluggo. They'd been going at it all morning, until he left to get his cheque.

"You know all it is?" I said. "It's just that we're nice to each other. That's all. People can treat us like shit, and sometimes we treat other people rough, too—but not each other." I stopped and drained my beer. I still haven't really slept. I should take the dreamcatcher down.

"Yeah! You hear that?" Jackie was saying, and Sluggo was agreeing and shaking his head at the same time, saying, "It's different! It's different!

Don't give me that shit, Jackie." And of course he's right, and I'm the one giving him that shit.

"Well, I'm not being too nice now," I said. "I'm supposed to meet her in five minutes, and it's half an hour to Osgoode."

"You asshole," said Jackie.

I borrowed a bike and made it to City Hall in ten minutes.

"Hey, sweetie," said Sherry. "Nice bike. You're looped, aren't you?"

"Yeah, but guess what? The old crew thinks we're the best couple in Tent City."

"Thank God for that," said Sherry.

And then, while we were waiting in line at Osgoode, Pops came hobbling up with a walker. It looked like he'd aged ten years.

"Jesus Christ, Pops! How you doing?" He cackled, grinned, and made eyes at Sherry, bouncing his walker on the pavement. I asked him if he'd seen Hawk around.

"He's right there, Shauny. He's right behind you," he said, smiling like the Buddha had snuck up on me. I turned around, and there was Hawk.

We looked at each other and that thing flooded through his eyes that I can never quite read—like the quick assessment before an attack, or the beginning of a laugh. He laughed, and grabbed me in his arms.

"Hawk."

"Shauny."

"How are you?"

"I've been rough," he said. "I've been coming to see a doctor. Something in here." He jabbed a thumb into his belly.

"You going to be okay, Hawk? You look slower."

"Yeah." He peered into my eyes. "Can't get that left up so fast, eh?" He faked a quick jab.

"You remember Sherry?"

Hawk stepped forward and shook her hand. "I'm glad to see you."

"Hi, Hawk," she said.

"Where are you staying? What happened to the place up—"

"It's your turn to eat," said Hawk, cutting me off. "Come see me after."

"Where will you be?"

"Over there," he said, pointing toward City Hall, and we went in for dinner.

After we ate I unlocked the bike and we walked it over to where Hawk was holding court. Pops was there, as well as a few other bums, and there were sleeping bags on the ground.

"You staying here?"

"Sure, Shauny," he said, killing a cigarette between his tree-trunk fingers. "You know me—I can stay anywhere. How 'bout you? You running things down there yet?"

"No, Hawk. Not running things . . ."

"Yeah," he said loudly. "Hear the place been going down since I left."

"Yeah."

And then he dropped his voice "How are things, Shauny?"

"They're the same," I said. "And they're different."

"Place is going down, Shauny. It's going to hit the ground."

"Yeah, maybe."

"What you going to do?"

"I'm going to try to double Sherry all the way home," I said. And Hawk and Pops and the rest of the bums at City Hall laughed as we struggled onto the bike, then applauded as we rode away.

x
   x
     x

As we ride through the front gates, still somehow alive, I notice that Jimmy D has managed to build a wall around Hawk's old place. And it isn't just any wall—it is a massive and awkward-looking fortress of oak rounds piled on top of each other. I can see his dirty Tilley hat poking over the top.

I stop the bike and start to fall, but Sherry catches us both.

"Hey, Jimmy," I say, peering over the wall. "Having trouble with the thieves?"

"Rahhh!" he growls. "How you doin', man?"

"If the silo guy comes over, be nice to him. He's a friend of mine, okay?"

"Rahhh! Who the hell are you?"

"I'm me, Jimmy."

"Okay, man. No problem."

x
   x
     x

Sherry and I have some drinks over at Sluggo and Jackie's until Sluggo passes out. Then Jackie gives me another half-bottle of whisky and disappears once more with the rest of the booze.

Olivia comes by to tell me that she got more food from the food bank, only to have it stolen again. "Except the beans," she says. "It's someone who doesn't like beans." Some guy drives by in a car and gives Olivia the finger, and Spider chases his bumper all the way out of Tent City, swinging a six-iron.

Les struts past with a bandaged foot and a fuzzy-haired doll in his arms. "You seen Jo-Jo?"

Jo-Jo prances by in a sequined cocktail dress. "You seen my doll?"

Randy comes over and sits on the couch and talks about his daughters.

Petra brings over some more hash, and a pair of in-line skates.

A fight breaks out over at the lost boys' trailer.

A police boat sails up and down the shore.

Crackheads and johns come and go in their cars.

Jimmy D's famous voice travels up over his oak fortress and across Tent City. He sounds displeased.

Eddie bounces by, carrying a vacuum cleaner.

We get drunk again.

The party boat arrives. We swear at it, moon it and give it the finger. We dance and throw bottles. The party boat sails away.

Jackie shows up. "Shauny. Can I . . . use your shack?"

"All right," I say. "But just this once . . . I mean, this is the last time, okay?"

"Sure," says Jackie. "I understand." And she closes the door behind her.

Randy is staring at the ground. He sighs and says, "Life is what you make of it. But then, it's hard to change what you made." He looks up at us in surprise. "Hey!" he says. "That was kind of wise, eh?"

"Sure," I say. "In a Forrest-Gump-on-Quaaludes sort of way."

Sherry punches my arm, and says, "It *was* wise, Randy."

"But what have we made?" says Randy, looking back down at the earth between his feet. "What do you think we've made?"

September 19

As I was walking through Tent City today, my mind hazy from lack of sleep and too much drink the night before, three policemen came out of the bushes across the road from Randy's place. It took me a moment to realize what I was seeing. I stopped and watched as they followed a wire on the ground, gathering it up like a trail of bread crumbs.

"Just a sec," I said to Sherry, and walked over.

One of the cops looked up, flicked his hand at me like he was swatting a fly and said, "Move on."

"What's going on?" I said. "What are you guys doing?"

"What's it to you?" he said, his eyes narrowing. The others were glaring, too.

"Well, I live here. So . . ."

"Let's get this straight!" said the cop, stepping forward as the other two let out derisive laughs. "You don't live here—you got that! You don't . . ."

" . . . live here. But I do."

"Not for long," said one of the other cops.

September 22

Over the past two days there have been damning newspaper reports on Tent City in both the *Toronto Sun* and the *National Post*. The *Sun* mocked this place as "paradise" while the *Post* called it "a five-acre patch of hell." It's telling that the *Post* made the same acreage mistake that the *New York Times* did in its piece. The *Post* article also called Tent City "Toronto's shame" and a "mistake by the lake," and referred to "this stinking public health hazard and the hopeless people who live there."

Ironically, this story appeared in the *Post* on Tent City's proudest morning. It was cleanup day again, and this time we managed to transform our patch of hell into a hopeful kind of shantytown.

There were volunteers from all over: off-duty nurses and paramedics, suits from the Rotary Club, freelance writers, reporters, a group of very nice Ford workers up from Michigan and a bunch of churchies. We all worked together, digging and scraping our toxic earth. And although it took the offer of money to inspire some of us to action, that's the way it tends to work on the other side of the fence, too. Everyone was in a good mood, and we tried our best to entertain the volunteers. We had obstacle-course shopping-cart races, played "vagrant sandwich" with the dirty mattresses and blew up expired cans of Zoodles in the barrel fires. The president of the Rotary Club joined us on our coffee breaks and stretched himself out on Randy's couch, laughing at all our stupid jokes.

Halfway through the day, we lined up for a lavish buffet of burgers and salad served by real chefs in those big white hats, and there were no fights, even among the dogs. When I dropped a door on Randy's foot, all he did was curse and throw an apple at my head. A group was organized to try to clean up the charred remnants of the Brothers' compound, and when the bins were full we pushed the rest of the mess into a few small mountains of trash near the porta-potties. Practically the only people who didn't help out were the dealers at Crack Corner.

But of course this *is* Tent City. As people started packing it in, one of the volunteers I'd been talking to earlier—a writer for a non-profit, socially active newspaper—walked up next to me and said, "Damnit!"

"What is it?"

"It's my own fault. I was stupid. I left my bag over by the buffet table..."

"And someone took it."

"I don't know what I was thinking. I'm not usually so dumb."

"Screw that. You've been cleaning up our mess all day. You don't deserve—"

She put her hand on my arm as if to console me. "I've got no right to be righteous. I was just stupid," she said, and I liked her immediately.

"I'll try to find the bag," I said. "What was in it?"

"My wallet with all my cards, and just $5, my Daytimer, some writing, and—oh, shit, my house keys! Damnit! I've been handing out my card to people all day—for help, you know—and it's got my address on it. You think I should change my locks?"

"Wait," I said, hoping they weren't already in her house. "I'll see what I can do."

I went around to all the usual suspects, or at least the ones I could find, but came up with nothing. When everyone gathered around Beric and Patrick (who was in charge of the list of thirty) to collect their pay,

I asked for their attention to make an appeal: "If anyone comes across that nice lady's bag that was left by the buffet table, you can bring it over to me—no questions asked. And you can keep the money in the wallet. I'd appreciate it—"

"Listen here," said Patrick, cutting me off, and I thought maybe he was pissed that I'd stolen his spotlight (it's not often you get thirty of us together and attentive). But he was just backing me up. "That's a nice lady!" he said. "She came down to help us all out. So whoever took her bag better do right."

"Everyone got it?" I said, and we all nodded. Once we'd got paid, people started coming up to me, one at a time on their way to the liquor store, with theories on the missing bag. Nobody was offended when the whispers led to them. As Curly said, "Of course you're asking—you know us. And you know we'd up it for you in a second."

I found a pager, a case full of CDs and a pair of sunglasses, but not what I was looking for. We've got nothing to hide from each other, and most anyone down here would do me this favour . . . So why couldn't I find it?

"It's okay," the lady said. "I didn't expect you to. It's my own stupid fault."

"It's probably someone I don't know. I guess you should change your locks . . ."

"Damnit, I wish I wasn't so stupid . . . but thank you so much, for all your help."

"I didn't do anything, but thanks for helping us clean up . . . I'm sorry, for all of us . . ."

"Don't be," she said. "You guys are great."

I took my $30 and started walking around. I went up to Eddie, who was over by Heartbeat's old place, where Norm and Sandy live now.

"Listen, Eddie," I said. "Can you spread the word that I've got $10 for the bag, and they can still keep any cash that was in it."

"What else was there?" he said.

"Daytimer, keys to her house—she'll have to get the locks changed . . ."

"That'll cost a lot. That's tough, eh?"

"Yeah, so . . ."

"Well, if I find it you can forget about the $10."

"Uh . . . why?"

"She helped out. You're just trying to do right? I understand that."

"Uh, right . . ."

"But you know, I can pretty well guarantee the Daytimer's gone by now . . ."

"Eddie . . ."

"Yeah?"

"You going to give me her bag?"

"Yeah, I am, you little prick . . . I was just . . . I was embarrassed before . . . with all the attention . . . and you. I was just . . ."

"Embarrassed."

"Yeah."

I could see the last half-ounce of Eddie's soul, burnt and smoking, still alive behind his blue-sky eyes, making him feel . . . embarrassed. "You go into my shack—Wilf's old place—and in the back left corner there's a cardboard box under a jacket."

"Thanks, Eddie," I said.

"No problem, asshole."

I ran and caught up to the nice writer lady just as she was heading toward the gates, and told her to meet me at my shack. Then I cut through the bushes to Wilf's old place.

Karen was inside smoking crack with some of the guys.

"Hey, Shaun," said Karen. "You know that guy on the Glad commercials?"

"I got to get something, Karen. Eddie sent me to get something."

I went to the corner, dug under a leather jacket and came up with the cardboard box. I carried the box back over to my shack, and waved the writer lady over.

"Oh my God!" she said. "How'd you find it?"

"Somebody had it. He's sorry."

"What can I do for you? Can I give you some money or something?"

"No thanks. It's not like that."

"I told you you guys are great," she said. "I *told* you."

x x x

I can't help but think of the cleanup we had just after little Caleb was born, when Eddie and I vowed to get clean. But it was never a fair pact—

I was lost, but never like Eddie. I was digging a hole, but not the size of this place.

It's amazing how much has changed since we last raked this contaminated ground and then dived into the polluted canal. I have a deck now, a fence, a shower, a rattan couch, a girlfriend and trees that drop tired green leaves on my front yard. I have the Dirty Thirty backing me up, and barely a thing to prove. It's like I'm rising as this place goes down—the dealers, cops, crackheads, and even the odd journalist, burying this earth in dirt.

But maybe you can never get clean—not in a place like this. After all, I've still got insomnia, a lost friend's dreams caught above my bed, too high a blood-alcohol count for far too long and the inability to change a thing.

x   x   x

After the lady left, people kept dropping by to share a drink. Everyone was in a good mood, had a bit of money and was glad I'd found the missing bag.

"Got to do what's right," said Randy.

"To be good to good people," said Curly.

"To make us look good," said Sluggo.

"Or just not too bad," said Olivia.

"You got any margarine?" said Jackie.

"Pass me a beer," said Les.

"Rahhh!" said Jimmy D.

The sun was warm, but not too hot. There were ducks and geese out on the canal, and the gulls swarmed in when we scattered bits of hamburger buns on the water like coins tossed to floating derelicts. They all went for each other, gulls on geese on ducks, and we laughed righteously, on dry land, each of us with enough for now, treating each other good, on a nice warm day.

We got drunk, but not too plastered. High, but not too close to the sun. There was fresh toilet paper in the outhouses, leftover food for everyone and enough apples to start a good-natured battle. People went for walks through Tent City, just to walk, just to see what it looked like clean. For a small stretch of time it seemed like everyone had what they needed—a few bucks, a job well done, a clean yard, a bit of a buzz and sunlight hitting the water. At the end of twilight, we lit a few fires and sat watching the smoke rise, drinking and waiting.

September 24

That is all.

September 25

The Toronto Star, front page:

TENT CITY FOLDS, SQUATTERS FORCED OUT OF RAMSHACKLE HOMES

Private security guards and police swept through Toronto's Tent City shantytown yesterday, peacefully evicting squatters who vowed for years that they wouldn't leave without a bloody battle.

Hired by the building supplies store Home Depot, which owns the 4.45-hectare waterfront property and accompanied by Toronto police officers, the guards removed about 50 residents who were home during the 11 am raid . . .

The Globe and Mail, front page:

TORONTO'S TENT CITY SEALED OFF, SQUATTERS EJECTED

A shantytown that had become an embarrassment for Toronto was cleared yesterday in an operation Mayor Mel Lastman praised and poverty activists condemned.

About 100 people looked dishevelled, dazed and angry as security officials hired by the landowners, Home Depot Canada, rousted them from the camp in a rubble-strewn field near the harbour.

Some wept and others yelled in contempt as a police cordon kept them from retrieving their belongings from the makeshift shanties that had been home to some for as long as two years . . .

National Post, front page:

HOME DEPOT, POLICE EVICT SQUATTERS FROM TENT CITY

Police and private security officials evicted more than 100 homeless
people yesterday morning from Tent City, a community of makeshift
shelters on contaminated land near the city's port.

Bulldozers demolished many of the shelters and police stood
guard as a fence was erected around the land, which Home Depot
owns . . .

The Toronto Sun, full front page:

TENT CITY, POP: 0

x   x
x

They came without warning, in the middle of the morning. They came
in waves of white, then blue, dozens of them, like whitecaps curling over
Tent City in the sun. They came with flak jackets and guns, black gloves
and the blessing of the law.

When they came, we were hungover and tired, wired and distracted,
putting a pot on the grill, rolling a smoke, washing our hair, fixing a bike,
going to the bathroom, feeding the birds, building a shack. When they
came, we were walking downtown, cycling uptown, carrying a bag from
the food bank, pushing a cart to the beer store, digging dirt in a construction site, sweeping out a warehouse, showering in a community
centre, taking the dog for a walk.

When they came, half of us were home, inside the fence. They surrounded each of us separately and marched us toward the gates, one
on each side like a new game of vagrant sandwich. We could take
nothing with us. We went peacefully, except for April who was put in
handcuffs because she was drunk and angry when they woke her. And
we couldn't turn back, except for Curly who was finally allowed to go
back for his pants when a policeman he knew intervened. "Have some

respect," said the cop to the security guards. "The man *is* human."

When they came, half of us were outside the fence. I was at the gym, trying to be good—trying to sweat out the booze, get healthy and strong, get myself out of the web of chain-link and mixed-up dreams. When I walked out of the community centre onto the Esplanade I saw Frizz going one way and Eddie another. "It's over, kid," said Eddie. "That's all of it. That is all."

When they came, the half of us inside the fence walked like jail-birds, tough guys and tramps, victims and vagrants, drunks, drug addicts and homeless people, slowly toward the gates. Those of us out-side rushed from all over, back home, toward Tent City. And by noon we were all there together, with nowhere to go, outside the fence.

I think we were in a state of shock, and probably still are. We were outside the fence all day, and into the night, and it was all a blur.

x
x
x

We are walking the chain-link fence, up and down, staring at our home, like aliens suddenly dropped on a strange new planet, gazing back into the heavens. Karen walks by, treading the ground out here like she's test-ing it for the first time. "Feel weird to be on this side?" says Curly, and he means to tease her a bit, but his voice drops and he sounds serious and caring, floating in space. Karen doesn't even hear.

Jackie comes toward me. She puts her arms out low, and as she falls in to hug me she begins to sob. "Jacks," I say, and she sobs. "I know," I say, and she sobs.

"Shauny," she says, and I want to cry.

"Where's Sluggo?"

"He took Cleo," she says, drying her eyes on my shirt, "to the humane society." She sobs.

I walk, step, step, step, toward the Cherry Street gate. I can see my shack from here, but a wall of men in white uniforms stops me. There are so many of them. And they are silent. The crests on their arms read "Shadow Security." They stand shoulder to shoulder, staring straight ahead, and they won't say a thing, won't even look at us. Even when we ask them if we can go in and grab a jacket, our cat, our medication. No answer. We ask them who's in charge, what's going on? No answer. We call them dumb-asses, security goofs, rent-a-cops. And they still don't say a thing. "They can't talk." I say, and we all look at them in awe.

They're bringing trucks in through the gates and have started cutting down trees and bushes, and mowing the high grass around the inside perimeter of the fence. On this side, more and more people keep arriving. There are dozens of reporters—TV, print, radio—more coming in vanloads, cars, on foot, by the minute. The Street Help vans that stopped coming down a couple of months ago are here now. Everyone's here—volunteers from the soup kitchens, the nice lady whose bag I found, Jane, Goran, his wife, Julie . . . There are riot cops on horses and police camped out across the street, hidden under the Gardiner with water hoses, tear gas and heavy artillery.

The TDRC is here, and they've got a team of professional protestors with them, like rented mourners at a funeral. They've got placards, banners and slogans. "Shame! Shame!" they shout. "No Home Depot!" they try. "No Home Depot!" They finally change it to "*Homeless* Depot! *Homeless* Depot!"—a bit catchier—and begin to march around in a circle.

Men in white jumpsuits and white face masks start to build the fence higher, adding chain-link on top of chain-link. Beric and the other protestors take turns with the megaphone. Spider is shouting at the voiceless Shadow Security men about his kittens, who are somewhere inside. The cops close in tighter and I hold Spider back. A few of us are kicking at the fence. Someone's bellowing through the megaphone about City Hall and Home Depot, while the circle of protestors continues to yell out, "*Homeless* Depot! *Homeless* Depot!" The reporters are stepping on each other's feet, jabbing microphones and cameras in the air like megaphones, placards, batons, guns and fence posts. Suddenly Phil—the quiet guy who makes the beautiful, crazy, Dr. Seuss percussion bikes, and drums on them at twilight—grabs the megaphone. "All of you," he yells at the protestors, "are hijacking us! You are hijacking Tent City. You don't know what it was!" And then the megaphone is gone from his hands, and he is drowned out by the protestors.

We walk along the outside of the fence. I can see my shack; we can all see our shacks through the fence as they build it higher. Backhoes and bulldozers roll through the gates. We stumble toward them in a daze and are pushed back by the wall of Shadowmen standing shoulder to shoulder, staring straight ahead. Finally one of them speaks—the commander-in-chief of Shadow Security, hired by Home Depot to secure the site. He says that once the fence has been completed we will be allowed back in, one at a time, to collect as much as we can carry. He says the shacks will not be bulldozed, yet. He says we can call him by his Shadow Security badge number: 2001.

The police are going through the trailers at Crack Corner, carrying out garbage bags and boxes. I can see Big G across Lakeshore, sitting on a guardrail beside his bike, watching all of us, alone.

Marty is drinking cans of Crest, holding his dog, flanked by reporters. Crazy Chris is lying on his back, stoned and drunk in the shade of a tree that the men in white jumpsuits are zealously pruning to make room for the razor wire. I step toward the fence, away from it. I find $7 in my pocket and give it to Karen to go to the beer store. She asks Jane to give her a lift.

People are handing out sandwiches and juice. Others are trying to find out about beds for us in shelters. Everyone's asking if we're okay. The reporters keep jabbing their microphones at us. I borrow someone's cellphone and call Sherry.

"Oh, God, sweetie . . . ," she says. "Are you okay?" I tell her not to come down. "Why?" she says. "Are you sure?"

"It's too much," I say. "It's a blur. I don't know," and then I start drinking the beer that Karen bought.

I drift toward the fence. I bump against the security guards, get pushed back. I can see my shack. Ishmael the Hungarian is here, and I offer him a drink, but he declines. "I'm Shaun," I say, and we shake hands. "I was a friend of Ron's."

"Me, too," he says.

"Why did he kill himself?"

"I don't know," he says, and we stand side by side, staring through the fence. He has a deliberate and intelligent way of speaking, and I begin to wish I'd known him before, in there.

"Didn't he leave you a note?"

"Yes, it was three pages. But I didn't read it."

I wait. And watch. It's like a military operation on the other side of the fence. Finally I ask. "Why not?"

"I couldn't read it then. And then the policemen took it. I suppose I should . . . follow up on it."

"He seemed fine," I say.

"Yes. We had been talking about how things might be okay. About getting jobs, and . . ."

"Do you know how he did it?"

"I think probably with pills, yes. He knew a lot about that. He knew a lot about different pills and poisons, he was very into that. He knew . . ."

"About a lot of things."

"Yes."

"But he wasn't a drug addict, was he? Or an alcoholic?"

"He knew a lot about pills. And he drank a lot . . ."

"I didn't think . . ."

"In a way that people wouldn't really know. He was good at it. He was a drunk more like you are."

"Oh."

And we stare through the fence, which is finished now. It is about 3 feet higher than it used to be, reinforced, with a staggered, razor-wire top. And they are about to let us back in.

"One at a time!" says 2001 as we push toward the gate. "You will be escorted in, and you will be escorted out." He points at me and a few others, calling out numbers, and people are yelling.

"He has to get his medication and his cats," I say to 2001, holding Spider back. "And she has to get her medication, too," I say, pointing to Lisa. "And him, too . . . and him." Some of the numbers are changed around, and we wait, staring through the gate. The protestors are still chanting behind us. Someone on the megaphone is yelling at the cops. The reporters are still shouting out questions, muttering orders at their cameramen. But we are quiet as we wait, like we're suddenly nervous to go back in, each of us alone.

x   x   x

When my time comes, I cross through the fence with two Shadows and a cop.

I'm inside now, and as I walk, the noise disappears behind me. Even with the trucks, bulldozers, chainsaws and weed-eaters, it all seems so quiet in here. I can hear my breathing and my footsteps, and I walk purposefully slow.

The two Shadows walk on either side of me, the cop behind us. Nobody says a thing until we reach a large fold-out table in the middle of Crack Corner. Four young men in white Shadow Security uniforms sit behind the table like they've just set up shop. They're eating cookies and pizza. They ask me my name and take a Polaroid of me, then tell me to sign something. I begin to read it. It appears to be some sort of confession—that I know what's going on, that I was trespassing, that I'm a vagrant, a derelict . . . I ask if I have to sign it. One of them glares at me, two of them pretend I'm not there, and the fourth just shrugs. I shrug back, and scribble something illegible on the bottom of the sheet. They hand me a pink ticket, which I stuff into my pocket.

There is a large aerial photo of Tent City taped across the surface of the table, like a map in a war room. I notice that the Shadows behind the table each have an eight-by-eleven copy of it on a clipboard. They ask me which dwelling was mine. Instead of locating it on the map, I point at my blue roof through the trees, and begin to walk down the road. The two Shadows quickly join me, the cop still behind. I walk slowly, stare straight ahead, listen to my footsteps and my breath.

I walk past Roger's, past the place the Frenchman built, where Spider and Olivia lived, past a couple tents, past Heartbeat's old prefab and Marty's old trailer, where Curly, Lisa, Norm and Sandy had been living. I walk along the road by the water, but I don't turn my head until I'm . . . home.

When I see it, it's like a stone hits the back of my throat. I somehow feel like I haven't been here in years. Yet it's pretty much how I left it. The log fence encircles my yard. There's a couple of beer bottles on the table from the night before. Behind the couch, Dude's old Moosehead beer pitcher is sitting on a stand-up bookshelf along with a broken eight-ball trophy I found and a big plastic hand that Frizz gave me. Hawk gave me the couch. I step onto the porch. There are two small Canadian flags tucked into the window frame, there since Canada Day. An oar Eddie gave me is leaning against the front wall. Randy gave me the door. There is yellow caution tape encircling the whole shack. I unlock the door and break the tape as I pull it open.

One of the Shadows follows me in. I turn and face him. I look down at his feet, standing on my floor. Nobody ever walked in here uninvited—except for Eddie when he did his Fonzie knock, and this guy is no Eddie. I'm about to tell him this, but then stop. Only now does it start to hit me—this isn't my shack. And now I'm moving faster, like I want to get out of whoever's place this is. I grab two bags from the foot of my . . . the bed, and look for something to put in them. But what do you take? What do you bring with you to the other side? I stop moving and stand in the middle of the room. I look at the Shadow standing next to me, the other by the door, and they both look away.

I look at my books, my stove, at the radio, at the cigarette roller, at the avenging angel on my wall—Babylon burning beneath her—at Eddie's dreamcatcher in the corner, and Hawk's tool belt. I fill one bag with booze (a quart of Lucky I was holding in hock for Randy, a half mickey of whisky and some bottles of homemade cider I'd been saving for a rainy day). In the other bag I stuff two pairs of underwear, a T-shirt, my leather jacket and nineteen spiral-bound notebooks filled with writing. I glance at the Shadows looming over me, then stand up and walk out the door. They fall in behind as I move through this living ghost of Tent City, back toward the fence.

x   x   x

The "retrieval process," as 2001 refers to it, is taking forever. Everyone is spending as long as they can inside. Once they're there, they don't want to leave again.

A 20-foot-wide swath of land around the inside of the fence has been razed and covered in gravel, and the white-clad Shadowmen are patrolling the perimeter. They are escorting us one at a time, telling us to stand here, then there, then here, then wait, then there. The razor-wire fence can't help but make the place look like a gulag. About a hundred police stand by, to keep the peace.

We've been out here for hours now, and more people keep showing up—not just reporters, aid workers and protestors, but more of us, too. This young guy, Jerry, who hasn't been here for months, comes pushing through the crowd, yelling that his cat is still in there. He's ranting, and trying to get through to the security guards. The cameras push in close to catch the confrontations.

"Shaun!" yells Jackie. Since I got my stuff out, I've found myself mediating between us and the Shadows. 2001 has trouble understanding what people are yelling at him, but I know what everyone's complaint is, and how to calm them down. I've been to the other side, I know what it's like. So I stand at the gate, on the border, trying to help. I move in front of Jerry, put my arms around his shoulders and whisper in his ear as he yells. I tell him to get his cat, and to be careful in there, controlled—there are no cameras in there, or any of us to back him up. You're on your own. He calms down. And I wonder if there's a difference between mediating and betraying your people.

I move away from the fence, and glug down another beer. I pass out a few ciders. The protestors are still chanting about Homeless Depot. Olivia sits down in the centre of their circular march and starts singing, "All we are say-ing, is give homeless a chance!" None of us know what this means, but we sing along and then break down laughing. I drink another beer, then a cider, and we try "It's the End of the World as We Know It," but we don't know the words. Mike the junkman walks up and tells me how horrible all this is, how it's the worst thing that could have happened—a tragedy. I nod in agreement. Les comes strutting over the Cherry Street bridge, coming from God knows where. "Hey there, Lester," I say. "How you doing?"

"Actually, hm-hee, pretty good," he says with a half-hidden grin. "I finally got her out of there. I mean, hm-yah, it's too bad. But I finally got her out of there."

Jerry is escorted back out of Tent City, carrying his cat in his arms, and the crowd breaks into applause, flashbulbs go off. The next day, his photo will be on the front page of the *Toronto Sun*. As he walks away from the fence, I say, "I thought you won the lottery and bought a condo." He looks at me like I'm insane. I drink another cider.

Silo Greg comes through the crowd, toward the gate, and he's angry. He's saying someone told him he could stay until the weekend, but he just got kicked out with no warning. I move toward him, to put my hand on his back. Then I stop. Why should I calm him down—this guy who's been nothing but calm for too long, sitting in 2 feet of water in an abandoned grain elevator? I step back, and we all look at him as he explains angrily that he's just been kicked out of his home. Nobody tells him to join the club, or take a number, or anything like that. "Gee," says Les. "That sucks."

"Yeah," answers Greg. "It does." I give them each a cider and open another one. And once more everything is blurring together, moving in waves. I step toward the fence, away from it. I hear Greg say, "Where are you going to sleep?" and hear someone else answer, "I don't fucking know." Julie has just been arrested for marijuana possession and Patrick is insisting it was his, trying to take her place in the paddy wagon. Crazy Chris has passed out, Spider is yelling again, Jackie is crying. Karl is ranting incoherently into the megaphone. Dozens of us are sitting like we have been for hours, all day, maybe forever, staring at the fence. We stand up, we sit down. We walk toward the fence, we step back. We answer reporters' questions, or wave them away.

And now something strange is happening. For the first time in months, in forever it seems, it is starting to get . . . cold. Not only is it no longer sweltering and humid, but it is cold. Some of us are starting to shiver. And as we realize this, a sort of panic begins to course through us—the sudden yet slow realization of the night coming, and winter, and nowhere to sleep, out here in the big world beyond the fence. We are still in shock, but now also numb and cold and scared all at the same time. Some of us are trying to stand, searching for sweatshirts, blankets.

I've got the cider to warm me. I want to keep it together, especially at a time like this, but it's not easy. I realize I haven't said a coherent sentence to any of them—to Jane, Goran, the aid workers or anyone else who belongs out here—in all this time. They keep asking if I'm okay. Every one of them—even the nice writer lady—has offered me a couch to sleep on. But I just nod, stammer and shrug. It's like it can only make sense to us. And now we're shivering and shaking, and I'm getting drunk, and I think I'm cracking up.

Beric makes some announcements I don't really understand, about emergency response and shelter beds and a community centre, and maybe even hotel rooms. He finishes by saying, "It may take some time, but it's in the works." Many of us, though, still haven't been let back inside. Marty has come off his fast drunk and is sitting beside Jane, shaking horribly in the cold.

I get my leather jacket out of my bag and bring it over to him. I haven't worn it since last winter, and as I drape it over his shoulders, a spider crawls out from the cuff and onto my hand, then another. I pull the jacket off and, as I hold it up to look at the lining, Jackie lets out a scream. The whole inside of the jacket is covered with dozens of white, spindly cocoons, each one containing a small, suddenly frantic spider. There are legs pushing out, and heads. I laugh, and begin to break each one open carefully, systematically, releasing the spiders who crawl across my arms and fall to the ground. "Sorry, Marty," I say. "I really should move out of that place."

I sit down and stare through the fence. It is twilight, and dozens of white Shadows are moving around on the other side, among our shacks and tents and fire barrels, like shades of our former selves. I look up at the reinforced fence, and notice that they've built the razor-wire top the wrong way around. It angles inward—like around a prison yard—as if built not to keep us out, but to keep the Shadows in.

x   x   x

I stay at the site of Tent City until well after dark. There are floodlights set up and the Shadowmen are still patrolling the perimeter. Emergency response has been put into action, and buses are taking us to the WoodGreen Community Centre on Queen East. I get the last ride and try not to look back.

When I arrive at the centre, some people are trying to eat the sandwiches that have been laid out on tables, some are being processed so they can spend the night on blue mats on the floor, and some of us go outside to drink my cider and smoke cigarettes. There are no fights and very few arguments. Everyone is still moving in a daze. Curly tells me that Big G is going to go down, and he laughs. "I told him," he says. "He had a proof-of-purchase right there in the big trailer he bought. And I told him, you don't keep a proof-of-purchase in your crack house. But he wouldn't get rid of it. He was probably the only one in Tent City with his name on anything."

I ask around for a cigarette. Olivia goes to the store on the corner and comes back with a whole pack of smokes for me. Lisa says, "I haven't smoked crack all day, and I don't want to." Several others echo the sentiment. Inside, a crowd is gathered around the TV, watching themselves over and over again on the news. Every time they show the clip in which Spider yells at the security guards, "You think this is funny? You think this is funny? Just watch out, you goofs—'cause I *will* jump you!" everyone bursts out laughing and whistling.

I ask where Randy is and people say they haven't seen him all day. The emergency aid workers start a series of interviews with some of the couples, to decide who's eligible to stay in a hotel for the night—they have fourteen rooms available. A few people whom I don't even recognize from Tent City are lining up, but still there are no fights. It's like the fight has left us. Except for Jimmy D. If you didn't know him, he would be an inspiration. He's out on the sidewalk, puffing out his chest and throwing his hands in the air. "Hell, I don't care!" he growls. "They can't keep us down! Just move on to the next thing, just move on! It'll be fucking fun!"

"Yeah, Jimmy D!" we all say. Crazy Chris cackles, but then comes up to me and says, "I gotta stay with him tonight. So I'm there in the morning when he's hitting withdrawal—fuckin' DTs, eh?" Crazy Chris, of all people, is thinking about tomorrow and about taking care of Jimmy D. I tell myself never to assume anything about this world. Never presume to know. I just hope I can remember this—at least long enough to write it down.

And now Eddie is talking the talk, too, saying there's no way he's going to hang around here, stay in a shelter, live by anyone's rules. No way! He's going to start up another Tent City, and just you see—everyone'll be building there in no time, in Eddie's new Tent City! And then the caseworker calls him and Karen in for their hotel-eligibility interview. Karen hugs me, and then Marty asks if I want to go find a bar with him. But all of a sudden I'm just so exhausted. I've got nothing left inside me, and I don't want to be here, to see this.

I don't want to see us sleeping on plastic mats in a community centre. I don't want to see us gathered around the TV for the next few days, watching ourselves on the news. I don't want to see us filling out forms. I don't want to see us blown apart, scattered to the cold wind, in all directions.

x
x
x

By 2 a.m., all but one of the street patrol vans has left with those who are going to hotels and motels, and most of the rest are lying down on blue mats on the floor. I don't want to lie down here. I don't have a hotel room, but I get in the van anyway, with Norm and Sandy, and Sluggo and Jackie, and two people I've never met. I don't want to stay here and I don't want to say goodbye. So I get in the van to go nowhere.

I sit in the back with Sluggo and Jackie. The person next to the driver has a clipboard and is asking us our full names and our ages. We laugh at how young Sandy is, how old Sluggo. For some reason, when it gets to my turn, I decline, and say it doesn't matter—since I won't be staying at the hotel. Maybe I want to keep something for myself, for life on this side of the fence. I pass around the last of the booze.

As we drive through the streets, Jackie points out a place she used to live, Norm points out a bar he used to bounce in, and Sluggo points out a high school. "I did renovations in that place," he says. "I used to skip out every chance I could, strip down and go swimming in the pool. Bossman was always yelling at me, 'Mackenzie! Mackenzie! Get your skinny ass out of the pool!'" He says it like he's testing his last name, seeing how it sounds, out here in the new world.

We drive all the way out to Scarborough, and the driver says, "The motel's just five more minutes up this way." And now we're all checking out the new neighbourhood. "There's the Beer Store!" says Sluggo. "Yeah, that's where you'll be walking to," says Jackie. "No way," says Sluggo. "We're not in Tent City anymore! You're doing the walking now, honey!" and we all laugh. "There's the Pizza Hut!" says Jackie, and we stare out the window like now this is where we're going to live. "Where's the water hose?" says Norm. "Where's the woodpile?" says Sluggo, and we all bust up laughing again, as if there's nothing to worry about.

When we get to the motel, the driver checks them in. I say goodbye and I hug Jackie. "You okay?" she says, "You want to stay with us?"

"No," I say. "But thanks, Jacks." There are tears falling from her blue eyes.

"I'll see you soon, right?" she says.

"I'll see you, Jacks," I say.

I watch as they go to their rooms.

Then I turn and walk with my leather jacket buttoned up and the bags slung over my shoulder, toward where I think Sherry lives. It's cold and I'm exhausted. I'm not sure where I am, but I know it's a long way. I just hope she's there when I arrive, so I don't have to sleep out here.

The Other Side

It's been a long time and a lot has changed. The 27 acres have been bull-dozed. Nothing grows there now—it is the most barren patch of earth you'll ever see.

It has taken a while for me to start living again, on this side of the fence—to become comfortable with comfort, to have high walls around me and heat and running water, to just hang out in a restaurant or a bar, to relax and stop looking over my shoulder, to go for a walk and breathe the easy air.

After the eviction I tried to hold on to everyone, following them to wherever they fell. But I couldn't help at all, and finally I just stopped. I collapsed and didn't get up for a long time. I imagined us all on our backs, strewn throughout the city, trying to catch our breath.

When I was able to get up again, it was like I'd awoken in some sep-arate yet familiar dawn. I walked toward the outskirts of the life I used to have, and my family was there, and a few of my friends. I got the hint of a future, as if my life had been going on without me, and I started edg-ing back into it. I pushed doors that said "Pull," I laughed at the wrong things, until finally I became something like myself again. But there are always shadows behind you, no matter how fast you walk forward.

x
x
x

During the days that followed the end, people all over the country become experts on Tent City. Both the media and the public were increasingly adamant about the whole affair—half in support of those evicted and half in angry condemnation. I quickly stopped reading the papers and I didn't watch the news, and although I have a folder full of clippings, I haven't been able to read them all. There are some insightful and inspiring pieces in there, and some pleasantly naive. But there is also such an outpouring of hate and ignorance that to keep reading drowns the spirit.

We were the hot topic, for a while, of barroom and council debate, until finally it became clear to the city that it had to end. Then, just like that, millions of municipal dollars appeared—their purpose, as if preordained, to house the "refugees." A rent-supplement plan and a housing task force was assembled, and within a month they started moving the former residents of Tent City into apartments.

Soon, however, the housing workers realized that many of those with promissory letters had never been to Tent City, and weren't even homeless. That's when they hired Jane to help figure it out, since she knew some of those who'd lived there. She did a great job, and thanks to her and the other housing workers, as well as Beric, the TDRC and a municipal plan surprisingly short on bureaucracy, practically every resident of Tent City soon had a subsidized apartment. The blemish on Toronto's face had been dug out clean; the land had been razed, the people housed and the public outcry had died. And for the most part, we, of the disappeared shantytown, were still alive.

x
x
x

Some six months after the eviction, I was invited to a Tent City reunion organized by the TDRC. I was apprehensive about it. In fact, I didn't want to go.

Sure, they had apartments. But I'd already decided that the problem wasn't just a lack of housing. It was life, the mess inside, the cosmic humour and the daily horror and all those things that stack the deck against you. I was scared that my friends—although they weren't officially vagrants any more—might have gone down even further since Tent City. And I hadn't been there for them. I hadn't done a thing.

If they had stayed the same, I didn't want to see that either—just as I didn't want them to see how much I'd changed. I also had some vague hallucinatory fear that if we all got back together, in one place, the chain-link fence would rise around us and Tent City would form once more.

But that didn't happen. In fact it was a great and glorious night.

The reunion was held at the Winchester on Parliament Street. A band was playing, and some of the street nurses were handing out drink tickets at the door. As soon as I walked in, Jackie came flying through the crowd and lifted me into her arms. "Shauny!" she yelled.

Almost everyone was there and it didn't take me long to realize that I'd figured things wrong, and that I missed them all so much.

Jackie told me about the little girl she's babysitting, who lives in her building. She said she's going to take a course in social work and hasn't done crack since Tent City—except once. She said Sluggo hadn't got mad at her when she fell, he was just sad for a while. He told her that once in six months isn't so bad, and that now they'd try for a year—and after that a lifetime.

Sluggo is going to school five days a week, studying communications. He told me they've just started on computers and if I send him an e-mail he should be learning how to send a reply sometime next week. He told me he hasn't really been drunk in six months, and Jackie concurred.

Curly has gone back to school, too. He studied sociology in university and is now working toward becoming a certified social worker. He is volunteering with the Street Help crews, doing harm reduction. He looked fit and trim, and when I asked him about it, he said he's back in the gym, hitting the old heavy bag.

Patrick and Julie told me they have a nice place and that their puppy has grown into a dog. Patrick is working construction and Julie is looking fine as ever.

I didn't spend much time talking with Les and Jo-Jo, but I did dance with them a lot. They are living in the same building, though in different apartments, and it seems they'll spend the rest of eternity devouring and adoring each other.

I also danced with Bonnie, who has left her Hamilton man and moved into a place of her own. She seems happy and is planning a swift return to the front lines of harm reduction.

I told Frizz that in my book he's Wolverine, and he called over a few of the boys so I could repeat what I'd said. He's living in a room above a bar, but says that he's going to pitch a tent in the nearest park and start a new shantytown just for the hell of it. He looks tough as ever and like he could do anything he wants, just for the hell of it.

Olivia was dancing all night. She said that Spider is touring with a carnival, that he doesn't drink Bingo anymore and is registering for school in the fall. She told me that during the first week in their apartment he flushed the toilet every hour on the hour, just to see it swirl. She said she's begun her life again and is loving it. And then, near the end of the night, she was kicked out of the bar for illicit activities in the men's bathroom.

Randy and Marty were too drunk to talk, and the bartender cut them off before most of us even started drinking. I went to the liquor store across the street to buy them some beer and they filled their cups beneath the table.

Nancy was also trashed, and in a state of mourning. She hung on to me for a long time, telling me how Steve was in the hospital dying of cancer. When Jack Layton showed up, she held on to him instead. Layton has recently become the leader of the federal New Democratic Party and he came all the way from Ottawa to celebrate with us at the Winchester. As he concluded his speech from the stage, Nancy clung sobbing to his chest.

Heartbeat, too, is dying of cancer. He was gracious and friendly as ever. Terry has moved into the place next to him, and is trying to support them both with his roofing job.

Jerry has acquired a girlfriend, and kept thumping people on the back too hard.

Jimmy D was drunk and trying to remember people's names as he strutted around the bar. Roger was there. And so was Dry. And also Phil—who built the crazy musical cycling machines. Some of the rec centre girls were dancing.

Crazy Chris was in jail.

And so were a few others.

On a table by the door was a photo of Hoyt, who died a few months ago. Apparently his intestines got twisted and his stomach just exploded. I am glad that I never hit him. I hope he's the man he wants to be now, and in a better place.

None of the dealers came to the reunion, and neither did Hawk, Pops or Karl.

Everybody said Karen and Eddie were going to be there, but they never showed up. Any day now, Karen is going to have another child. It turns out she was pregnant before they even gave up on Caleb, but nobody else knew until now. It's as if the baby wouldn't show itself, somehow hiding beneath Karen's bones and her tough pale flesh. I hear they're living outside the city, in some crack-fuelled housing project. I guess I'll have to find them myself.

Although some of us were missing, the reunion at the Winchester was a celebration to the end. There were plenty of people there who'd never been to Tent City, and those of us who'd lived there felt like survivors of some mythical battle. We all told stories about it, and nobody argued and nobody fought, and the more we drank the kinder and crazier the stories became. And by the end of the night we all were dancing.

x
x
x

I was visiting my family in Vancouver recently. One evening, just as we were sitting down to dinner, the phone rang.

"It's someone who says he's your big brother," said my mum. "You'd think I'd know him." I picked up the phone and Calvin started laughing into my ear.

He never did get to B.C. Apparently he met a girl in Calgary and decided he'd come far enough. "She's a real sweet one," he said. "You'd like her, Lucky."

"You know it's gone, eh, Cal?" I said.

"I know, b'y," said Calvin. "But we're still here."

x
x
x

Having lived down there, it is hard to be objective about Tent City. The other day I had a talk with Goran. He remembers framing a shot of our shacks, the downtown skyscrapers behind, then having to stop—amazed anew by what he saw. "I had the feeling that, despite how bizarre the place was, it was sure to outlast the city." Even he, a perennial observer, felt that Tent City would always be here, that it belonged on this earth.

In this new world of cosmetic surgery, reality TV and suicide bombings, the bizarre becomes normal so fast, and the remarkable turns into the skyline. I can't believe Tent City was allowed to exist for so long, and yet some of us could have lived there forever.

I have written a lot. I came out of those gates with a thousand handwritten pages. And yet I'll never be able to fully explain what it felt like in there . . . those quiet, still moments when I'd walk out of my shack and breathe the night air. It was a breath like no other—the wilderness and the city together, the breeze off the lake and the hum of the overpass, the fire barrels crackling and the moonlight on the water. The air felt both infinite and volatile, like we'd slipped from the edge of this world onto a whole other planet. And I will always miss that place.

x   x
  x

People keep asking me if I regret having lived in Tent City, and I keep saying no. But now that I've read this book, I do regret some things.

I never took the time to mourn Ron's death. After I read over that part, I stopped turning the pages. I stopped everything for a while. Out of everyone down there, Ron was the kind of man I could easily have been friends with, if I hadn't been so intent on finding something new. I can't help feeling that if I had truly been myself I could have done something. Maybe that's why I was there, and I just didn't see it. And so he died.

I am deeply sorry about that.

And though I didn't go in with any particular questions, I wish I'd come out with some answers. I still don't know why people sink into despair, or how they manage to scratch their way out of squalor.

I am glad I was wrong about the importance of city housing. I never thought it would make much difference, since the people in Tent City had their own houses—albeit precarious ones—and their battle seemed more with their demons than their environment. But now that they've got their own apartments, it seems at least half of them are doing better than they were.

I think there are two reasons for that, and both have to do with Tent City.

It was a circus in there, and we were all swept up in it. When the show was strong we all laughed along and kept on raging. And when it fell apart we all fell apart with it, raging even more. But once we left, the circus was gone. And then it came down to each one of us, and what we could accomplish on our own—which has to do with my second reason.

Many of the people who survived in Tent City learned something about living that others may never learn, and they brought that strength and dignity—no matter how tarnished, or incongruous in normal society—with them to this side of the fence. And so they're making the best of it.

But regarding the tougher questions, and the half still sinking, I really don't know.

Maybe it comes down to this: Very few of those who were not born healthy and well off, to a kind and loving family, can transcend the squalor without help—and for some it will come too late.

I had every opportunity in the world. I have been to all sorts of places and done all sorts of things. But, when it came down to this, even I could barely make it through. So be good to people, be good to vagrants, beggars, winos, buskers, con men and tramps. They are like you, or else you are like me, and I am just lucky.

Acknowledgements

To my mum and dad, and the three other people without whom this book would not exist: Don Sedgwick, Shaun Bradley and Anne Collins. Quite simply, I owe you my life.

To Cassidy, Reilley, Josh, Nana and the rest of my family. To Mike Wasko, Max Lenderman, Janine Kobylka, Saskia Wolsak and Marci Denesiuk, who somehow never lose faith—no matter what I do. And to Sherry Izumsky, the bravest girl I know. I love you all madly.

To Ernest Hillen, for his constant support and guidance. And to Elizabeth Nash for her generosity.

My deepest thanks to the following friends, editors, mentors and ex-girlfriends: Goran Petkovski, Julie Choquette, Paul Quarrington, Stacey Cameron, Craig Pyette, Adam Sternbergh, Jane Mountain, Diane Defenoyl, Paul Wilson, Patricia Grant, John Fraser, David Wright, Mary-Lou Zeitoun, Adam Starr, Mark Sumner, Anna Lisa Manfredini, Ryan Carter, Mike Meehan, Deborah and Rosie Trudel, Wil Wigle, Ibi Kaslik, Merrily Weisbord, Adrien Trembling, Josée and Anaïs Trépanier, Jodie and David Stall, and the kids at the Copa. I owe you all a drink.

Thanks to those who made outlasting Tent City just a little bit easier: Sister H, Dr. Paul Wright, Dr. Jennifer Bayani, Alicia Hogan, Kathy Hardill and Cathie Simpson of Regent Park Community Health Centre, Lee Hogan, Terry McWilliam, Toby and Vicki of Street Survivor, the WoodGreen housing workers, the TDRC and the Toronto Community Housing, the staff of the St. Lawrence Community Centre and the St. Lawrence Library, the owners of the Good Tymez Café, the people of the Good Shepherd, and the old boys at Henry's.

And finally, my gratitude and respect to the Dirty Thirty: Jackie, Sluggo, Eddie, Karen, Calvin, Spider, Olivia, Randy, Chris, Hawk, Pops, Les, Jo-Jo, Marty, Bonnie, Heartbeat, Terry, Curly, Jimmy D, Petra, Patrick, Julie, Lisa, Brenda, Jake, Frizz and Nancy. And to Hoyt, Steve and Ron—may you rest in peace.

SHAUGHNESSY BISHOP-STALL hitchhiked from Canada to Costa Rica at the age of 18. Since then he has picked olives in Spain, painted villas in Italy, hopped freight trains in Arizona, taught English in Mexico and built a shack from scrap lumber on the edge of Lake Ontario. His non-fiction has appeared in *Saturday Night*, *Utne* magazine, *Toro*, the *National Post* and the *Globe and Mail*. Most recently, he has played a well-dressed segment producer on CBC TV's award-winning comedy *The Newsroom*.